THE WORLD IN VOGUE

THE WORLD

↑ 807243

Vogue.

IN VOGUE

COMPILED BY THE VIKING PRESS AND VOGUE

EDITORS FOR VIKING: BRYAN HOLME AND KATHARINE TWEED
EDITORS FOR VOGUE: JESSICA DAVES AND ALEXANDER LIBERMAN

THE VIKING PRESS   NEW YORK

BOOK DESIGNED BY AUDREY ROSENSON
In the making of any book, many minds: in this particular book, the efforts, the ideas of almost uncounted people. For the final summing up, however, there is a group of workers without whom the book could not have gone to press. Some of them are acknowledged elsewhere in the volume; others we list here, with special thanks. For Vogue: *Evelyn Raphael, Kathleen Marvin, archivists; Marcel Guillaume, Richard Cole, technical aide, photographs; Elsa Blaisdell, research and manuscript preparation; Alice Stewart, research; Samuel N. Antupit, jacket design and layout supervision; Albert Hamowy, special layouts. For* Viking: *Beatrice Trueblood, Mary Kopecky, and Catharine Carver, research and manuscript preparation; Edwin Kennebeck, copy-editing; John Meyer, co-ordination; Libra Studios, mechanical preparation; Christopher Harris, production.*

EXECUTIVE EDITOR: PAUL H. BONNER, JR.

Copyright © 1963 by The Viking Press, Inc.

Copyright © each year 1893-1963 by The Condé Nast Publications, Inc.

Additional copyright information will be found under "Notes and Acknowledgments," page 410

All rights reserved

Published in 1963 by The Viking Press, Inc., 625 Madison Avenue, New York 22, N.Y.

Published simultaneously in Canada by The Macmillan Company of Canada Limited

Library of Congress catalog card number: 63-19603

Printed in the U.S.A. by Herst Litho Inc. Color pages by Civic Printing Co.

CONTENTS

Foreword *I. S. V.-Patcévitch*	7
The World in Vogue *Jessica Daves*	9
Seven Decades: People and Events: 1893-1963 . .	10
The Looking-Glass *Alphonse Daudet*	22
Ware Holes *Arthur Conan Doyle*	24
"Lady Windermere's Fan"	25
Breakfast at Delmonico's: 1893	27
On Stage: 1900-1907	28
"Woman Fishing" *Georges Seurat*	32
"Spring Flowers" *Henri Rousseau*	33
"Four Jockeys" *Edgar Degas*	34
Steeplechase Day — Paris *Edward Steichen* . . .	35
Her Diary: Leaves Culled from the Journal of a Lady of Fashion	37
Portraits of Royalty: 1906-1907	46
The San Francisco Fire: 1906 *Arnold Genthe* . .	48
Sky-Sailing: a Feminine Fad	50
The Progress of the Flying Machine *Elizabeth H. Gregory*	53
Candid Photography	56
1900-1910: Fashion: Hourglass Figures; Outrageous Hats	58
In London for the Coronation	61
"The Girl of the Golden West": Première of Giacomo Puccini's Opera, 1910 . . .	62
The Motor-Car: 1906-1913	64
The Armory Show, 1913: From One Extremist to the Other *Guy Pène du Bois*	67
Enter Gwendolen! *Emily Post*	70
People and Places	72
The Russian Ballet	76
Noted English Authors	78
The Riddle of the Sphinx *Huntly Murray* . . .	79
War: 1914-1918	80
Family Portraits	84
Yvette Guilbert *Clayton Hamilton*	86
The New Motion Pictures: 1918-1919	88
The Mode as an Art *Lady Candour*	91
The Tragedy of Modigliani	92
Rodin and Brancusi: A Study in Contrasts . . .	94
1915-1920: Fashion: Women Are Cocoons . . .	96
Life on a Permanent Wave *Dorothy Parker* . . .	99
Ten Thousand Nights in a Dinner-Coat *Frank Crowninshield*	102
Portraits by *Baron de Meyer*	108
La Duse *Kenneth Macgowan*	113
The Marrying Age *Paul Géraldy*	115
Love in the Twenties: As Hollywood Sees It . . .	118
Champions' Champions	120
Mannequins *Colette*	121

1929: Fashion: The Short and the Long of It . . .	124
On Stage: 1928-1931	128
What Makes or Breaks a Party? *Elsa Maxwell* . .	132
Are the English Hypocrites? *Harold Nicolson* . .	135
At the Opera Ball: 1933	138
Fashion and the Fine Arts *André Maurois* . . .	140
Sophisticated Ladies Kiss Everybody *Mary Borden*	143
"Les Coqueluches des Dames"	146
Don't Flatter Yourselves, Girls *Paul Gallico* . . .	149
"The Hindu Pose" *Henri Matisse*	151
The Clark's Fork Valley, Wyoming *Ernest Hemingway*	153
Marine Life, from A to E *Alajalov*	154
Eugene O'Neill	156
Shakespeare on Stage and in the Films	158
Old Home Town *William Saroyan*	159
The Wedding at Candé: 1937: The Duke and Duchess of Windsor *Cecil Beaton* .	162
Conversational Kleptomania *G. B. Stern*	165
A Party in Honour of Mr. Cole Porter	166
Paris Collections *Bettina Wilson*	169
"Fanny — You Fool!" *Marjorie Kinnan Rawlings*	172
"Still Life With Three Puppies" *Paul Gauguin* . .	173
There Was No More Sea *Mary Ellen Chase* . . .	175
1938 Fashion: Wide Shoulders; Narrow Skirts . .	178
Air History	180
Family Fugue: Variations on the Joseph Kennedys *Lesley Blanch*	182
They Pack Them In *Howard Taubman*	187
Picasso: Four Sketches and a Painting	190
The House of Vanderbilt *Frank Crowninshield* . .	193
Thanks to Casey Jones *John Mason Brown* . . .	197
Jewels *Salvador Dali with the Duc di Verdura* . .	200
The Charmed Life *Katherine Anne Porter* . . .	201
On Stage: 1939-1941	204
A Song History of Irving Berlin *Allene Talmey* .	206
About Band Leaders *Jan Spiess*	211
Ten Americans with a Sixth Clothes Sense . . .	212
Exodus *Lee and Carl Erickson*	219
War	220
The Crisis of Man *Albert Camus*	226
Pierre Balmain *Gertrude Stein*	228
Mail Gossipings *Alexander Woollcott*	233
1947: Fashion: The New Look	234
Opera Addict *W. H. Auden*	237
Epigrams *W. Somerset Maugham*	240
Gouache *Joan Miró*	241
Just Idling Along *Daphne du Maurier*	244
Men of Letters	246
Meditation on Simplicity *Rumer Godden* . . .	247
Three Dramas with Familiar American Settings . .	248
Man's Burden *Saul Steinberg*	250
Food, Artists, and the Baroness *Alice B. Toklas* .	252
Famous Models	254
My Grandmother and Mr. Gladstone *Bertrand Russell*	257
New York *Truman Capote*	261

Italian Films *Richard Winnington*	262
The Best of Talk *Jean Cocteau*	264
G.B.S.: 1856-1950	266
Younger and Charminger, I *Franklin P. Adams* .	269
Nobel Prize Acceptance Speech, 1950 *William Faulkner*	273
"Between the Birds and the Poets": A Millay Memoir *Vincent Sheean*	274
Revisitation *Anne Morrow Lindbergh*	281
Laughter *Christopher Fry*	282
The Twenty Years: 1933-1953 *Russell Lynes* . .	286
The Light in the Dark *Elizabeth Bowen* . . .	291
The Art of Scepticism *Rebecca West*	294
In Braque's House *Alexander Liberman*	298
People I Wish I Had Known *Jacqueline Lee Bouvier*	301
Funny Bones	302
One Man's Money: The Rockefeller Philanthropy .	304
The Man Who Planted Hope *Jean Giono* . . .	308
Revolution of the Women *Joyce Cary*	314
Coronation Portfolio: 1953	317
Rosemary *Marianne Moore*	321
"Brothers, I Presume?" *Senator John F. Kennedy*	323
Costume Ball in Biarritz	326
The Art of Ballet *Agnes De Mille*	329
The New Vamp *Anita Loos*	337
1957-1958: Fashion; No-Shape Dresses	338
On Stage: "The Confidential Clerk," "My Fair Lady" . . .	340
G.B.S. on Women	340
People and Sports	342
Gian-Carlo Menotti and Leonard Bernstein . . .	344
What Is an Englishman? *Pierre Daninos* . . .	346
Portraits by Penn	350
You and the Queen of Sheba *Harlow Shapley* . .	355
The Eye of a Soldier *Geoffrey Household* . . .	359
"The White Tablecloth" *Pierre Bonnard*	361
Collector's House: Wright Ludington	362
"Merritt Parkway" *Willem De Kooning*	364
How to Get Along with a Man *Phyllis McGinley* .	365
Wolfe and the Angel *Allene Talmey*	368
The Royal Wedding, 1960: Princess Margaret and Antony Armstrong-Jones *Sarah Russell*	370
Modern Architecture in America *Peter Blake* . .	372
Popularity *Sir Osbert Sitwell*	379
On Stage: 1958-1962	382
How to Face Outer Space *Anthony West* . . .	385
A Little Game *Lawrence Durrell*	388
Nobel Prize Acceptance Speech, 1962 *John Steinbeck*	393
Space Heroes: Colonel Glenn and Major Cooper . .	396
Robert Frost	398
There Is *So* Alas about a Pigeon *Patricia Collinge*	400
1958-1960s: Fashion: "Plus ça Change"	404
Life Must Surpass Itself *René Dubos*	406
Notes and Acknowledgments	410
Index: The People in This Book	412

FOREWORD

The making of magazines is, I daresay, quite different from manufacturing almost anything else. Our product seems, at first glance, so frail, so ephemeral. It cannot be eaten or worn, or used as a building material, or driven along a highway. A magazine in its physical form — even such as *Vogue* — is, before all, simply a number of sheets of paper imprinted with illustrations and text, neatly stapled together and collected beneath an eye-catching cover. It appears on and disappears from the newsstands with dreamlike rapidity. Unless carefully stored or preserved in a binding, it is perishable. With heavy or prolonged use and handling, it disintegrates.

Yet, each issue of *Vogue*, this fragile and transistory product, performs a certain historical function. It holds a mirror up to its time; a small mirror, perhaps, but a singularly clear, brilliant, and revealing one. Its purpose is not to reflect a vast panorama, an epoch, or even a year, but a small segment of time — two weeks, a month; and to reflect only certain events, certain people, certain aspects of that time. Every two weeks, as the current issue of *Vogue* has served its purpose, it is replaced by a new one, and much that was in the previous issue is relegated to the archives of memory.

Much, but not all. A surprising amount of the content of each issue of *Vogue*, both editorial and pictorial, stays fresh and fascinating, for a year, ten years, twenty years or longer, after its publication date. Some of the pages in almost every issue will, I believe, retain their excitement, their interest, as long as our particular civilization endures. What is really superficial is swept away, like leaves and twigs from the surface of an onrushing stream. What remains is the stream itself, bright and swift, changeless and changeable.

The proof of this lies in your hands. From seventy years of bound volumes of *Vogue*, the present anthology has been drawn. During those years, *Vogue* has reflected and recorded the best of its own time, its own world. From this vast and unique reservoir of material, the editors of this book have extracted and re-distilled the best. They have read and appraised, winnowed and sifted through the brief but elegant epoch of Arthur B. Turnure, first publisher of *Vogue*; through the long and glorious years when Condé Nast was its publisher and Edna Woolman Chase its editor; through the years of my own incumbency, from Nast's death in 1942 until the present.

They have been years of high prosperity and deep depression, of two World Wars, of revolutions both political and industrial; and these things, too, are reflected obliquely in *Vogue*'s mirror. If *The World in Vogue* is accepted as an enduring record of an extraordinary passage in the history of our day, we will have achieved our purpose in publishing it.

I cannot conclude this brief foreword without a grateful recognition of those who have made *Vogue* what it is and through it made possible the publication of this colorful record — a grateful recognition not of any one editor, not of any one art director, artist or photographer, layout man or copywriter, but of a vast group of women and men, all over the world, whose hearts and minds and talents have flowed into this magazine over the years.

I. S. V.-PATCÉVITCH, President, The Condé Nast Publications, Inc., Publishers of Vogue

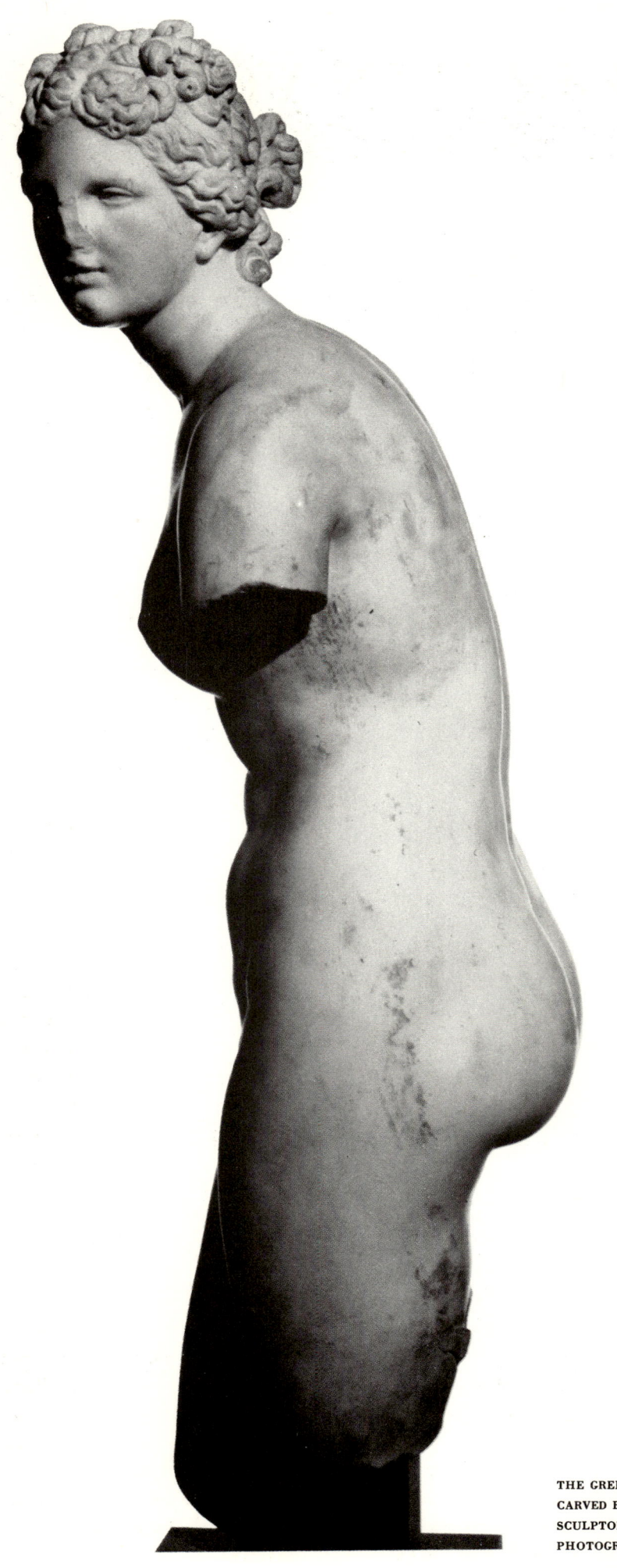

THE GREEK GODDESS APHRODITE,
CARVED BY A ROMAN
SCULPTOR OF THE FIRST CENTURY A.D
PHOTOGRAPHED BY PENN

Metropolitan Museum of Art

THE WORLD IN VOGUE

It is accidental history that the beginnings of the magazine *Vogue* (and of this book) came at the beginning of an onrush of technical changes — the most radical changes in exterior life that the world has known since what *is* known has been recorded. Let us say immediately that those outward evolutions do not compare, certainly, in majesty with the early Greeks' recognition of the dignity of man. That was a transformation of the spirit; a recast of values that has left its mark on every succeeding hour of every succeeding day. But the inventions, the discoveries that have come upon us since 1893 have had the quality of magic, enlarging the natural powers to supernatural proportions. It is as if the witches on the heath had taken command and had melted the world into a single element, erasing the partitions that separate the individual allotments of time, the individual cubicles of space. It is the cliché of our decades that we hear around the world, see around the world, speak around the world, travel distances greater than the mind can comprehend.

These magnified powers, it is true, have made of man a creature sharply different, in most objective areas, from his antecedents; but in the subjective world, in the slipstream of the inner consciousness, the prevailing emotions tend to be unaffected by these waves of worldly progress. From generation to generation, the race continues to be moved by hunger, love, and fear; to seek amusement; to feel envy, desire, curiosity, and an avid interest in the new. In its pages, *Vogue* has as a matter of course reported the exterior changes; but the current of news has been only one of *Vogue*'s reasons for being. There has been, more deeply, the hope to cherish the sense of beauty, to feed the mind, to stir the imagination. And governing all has been a high regard for the best — the best of its kind, whatever the kind. The pages were asked not only to amuse, to stimulate, to please, to bring news, but to present a level judgment of quality in people, places, manners, milieu. Playwrights, laugh-makers, ballerinas, pianists, painters; leading ladies and prima donnas; writers to prick the mind, ideas to fire the pulse — all these have been weighed on the scale of quality. The stirring beauties, the diplomats, the captains, and the kings are in the record; women who make an art of presenting themselves; some who have made an art of life. Out of that scrutinous choice of seventy years has come this book, an essence of a stirring time. In the first of those seventy years, the automobile was barely born, the aeroplane unknown; the motion picture was a Kinetoscope. No one had ever heard a radio or looked at television; had ever talked across the ocean or across the continent — and very few had even talked across a city. The only frozen foods they knew were accidental victims of weather; air-conditioning was the movement of a painted fan. But people seemed to manage very well without these 1963 accessories to living. And that is part of what this book is about; a record of the continuance and the change, the continuance of elegance and wit, the change in their manifestations.

Vogue has sometimes been called a civilizing force. If that is true, perhaps it is because a civilization, to endure, needs voices to sing its praise. "They had no poet and they died," is Gogarty's epitaph for the lost treasures of the unrecorded past. A part of civilization is a regard for the gifted, an admiration of beauty, an understanding of the arts — the arts of daily living as well as the arts of painting or sculpture, writing or music or architecture. Civilization has in it, too, respect for the boldness of the frontiersmen in the sciences and in all the worlds of abstract ideas. These things *Vogue* has recorded, dramatized, applauded. Some of the best of the record is in the pages of this book.

JESSICA DAVES

SEVEN DECADES

1893 1913

As the era began, the world, for a brief moment, was not engaged in any major war. But in a few years both Cuba and the Philippines rebelled against and shook off Spain. The Chinese "Boxer Rebellion" started in 1899 and ended in 1901 with the Dowager Empress of China agreeing to allied demands. The Boer War (1899-1902) added the South African republics to the British Empire. But all was not politics or war. In 1893, Mrs. Potter Palmer gave the Chicago World's Fair her approval. In 1894, Debussy wrote "Afternoon of a Faun." In 1895 X-rays were discovered. And in 1896 Marconi filed his first wireless patent. King Victor Emmanuel III, Italy's last king, was crowned in 1900. U.S. President McKinley, assassinated in 1901, had stated ahead of his times, "Isolation is no longer possible or desirable." Calvé sang *Carmen*; people talked about the Dreyfus case and Lizzie Borden's trial. It was the fashion to be dressed by Paris couturiers Worth, Redfern, and Callot. Children read *Little Lord Fauntleroy*, their elders *Graustark* and Stephen Crane's *Red Badge of Courage*. In 1909 Peary reached the North Pole. And in 1912 the "unsinkable" *Titanic* struck an iceberg and sank. 1503 lives were lost.

Horse-and-carriage days see beginning of the end of their era.

Kipling: "Empire's best salesman." Zola: *Nana* is notorious classic.

1906. The *Lusitania* is launched. (Sunk in 1915 by German U-boat.)

Wright brothers fly, 1903. Medal for first 100-mile flight, 1909.

French Madame Méliès appears in husband's films. Here in *Tragède*.

Davis Cup (established 1900) gave tennis international importance.

1906. The newest hair fashion: Paris invents permanent wave.

William Howard Taft, President, 1909; with family in touring car.

Whistler's "Lady Meux"; Sargent's portrait of sister. He and Boldini painted many fashionables.

Mrs. Pankhurst, English suffering suffragette, speaking in the U.S.

Ladies' skirts flick the streets.

Bathing suit regarded askance; not admitted on several beaches.

1901 sees end of the fabulous 64-year reign of Queen Victoria.

1908. Henry Ford's new Model-T; world's first mass-produced car.

Pavlova, Russian prima ballerina, makes a sensational world tour.

1898. Mme. Curie and her husband Pierre discover radium in Paris.

President Theodore Roosevelt is cartooned at the Panama Canal—authorized 1904, completed 1914.

1910. King Edward VII dies. At funeral, heads of leading nations.

1913. Suffragettes on New York's Fifth Avenue protest child labor.

MRS. GROVER CLEVELAND, WIFE OF THE TWENTY-SECOND PRESIDENT OF THE UNITED STATES

1913 1923

Status symbol for the very rich — the private railroad car.

1913. U.S. Income Tax ratified; Congress taxes all money earned.

Mary Pickford, World Sweetheart.

April 6, 1917. President Woodrow Wilson asks U.S. Congress for declaration of war against Germany.

"Over There" by George M. Cohan becomes a wartime theme song.

Russian Royal Family is murdered during the Bolshevik revolution.

Irene Castle has bobbed her hair. The tango is international craze.

Versailles Treaty. Lloyd George, Orlando, Clemenceau, and Wilson.

1920. 18th Amendment to Constitution prohibits U.S. liquor sales.

1920. 19th Amendment to Constitution gives U.S. women vote. (English women's full rights, 1928.)

Legal scrutiny of bathing suits.

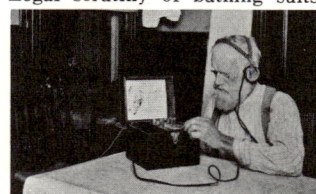

Radio, with ear pieces, is in.

1921. Man O'War, great race horse, cost $5000, later made a million.

1922. Marcel Proust dies in Paris.

Shaw writes *Saint Joan*, Fitzgerald *The Beautiful and Damned*.

1923. The Duke of York weds nonroyal Lady Elizabeth Bowes-Lyon.

Ten years that saw the world uprooted by the Great War. The assassination of Archduke Ferdinand set off the fuse, and in 1914 the war began. The U.S. entered in 1917, and the Armistice was signed November 11, 1918. Meanwhile other pursuits continued. Automobile production started to soar (over a million cars in the U.S. in 1913). Shaw's *Pygmalion* commenced its long life in 1913. Will Rogers stopped the show, appearing in *The Ziegfeld Follies* of 1914. And movie history was made by *The Birth of a Nation* in 1915. In 1919 two Englishmen, John Alcock and Arthur W. Brown, were first to fly the Atlantic. Jazz bands and the shimmy took over. New, curveless modern furniture horrified the lovers of Victoriana. Galli-Curci's silver-thread voice was heard in *Lucia*. *Abie's Irish Rose* played an unbelievable 2327 times. People talked about Einstein's theory of relativity without imagining the atom bomb it foreshadowed. Radio reporting started in 1920 with the broadcast of the Harding election returns. In 1922 James Joyce's *Ulysses* set the literary world on its ear. Also discussed were: Wilson's Fourteen Points and Liberty Bonds, bootleggers, Mussolini and Fascism. Canada's Dr. Banting discovered insulin, gave diabetics new life. And Herbert Hoover continued his work as Director of War Relief (started in 1914) — a work which lasted through 1923 and which fed and clothed millions in the devastated lands of Europe and Russia.

LADY DIANA MANNERS,
YOUNGEST DAUGHTER OF
THE DUKE OF RUTLAND

Steichen

1925. KATHARINE CORNELL IN "THE GREEN HAT"

14

1923 1933

The era began in the U.S. with the end of President Harding's scandal-ridden regime. In England a general strike paralyzed the country for a week in 1926; Parliament then declared general strikes a criminal conspiracy. Meanwhile, three American aviators made the first round-the-world flight (175 days). Dry ice was invented. In 1923 Edna St. Vincent Millay won the Pulitzer Prize for poetry. People laughed at Charlie Chaplin and at Harold Lloyd in the films. In 1927, the first transatlantic phone call, New York–London; the first air-conditioned office building, San Antonio, Texas. Everyone was obsessed with "I Got Rhythm." Skiing became a rage. The Riviera sprang to life again; lunching at Maxine Elliott's in Cannes was the thing. In 1927 Babe Ruth set a memorable 60-home-run baseball record. In 1929 the Papal State, extinct since 1870, was revived. Ernest Hemingway wrote *A Farewell to Arms*. China and Japan went to war in 1932, three years after the Kellogg-Briand Treaty in which 62 powers renounced war. Young talents gathered in Paris, believing they could create only by starving in a Paris garret. And Ring Lardner died in 1933, leaving a heritage of sardonic writing still to be surpassed.

1923. Handsome President Harding, too affable for his own repute, dies. Calvin Coolidge takes over.

1924. Lenin dies; Joseph Stalin becomes undisputed dictator of U.S.S.R. for next thirty years.

1925. Scopes' Trial makes teaching of evolution illegal. Lawyers: Clarence Darrow for defense, William Jennings Bryan, prosecutor.

Sinclair Lewis refuses Pulitzer Prize, 1926; accepts Nobel, 1930.

1926. Josephine Baker, Harlem night clubs, the Charleston, and jazz bands make world-wide news.

1927. Dempsey, "Manassa Mauler," the world heavyweight champ.

1927. The first talking picture, with Al Jolson as singing star.

1927. Lindbergh makes historic first solo flight across Atlantic.

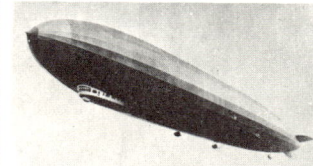

1928. Germany's Graf Zeppelin is the earliest transatlantic dirigible.

1929. Short skirts; bobbed hair; hats cover ears. Next year Patou bomb drops — skirts reach ankles.

Sir Alexander Fleming announces discovery of penicillin in 1929, first of the miracle antibiotics.

1929. *Variety*'s famous, succinct headline marks the most publicized market drop in history and start of world-wide depression.

1929. First movie Oscar given to Janet Gaynor for *Seventh Heaven*.

1929. Ramsay MacDonald, British Labour Prime Minister, speaking before Congress; historic first.

1931. Empire State Building with 102 stories is tallest in world.

1932. Amelia Earhart, first woman to fly alone across the Atlantic.

1933. Mae West, top box-office news, makes the world love curves.

1933 1943

Beneath the outer crust of the familiar world, seismic tremors of earthquakes to come; breadlines followed the 1929 market crash; in 1933 Adolf Hitler became Chancellor of Germany; in 1934 Fermi smashed the atom; in 1936 revolution came in Spain, Mussolini invaded Ethiopia. Yet King Edward VIII's love story made more headlines than either Hitler or the breadlines. Color film for ordinary cameras became a fact; the dancing Rockettes in New York's Radio City were a byword for precision. People were singing "Three Little Fishes"; doing the Lambeth Walk; reading *Anthony Adverse, Rebecca,* and Gertrude Stein; listening to Gershwin's *Porgy and Bess.* Women wore shoes with four-inch cork soles. Surrealist Dali was painting limp watches; Oppenheim made fur-lined teacups. On June 28, 1939, a Pan American plane made the first transatlantic passenger flight, with 22 aboard. Nylon stockings first appeared in 1940; shortly disappeared as nylon went into parachutes. World War II began September 1, 1939, as Hitler blitzed Poland with his Stukas; two days later Great Britain and France declared war on Germany and the holocaust was on. Japan bombed Pearl Harbor on December 7, 1941, and the U.S.A. was in the war.

1933. Franklin D. Roosevelt ushers in his New Deal. With him, President Hoover on Inauguration Day.

Breadlines form in city streets, symbol of the great depression.

1933. Adolf Hitler is Chancellor of Germany — first step to terror.

1935. Will Rogers, salty philosopher-humorist, dies in air crash.

1936. Jesse Owens, in Olympics at Berlin, wins three events for U.S.

1937. Duke of Windsor, England's ex-King, marries Wallis Simpson.

Jean Harlow, first of the Hollywood platinum blondes, dies at 26.

Mickey Mouse, Walt Disney pet, becomes an international figure.

1938. The Cunard Line launches biggest liner, *Queen Elizabeth.*

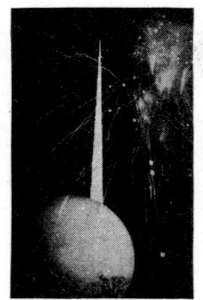

New York World's Fair welcomes the King and Queen, first reigning English monarchs to see U.S.

1939. Britain's Vivien Leigh is Scarlett O'Hara, Southern belle, in movie, *Gone with the Wind.*

Sun bathing: new craze. Minimum-coverage suits seen on beaches.

1939. New Museum of Modern Art is bulwark for the avant-garde.

Dec. 7, 1941. Japan bombs Pearl Harbor while her ambassador still talks peace at the White House.

U.S. enters World War II a day after Pearl Harbor is attacked.

Prime Minister Churchill at helm as German planes blitz London.

1941. The King and Queen inspect havoc caused by German bombs after night raid over England.

1942. Ration stamps are familiar. Limited food, and sparse dresses.

Nobel Prize winner for atom research, Fermi, directs first controlled nuclear chain reaction at University of Chicago, 1942.

1943. Lady Cavendish (Adele Astaire) entertains GIs in London.

GRETA GARBO
PHOTOGRAPHED BY CECIL BEATON

1943
1953

February 1945. Yalta Conference Churchill, Roosevelt, and Stalin.

April 13, 1945. Truman sworn in as President following death of Franklin Roosevelt on April 12.

July 16, 1945. First atomic bomb explosion, New Mexico. August 6, Hiroshima; August 8, Nagasaki.

Victory celebrations: August 14. V-J Day follows on September 2.

1945. General de Gaulle is head of Provisional French Government.

1945. First United Nations session, April–June, San Francisco. 50 member nations sign charter.

Frank Sinatra fans queue up for blocks to hear bobby-soxer idol.

1947. Dior new look nips waists, lengthens skirts, and pads hips.

1948. Gandhi, the great Indian leader, killed by Hindu fanatic.

One result of population explosion: mass housing developments.

1948. Israel Free State a fact, with Ben-Gurion Prime Minister.

Television captures the world and housetop aerials dot landscape.

1952. Albert Schweitzer, medical missionary to Africa and a Bach authority, gets Nobel peace prize.

Korean War: American wounded are evacuated from front by air.

Bob Hope, English-born American, beloved Army-camp-show personality, travelled 2,000,000 miles around world to entertain troops.

Blue jeans become a new fad for women. 1952 news: Stiletto heels.

1952. The *United States* on her maiden voyage sets speed record.

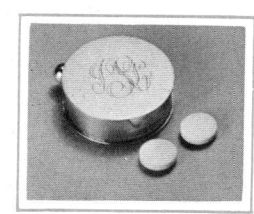
Handbag pillbox is now usual for holding tranquillizers, vitamins.

The atomic era begins. With two more years of war ahead, great nations and small nations were engaged in a bloody life struggle on the sea, in the air, on land. F.D.R.'s time was running out; the Yalta Conference with Churchill and Stalin in February 1945 showed him pitifully haggard. He died on April 12. The Germans surrendered on May 6. In August, atom bombs were unleashed on Hiroshima and Nagasaki. Japan surrendered on August 14. Later that year Prime Minister Churchill, Britain's symbol of victory, was swept aside and the Labour Party with Clement Attlee took over. In 1946 the republic of the Philippines became an independent nation and in 1948 the Free State of Israel was created. But again major world events did not shut out other absorbing interests. *Oklahoma!* opened, setting a new style in musicals (it ran more than four years). Bright colour appeared in men's clothes, on the beach and in the country. Press agents became Public Relations Counsels. And Dr. Spock's *Common Sense Book of Baby and Child Care* made his name famous. A radar beam reached the moon in 1946. Hatlessness became usual, even on city streets. The first wave of brutal post-war books began in 1948 with *The Naked and the Dead* by Norman Mailer. In 1951 President Harry Truman relieved General MacArthur of his Far East Command. And in 1952 talk began about a European Common Market.

LEFT: MARINA, THE DUCHESS OF KENT

1953
1963

In 1963 anything seems possible—a holiday on a planet (not Venus or Mars, we are told) or a space cruise of a few million miles over a week-end. Or we might all vanish with the hydrogen bomb. "What's past is prologue": the space era began in men's minds, perhaps with Galileo, da Vinci, or with pre-history scientists. But the 20th century has made space travel a fact. The first satellite to orbit the earth was Russia's Sputnik in 1957; next, in 1958, the American satellite Explorer (still orbiting). Then came the human orbiters: Russia's Gagarin in 1961; U.S.'s Glenn in 1962 and, in 1963, Cooper, who orbitted the earth twenty-two times in thirty-four hours. Space stirs the imagination; automation gives us pause. Possible future developments: universal person-to-person communication by dialing a universal number; decentralization of cities; minimum human contact in factories, in shops. Today computers could supervise most non-creative processes, but those computers are designing computers even smarter than they are — machines that might compete with man. The decade will also be remembered for the conquest of Everest in 1953 by Sir Edmund Hillary; for the Supreme Court decision (1954) declaring racial segregation in U.S. public schools unconstitutional; for credit cards (deferred payments); for young scientists, new campus heroes; for beatniks and the Twist; for mental illness treated with medicines. Other facts: In 1958, Pasternak, author of *Dr. Zhivago*, was named for the Nobel Prize, but the Soviet refused acceptance. In 1961 twenty American republics organized the "Alliance for Progress," and in 1963 the Federation of Malaysia became the promise of power in Asia. Churchill, in 1963, was made honorary citizen of the U.S., the first since Lafayette. And today the English Royal Family, and America's First Family, remain young enough, handsome enough to be favorite "pin-ups" of the world.

1953. Eisenhower inaugurated for first term as U.S. President. Richard Nixon is Vice President.

Paperback book boom, worldwide.

1954. First atomic submarine, Rickover's dream, is launched by U.S.

1954. Egypt's new Premier Nasser talks with free India's Nehru.

Skirts are shortest since 1929, often several inches above knee.

Dr. Jonas Salk's new anti-polio vaccine is announced a success.

1957. Macmillan, England's Prime Minister, takes over from Eden.

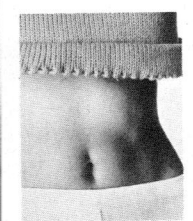
Two-piece beach suits, showing navel, accepted on most beaches. 1957. The chemise dress is back.

1958. First passenger jet across Atlantic; BOAC Comet, 6 h. 12 m.

Mao Tse-tung, Khrushchev, heads of Communist alliance of 1959.

Jean Monnet, France's financial brain behind Europe's powerful new six-member Common Market.

Brasilia, a modern city built in jungle. Kubitschek, the Brazilian President, was prime moving force.

Astronauts. Lower row: Cooper, Grissom, Carpenter, Schirra, Glenn, Shepard, and Slayton.

The African map changes—one of greatest continental upheavals. 33 African nations UN members.

1960. Incoming President Kennedy, outgoing President Eisenhower in engaging pre-inauguration photo.

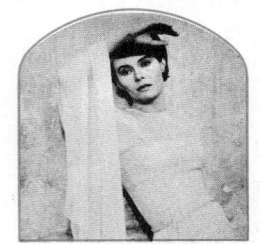
Last Year at Marienbad, the new motion picture affirming "*Nouvelle Vague*" of dream-like unreality.

1962. Rome. Pope John calls first Ecumenical Council since 1870.

Telstar, satellite world-wide TV relay station, 3000 miles in space, created by Bell System in U.S.

RIGHT: MRS. JOHN F. KENNEDY,
WIFE OF THE THIRTY-FIFTH
PRESIDENT OF THE UNITED STATES

Elio Sorci PIP

THE LOOKING-GLASS

BY ALPHONSE DAUDET

To the North, to the banks of the Niemen, comes a little Creole, as pink and white as an almond blossom. She comes from the land of the humming-birds, borne by a wind of love. The people of her island said to her: "Do not go; it is cold on the Continent; the winter will kill you." But the little Creole did not believe in winter, and only knew of cold from having eaten sherbets; and then she was in love; she had no fear of dying. And now she is landing far up among the fogs of the Niemen, with her fans, her hammock, her mosquito nets and a cage of gilded lattice-work full of the birds of her country.

When old Father North saw the arrival of this flower of the isles, which the South had sent him in a ray of sunlight, his heart was moved with pity; and as he knew very well that the cold would make only a mouthful of the little girl and her humming-birds, he hastened to light up his big yellow sun and to clothe himself in his summer garments to receive them. The Creole was deceived; she mistook this heat of the North, brutal and heavy, for a lasting warmth, and hanging her hammock deep in the park between two pine trees, all day long she swung and fanned herself.

"Why, it is very warm in the North," she says, laughing. But one thing worries her. Why is it that in this strange country the houses have no verandas? Why these thick walls, these carpets, these heavy hangings? These great porcelain stoves, and the high heaps of wood piled up in the courtyards, and the blue fox-skins, the thick cloaks, the furs that sleep in the bottom of the wardrobes — what is the use of them all? Poor little one, she is soon to know.

One morning, on awakening, the little Creole is siezed with a sudden chill. The sun has disappeared, and from the low, dark sky, which seems to have drawn nearer the earth during the night, there falls in flakes a white, silent substance like that under the cotton plants. Winter is here, winter is here! The wind whistles, the stoves roar. In their great cage of gilded lattice the humming-birds sing no more. Their little wings of blue and rose and ruby and sea-green are motionless, and it is pitiful to see them, benumbed and puffed up by the cold, with their delicate beaks and their eyes like the head of a pin. Down in the park the hammock is shivering, full of hoar frost, and the pine branches are like spun glass. The little Creole is cold; she will not leave the house.

Curled up by the fire like one of her own birds, she spends her time gazing at the flame, and makes herself sunshine with her memories. In the hot, bright fireplace she can see all her native country: the wide docks full of sunshine, and the brown sugar of the dripping canes, and the grains of Indian corn floating in a golden dust, and then the afternoon siestas, the starry nights, the fireflies, and millions of little wings that hum among the flowers, and in the lacey meshes of the mosquito nets.

And while she is dreaming thus before the fire, the winter days follow one another. Every morning a dead humming-bird is picked up from the bottom of the cage; soon there are only two left, two tufts of green feathers bristling close together in a corner.

This morning the little Creole cannot rise. Like a little summer craft caught in the ice of the North the cold clasps her, paralyses her. It is dark; the room is sad. The frost has spread a thick curtain of dull silk on the panes. In her bed, to amuse herself, the Creole makes the spangles of her fan sparkle, and spends her time looking at herself in looking-glasses of her own land framed in great Indian feathers.

Ever shorter, ever blacker, the winter days follow one another. Within her lace curtains the little Creole languishes and grieves. What saddens her the most is that from her bed she cannot see the fire. It seems to her that she has lost her native country a second time. Every now and then she asks: "Is there a fire in the room?" "Why, yes, little one, of course there is. The fireplace is flaming. Don't you hear the wood snapping and the pine cones bursting?" "Oh, let me see, let me see!" But no matter how she tries, the flame is too far from her; she cannot see it, and she is in despair. Now, one evening, as she lies there, pensive and pale, her head on the edge of the pillow and her eyes ever turned in the direction of the beautiful invisible flame, her lover comes near her and takes up one of the looking-glasses from the bed. "You want to see the fire, darling? Well, wait a minute." And, kneeling on the hearth, he tries to send her with the glass a reflection of the magic flame. "Can you see it?" "No! I don't see it." "And now — " "No! not yet." Then, suddenly receiving full in her face a jet of light which enwraps her: "Oh, I see it!" says the Creole, joyfully, and she dies, laughing, with two little flames in the depths of her eyes.

[*Translated by S. G. Lawrence.*]

SELF PORTRAIT:
A DARING STUDY IN PHOTOGRAPHY
BY ALFRED STIEGLITZ

[1893–1913] 23

WARE HOLES BY A. CONAN DOYLE

"THE STORM" (ALSO KNOWN AS "PAUL ET VIRGINIE")
ONE OF THE MOST POPULAR PAINTINGS OF THE DAY,
WAS PAINTED BY PIERRE AUGUSTE COT IN 1880

A sportin' death! My word it was!
   An' taken in a sportin' way.
Mind you, I wasn't there to see;
   I only tell you what they say.

They found that day at Shillinglee,
   An' ran 'im down to Chillinghurst;
The fox was goin' straight an' free
   For ninety minutes at a burst.
      *   *   *
'E was a stranger to the 'Unt,
   There weren't a person as 'e knew there;
But e' could ride, that London gent —
   An' sat 'is mare as if 'e grew there.

They seed the 'ounds upon the scent,
   But found a fence across their track,
And 'ad to fly it; else it meant
   A turnin' and a 'arkin' back.

'E was the foremost at the fence,
   An' as 'is mare just cleared the rail
He turned to them that rode be'ind,
   For three was at 'is very tail.

"Ware 'oles!" says 'e, an' with the word,
   Still sittin' easy on his mare,
Down, down 'e went, an' down an' down,
   Into the quarry yawnin' there.

Some say it was two 'undred foot;
   The bottom lay as black as ink.
I guess they 'ad some ugly dreams,
   Who reined their 'orses on the brink.

'E'd only time for that one cry;
   "Ware 'oles!" says 'e an' saves all three.
There may be better deaths to die,
   But that one's good enough for me.

For mind you, 't was a sportin' end,
   Upon a right good sportin' day;
They think a deal of 'im down 'ere,
   That gent what came from London way.

["*Ware holes*" *is the expression used in the hunting field to warn those behind against rabbit burrows or other such dangers.*]

LADY WINDERMERE'S FAN

JULIA ARTHUR AS LADY WINDERMERE IN OSCAR WILDE'S CONTROVERSIAL PLAY

OSCAR WILDE

It has been said that Oscar Wilde's *Lady Windermere's Fan* is an immoral play, and for that reason has no place upon the stage. If this is true, I suppose it may be said that *Romeo and Juliet*, *The School for Scandal*, *Frou-Frou*, and *The Squire* are also an insult to the theatre-goers. Hadden Chambers, the author of *Captain Swift*, had quite a good deal to say once about this question of morality and immorality in plays. It is the purpose of a drama, said Chambers, to show both the good and the bad in humanity. Otherwise there would be no clash of interest or catastrophe. It all depends upon the way in which the theme is treated. The only fault that can be found with Oscar Wilde is that in this play he has not indicated sufficiently clearly that he satirizes the phase of society rather than the entire social structure.

[1893 – 1913]

BREAKFAST AT DELMONICO'S—1893

There are very few things, in the aspect of her native city, that astonish an old New Yorker so much as the crowd of idle men who invade Delmonico's restaurant at the luncheon hour; fill the windows of the Union, Knickerbocker, and other fashionable clubs during the afternoons; or are seen spinning through Central Park, in coaches, T carts, and even broughams, at any hour between twelve and six.

Twenty years ago an idle gentleman was almost unknown among us. Idleness in those days was the particular property of tramps, loungers or loafers, as they were then called, or of Congressmen and Assemblymen off on a spree. At the present time one has only to drop in at Del.'s about two o'clock, p.m., to see every table occupied, and a throng of waiting ladies, almost all of them accompanied by men, standing in the hall and doorway. Within, the restaurant presents a gay scene, and the hum of conversation with an occasional burst of laughter reminds one of the Metropolitan Opera House, when one of Wagner's gems was in process of interpretation.

On a recent occasion, when I was lunching there with a party of friends, I saw at least a dozen young fellows, personally known to me, who were evidently breakfasting at that advanced hour, and who apparently had nothing in the world to do but to enjoy themselves. At one table sat De Courcy Forbes, Fred. Beach, R. T. Wilson, Jr., Julian Potter, and Hamilton Cary. They were all in faultless morning dress; were groomed to perfection, and one and all recalled the London man about town, who, although he never breakfasts in a restaurant, is to be seen in his club window, or strolling down Piccadilly or St. James Street, at a corresponding hour of the afternoon. At another table sat the Hon. James Otis, a Union League veteran, infinitely manly and attractive. Mr. Thomas Cushing, most admirably gotten up, came in soon after. Both these gentlemen are widowers, and very popular in society. Sprinkled about, among the ladies, were a half-a-dozen English swells whose flashy ties, and rather startling shirt fronts, astonished my unaccustomed eyes. Among them was a very good style of man, whose silk tie had a twist in it, however, that no native American could possibly imitate; under each ear was a sailor's knot from which depended two long ends — that were crossed together in front and held together by a gold safety pin — which looked quite out of place in the duty assigned to it. Another young fellow, who was lunching with this Englishman, wore a marvellous shirt front of lilac cambric, on which were woven all the flowers of the field, arranged in bouquets. A white shirt was rather the exception, but "spats" were of snowy whiteness, and those among the crowd, who accompanied ladies and were evidently bound for matinées and receptions, wore frock coats, high hats, and white linen of course. If one or two of the fathers and grandfathers of the present generation, who sat in their counting-houses from nine in the morning until the family dinner hour at three p.m., and then returned to their desks for the afternoon hours, could have looked through Delmonico's windows at the time I speak of, they would have been quite sure that they had come to life in a new world, far away from their old homes.

SARAH BERNHARDT, THE GREAT LADY OF THE FRENCH STAGE, IN HER APARTMENT ON THE BOULEVARD PEREIRE, PARIS
Collection Ochsé

ON STAGE 1900-1907

The five charming people photographed here are: Edna Wallace Hopper in the turn-of-the-century review, *Florodora*; Mrs. Patrick Campbell, who strode into the limelight as *The Second Mrs. Tanqueray* — Sir Arthur Pinero's play which opened in London and was recently part of her repertory in New York; Lionel Barrymore, whose latest vehicle is J. M. Barrie's *Pantaloon*; Ethel Barrymore, who once again is appearing in *Captain Jinks of the Horse Marines*, the play in which she became a star in 1901; and the lovely Geraldine Farrar, opera's youngest prima donna, shortly to make her début with the Metropolitan Opera in *Romeo and Juliet*.

EDNA WALLACE HOPPER
Brown Brothers

28 [1893 – 1913]

MRS. PATRICK CAMPBELL

LIONEL BARRYMORE

ETHEL BARRYMORE
Brown Brothers

BARNEY OLDFIELD RACING
IN THE WINTON BULLET NO. 2
AT DAYTONA BEACH, FLORIDA, 1904.
HE RECENTLY SET THE SPEED RECORD
OF NEARLY SIXTY-FIVE MILES PER HOUR

"WOMAN FISHING." A CONTE DRAWING BY GEORGES SEURAT

Museum of Modern Art (Lillie P. Bliss Collection)

"SPRING FLOWERS" BY HENRI ROUSSEAU

Albright Art Gallery, Buffalo, N.Y.

"FOUR JOCKEYS"
AN OIL PAINTING
BY EDGAR DEGAS

STEEPLECHASE DAY — PARIS,
AFTER THE RACES, 1905.
A PHOTOGRAPH
BY EDWARD STEICHEN

[1893 – 1913]   35

HER DIARY

LEAVES CULLED FROM
THE JOURNAL OF A LADY OF FASHION

1893: SKIRT DANCING, THE TALK OF THE TOWN

Harry McVickar

December 31st, 1892.

If one had to make New Year resolutions I think I'd make one to go on doing what I am doing — only more of it — till I'm sixty. From the night of my first ball till now I've had a perfectly delightful time.

Last night I went to a young dance at Mrs. Pierpont Morgan's, which was very pleasant. But I find it pleasant going to meet really older people, too; their gossip is so interesting. And I like meeting the people who are characters in society, old wits and beaux of my mother's time or earlier. There is Mr. Ward McAllister, for instance, who has made himself a sort of ruler in social matters, and Mr. Peter Marié, who is one of the kindest and most cultivated old bachelors of a former day, and Mr. James Parker, who used to live in Paris and has brought over traditions of great buckishness with him. Hearing them all spoken of made me wonder what they would be like when I met them. But they are not at all alarming at close quarters. The other evening at Mr. Peter Marié's dinner I thought I wasn't going to get on very well, sitting between Mr. James Parker and a secretary from one of the foreign embassies — Russian, I think, though it didn't matter, because he spoke English so well — but, on the contrary, I had a delightful time. Mr. Parker is most amusing. He's like a handsome, scampish old parrot, with a brilliant black eye that comes round the corner suddenly at you when he turns his head. I was very much flattered, too, before dinner by Mr. Marié's asking me to sit for a miniature. He has a famous collection, and any girl he adds to it is supposed to be really pretty, if not beautiful.

January 10th.

So many things have happened, one after the other, that nobody could put them all down.

Wednesday night I went to the dinner-dance at Mrs. Ogden Mills'. It's a lovely house for a dance, more like a London house than most in New York, one of the few where you find dressing-rooms on the ground floor as you enter. She has servants in knee-breeches, too, which I think looks very well. Mrs. Stuyvesant Fish says hers hate wearing powder, and that's a pity, because all that sort of ceremonious costuming of servants is part of the great social game, and I do think it's amusing to see it played well.

We had lovely favours — ribbons, and bells, and silver toys, and silk bags, and boutonnières, and bunches of roses, and shepherdess hats and crooks — and when I jingled home at three o'clock or later, Mama knew I had had a splendid time, because my train had all the balayeuse ruffles torn, one of my double-puffed velvet sleeves was ruined, from my having carried my roses over my shoulder, and I'd danced holes in

THE DUCHESS OF MARLBOROUGH,
THE FORMER CONSUELO VANDERBILT.
A PASTEL PORTRAIT BY HELLEU

MR. AND MRS. CLEMENT C. MOORE
AT NEWPORT

Brown Brothers

"THE BREAKERS" —
THE NEW CORNELIUS VANDERBILT
SUMMER COTTAGE

Brown Brothers

Galloway

"EVERYBODY'S BICYCLING
MORE THAN EVER"

both of my slippers. I'd had Brock Cutting for a partner (who is without doubt the most charming young man in New York, and as he seldom asks any one to dance a cotillion this was a really great triumph) and I'd had a front seat, and been taken out a lot of times, and so of course I was very proud and could not go to sleep for the grinding of the waltz and polka tunes in my head.

On Thursday I went to the Harry Cannons' to dinner before going to the Assembly. The Assemblies are given in the Madison Square ballroom this year. Elisha Dyer, who seems to lead all the cotillions now, led this one, too, and he always gives me a good seat when he can; but I think private balls are nicer on the whole.

Last night it was the Patriarchs' at Delmonico's, and Elisha led again. They had the cotillion before supper, which may be better for business men, but somehow doesn't seem so gay. These subscription dances, where the people who belong send out so many invitations, do not really test a girl's popularity because, of course, the men you send tickets to feel they must ask you for supper or for the cotillion. One is very glad they do, of course, and it's a great comfort.

Mrs. Van Rensselaer Cruger looked very handsome in a white satin dress with brilliant steel embroidery. The famous string of pearls was in evidence — the one she said came from literature. It must be wonderful to make enough money by writing to buy pearls! *A Diplomat's Diary*, her first book, is very interesting, I know, because I've read it. But not serious, and it isn't so long, either.

January 28th.

The weather has been so cold that sleighing and skating have actually been giving those who like sleighing and skating a lot to do. The St. Nicholas Rink, an out-of-doors place at Fifty-seventh Street, has been full of people. But Mama nearly always makes me pay visits of an afternoon. I don't see much good in driving about from house to house leaving the family cards. However, she thinks we should, so we do. Mrs. Paran Stevens, a great personality in her way, happened to be at home, we got there so late. There was an English girl staying there, in such a lovely dress. I don't mean she stayed in it always — she had it on. A bright red silk, with sleeves as big as balloons. It was trimmed with bands of black fur headed with jet *passementerie* — "Exceedingly *fin de siècle*," so somebody called it. Mrs. Stevens was very funny about some rude man behind her at a matinee who had asked her to take her bonnet off. "Sir," she said, "a lady does not take off her bonnet in public." That was all she said to him, but the things she said about him would have made his ears burn, and they were big enough, she declared, to obstruct her view. Only, as she didn't think *The Fencing Master*, even with Marie Tempest, very good, she hadn't asked him to remove them.

Newport, August 10th, 1895.

Nothing could be more tiresome than the journey to Newport but fortunately I got a seat in the car which goes direct to Wickford Landing, so I didn't have to change my bags and things at the Junction, which was one blessing! The good old *General* was creaking at the wharf — I always wonder when it's going to shake itself to pieces and drown all the summer colony and their guests, but, as usual, it got safely to its destination. Constance met me, and we trotted comfortably home in her phaeton; we are going to dine on board the Gerrys' yacht (Mr. Gerry is Commodore of the Yacht Club), and I don't want to be too late. Just late enough to make people wish for one without being angry at one, is the ideal time to arrive. Mr. Higgins, I hear, is going to have great luncheons on board the *Sapphire* during yacht race week. Well, I'd always rather do my yachting in the harbour, for I'm no sailor.

Newport is very gay. The New Breakers, the Cornelius Vanderbilt house, isn't finished yet, because they are going to try putting in electric light as well as gas, and that holds up the work; but we are going to dine there Thursday, so I shall see some of the alterations, which they say are wonderful. I hope I shall sit near Mr. Vanderbilt, who is one of the most dignified and delightful of men. I shall wear my best! Sleeves as big as skirts, and skirts nine yards round, the very latest thing from Paris.

For the rest, there'll be polo to go to, which I love, and there's the tennis tournament, and the coaching parade on the 14th. Constance says everybody bicycles more than ever, and that Mrs. W. K. (only I think she calls herself Mrs. Alva Vanderbilt now that she has separated from Mr. Vanderbilt) rides eight miles a day, and that a number of people have asked Mr. Van Alen to get up a Bicycle Meet, like the one they had here last year, and— But here come my trunks, at last, and I can dress. Heaven send my sleeves are not crushed!

August 20th.

It's impossible to write much when one gets into the whirl of things. The Coaching Parade was really the nicest I've ever been to. I remember, in the spring of the year I came out, when kind Mr. James Parker asked me to the Parade of the New York Coaching Club, I was prouder than a peacock. It was considered awfully smart, and the women's costumes were said to set the fashion for the whole summer. The coaches all met at Eighth Avenue and Fifty-ninth Street and drove up to Claremont, where we lunched. My sister says, though, that it was nothing to the parade in her day, when they met

"THE DEFENDER" AT THE 1901 NEWPORT RACES

MR. ALFRED G. VANDERBILT'S
FAMOUS ROAD FOUR,
1907

Culver

at Washington or Madison Square, in the afternoon, drove up Fifth Avenue to the Park, and afterwards had dinner at the Buckingham. But that was a small affair to the one here. We had twelve coaches in line. The parade formed at noon, at Narragansett and Bellevue Avenues, and we drove round the Ocean Drive to the Country Club, where we lunched. We didn't leave till half-past four, and then at least half of us drove to the Polo Grounds and watched the match. A most pleasant day.

The first trial race for the Cup Defence was sailed to-day. They say the *Vigilant* will be withdrawn in favour of the *Defender*, which has caused a lot of talk. There have been awfully nice luncheons — for good sailors — on the *Nourmahal*, the Astor yacht; and Constance, who went on the Goelet yacht, the *White Ladye*, says their party for the Duke of Marlborough was great fun. I wish I liked the sea, but the truth is one look makes me ill.

Mr. Oliver Belmont's ball at the Stable will be the last I can go to before I go home. No ball in town is half so pleasant as the ball at Newport. Illuminated grounds, supper on terraces, great windows open on the verandas so that one can dance out into the fresh air — it's much more informal, and much more fun! I shall hate to leave it all. The latest gossip says the Duke of Marlborough is, or will be, engaged to Consuelo Vanderbilt. My sister says she once stayed at Mrs. Paran Stevens', when his father, the late Duke, was out here, just before he married Mrs. Hammersley. It's odd to think that Mrs. Hammersley, as a girl, was told by a gipsy that she would marry three times and her second husband would be a Duke.

New York, November 7th.

The Marlborough-Vanderbilt wedding yesterday was a wonderful sight. I never saw such a crowd in my life as the one collected at the door of Saint Thomas's Church. Of course it was beautifully decorated, with wonderful arches and wreaths, and the wedding procession looked charming — as much as one could see of it — coming up the

MRS. CORNELIUS VANDERBILT II
AND HER DAUGHTER GLADYS

MISS ALICE ROOSEVELT   Brown Brothers

42 [1893 – 1913]

aisle. The effect of white, all glistening, in satin, or frosted in lace, was lovely. The bridesmaids had pale blue sashes and lovely lace fichus, and the blue velvet hats worn with them had pale blue feathers, and were most becoming to all the girls. The bride herself, with her delicate little Japanese face perched like a flower on her long neck, looked so sweet that even if one had not known her one would still have been enthusiastic in wishing her well. A fine, notable wedding, as Mr. Pepys would say, and a great many clergymen to marry them — Bishop Littlejohn, Bishop Potter, and the Reverend Doctor Wesley Brown.

The breakfast was at Mrs. Vanderbilt's house, in Seventy-second Street, as, of course, she is no longer in the Fifth Avenue house. All the smart world was there, and everybody seemed in the best spirits.

November 16th.

At the Horse Show last night, the box where the Marlboroughs sat was so mobbed that no one could get past it, and no one looked at the horses. It was as gay a night there as can possibly be imagined. I do wonder how many dressmakers have nervous prostration after they have sent us home our Horse Show dresses? Of course, as an event, it really does start the Season — that, and the Opera — and the luncheons and dinners we have, at the nearby restaurants, before going to the afternoon and evening sessions, are great fun. The last nights, with the high-jumping contests, are the most exciting of all, and always crowded.

February 26th, 1897.

There is talk of a war with Spain, and everything is very quiet. Poor Mrs. Bradley Martin is being much misunderstood because of the fancy ball she gave at the Waldorf. She really wanted to help, and give work to many people who were out of employment on account of the dull season — people like dressmakers, caterers, florists. But of course, instead of giving her the credit for that, the outside world is being abusive. I don't wonder she wants to sell her houses here and make her home in England. I should too. It's lovely there.

It was an enormous ball, and fearfully crowded. There was a sort of royal quadrille and a minuet, and Mrs. Jack Astor, who was to have danced in the minuet, couldn't come at the last moment, so Edith Hall took her place. All the women employed the same hairdresser, and I hear that some of them kept him waiting so long he couldn't get to others, who naturally were furious. I know we waited ages for the minuet to begin. Mrs. Martin was in black and flame colour as Mary Stuart, perhaps not the best costume she could have chosen for her height, though her face was sweet under the cap. Kate Brice was quite wonderful as a Spanish Infanta, but had to stand up all evening on account of her crinolines. Anne Morgan went as an Indian girl, and Mr. Welling as a chief. But his headdress was so high above his six feet and more of self that he couldn't get it into any shut-up cab and had to drive to the ball in an open one, to the delight of the populace. The ball was one of those great sights one is always very glad to have seen. If a person goes to any much-talked-of entertainment, it may or may not be amusing, but at least it is a comfort to be in a position to judge.

December 30th, 1901.

This winter we are wearing bellish skirts and rather bustly effects, trimming round our knees and circular flounces, which no living woman can hold up in the street. And thinking about streets, and walking in them, makes me wish I had one of those new little electric automobiles; not for town use, but for next spring in the country. The women at Newport have them and I shall begin to drop hints about it into Papa's mind in a month or so.

I wonder if I'm getting old; I mean, if anyone else would think so? Of course, *I* don't. Still, it is ten years since I came out, and that makes me— Well, not thirty, at any rate, but of an age when my great-grandmother would have begun to think of caps, very likely, while I am thinking of quite a different head-adornment. I enjoy going out as much as ever — almost — especially to the

MRS. EDITH WHARTON, THE AUTHORESS, RIDING AT NEWPORT

MISS MAUDE ADAMS   Culver

MRS. AVA WILLING ASTOR   Campbell Studios

[1893 – 1913]

Opera, though I am not wise enough musically to appreciate Wagner, as the real musicians say one should. A friend of mine assured me the other night that if one shut one's eyes and listened very hard to the orchestra, one didn't mind the singing half so much. Not having tried it, I don't know, but I should think that to be able to concentrate the attention elsewhere just while moral people, like King Mark, or Wotan's Model Spouse, are scolding delinquent connections, would be an immense comfort.

Everyone is breaking out into Musicales this season. Mrs. Oliver Belmont has had one, and Mrs. Clarence Mackay had a wonderful one on Christmas Day at Harbor Hill, the beautiful place her father-in-law gave her near Roslyn. Then Mr. Bagby's Musical Mornings at the Waldorf-Astoria are very pleasant, and altogether one's bump of harmony seems in a fair way to be developed.

I never go to the Waldorf-Astoria without thinking of the two Astor houses as they were, and some anecdotes of each of the Mrs. Astors told me by Mama. She said that Mrs. John Astor, the mother of William Waldorf, being very busy on a thousand committees for different good works, spent but little time at home, and one day showed her a small table in the corner of her library, saying, "This, my dear, I call my 'pelican table,' because I stand on one leg when hastily eating my lunch there." And Mrs. William Astor, the present Mrs. Jack's mother-in-law (also involved in many charities), was found quite discouraged one day because, in supplying all the artificial legs, arms, and eyes for certain wards in a hospital, she had come in contact with a very angry young Irishwoman who wanted a blue eye to replace one of her black ones. They finally gave it to her, though they warned her it would not look well. "And now she blames me very much," said Mrs. Astor, "because she can't see out of it."

January 10th, 1902.

I did not go to Washington for the ball the Roosevelt's gave Alice, though a lot of people did. The Bachelors' Ball has been the best here so far. Mrs. Ogden Mills, Mrs. Neily Vanderbilt, Jr., Mrs. Jack Astor, and Mrs. Clarence Mackay received, and the list of men who gave it ought to be framed and hung before the writing table of any women bent upon entertaining. I think it is a delightful way for men to return the politeness they have received, and, if there are enough, it cannot weigh heavily on any one. It might be amusing to have a Spinster's Ball, too. But, to speak gently for fear of attracting Fate's adverse attention, I shall not be a spinster long, so I'd better not start this particular ball rolling. I am glad I am marrying rather late. If I had taken the very first gentleman who asked I might have been most unhappy now, and as my family do not countenance divorce — except in other families whose standards they deplore — I suppose I should have had to stay unhappy.

February 27th.

Great excitement about the arrival of Prince Henry of Prussia. Mrs. Mills is to give him a breakfast, and Mrs. Neily Vanderbilt a fine dinner, and all the town is agog. I rather liked his yellow beard and his square, military shoulders myself.

May 22nd.

It's much nicer going to places with a man. I always knew it would be. And I know it's going to be delightful going to Europe, though we shall miss our Newport, too. I think I'll be married on the 15th of June.

January 12th, 1907.

Matrimony seems to be a pleasant institution, even after several years of it. The winter has been mild, on the whole. Indeed, they had a drag-hunt at Hempstead only ten days ago. Settled old couples like ourselves (though if any one else called us that we'd smite him to the earth) followed comfortably along the road.

There's a pleasant sparkle about the air of New York, though. We came back late — as people are doing more and more — so I hardly feel more than settled. Of course we did all the theatres, at once; saw *The Rose of the Rancho*, and *The New York Idea*, Langdon Mitchell's play, with Mrs. Fiske and George Arliss, and also Maude Adams in *Peter Pan*. I hope she'll go on playing it till I can take my daughter to see her. The opera, where we went the other night, was brilliant. All the boxes gleaming and glistening with silks and satins, jewels and waving fans. The dresses seemed to me beautiful, and there's something very graceful about the way women's figures curve in at the waist and out again generously to full hip and rounded shoulder. The eighteen-inch waist of my sister's day will never come back, I suppose, but the present small-waisted effect is certainly most delicate and charming. We heard a rather new young star, Geraldine Farrar, who has a fresh, sweet voice.

May 9th.

We returned to New York last month from a Southern trip, and have heard Calvé — no one will ever surpass her Carmen — and Cissie Loftus, who amused us mightily; and I, personally, have been extremely interested in the Parade of the Ladies' Four-in-Hands and their luncheon afterwards at the Colony Club. I wasn't here when they opened the Colony Club, on March 9th, but I hear the Dedication Dinner was a great success and Daisy Harriman made a good speech.

They had nine coaches in the parade. It was beautifully done, and a long drive, too, round the Park to the Circle, where they were reviewed, and down Fifth Avenue to the Colony Club at Madison Avenue and Thirtieth Street. It's extraordinary to me how well women do a lot of things we used to think only men could. Motoring, as they are beginning to do more and more, driving, riding, boating — and when I was little, tennis was just coming in as a woman's game!

I wish I knew whether we were going to Lenox this summer. I should like to be near Mrs. Edith Wharton at the "Mount"; never was there a more stimulating and delightful neighbour, or one with more exquisite taste in the surroundings she creates for herself.

LILLIAN RUSSELL PLAYS THE ROLE
OF A CHARMING YOUNG WIDOW,
THE OWNER OF A RACING STABLE,
IN "WILDFIRE" AT NEW YORK'S LIBERTY THEATRE

PORTRAITS OF ROYALITY

1906-1907

AFTER ONE OF KING EDWARD'S LUNCHEON PARTIES
AT WINDSOR: KING EDWARD VII, KAISER WILHELM II,
QUEEN ALEXANDRA, AND (SEATED) THE QUEEN OF SPAIN,
THE GERMAN EMPRESS, THE QUEEN OF PORTUGAL,
KING ALFONSO, AND THE QUEEN OF NORWAY

THE IMPERIAL FAMILY OF RUSSIA:
NICHOLAS II AND THE EMPRESS ALIX
HOLDING THE GRAND DUKE ALEXIS.
THE GRAND DUKE'S SISTERS
ARE, LEFT TO RIGHT: GRAND DUCHESS
TATIANA, MARIE, ANASTASIA, OLGA

Brown Brothers

THE CROWN PRINCE AND PRINCESS
OF RUMANIA AND FAMILY:
PRINCE CAROL, PRINCESS MARIE, PRINCE
NICOLAS, AND PRINCESS ELIZABETH

[1893 – 1913]   47

VIEW DOWN SACRAMENTO STREET.
AN EXTRAORDINARY PHOTOGRAPH
BY ARNOLD GENTHE, TAKEN ON THE DAY OF
THE GREAT DISASTER, APRIL 18, 1906

THE SAN FRANCISCO FIRE

SKY-SAILING
A FEMININE FAD

The interest in aerial flight has been rekindled in the past few days by the spectacular flight over the English Channel of M. Louis Blériot and is attested in another manner by the persistent news accounts of aerial trips in which women have taken leading roles.

It is in Paris, that the woman balloonist has come to the front. French women of means and of leisure have gone in for sky-sailing with a vim. It is they who have formed such workmanlike organizations as the "Stella" *aéro club feminin*, an association which holds regular meetings and conducts monthly ascensions during the season, which extends from the earliest spring until late into the autumn. The society has for its president the noted Madame Surcouf, a balloonist of rare skill, whose ascensions number more than thirty. During the month of June Madame Surcouf won the brevet of pilot of the Aero Club of France, in recognition of her ability; and to a French aeronaut the one qualification indispensable for recognition is the right to place after his or her name those mystic letters, "*pilote de l'Ae.—C.-F.*" Some of Mme. Surcouf's ventures in aviation have been at night and at least one of these trips, during which there was but one other person aboard, lasted an entire night.

This record is nearly equalled by that of Mme. Louis Blériot, wife of the monoplane aviator. Mme. Blériot is a vice-president of the "Stella," and an enthusiastic balloon traveller. She has made many ascensions, on some of which she has been accompanied by her husband. She has not, however, up to the present time been his companion on any of his aeroplane flights, and has even, according to report, extracted from M. Blériot a promise that shortly he will cease altogether his trips in the monoplane. One of the notable flights to the credit of the "Stella" was made on June 16th and 17th by M. and Mme. Blériot. With a pilot the couple ascended from the Aero Club of France at Saint-Cloud in the flower-bedecked balloon, *Les Hortensias*. After a night spent in sailing through the clouds the party landed the next day at Villemontais in the Loire, having gathered fresh laurels for the "Stella" by the long trip.

At a recent fête given by the "Stella" at the park of the Aero Club of France, flowers were made the keynote of the entertainment. Members of the club in six parties made ascensions, and all of the balloons were named for and decorated with flowers. Thus Mme. Surcouf sailed away in *Les Bluets,* and her balloon was decked with cornflowers. Mme. Desfossés-Dalloz, a vice-president of the "Stella," and Mme. Omer-Decugis, also of the club, were borne aloft in *Les Roses,* and the car of their air chariot was smothered under La France roses. Mme. Abulféda and Mme. Dumas, other members, occupied *Les Paquerettes,* and employed Easter lilies for its decoration. The Comte de Castillon de Saint-Victor acted as pilot of the balloon occupied by another "Stella" enthusiast, Mme. Monnot; on her car, *Les Pivoines,* she had lavished a wealth of peonies. Every car in the fête had its bank of flowers, and as the balloons rose over the beautiful park showers of colorful blossoms descended to the feet of the spectators.

The aeronautes of the "Stella" have set the fashion in their ascensions of wearing dainty and becoming apparel. Once a woman preparing for a balloon trip donned heavy boots, corduroy skirts or knickers, thick woolen or flannel sacques, and velveteen or leather jackets. Not so with the "Stellas." A trip in the clouds means less to them than a trip in a motor car, so far as change of raiment is concerned. A long veil, which may be used to tie on the hat and to keep rebellious locks confined, and a heavy coat that will keep one warm when passing through a cloudbank of mist or when in the higher and colder levels — and any afternoon toilette is transformed into a modern sky-sailor's equipment.

With the wealthier French women ballooning is the fad of the hour. As a sport it has replaced motoring, which now is considered slow and *passé*. A glance at any smart Parisian journal will reveal the popularity of balloon riding, for the papers are filled with accounts of daily ascensions, while the advertising pages display notices of where balloons may be bought or hired, tell of what parks offer facilities for ascensions, and print schedules of rates at which skilled pilots may be hired.

Week-end balloon parties are just as common as are week-end house parties in this country. The hostess need not ask her guests if they fly; it is taken for granted that they do, and that they will take a part in the fête as a matter of course. And as a matter of course they do take part.

50 [1893–1913]

BALLOONING HAS MADE
AVIATION
A SOCIAL PASTIME

Underwood and Underwood

THE PROGRESS OF THE FLYING MACHINE

BY ELIZABETH H. GREGORY

Not so very long ago the man who proclaimed himself an airship inventor was classed as a crank or dreamer, but with the rapid progress of science during the past two years, air navigation has taken on a different aspect. For it is within this period that flying has become an accomplished fact, and almost unbelievable wonders have raised both layman and inventor to heights of enthusiasm. It may be said that it was America, finally, who gave to the world both the means for flight and its application.

Prof. S. P. Langley, to whom the U.S. government appropriated fifty thousand dollars for experimental purposes, was the first man to bring about a realization of the practical side of the subject, and it was he who first proved that the solution of the problem was not impossible. The Langley machine, had it not been for an accident in the launching, would probably have flown and, though it was not a machine of commercial value, from it a practical one could have been evolved. This inventor whose work was unjustly criticized by the press as a failure and who was referred to satirically as the "buzzard," died before receiving proper public recognition or himself realizing the results that were later to be built upon his experiments.

Nothing in the world has done more to stimulate aeronautics in both America and Europe than the marvellous flights of Wilbur and Orville Wright, who hold the world's record of approximately one hundred miles. Their magnificent achievements have served to awaken other inventors to action as well as to inspire confidence in a doubting public. These two men, who but a few years ago were regarded as cranks, have now returned to their country loaded with honours and with profits from their invention. Before the President of France the Americans have shown what they can do; King Edward has been an interested watcher of their flights; King Alfonso journeyed from Pau to witness their manœuvres, and King Victor Emmanuel was delighted with their exhibition. They have brought with them to America the premier trophy of aeronautics for the longest flight in the year 1908, the Michelin Cup. Unlike any other machine the Wrights' is launched from a monorail, and it was this feature that caused them to refuse to compete for the five-thousand-dollar aviation cup offered this year by James Gordon Bennett. All of the European machines, being mounted on wheels, can run a distance on the ground before rising in the air, while the Wright machine leaves the ground at once. However, in some of their more recent flights, the Wrights have dispensed with the derrick and monorail.

Wilbur Wright has taken up six women, including his sister, Miss Katherine Wright, Mrs. Leon Bollee, Mrs. Lazar Weiler, Countess Lambert, and Mrs. Hart Berg. While staying in Paris, Miss Anne Morgan witnessed a flight and immediately asked Mr. Wright to take her up, but at that time it was not considered safe to do so. Miss Morgan is deeply interested in the subject, and it is said that she wishes to form an aeronautic club. Miss E. L. Todd, of New

ORVILLE WRIGHT
AND LIEUTENANT SELFRIDGE
IN FLIGHT AT FORT MYER, VIRGINIA – 1908

PAULHAN (FAR LEFT) AND HIS
PRIZE-WINNING BIPLANE

BLÉRIOT, WHO CROSSED
THE CHANNEL,
AND HIS MONOPLANE

York, is the first woman to invent an aeroplane. She now has her machine ready for the installment of the motor, and expects to drive it herself.

Now that "flying" promises to become a popular pastime, what to wear is a matter of concern to women aviators. A well-tailored gown with a short or divided skirt is considered the appropriate toggery by those who have had experience in this sport. The use of the divided skirt is a matter of preference. A close-fitting hat or cap is advisable for headgear. A French woman, Madame Theresa Peltier, who made an ascent with Delagrange, has adopted the divided skirt with leather leggings, and this is decidely picturesque.

It is interesting to know that it was a woman, Mrs. Alexander Graham Bell, who conceived the idea of forming the Aerial Experiment Association, and made the proposition to provide funds with which to carry on the experiments. The organization was founded, and four machines, the Red Wing, the June Bug, the Silver Dart, and the Cygnet, or Dr. Bell's tetrahedral kite, were built. The June Bug, the invention of Glenn H. Curtiss, won the Scientific American trophy in 1908 in a flight of more than a kilometre.

Now that suitable grounds have been obtained for flying purposes the interest in the subject undoubtedly will be broadened. The Aeronautic Society has leased the Old Morris Park grounds and will give exhibitions every Saturday afternoon during the summer. It has purchased an aeroplane and a dirigible for the use of its members, and it will be only a short time before women will be given an opportunity to learn how to operate a machine. The Aero Club of America has secured a tract of land from the Motor Parkway Association for practice purposes. The grounds are located within a comfortable distance of the city, and it is calculated that a member may go out in the afternoon for a "fly" and return home in time for dinner. It is hoped also to establish aeroplane and dirigible balloon races. The membership of the Aero Club includes William K. Vanderbilt, Jr., John Jacob Astor, Harry Payne Whitney, Charles G. Gates, and Peter Cooper Hewitt.

The return of the Wright brothers to America has created an active interest in aeronautic circles, and at last their own country has been given the privilege of honouring the inventors. In the East Room of the White House, on June 10, President Taft presented the brothers with the two beautiful gold medals offered by the Aero Club of America. The medals, which show the heads of the inventors on one side and their aeroplane in flight on the other, are said to have cost $1000 each. The President in presenting the medals said, "I esteem it a great honor and an opportunity to present these medals to you as an evidence of what you have done. I am glad — perhaps at a delayed hour — to show that in America it is not true that 'a prophet is not without honour save in his own country.'

"I don't like to think, and I decline to think, that these instrumentalities that you have invented for human use are to be confined in their utility to war. I presume that they will have great value in war, and I suppose that all of us representatives of the various governments ought to look at this matter, following the rules of governments of to-day from the standpoint of their utility in war; but I sincerely hope that these machines will be increased in usefulness to such a point that even those of us who now look at them as not for us, may count on their ability to carry more than 'thin' passengers in times of peace.

"Many great discoveries have come by accident. Men working in one direction have happened on a truth that developed itself into a great discovery, but you gentlemen have illustrated the other and on the whole much more commendable method. You planned what you wished to find and then you worked it out until you found it.

"I congratulate you on the result. I congratulate you on the recognition that you have received from all the crowned heads of Europe, and I congratulate you that in receiving it you maintained the modest and dignified demeanour worthy of American citizenship."

The Wrights were also presented with medals from the government in recognition of their great scientific achievements. These medals awarded to the Wrights mark the thirteenth given for non-warlike accomplishments. They are the first civilians to receive this award in more than twenty-four years, the last being Joseph Francis of Boston, inventor of the life car. The Wright brothers returned to America in order to fulfil their contracts with the government for a heavier-than-air machine, to be delivered at Fort Myer.

With so much that is practical already accomplished, even the doubting Thomases must admit that the science of flying is no longer in the dream state.

54 [1893 – 1913]

FARMAN,
SUCCESSFUL ENGLISH AVIATOR,
IN HIS AEROPLANE

ORVILLE WRIGHT (BELOW)
IN A GORDON BENNETT RACER
AT BELMONT PARK, 1910

Culver

GLENN CURTISS,
WHO WON
THE SPEED PRIZE
AT RHEIMS

LATHAM, IN HIS
ANTOINETTE,
ROUNDING THE
POST IN A
SPEED TRIAL

THE FRONT SEAT

COLLEGE GIRLS
HOLIDAYING
IN 1906

56 [1893 – 1913]

CANDID PHOTOGRAPHY
WHEREIN IT IS SHOWN THAT THE CAMERA DOES NOT LIE

MRS. GEORGE PELL
AT THE DOG SHOW

CLAM-DIGGERS

SOCIETY PHOTOGRAPHER
DRESSED FOR THE BEACH

MRS. HERMANN OELRICHS
AT THE BELMONT RACES

THE MISSES VANDERBILT
SHARE A JOKE

[1893 – 1913] 57

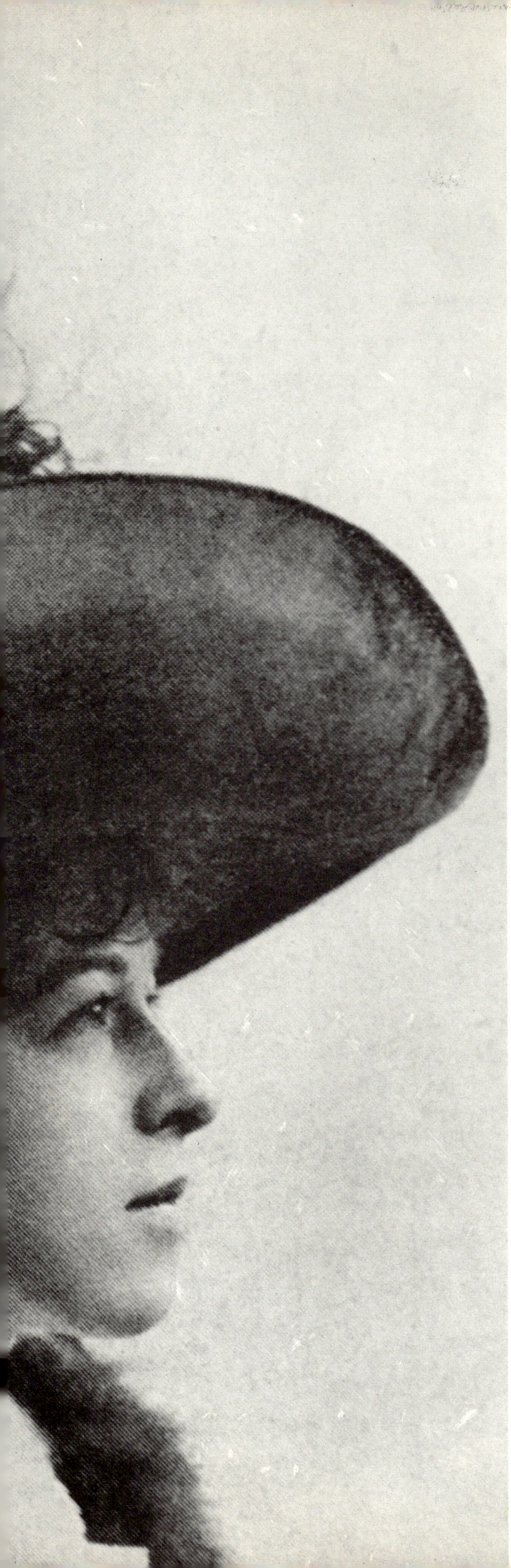

1900-1910:
WOMEN ARE HOURGLASS FIGURES UNDER OUTRAGEOUS HATS

HAT: LEWIS MODEL, 1909

MRS. STUYVESANT FISH, 1906

[1893 – 1913] 59

IN LONDON FOR THE CORONATION

Coronation guests from the whole world over have gone away from London deeply impressed with the Englishman's loyalty to and love for his new King and Queen.

How the people love Queen Mary was plainly evident on Coronation Day, and even more so on the second day's procession through the poorer part of Their Majesties' capital, for Queen Mary is in her element among the poorer subjects of the King, more so indeed than in the Mayfair drawing-room, where her dress, her manner, and her modes of employing her time are crudely criticized by the idlers about town.

Throughout the whole fortnight of the Coronation festivities, Their Majesties never failed in their untiring attentions to their foreign visitors — a great foregathering of the world's elect — and to the Indian princes especially, who received the greatest marks of favour from all the royal family and were fêted everywhere.

Those who have discussed the ceremony with the Queen say that she was delighted to observe that, without exception, the gowns worn by those present, whether peeresses or commoners, were after the fashion approved by herself.

One of the early comers at Westminster Abbey was the Duchess of Marlborough. Her arrival was greeted with delight and surprise, for it was common talk that Her Grace would not be seen at the ceremony, not so much because she was passed by as a canopy bearer and her place filled by the Duchess of Hamilton, as because of her growing dislike for big royal and social functions. Her famous pearls fell in long loops almost to her knees, and her small diamond crown and fairy-like coronet that fitted into the center proved the most becoming of any worn that day.

The Duchess of Roxburghe was one of the most striking figures in the Abbey; her gown was one sparkling mass of diamonds and shimmering pearls, which showed well under the wide opening of her velvet robes. Many of the gems she wore were culled from the jewels in the royal crown of France.

The Duchess of Roxburghe was one of the many unfortunates who, after the historic and glittering ceremony was over, found themselves lost in the throng outside the entrance. The arrangements were disgraceful, and the Goldsticks were apparently far too busy looking after their own comfort, and striking attitudes for the benefit of the crowds, to attend to their duties. One aged peeress remarked that these "sticks" seemed to feel that the Coronation might proceed without the King and Queen, but without the presence of the Goldsticks it would be an impossibility. The sarcasm was overheard by two of these dandies, who then really set to work to help the poor ladies, many of whom, having arrived at seven-thirty in the morning, did not leave the Abbey until nearly five in the afternoon.

HIS ROYAL HIGHNESS, THE PRINCE OF WALES
IN THE FULL UNIFORM OF A LIEUTENANT
OF THE ROYAL NAVY, 1913

THEIR MAJESTIES KING GEORGE V AND QUEEN MARY
IN THEIR CORONATION ROBES – 1911
Brown Brothers

THE GIRL OF THE GOLDEN WEST

It is history now — the premiere of Giacomo Puccini's opera, *La Fanciulla del West* (*The Girl of the Golden West*), given to the musical world at the Metropolitan Opera House in New York on the evening of December 10, 1910. For the first time America has won the honour of introducing a work of international calibre.

Those among the fortunate who obtained places within the crowded Metropolitan auditorium will not forget the scenes that occurred. Regardless of the intrinsic musical merit, there can be no division of opinion as to the popular triumph of *La Fanciulla del West*. It swept the four thousand people into evidences of approbation and left a topic for discussion, continuous ever since. No opera heard here for the first time has raised such endless dispute, and the second presentation appears to have given added impulse to the debate.

The average patron of opera is interested, principally, in the quality of music Puccini has written for *La Fanciulla del West* as compared to his three popular works, *La Bohème*, *Tosca*, and *Madama Butterfly*. The consensus is that previous efforts have not been touched. "It is not a *Bohème*," says one person. "Give me *Tosca*," declares another, while a third person stands firm for *Butterfly*.

But precisely what Puccini has, or has not, done cannot be determined through a single hearing of his work. Every music critic who reviewed the premiere for the New York dailies had copies of the pianoforte arrangement of *La Fanciulla del West* a week before it took place. They heard rehearsals at every available opportunity, and, two days before the public presentation, a dress performance was given, largely for their special benefit. Thus fortitfied, they could speak with authority, and yet the most competent disclosed indecision in some important respects.

The experiment of taking as the basis for an opera a melodrama so replete with short, snappy dialogue as David Belasco's is unusual. The task of the composer in undertaking to fit to unlyrical "speeches" and "lines" music of essentially melodic quality is monumental. It is true that there seems to be less melody in *La Fanciulla del West* than in Puccini's earlier operas, but there is more melody in it than appears on the surface.

The waltz that occurs near the close of the first act, in the Polka Saloon, reappears frequently throughout the opera, and the final aria allotted to the tenor, "*Ch' ella mi creda libero*," is a manifestly fine piece of creative melodic writing. So, too, is Rance's aria in Act Three, "*Minnie, ora piangi tu.*" What is mistaken by some for lack of melody in *La Fanciulla del West* is fragmentary tunefulness. In the maze of musical sound it is not always easy to follow the melody, which, nevertheless, is there.

The few solos and the quick-fire recitative are handled in a manner to give an illusion of musical conversation. There are themes to typify Johnson, Minnie, Rance, and even the Indian, who is of slight consequence in the story of the opera; and they spring to the surface as often as an episode demands their use.

The melody heard while Minnie and Johnson are talking at the bar of the Polka Saloon, after "the boys" have left the place, is intended to be American, as is the camp minstrel melody, sung by Jake Wallace — "the homesick melody." In the solo bits for the lesser principals, the thumping of fists on tables gives a rather weird musical effect, but without traces of Americanism.

Manifestly endeavouring to apply local musical colour to the Belasco melodrama, Puccini has failed. The ruggedness of the life in the days when the action of *La Fanciulla del West* is supposed to have taken place is put into the music, but it is Italian in intensity rather than American in spontaneous, vigorous outburst. But in Europe, where the customs of this country are only scantily known, *La Fanciulla del West* is likely to be accepted as "the real thing."

Though often super-excellent, the music lacks consistent originality. There is not enough of the Puccini bigness of musical sweep — that freedom of stroke analogous to the painter's handling of the brush. A great deal of the success comes from the melodrama; and this,

too, despite the inability of the librettists, G. Zangarini and C. C. Civinini, to put certain American phrases into exact Italian translations. Had the opera been sung in English, it would have gained in power.

The elimination of David Belasco's short fourth act and the substitution of a third act different from the original was done for operatic purposes. The final act, in the California woodlands, brings Johnson his freedom, after Minnie has ridden to his rescue just as "the boys" have caught the outlaw and are about to hang him. The scene in which these rough men of the West weep as the renegade and his sweetheart walk slowly off to their new life together struck a false human note. They would not, certainly, have done such a thing in '49.

As for the performance, nothing better from vocal and dramatic standpoints has ever taken place on the operatic stage. There has been criticism because no American singer was chosen to create one or more of the roles in *La Fanciulla del West*, but this was unjust. No tenor living could have sung the music of Johnson with such tonal beauty, vigor and finish as did Caruso, and few could have equalled his easy impersonation of the character. Destinn, as Minnie, proved a surprise; her creation of the part is one of the finest achievements in her career.

Amato, first of baritones, carried off the honors of the performance as the sheriff, Rance, in a characterization so finished that even Frank Keenan — who made so much of this role in the play — could not have surpassed it. Amato dominated every scene in which he figured. As always, his singing was well-nigh flawless. Dinh Gilly, a baritone who has progressed rapidly since he joined the Metropolitan organization a year ago, was almost as effective in the smaller part of Sonora while de Segurola, as Wallace; Didur, as Ashby, the express agent; and the others in lesser roles, all acquitted themselves in a manner indicative of arduous training at the hands of David Belasco.

THE HANGING SCENE. CARUSO WITH DESTINN AND, IN TOP HAT, PASQUALE AMATO AS THE SHERIFF

[1893 – 1913] 63

SURREY WITH REMOVABLE TOP

THE MOTOR-CAR, 1906-1913

Conveyances of distinction fitted with such luxurious appointments as the age and the country afforded have ever been the prerogative of wealth and high degree. The maharajah of the east travels in a superb howdah, on a camel or an elephant; the rulers of Rome used chariots drawn by four horses; and the monarchs and beauties of the French court had nothing less than a golden coach with four horses and with outriders magnificently mounted to announce their approach.

Though these equipages appear picturesque from a distance, they are outdone not only in elegance, but in comfort and luxury, by the modern motor-car. To this luxury-loving age, the perfectly appointed car is most appropriate. Its interior is as dainty as a boudoir, as solidly comfortable as a library, while beneath its beautiful appearance is concealed the power to annihilate the old enemies, time and space. Even the elements beat in unavailing onslaught, as the motor runs through rain and wind, for snow alone impedes its progress.

64 [1893 – 1913]

FUR COAT AND CAP,
A NECESSARY PART OF THE
CHAUFFEUR'S OPEN-CAR
EQUIPMENT FOR WINTER

"NUDE DESCENDING A STAIRCASE," A CUBIST PAINTING BY MARCEL DUCHAMP, ONE OF
THE MOST CONTROVERSIAL EXHIBITS IN THE ARMORY SHOW

THE ARMORY SHOW

FROM ONE EXTREMIST TO THE OTHER

"THE WAY DOWN TO THE SEA" BY AUGUSTUS JOHN, THE MOST PROMINENT ENGLISH MODERNIST

BY GUY PENE DU BOIS

People have laughed and turned serious in a breath at the exhibition of modern art held in New York at the Sixty-ninth Regiment Armory. The exhibition has been called good and bad; it has been relegated to the realm of the worthless and placed on the pinnacle of the most high. The more sage critics have all pointed to the importance of its significance. Indeed, it is from this point of view that the exhibition was of particular importance. For the first time in their young art lives Americans have an opportunity to view, under one roof, the works of all the modernists.

For a number of years, Paris, which admittedly is the hub of the wheel of art, has been the storm center of a galaxy of revolutionary movements in art.

The new art is so new that it must inevitably be shocking to untrained eyes, especially that of the most extreme post-impressionists, neo-impressionists, futurists, and cubists. They have left the beaten paths of art in technique and in point of view, in attack, and in vision. Heretofore, this has been, even in the case of the symbolists, representative. The moderns say that it must not be representative; they say, with Oscar Wilde, that art begins where representation ceases. They are, in a sense, trying to do with paint and with plaster what musicians do with notes. Above everything, perhaps, they seek rhythm.

The exhibition in chronological sequence, as arranged by Mr. Arthur B. Davies, the President of the Association of American Painters and Sculptors, showed the roots of the present movement to be the classicist, Ingres; the romanticist, Delacroix; the realist, Courbet.

Following Ingres, according to the chronology of Mr. Davies (and that is the chronology of the show), were Puvis de Chavannes, Degas, who was also influenced by Courbet, and Serret; after Courbet came Manet, Monet, Sisley, Pissarro, Signac, Cassatt, Toulouse-Lautrec, and Morisot; and in the wake of Delacroix came Daumier, Redon, and Renoir.

Cézanne, who was influenced by the realism of the Impressionists, by their scientific truth, and by the order of the classicists, gave a new impetus to the art of his day. Indeed, Cézanne may be said to be the god of all those of the new army which literary people have divided into many very confusing lists. Cézanne led a more positive return to nature than any of his predecessors. He spent a number of years in Paris in communion with that group of great spirits which included Manet, Monet, Courbet, and Degas. During this period he was tyrannizd by their influence and that of Daumier and Delacroix, even

"RED TOP" BY ROBERT HENRI,
PROBABLY THE BEST KNOWN
OF THE AMERICAN INDEPENDENTS

GEORGE LUKS SHOWED HIS REMARKABLE "PHILOSOPHER"

AFTER THE CUBISTS, BUT FOR QUITE OTHER REASONS,
ROBERT L. CHANDLER'S DECORATIVE PANELS (BELOW)
ATTRACTED MOST ATTENTION

"PORTRAIT OF MAURICE DENIS" BY REDON,
WHOSE WORK, IT IS SAID,
HAS BEEN UNFAIRLY SUPPRESSED

VINCENT VAN GOGH'S "LABORERS" (BELOW)
IS CHARACTERISTIC OF THIS ARTIST'S
INTEREST IN THE VITAL ASPECTS OF NATURE

of Rubens, Veronese, and Michelangelo. Then in 1879 he retired to Aix-en-Provence to work out his own salvation. Here in seclusion he found the new rhythm so much admired by the moderns of today, and here, as much as man can, he got rid of the traditions of art that had hampered him so long, threw off the influence of other men, and began intimately to understand his subject.

The work of this period, which is Cézanne's great work, has something in it of the archaic quality of Puvis, if you will, or of primitive man. It is nature ordered by law, made rhythmical and complete, in arrangements of forms and colors that, by their juxtaposition and their harmonious concordance, lend the beauty and the nobility of life, and complete the picture. There can be no doubt of the greatness of Cézanne, just as there can be no doubt of the value of the wonderful romanticists, Gauguin and Van Gogh, whose intensity hurried his death. Now that we see these three giants of this exhibition, we in America can but wonder that we have waited so long for the pleasure.

In the case of the cubists and the other extremists, wonder is not paramount. Their methods are so obvious. Their influence will prove greater than their work. They have concocted formulas and carried them too far beyond the pale of life, and beyond the possibility of appreciation by the multitude. One of the sensations of the show — Marcel Duchamp's "Nude Descending a Staircase," shown in the cubists' room, was not even interesting as a picture puzzle, because there is possibility of solving a picture puzzle, whereas there was no such possibility in this picture.

On the other hand, familiarity with the purely cubistic productions of Picabia led to a certain understanding or, shall I say, deciphering of them. Out of the rhythmic mass of his cubes in red and pink and white and black, figures at last became discernible, and, not seldom, a sense of beauty borrowed from the classicists. But the sense of life, if it was there, was very successfully hidden beneath the disconcerting design. This is not so true of the work of Picasso, the father of the cubists, who sometimes recalls Ingres.

The most that may be said of the art of the extremists among the cubists, if it may be said at all, is that it is art in embryonic form. Cézanne said that nature might be divided into cubes. The cubists have taken him too literally. Cézanne once said that fat form and fat color, thin form and thin color were indissolubly linked. Again the cubists have taken him too literally, and, like most imitators, have attained only a surface understanding. They have grasped, not the substance, but only the superficialities; they have imitated the manner and forgotten the underlying quality, the inspiration which, in reality, is the only quality worth considering.

Particular beauty was lent the collection by the decorative pieces of the very human Maurice Denis; and power by the contributions of the Englishman, Augustus John. That so-much-heralded post-impressionist, Henri Matisse, was represented by over a dozen disappointing works, thin and unconvincing.

The revelation of the American section came in the screens of Robert L. Chandler. They were painted with great luxuriance and vigor and immense decorative value. The standard of the American pictures, on the whole, was unusually good.

The catalogue of the entire exhibition contained 1040 numbers. The exhibition was richer in diversity and in modernity than any ever held in this country. Indeed, there can be no doubt that it will go down in the annals of American art as one of the most important exhibitions ever held here, if not the most important. Those who scoffed are those who are not in sympathy with modern art, for modern art was the controlling spirit of the show.

CEZANNE'S "WOMAN WITH THE ROSARY" IS, EVEN CONSERVATIVES ADMIT, A GREAT PICTURE FOR ALL TIME

ENTER GWENDOLEN! BY EMILY POST

Gwendolen was in tears. Her bills for clothes swamped her. Throughout the winter, in raiment that would have turned Bakst multicoloured and obliquely cubed with envy, she had tangoed and maxixed lightly, beautifully, and ceaselessly as a bit of foam upon the crest of the wave of fashion. And now that the derelicts of her winter wardrobe lay like washed-up flotsam after the season's storm, she must pay the salvage!

Moreover, she had been brought face to face with her insolvency at the same moment that her head was full of the Spender Cutadashes' Field-of-the-Cloth-of-Gold Ball. Gwendolen, who had (of course) been asked to be in the opening quadrille, had been ecstatically planning a costume of golden magnificence — and now, it would be months before she could even begin to feed the rapacious maws of that ever-yawning debit column.

It really was a case for tears. Here was poor Gwendolen, who had been to only twenty-odd balls in thirty days, and here was the most expensive and gorgeous one of them all rising like a golden sun, and she, poor dear, banished for want of the price of another dress. There had been a Russian ball, an Omar Khayyam ball, an 1830 ball, and a ball of one of the Louises — and each ball had cut her resources like a storm into the sands of the Jersey Coast.

She chewed the end of her pencil and read her balance — or rather her lack of a balance — over again. Then she dumped out her mesh purse and counted over every cent. She had one dollar and eighty-four cents. This for a costume for the most expensive ball New York had ever attended!

"If only it were fashionable," thought she, "to go in one's skin!" She had nice skin, had Gwendolen. However, the Cutadashes were not giving a Venus party. It looked very much indeed like the setting of a very bright particular social star. Who was the smartest woman at the opera on Monday? Gwendolen. Who was it that really gave cachet to the whole party that the Blatants took south? Gwendolen, of course. And at the Spifflings' masquerade, who wore that marvellously chic minaret of pearls and the emerald wig? Who, indeed, but Gwendolen?

No one understood better than she that to attempt to go to a party badly dressed would be like leaving one's ticket of admission at home.

The situation was certainly distressing. What was Gwendolen to do? Stay at home forever? Stay at home, this time at least! That was the only answer.

Her eyes wandered mournfully from the balance in her check book to the gold-emblazoned invitation, and with a sigh that came from the very depths of her little butterfly being, she wrote the first three lines of her regret —

At this point she was interrupted by a Mere Man. She welcomed him dolefully.

He saw her distress and inquired sympathetically.

She answered evasively as to one not capable of sounding the acute depths of her misery.

"Are you going to the Spender Cutadashes'?" he blundered.

"No."

"No?"

Whereupon she did the unexpected (as usual) and told him the whole sad story. "If it only wasn't gold," she wailed. "No materials are so expensive as gold — "

"There is a yellow art cheese-cloth that is said to look very like gold gauze — what is all your silly talk about not being able to arrange something to wear to the Cutadashes'?"

She turned the mesh purse out again. "There," she said, "do you see that overpowering wealth? Well, that and a few pearl beads is everything I have or can get that would be available. What sort of an appearance can I make in that?"

"A rather natural costume garnished with a few beads and a sweet smile — would certainly make a stir. But somehow, does it sound advisable?"

In that instant Gwendolen bounded to her feet, her face radiant. "Will you bet me — will you, will you, will you?" she cried.

"Bet?" The Mere Man seemed bewildered, but, being Mere Man, quite keen for a gamble. "I will bet you," said she, "whatever you like, that I go to the Cutadash ball after all, and that my costume will not only be all of gold but — quite all right, and I will not spend a bit over one dollar and eighty-four cents."

The Mere Man, being a millionaire, was very careful about squandering his pennies. "You mean," he inquired cautiously, "that you have a dress of gold stuff left over from some past reckless expenditure?"

"I have eight or nine strings of pearl beads — they are quite big pearl beads."

"Nothing else?" he gasped.

She made her eyes look quite like a sleepy cat's that told nothing, and murmured, "And the dollar eighty-four."

Like a gorgeous, glittering snake the guests at the Spender Cutadashes' moved slowly in to dinner. Mrs. Cutadash had counted heads and found one missing, but she could wait no longer. The Mere Man from his place at the end of the golden file looked everywhere for that missing head, but he saw none that even remotely resembled hers. She had evidently found it impossible to make an appearance in a few beads and fewer pennies; and so, although it was a really lovely party, he felt quite depressed.

At table, the neighbour on his left broke into his reverie.

"A really glittering spectacle," she said. "It does seem though, rather extravagant when you think of the terrific cost of all these golden dresses that will probably never be worn but this once." Then looking about, she added, "I don't see Gwendolen anywhere."

"I am afraid she is not coming."

"Not coming? Why she has not missed a thing this year!"

"That is just it. There wasn't a crumb of money left to buy another dress."

"She is horribly extravagant. No one could dress the way she does on less than a fortune."

"If she comes tonight, her dress is all to be made for less than two dollars."

"I wish," said his neighbour, not listening to him, but with evident meaning, "that some nice man with lots of money would marry her."

"Maybe she has quite different ideas on the subject." And then he went on cryptically as though to himself, "The other day was almost crucial, and if the dollar eighty-four costume should prove a failure — " Then suddenly he ejaculated, "Oh, the fraud! I ask you! There is the young woman who said it would be unprincipled to spend over a dollar eighty-four for her costume!"

In the doorway stood a fantasy of the goldsmith's workmanship — a beautifully wrought figure, all solid gold, except the face which, marvellously resembling a bit of Chinese lacquer in texture and colouring, was recognizably that of Gwendolen.

Under a crown of pearls and coral, the curls of a solid gold metal wig fell to her waist. She seemed to have been poured into a clinging underdress of the same metal. The bodice, almost high-necked, had long, tight sleeves that reached below her knuckles, and all ten fingers were loaded with rings. Below and between the slashings of the long heavy strips of gold plates that formed her skirt, she wore clinging, smooth-fitting trousers of a metallic material like the sleeves. These were finished at the ankles with bands of pearls and coral.

Over the clinging underbodice and partially covering the slashed skirt of heavy metal was a transparent, sleeveless tunic of open-mesh gold gauze, embellished with a tracery of gold metal leaves and clusters of pearl and coral berries.

Across the tables Gwendolen caught the eye of Mere Man.

"Do I win?" Her triumphant lips formed the words mutely.

"No." He answered mutely back.

Her mouth and eyes were rounds of protest.

"Fraud," he articulated.

Pointing at her derisively, his lips protested, "Dollar eighty-four!"

She pointed her ivory-coloured, coral-tipped, ring-laden fingers to herself, and laughing, nodded, "Yes."

"What is all this sign language about?" asked his neighbour.

"A question of price. Would you say it was cheap, her dress?"

"Fabulous! You have only to look at the fit of it — "

"It is just that that makes me wonder," mused the Mere Man, suddenly disconcerted.

After the dinner there was the quadrille, and after that the voting contest for the best costume (which Gwendolen won), and not until after that did the Mere Man succeed in approaching the triumphant Gwendolen.

"Well," said her smiling, coral lips, "did you ever see a dollar eighty-four more audaciously or divinely spent?"

"You will, I suppose, explain?" asked he.

"Certainly," said she. "Have you a pencil ready?"

"For that dollar-eighty-four farce?" However, he pretended to humour her in whatever her game might be. "Item one, then, where did you get the crown?"

"It's made of the pearls I told you about — you allowed me those."

"Oh!" he said loftily, "thought as much. And the coral stones, and the manufacturer?"

"Manufacturer, myself. The coral stones are dried beans painted with coral enamel paint. Score one?"

"And the wig?"

"Oh, the wig was very expensive. It

MRS. EMILY POST

cost thirty-eight cents for gold paint and shellac. But a very nice carpenter gave me all the shavings — long, strong ones."

An expression, amazement and awe combined, was creeping into the face of the Mere Man. She continued, "And the gauze is ten cents a yard, white cotton veiling gilded, and the smilax — three bunches at the Ten Cent Store, also gilded."

"And your underdress?"

"Oh my under — "

"That slashed, metal, warrior-like thing."

"Oh, that is of embossed gold paper strips pasted on tarlatan and weighted."

"And all the real foundation of your dress?"

"Oh, you mean" — she faltered — "you mean my — they are — that is" — her voice trailed off rather low — "mostly gold paint — there is a little gauze. You know, I think that *peau de femme* is going to be the rage this year. It quite solves the problem of the high cost of dressing. A pot of paint and a brush — and every woman becomes her own dressmaker. Easily fitted, cool, economical and comes in all the fashionable colours — "

"Gwendolen you are — "

"But I win?"

As everyone heard later, they both won — which is usually the way when a woman bets.

[1893 – 1913] 71

PEOPLE AND PLACES

AT BELMONT PARK, SOCIETY
TURNS ITS BACK —
BUT NOT
ON THE HORSES

Underwood and Underwood and INS

MR. AND MRS. VINCENT
ASTOR ATTEND THE DAVIS CUP AT
FOREST HILLS

TOP: MR. HENRY CLAY FRICK
PLAYING A ROUND OF GOLF WITH MEMBERS
OF HIS PRIVATE CAR PARTY

ABOVE: MISS HELEN AND
MASTER THOMAS HITCHCOCK,
WHOSE MOTHER, MRS. THOMAS HITCHCOCK,
IS THE NOTED HORSEWOMAN

MRS. W. K. VANDERBILT
AT THE TENNIS MATCH
WHICH SEES AUSTRALIA
WIN THE DAVIS CUP
FROM AMERICA

OPPOSITE: MISS CLARA
FARGO AND MR. ROBERT
BREESE, GRACEFUL
SKATERS AT TUXEDO, BRING
THE DANCE
INTO THE OPEN AIR

72   [1913 – 1923]

MR. AND MRS. JAMES A. ROOSEVELT
AND MR. LORILLARD SPENCER
AT MEADOWBROOK

MRS. JOSEPH E. DAVIS
AND MR. THOMAS HITCHCOCK
AT BELMONT PARK

ABOVE: MRS. E. J. BERWIND
AND MR. KING AT THE NEWPORT
HORSE SHOW, A SOCIETY EVENT
OF GREATEST INTEREST

ABOVE RIGHT: MISS FLORA WHITNEY
AND MR. ARCHIBALD ROOSEVELT
AT THE PIPING ROCK RACE MEET.
YOUNG ROOSEVELT, THIRD SON OF
COLONEL THEODORE ROOSEVELT,
APPEARS TO HAVE INHERITED
HIS FAMOUS FATHER'S SMILE

RIGHT: MR. FRANKLIN D. ROOSEVELT,
NEW ASSISTANT SECRETARY OF THE
NAVY, AND SENATOR LODGE OF
MASSACHUSETTS AT THE WEDDING OF
MISS ETHEL ROOSEVELT TO
DR. RICHARD DERBY

FAR RIGHT: AT MEADOWBROOK, MRS.
DEVEREUX MILBURN, WIFE OF THE
FAMOUS POLO PLAYER;
MR. HARRISON TWEED, A POLO PLAYER
OF NOTE; MR. VICTOR C. MATHER

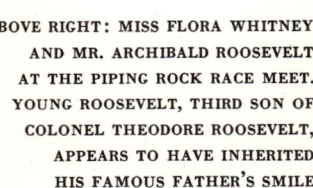

Underwood and Underwood and INS

Underwood and Underwood and INS

LEFT: MR. BAYARD TUCKERMAN,
MR. FRANK APPLETON,
MR. HAROLD VANDERBILT,
MRS. PAYNE WHITNEY AT THE
MEADOWBROOK HUNT CUP

ABOVE: MRS. RUSSELL ELLIS SARD
AS SHE VENTURES FORTH
FOR THE NEW SPORT OF SKIING

SECOND FROM LEFT: MRS. JACK
GARDNER, WHO OWNS ONE OF THE
MOST FAMOUS PRIVATE MUSEUMS
IN AMERICA, AT THE BROOKLINE
COUNTRY CLUB HORSE SHOW

LEFT: MISS ELEONORA
SEARS, ONE OF THE VERY BEST
SPORTSWOMEN
AT THE NEWPORT HORSE SHOW

wood and Underwood and INS

Baron de Meyer

ABOVE: MRS. HARRY PAYNE WHITNEY,
ONE OF THE PROMINENT HOSTESSES OF
NEW YORK AS WELL AS AN ABLE SCULPTOR,
IN A PERSIAN COSTUME WORN AT HER
OWN FANCY-DRESS PARTY

PEOPLE AND PLACES

MRS. WALDORF ASTOR AND HER LITTLE SON
WILLIAM ARRIVE ON THE S.S. "LUSITANIA."
SHE WAS MET BY CHARLES DANA GIBSON
AND HER SISTER MRS. GIBSON, THE ORIGINAL
MODEL FOR THE "GIBSON GIRL"

[1913 – 1923] 75

THE RUSSIAN BALLET

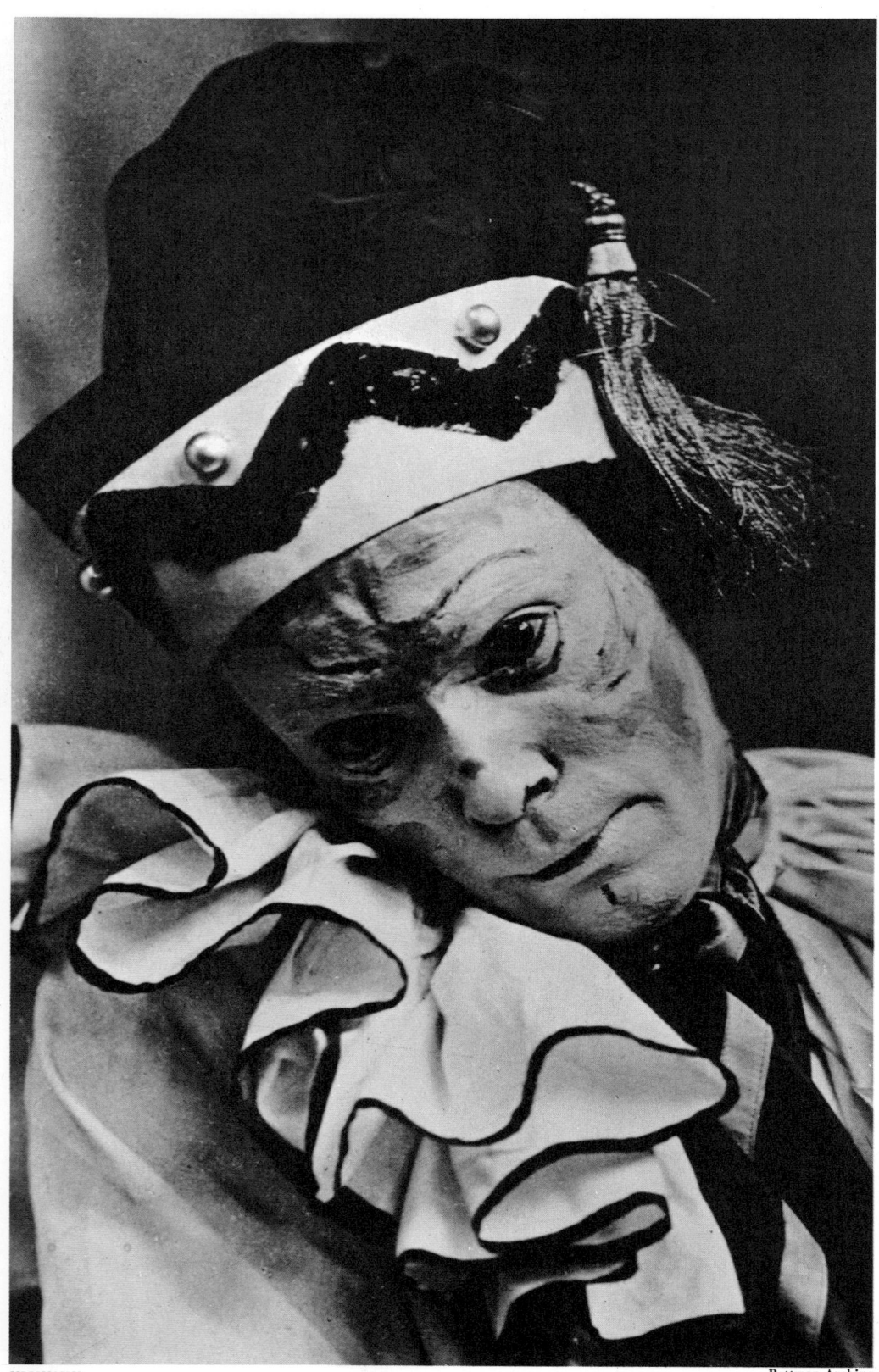

NIJINSKY
IN "PETROUCHKA"

The quickest way to grow acquainted with any race or any nation is to study its art. Art is the one thing in the world that cannot lie. It tells us both the best about a people and the worst. In studying the art of any nation, we are reading a page in the eternal book of the Recording Angel. What God remembers of great Greece is revealed to us by the Parthenon, the Hermes of Praxiteles, the dialogues of Plato, the "Trojan Women" of Euripides. All that the Recording Angel thought of mediaeval France was written on the face of that great monument at Rheims, which even the wayward winds and ranting rains respected for seven hundred years. To understand Elizabethan England, we read Shakespeare; to understand Venice we gaze upon the glittering canvases of Veronese. Historians may lie, biographers may sentimentalize, even philosophers may argue and scholars may dispute; but, after the tumult and the shouting die, Art remains, and tells the simple truth.

The Slavs are a new people, and the three arts they have most assiduously cultivated to date are literature, music, and the dance. It is in terms of the great art of the dance that the Russians have expressed themselves most vividly; and the huge welcome accorded by the West to the Russian Ballet of Diaghilev is a token of our deep desire to understand what Russia means, what Russia is. We want to know the truth about these semi-Asiatic and semi-European people. Let us therefore study the chief art that they have chosen.

The art of the Russian Ballet is undeniably barbaric; but having granted this, it becomes necessary to think

AS PRESENTED BY DIAGHILEV

about the word. There are two kinds of barbarism — first, the barbarism of a people ascending to civilization, and, second, the barbarism of a people descending from civilization. The descending sort of barbarism is decadent; the ascending sort is vigorous with pristine power. In literature, for instance, the barbarism of Rabelais is healthy and the barbarism of Frank Wedekind is sickly; it is simple to see which man is climbing up and which man is climbing down.

The imagined region of the Russian ballet is a region of primitive emotions. Beauty, anger, lust, terror, jollity, timidity stalk the stage naked and unashamed. This art is the antithesis of what, in the history of English literature, has been labeled with the name "Victorian." The note of Victorian literature is a note of almost harrowing self-consciousness. Of this disease of super-civilization these Russians are emphatically free. Their splendid and phantasmagoric dreams are undisturbed by forethought or underthought or afterthought. They do not worry; they achieve. They are pagan with the pure, untroubled paganism of the healthy child — the child still trailing clouds of glory, before climbing upward to that blinding sunshine which dispels all clouds, however glorious, until, in turn, it is enshadowed by returning night.

The barbarism of these Russian dancers is young with the youth of the world, and reminds us of the periodical return of Proserpine; but the technique of their art is trained and civilized. Here, as in the case of Russian music, we observe a huge and lawless impulse reined and harnessed by a sense of law. The message of this art may be semi-Asiatic; the method is more than semi-European. The material may be barbaric; the craftsmanship, if anything, is super-civilized.

The masters of the Russian Ballet have realized the dream of Richard Wagner. They have accomplished a synthesis of many arts, and have made what Wagner called a "music drama." Painting, sculpture, music, and the dance contribute obviously to the panorama. Literature is represented by the underlying note of narrative, and the technique of the whole is more than vaguely architectural. Somebody or other contributes the outline of a story; Golovine or Bakst imagines it in terms of painting; Stravinsky or Rimsky-Korsakov imagines it in terms of music; Diaghilev imagines it in the solid terms of architectural construction; the performers — Nijinsky, Karsavina, and the others of this amazing company — imagine it in terms of that art of rhythmic sculpture which is called the dance; and the compounded product is finally delivered to the world. Never before, in the history of art, has a pristine, pagan, and barbaric impulse been expressed so perfectly in terms of a technique that represents the final note in what may be called thorough cultivation.

The Russian Ballet, in a certain sense, says the latest word in art; for its material is supremely free from care and its method is supremely careful. If inspiration is synonymous with spontaneity, then this great art is inspired; if perfection is synonymous with the taking of infinite pains, then this great art is perfected. It is barbaric in content and civilized in form.

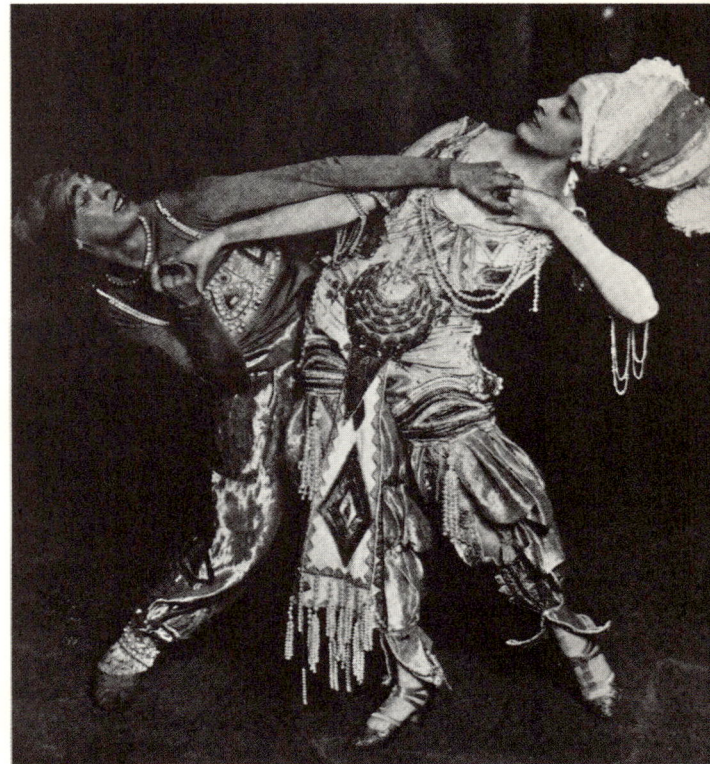

White and White

BOLM AND REVALLES IN SCHEHEREZADE

KARSAVINA IN "PAPILLONS" COSTUME DESIGNED BY LEON BAKST

Bransburg

NOTED ENGLISH AUTHORS

JOHN GALSWORTHY is well known both for his novels — *The Island Pharisees* and *The Man of Property* have attracted widest attention — and his plays, which include *Strife*, *Justice*, and *The Fugitive*.

Brown Brothers

HENRY JAMES, English by adoption and brother of William James, died in 1916 leaving two unfinished works, *The Ivory Tower* and *The Sense of the Past*, shortly to be published. His brother's major opus: *The Varieties of Religious Experience*.

Culver

Although trained in medicine, SOMERSET MAUGHAM started a writing career so successfully with the publication of *Lisa of Lambeth* in 1897 that novels and plays now claim his entire attention. His latest and most extraordinary novel: *Of Human Bondage*.

Brown Brothers

H. G. WELLS continues to write his astounding literary scientific predictions and his outspoken social and political theories for which his fiction has become so popular. Recently published: *The Research Magnificent* and *Mr. Britling Sees It Through*.

THE RIDDLE OF THE SPHINX

BY HUNTLY MURRAY

Let us acknowledge at the outset that any attempt to characterize the sexes, asserting that Men or Women, as such, are thus and so, must be profoundly futile. Acute observers have recognized several different kinds of women and almost as many kinds of men.

Our first step is to explode the superstition that women are mysterious. Women are about as mysterious as hippopotami. Their habits, though strange, are easy to observe and understand; and their psychology, though in some respects other than that of men, is yet reasonably simple. Of course, if you treat a hippopotamus like a man and a brother, it may not perfectly respond; and if you make the opposite mistake and treat it as a nightmare or an angel, you may even give offence.

The premise of the mystery of woman is habitually encouraged by women for precisely the same reason that it has always been encouraged by priesthoods, cabals, and secret societies. It flatters the vanity of the initiate and increases the power over those without the pale. And it is acquiesced in by the men from motives, curiously mixed, of indolence and cunning. By accepting the fiction that women are incomprehensible, they avoid at once the trouble and the obligation of attempting to comprehend them. At the same time, they pay an easy compliment and make such knowledge as they have doubly effective under cover of innocence. It is indeed surprising how few women realize that this weapon works both ways. Try it upon some man, and see. Tell him that you consider him a mystery beyond all feminine understanding, and observe his reactions. Observe also what you can do to him with seemingly innocent flattery.

It is commonly said that women are frivolous; and the patent absurdity of this serves to illuminate the first great distinction between them and the rest of humankind. Women are called frivolous because they manifestly expend much thought and energy upon frivolities. But the true explanation is not that they are frivolous, but that they are on the contrary almost insanely serious and responsible. A woman simply has to be serious about something; and in default of something more important in itself, she will be serious about a trifle. If she is not responsible for a child, she will be responsible for a chow dog; if she is not in love, she will expend herself upon the most ephemeral flirtations; if she is not in charge of the morals of the community, she will take charge of its manners with an equal zest; in a word, if she has no cause for work, she must work for a Cause. Nature has placed in her care the central and basic responsibility of all, the bearing and rearing of the race, and for that object has implanted in her a gravely furious instinct of devotion, deeper than sex itself.

A woman cannot even imagine the deep frivolity of men. Men play at their work, amuse themselves with love, dissipate life, and die with a jest upon their lips. Women make even amusement a vocation. Men have their hobbies, to which they lightly sacrifice important matters; but no woman ever has a hobby. For her, either a thing is seriously important or it is not. She cannot understand how a man plays a game, furiously yet with his tongue in his cheek, at once with effort and with unconcern.

That profoundly personal view of all human relations which is as characteristic of women as their sense of responsibility, is really part of the same principle. For responsibility is always personal. The celebrated incident of Cleopatra and her messenger slaves is not so much tyrannical as typically feminine. Her reasoning was simple; the bad news made her unhappy; the slaves brought the bad news; therefore let them die. The idea that the messengers were not themselves responsible for their ill tidings is an abstraction foreign to the feminine mind. A man, of course, thinks first of the principle involved. But a woman thinks only of two personal questions: how much she is hurt and who it is that has hurt her. She is in no wise disarmed by the apology, since an apology is to her merely a confession. And why should a fault be deemed less blameworthy for being confessed? She herself never apologizes, except as an unmeaning social formality. She may admit herself defeated; but it's too much to expect her to admit that she deserves defeat. And if her opponent is base enough to do so, she will merely change her sword into a scourge and go on fighting gloriously long after she has won.

WAR

AMERICA ENTERS
THE GREAT WAR.
FAREWELL PARADE,
27TH DIVISION,
AUGUST 30, 1917,
NEW YORK CITY

W. W. Brooks

1914-1918

LEFT: QUEEN MARY,
WITH ENGLISH OFFICERS,
REVIEWS WOUNDED
INDIAN TROOPS

MRS. WILLIAM K. VANDERBILT
WITH A CONVALESCENT SOLDIER
AT NEUILLY, IN FRANCE

ENGLISHWOMEN, ORGANIZED
UNDER THE FRIVOLOUS
TITLE OF "FANNIES," RUN FIRST-AID
STATIONS IN FRANCE

RIGHT: MISS MAUDE KAHN, DAUGHTER
OF MR. OTTO H. KAHN,
AND MISS MARIANNE MC KEEVER,
RED CROSS NURSES

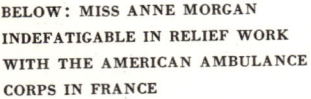

BELOW: MISS ANNE MORGAN
INDEFATIGABLE IN RELIEF WORK
WITH THE AMERICAN AMBULANCE
CORPS IN FRANCE

LEFT: THE WHOLE OF THE CONVOY
OF WOUNDED FOR THE ENORMOUS
CALAIS DISTRICT IS DONE BY
THESE STURDY GIRLS

MRS. J. BORDEN HARRIMAN
HAS TRAINED HUNDREDS OF WOMEN
IN AMBULANCE DRIVING

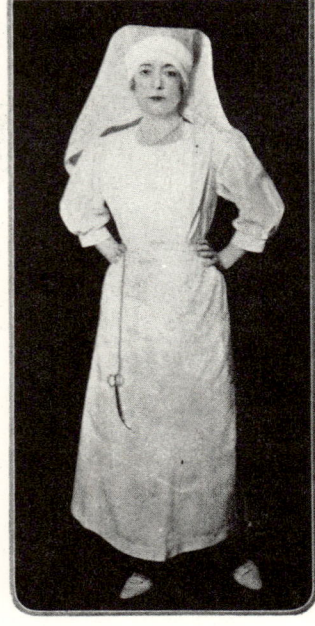

MISS ELSIE DE WOLFE, WHO
SERVED A NURSE'S APPRENTICESHIP
IN FRANCE, UNDER
DR. BARTHE DE SANTFORT

RIGHT: MRS. HENRY POTTER RUSSELL,
DAUGHTER OF MRS. J. BORDEN
HARRIMAN, IS A DEDICATED
WORKER IN WAR RELIEF

MRS. AUGUST BELMONT
WHO WAS MISS FLORA ROBSON,
HAS TOURED THROUGH FRANCE,
INSPECTING HOSPITALS AND
VISITING FAMILIES
UNDER RED CROSS CARE

PRESIDENT WILSON WITH
MR. JESSE JONES AND
BRIGADIER-GENERAL DYER,
[MAR]CH DOWN FIFTH AVENUE, NEW YORK,
LEADING THE SECOND RED CROSS
WAR FUND DRIVE, WHICH
LASTED EIGHT DAYS AND
RAISED ONE HUNDRED AND
FIFTY-FIVE MILLION DOLLARS
FOR THE RED CROSS

MISS MARY HOYT WIBORG
AIDED BY MRS. H. SQUIRES
AND ONLY TWO FRENCH NUNS,
CARED FOR SIX HUNDRED WOUNDED MEN
IN A HOSPITAL BEHIND THE MARNE

MISS HELEN PEABODY,
WHOSE FATHER IS HEAD OF
GROTON SCHOOL, WEARS
UNIFORM OF AMERICAN
WORKERS FOR THE Y.M.C.A.

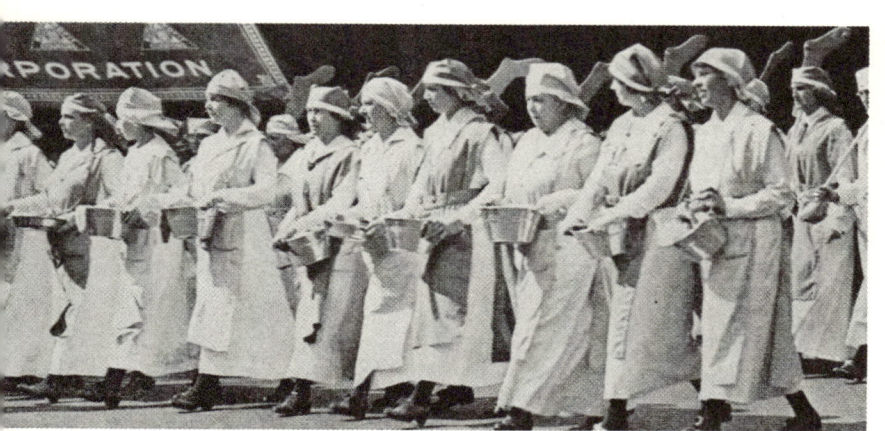

ABOVE: MEMBERS OF
NEW YORK'S COSMOPOLITAN
CLUB MARCHED TO
THE CLICK OF
KNITTING NEEDLES,
CARRYING THEIR FINISHED
PRODUCT MOUNTED ON
LONG POLES IN THE
RED CROSS PARADE

ABOVE: THE WOMEN OF THE RED TRIANGLE
GO EVERYWHERE IN THE WAR AREAS,
SHORT OF THE TRENCHES THEMSELVES.

CAPTAIN MAURICE BURKE ROCHE
AND HIS TWIN BROTHER,
ENSIGN FRANCIS BURKE ROCHE,
PHOTOGRAPHED IN 1918
BEFORE EITHER HAD
RECEIVED HIS COMMISSION

ABOVE, RIGHT: THIS Y.M.C.A. DUGOUT, WITHIN
SHELLING DISTANCE OF THE FRONT LINE, IS
ONE OF THE MERCIFUL RED TRIANGLE HUTS
SERVING COFFEE TO THE WALKING WOUNDED

[1913 – 1923]

FAMILY PORTRAITS

The photographs on these pages show members of some of America's most noted families. Mrs. Angier Biddle Duke and Mrs. Kermit Roosevelt are posed with their young sons. Mrs. Roosevelt is the daughter-in-law of Colonel Theodore Roosevelt. While her husband is serving with General Maude, Commander of the Mesopotamian forces, she visits her father, Ambassador Joseph E. Willard in Spain. Also pictured are Mrs. Leonard Thomas (née Blanche Oelrichs) and her two sons, at home, while Mr. Thomas serves with the American Expeditionary Force in France. Mrs. Thomas is the well-known authoress, Michael Strange. The lady surrounded by four children is Mrs. Arthur Iselin, who owns Bedford house, New York, where her great-grandfather, William Jay, the famous American statesman, lived during and after the Revolutionary War. The last and newest photograph of this collection shows Lt. Colonel and Mrs. Theodore Roosevelt together again with their children, after a long wartime separation. Lt. Colonel Roosevelt is now taking an active part in politics.

MRS. DUKE AND HER SON, ANGIER BIDDLE DUKE, JR.

MRS. LEONARD M. THOMAS
(MICHAEL STRANGE) WITH HER
SONS, ROBIN AND LEONARD

MRS. ROOSEVELT
AND HER SON
KERMIT
ROOSEVELT, JR.

BELOW LEFT: MRS. ARTHUR ISELIN
AND HER FOUR CHILDREN, DOROTHY,
JAY, ELEANOR, AND ARTHUR

BELOW: LT. COLONEL THEODORE
AND MRS. ROOSEVELT WITH
CORNELIUS, THEODORE, AND GRACE

YVETTE GUILBERT
BY CLAYTON HAMILTON

FRANCE'S PREMIERE DISEUSE

The stage is nearly empty. The backdrop (borrowed from some scenic storehouse) displays a conventional picture of a conventional French garden. There is no carpeting upon the bare boards of the platform. Forward, in one corner, a grand piano looks incongruously out of place; and at the instrument is seated a totally uninteresting man. The lights have been turned up, and a hush has quenched the buzzing in the auditorium.

A woman enters through the wings, walks downward to the center of the stage; and at once the house is filled with the sensation that this is one of the great women of the world. She has reached the center of the stage; she pauses and stands still; she is about to speak.

In a few sentences of finely chiselled French, she announces that she is going to render an old ballad of the people — a ballad of the fifteenth century — that tells the story of the birth of Christ. That is all; but you have experienced already a drift of great adventures. First, you have seen a woman walking greatly; and no other woman can do that, since Modjeska. Next, you have seen a woman greatly standing still; and no other woman can do that, except Duse. Then, you have heard a woman speak; and you have been reminded of the goal of your striving toward the imperious and elusive eloquence of words.

From the inconspicuous piano come a few notes; and the great woman has begun to enunciate the words of the ballad. The stage is not empty any longer. The piano has become invisible. You are looking forth, in a wonderful clear night of stars, over the hushed housetops of the town of Bethlehem. From somewhere in the distance comes the high-pitched, thin, and drowsy call of the night-watchman droning forth the hour. You are back in that year of years from which our time is dated. You see a heavy, weary woman toiling toward a tavern; you see her rebuffed rudely by a fat-pursed hostess; you share the timorous despair of her humble husband; you are relegated to the stable, and breathe the breath of cattle. There is a pause — a silence. Then, suddenly, there comes a chant as of a host of angels, trumpet-tongued, blaring forth the miracle of birth beneath the dancing of a million stars.

Once again, the great woman pauses, and is silent, and stands still, and speaks. Next, she tells you, she will render an old-time ballad of the death of Christ. This ballad, in the sixteenth century, was chanted every Eastertide before the portals of all the great cathedrals of France. There is a silence, and a pause. "Including the Cathedral of Rheims," the artist adds: and you feel great tears welling up into your eyes.

Thence, forward through the centuries, she leads you, projecting ballads of the people of France. And, every time, she seems to crowd the stage with many living people; and always she captivates and overwhelms the audience with the spirit of the piece that she is rendering.

There is no word in English for that medium of art of which Yvette Guilbert is the supreme and perfect master. It is not acting, it is not singing, it is not recitation; yet it combines the finest beauties of all three. It offers simultaneously an interpretation of literature and an interpretation of music; and it continually reminds you of what is loveliest in painting, in sculpture, and in dancing.

She has developed a universal language — a way of appealing simultaneously and with equal power to the deaf and to the blind.

Baron de Meyer

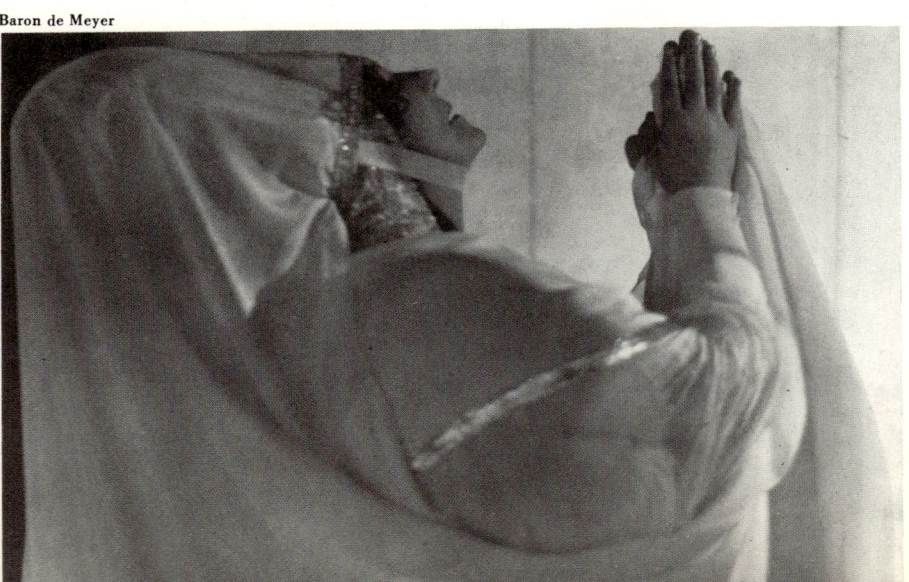

YVETTE GUILBERT

OPPOSITE: ETHEL BARRYMORE
AS MARGUERITE GAUTIER
AND CONWAY TEARLE AS ARMAND DUVAL
IN A RATHER MODERNIZED (1918)
VERSION OF ALEXANDRE DUMAS
FILS' "LA DAME AUX CAMÉLIAS"

Culver

THE NEW MOTION PICTURES
1918-1919

From Sardou to Harriet Beecher Stowe, everything has been screened. The results challenge comparison, scenically at least, with the best of the stage.

GLORIA SWANSON IN
"MALE AND FEMALE,"
DIRECTED BY CECIL B. DE MILLE

MARY GARDEN IN "THAIS"
Goldwyn Film Company

LINA CAVALIERI IN "A WOMAN OF IMPULSE"
Paramount

A SCENE FROM "UNCLE TOM'S CABIN"
Bettman Archive

LILLIAN GISH AND NOEL COWARD (AS AN EXTRA) IN "HEARTS OF THE WORLD"

VOGUE COVER DESIGN
BY GEORGE PLANK

THE MODE AS AN ART

BY LADY CANDOUR

There is always a curious tendency on the part of those women who apply individual ideas to their dress to despise fashion and throw it to the winds. They are often ignorant of the technique of style in the historical sense, and thus they blindly plunge into mere dowdyism, ruining their cause, which, *au fond*, is a good one. This leads to the question, How much is fashion worth?

Dress in all ages and among all peoples has been beautifully significant of their whole social fabric. Look at those most superb embroideries since time was — the Chinese. A thousand years before Christ, Chinese silks, brocades, and embroideries reached the height of textile and decorative beauty. Age after age their embroideries transcribed the history of the world as the Chinese knew it, conventional patterns representing chaos, the flood, the volcanic period, down to the first emperor, who came, in the guise of a dragon, to bring order, peace, fertility — an epic, a heroic poem in silks, revealing symbolically the science, religion, and artistic taste of a nation.

Look at the wonderful national costumes of certain peasants, made entirely of most exquisite *tapisserie* in fine wools and gold thread in a rich design that was national and traditional, and yet in every portion showed the individual taste of the craftsman. The whole costume is made of this *tapisserie* — skirt, bodice, apron, shawl, belt, gaiters, and bonnet — and its richness and beauty, the time it represented, the quality of the wool, the perfection of the dyes, all reveal as plainly as a printed page the several generations of home life of the women who produced it. The Greek national costume, loaded with gold bullion embroidery on cardinal velvet, some portions of it, in fact, stiff with gold that reveals nothing of the foundation fabric, cost enormous sums, and became a family possession for use at important fêtes, during a long period of settled national life, and no individual dreamed of altering the shape of a sleeve or adding a furbelow.

Look again at the licentious costumes worn for a few years in France immediately after the Revolution when the corset was abandoned, fleshings the only underclothes, and the robe so transparent that an apron was worn to serve the same purpose as the first savage *tablier* of skins or woven grasses. This came about inevitably as a part of the social disorder of things. Equally inevitable was the adoption of a bourgeois conservatism when the Restoration began; it influenced clothes to a point that amounted to prudishness, so that even the little children were done up in pantalettes. A race of people in the interior of Algiers, the Kabyles, who are supposed to be a remnant of the ancient Numidians, have lived so far outside the main stream of human progress that they still retain a costume that reveals its Roman origin, in the tunic or short *palla*, which is turned down from the top, fastened over the shoulders with brooches, and belted under the bust and about the hips.

These and many other lessons may be read from history to make us see that we are adding nothing to the evolution of a national style in parading as a primitive Greek, or as a mere nondescript bundle of inelegant garments that have not even the virtue of being authentic copies of a beautiful bygone type. Our clothes are more or less inevitable, and those of today in the West are what we should expect from prosperous and industrial nations where the fine arts, awaiting a moment of industrial quietude, are momentarily degraded to a second place. Good taste, or a consciousness of our limitations in battling with these conditions, bids many of us choose, even though with reluctance, the whole conventional fashion, rather than be a dowdy or a masquerader. But there is still a fourth path. Fashion at its extreme has always at least the piquancy that comes from sudden change and sharp contrast, as well as the decorative element that may always be found buried in the most eccentric or grotesque style.

The recognition of this last element in fashion is one of the most important for making the most of a style. And it is the lack of this recognition that is responsible for the making of half of the so-called dowdies. It is quite as bad, speaking from an artistic standpoint, to rob a fashion of its emphasis, thus destroying its character, as it is to misuse the fashion and push it eccentrically beyond the limits of harmony. If muffs are huge, wear them so, and hug them up becomingly against the breast, and get all the force of the action and gesture so imposed. Don't let them dangle on a cord from the third finger of a hand, in which case one looks simply encumbered. When turbans are in style do not exclaim at their queerness, do not insist upon having one and at the same time treat it as a hat, and place it on top of your head, so that it will show your ears and all your back hair, in the vain attempt to "modify it," "make it becoming," in other words, deprive it of all its turban qualities. Find out what a turban is, how it has been worn by many different people in many different countries, ancient and modern. Let all these pictures fill your mind, pictures of stately Arabs, mysterious solemn Hindus, aristocratic Persians, Yliates women whose muslin turbans have an end flowing free behind like a veil, flowing locks on each side of the face, and two long braids coming from behind and looped up to fasten across the front turban folds in a coronet effect. Some *Sahariennes* beauties wear actual coronets and dangling ornaments of coral, enamel, and silver outside of their turbans of muslin, as well as coiled braids of hair over each ear, these sometimes real, sometimes of goat or chamois hair, just as the eighteenth-century *perruque* was of fine hair or of wire, according to the fortune of the gentleman who wore it. Then there is the turban of the *moyen âge*, which was of cloth wound about the head with a scalloped end twisted into a cock's comb, or left hanging to wind about the throat for warmth. Look at Madame de Staël's turban of alternate twists of gauze and brocade; look at Mme. Le Brun's of white muslin. The Turks made theirs of every known material — silk, wool, muslin, embroidered, figured, or striped, and enough stuff, especially enough muslin, was used to make a man's whole robe. A strip of stuff sixteen feet long, with two people to twist it in opposite directions and then to wind it about the head, with some little personal touch in the actual disposition of the final folds, makes the Turk's headdress. With all this in one's mind, how can one help accepting such a "new fashion" boldly, making it modern and becoming, but never getting too far away from its own special character?

In carrying this principle throughout our dress, its ornamentation and coiffure, never getting away from our own age, and working side by side with Fashion, thus sartorial types can be created which will take their place with *les grands styles du monde dans le costume.*

THE TRAGEDY OF MODIGLIANI

Amedeo Modigliani, one of the most noted young painters in Paris, died in January 1920. Dragged from a straw pallet on the floor of a miserable studio in Montparnasse, he went to die in a hospital bed.

The Italian painter came to Paris when he was very young. Quickly he allied himself with artists living on the Butte Montmartre — Derain, Picasso, and others — but he showed nothing which would predict a brilliant career. But — and this is agonizing — from the day when he abandoned himself to certain forms of debauchery, an unexpected light came upon him, transforming his art. From that day on, Modigliani became one who must be counted among the masters of living art.

One often saw him ravaged by drunkenness. He drank wine, and, even more, just alcohol. He had tried the redoubtable hashish of which Baudelaire said, "It gives the taste of the infinite."

Modigliani had met Jeanne Hebuterne, a young girl who seemed, with her long braids, like one of those virgins painted by the primitives of the School of Cologne. The day came when Modigliani, sure that death had already put a hand on him, wanted to flee from his friends. Almost without resource, he locked himself with Jeanne in his studio. Jeanne, on the eve of being a mother, accepted this, ready for all torment, ready for all miracles, sad and confident, stretched out on the horrible pallet next to the one she loved above the whole world, her great man, her lover.

When Modigliani died, Jeanne returned home. She kissed her mother, then opened the window and leaped into space.

(*Condensed from Andre Salmon's article in* Vogue. *April 15, 1951.*)

AMEDEO MODIGLIANI

RODIN'S REALISTIC FIGURE OF BALZAC,
A DRAMATIC STATEMENT OF MASS,
PHOTOGRAPHED IN 1908 BY EDWARD STEICHEN,
WHO USED ONLY THE MOON FOR LIGHT

RODIN AND BRANCUSI
A STUDY IN CONTRASTS

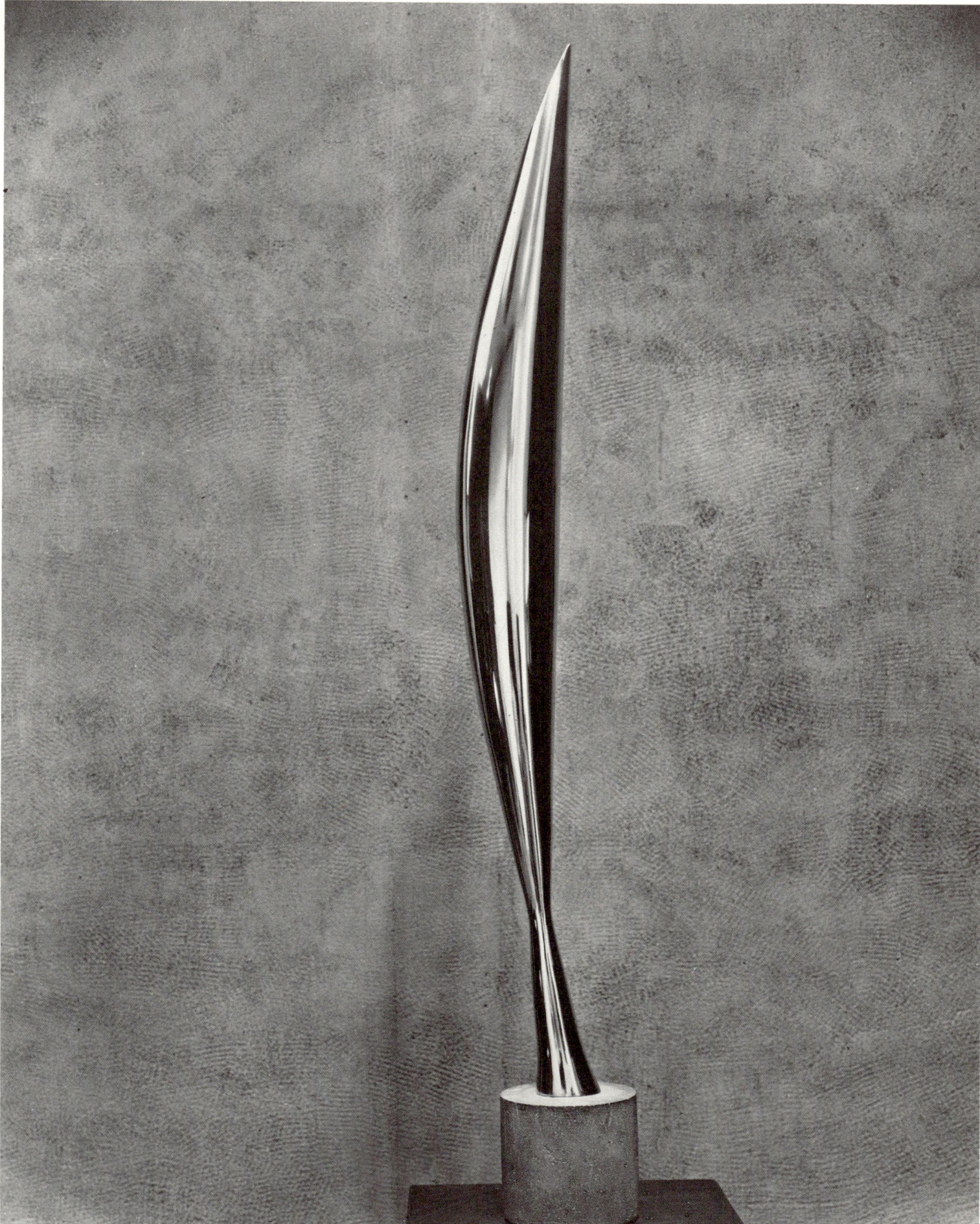

BRANCUSI'S IMPRESSIONISTIC "BIRD IN SPACE,"
COMPLETED IN 1919,
IS ELOQUENTLY SIMPLE
IN ITS ANALYSIS OF MOVEMENT

Photo: Courtesy Museum of Modern Art, New York

1915-1920:

WOMEN ARE
SHAPELESS COCOONS
WITH SKIRTS
HOBBLING THEIR ANKLES
(But the ankles and feet do show)

MODELS FROM:
PAQUIN, LANVIN,
MARTIAL ET ARMAND

LIFE ON A PERMANENT WAVE

BY DOROTHY PARKER

I gazed earnestly into the mirror and decided that I simply couldn't stand it any longer. Something would really have to be done about it. Nature had seen fit to curse me with straight hair, but you have to put Nature in her place every now and then. I would show her that she wasn't going to have the last word on the subject.

"I will come back a changed woman," I promised my mirror, and went bravely forth to become permanently waved.

With sublime optimism, I stopped and bought a magazine. You see, I knew many women who have braved the permanent wave, and I was so overcome with wonder at the results that I didn't think of asking how they were achieved. If I had thought that there could be any possible disagreeableness connected with the process — well, I never would have gone in for it, that's all. I am that sort of person. If I have a headache, I always suffer more than other people with headaches do; if I have a cold, I always know it is going to develop into far graver things than other people's colds could; if I bump my head, it always hurts me worse than it possibly could anybody else. I knew hazily that the process of permanent waving occupied three hours or thereabouts, and I thought I would while away the time with current fiction while the hair-dresser gently coaxed my willing tresses into the wave that won't come off. Ah, well, we live and learn.

I blithely entered the hair-dresser's where I was to meet my fate. A girl came towards me to tell me the glad news that Monsieur was getting ready for me, and my heart leaped with joy when I saw her, for I felt that I gazed on my future. Her hair lay in soft deep waves with irrepressible little curls bursting from bondage at her neck and temples. How clever it was of Monsieur to have her to greet his clients; she was indeed a good advertisement.

"How long ago did you have a permanent wave?" I asked her, as she disposed of my hat and coat.

"Oh, she said, "I never had one. My hair is naturally wavy."

She put me into a shapeless garment of white linen, which touched the floor, and which extended even unto long sleeves and a high, high neck. So clad, I looked startlingly like a charter member of the Ku Klux Klan. The garment had a strangely surgical air, and I grew a shade less joyous. From the room where the girl assured me Monsieur was making ready issued sinister clankings. I waxed thoughtful.

The girl removed my hairpins and my hair descended upon my shoulders; there it was, just about as wavy as a fountain pen. I gazed at it intently, impressing it on my memory, bidding farewell, a long farewell to all my straightness. Then the girl seized me and shampooed me so efficiently that every thought was washed out of my mind.

And then, as if to a flourish of trumpets, the door of the mysterious room was dramatically flung open and Monsieur appeared. No matter where one might see Monsieur, one would know immediately that he was a hair-dresser. He probably came into the world clutching a pair of curling-tongs. He spoke not a word of English, and I have no French, so I felt we would get along well together. No, I do myself an injustice to say I have no French; I know two phrases, *"Honi soit qui mal y pense,"* and *"Il faut souffrir pour être belle."* I found no use for the first, but I overworked the second.

The mysterious room was a bleak, bare place, just four blank walls, a monotonous floor, and an uninspiring ceiling. In the very middle of the floor stood a chair, much like a dentist's chair and just about as inviting. Directly above it, a strange machine hung from the ceiling — a mass of wires and coils and batteries, twisted and intermingled with diabolical ingenuity. Monsieur, with many superfluous gestures, motioned me to proceed, and as I entered the room, stumbling desperately over the linen gown, a horrid sentence flashed through my mind — "The condemned woman approached the chair with a faltering step." I wondered why on earth I had started this thing anyway.

They sat me in that hideous chair, and they bent my head back, clamped it into a headrest — a sort of modified

[1913 – 1923] 99

MARILYN MILLER, darling of the musical stage since her 1914 debut in *The Passing Show*, wears the newest hat, the turban, and a circular wrap, also of Oriental influence, deeply bordered with natural wolf.
Baron de Meyer

Iron Maiden. Then Monsieur got in back of me and began doing things that I couldn't see to the machine above me — a proceeding which made me extremely nervous. I asked for a mirror so that I could see what was going on but my request, merely the outcome of a natural and healthy curiosity, was greeted with shrieks of protest from the girl and with squeals of horror from Monsieur, to whom she translated it. It seemed that Monsieur had spent years and years in perfecting his marvellous process, and he guarded his secret with frenzied jealousy. No one should see how it was done while he lived — sacred name of a pig, no!

He divided my poor defenceless front hair into sections and twisted each one around some strange instrument, which, of course, I could only guess at — twisted it so hard and tight that my eyebrows were pulled up into an expression of permanent surprise. Meanwhile, the girl busied herself with an electric fan, trying its effectiveness on me from various angles. It was already pleasantly cool in the room, and I looked inquiringly at her.

"You see," she explained, "when it begins to get unbearably hot, all you have to do is tell me where it's burning you, and I'll turn the fan on the place."

"'Sunset,'" I murmured, "'sunset and evening star and one clear call for me —'"

Monsieur surrounded each twist with some strange and scratchy substance, twining and pulling and packing it with absolutely no regard for my feelings.

"Asbestos," said the girl, pleasantly.

"O Death, where is thy sting?" I sighed.

And then by some mysterious means they attached that brutal machine above me to the twists; it seemed to have cup-like appliances that fitted over them. It felt as if I were suspended from the ceiling by the hair of my head and I never would have lived through it, had not Monsieur thoughtfully given me other things to think of. He introduced some mystic liquid into the cup-like affairs, and then turned on a switch. Electricity leaped to his bidding and in no time at all the liquid was boiling merrily. I became conscious of a violent desire to go home. I thought of my hair, of the faithful friend it had been to me, of all the things it had done for me, of all the help it had been. I thought of all the happy hours we had spent together, my hair and I. I wondered if I should ever see it again. I grew lost in trying to decide what colour wig I should have. . . .

Monsieur strolled casually out of the room, and the girl started to follow him.

"It will be all right for a while," she said in answer to my wild look of entreaty. "When it starts to hurt, all you have to do is shout for me."

"Unaccustomed as I am to public shrieking," I began, but the heartless wretch had vanished.

There I sat, plunged in gloom. I don't suppose, looking back, that it was really so horrible, I should blithely go and have it done tomorrow. But you see, I know all about it now. Then, I didn't know just what was going to happen; I sat there and imagined. When one goes to be permanently waved, one should lock one's imagination in the top bureau drawer. Its place is in the home.

The girl came presently, and played the electric fan on me — she didn't think it necessary, but I did — and I tried not to think about the ache in my neck. Finally, when I had just decided this thing would have to cease and was about to say as much, Monsieur returned, turned off the current, and severed diplomatic relations between me and the machine. I rose immediately. My one idea was to get away then and there, even though the wave was only quarter accomplished. Straight hair was the least of my troubles; I wanted to go while I had my health.

But my spirit was broken. Partly because of Monsieur's entreaties, and partly because I was ashamed to acknowledge my cowardice to my friends, I fell back into the chair, and the process began all over again, this time with the hair in the middle of my head. When that agony was finished, they did my back hair. At last, when it was all over, I smiled tolerantly when I thought of the German atrocities.

They led me from the torture chamber and shampooed my hair again. I fully expected to see my hair come off in Monsieur's hands; I was all ready to say, "You see? I told you so." But it didn't. Monsieur dried it and then did tender things to it with a comb. I didn't have the heart to ask for a mirror; I expected the worst.

Eventually, Monsieur laid down his comb, and stepping back, regarded my hair as a mother looks at her first-born. Then, with dramatic suddenness, he flashed a mirror before me. I looked.

I know what Heaven will be like; I experienced it in that moment. I was incoherent with joy, the girl was vociferous with elation, and I think Monsieur shed tears. When things grew calmer, I left the place — oh, the wonder of seeing my hair curl beneath my hat brim — and motored home, a new woman.

I had a few qualms on the way home. I wondered how the wave could possibly endure for more than a day.

"Well, I had one good minute, anyway," I comforted myself.

But the fates are kind, and as for Monsieur — really, you know, he ought to be canonized. My hair is still with me, just as numerously as it was before, and it is behaving with almost human intelligence. It has opened up a new life for me. In the well-known words of the late Mr. Francis Scott Key, "Long may it wave!"

ANNA PAVLOVA, indisputably the world's prima ballerina, in an enchanting new photograph by Baron de Meyer. After leaving Diaghilev's Russian Ballet, Miss Pavlova has made regular personal appearances in England, Europe, and in America.

100   [1913 – 1923]

TEN THOUSAND NIGHTS IN A DINNER COAT

BY FRANK CROWNINSHIELD

I recently chanced — in the company of Mrs. Chase, the editor of *Vogue* — to spend a morning in the beautiful prison which some benevolent person has erected at Sing Sing. During our rambling tour of the prison, the warden drew my attention to an unhappy-looking man of approximately my own age, who was completing, in solitary confinement, a visit of thirty years to that famous Hudson River resort. The reason for his protracted stay was that he had once dismembered the body of a lady for whom he had formerly entertained the greatest feelings of affection.

"For thirty years," the warden told us, "this man has languished in solitary confinement. He has eaten nothing but the simplest food. He has never seen a theatrical entertainment, jazzed in a cabaret, consumed a bottle of champagne, cut in at a rubber of bridge, played a round of golf, seen a motor-car, smoked a Havana cigar, or eaten a dinner in the company of ladies."

"Sir," I said, "I can feel but scant pity for him; indeed, I would willingly change my lot for his. Consider my plight: For thirty years — simply because I am a bachelor in New York, with a change of dress-coats and some little private means — I have known no solitude whatever; I have been forced to eat only the richest food; I have tossed upon strange beds in the country houses of a thousand distracted hostesses; I have suffered intolerable and nightly agonies at the theatre; I have battled with French pastry, Greek waiters, Nubian bands, Welsh rarebits, Argentine tangos, and English noblemen at God knows how many cabarets. The costliest wines, pâtés, and cigars have been thrust down my throat. Inexorably I have been chained to my dinner-jacket, my week-ends, my auction bridge, and my saxophone dancing. I have spent ten thousand hours at collapsible bridge tables, three thousand hours in looking for lost golf balls, and fifteen thousand dollars on taxicabs. And as for dining out! Merciful heavens, I am prepared to swear that I haven't dined alone in thirty years!"

"Stop, stop," cried the editor of *Vogue*. "Say no more. Write all that down and make an article out of it. Show all the changes in our social structure; divide society into periods. Make the whole article historical, moral, discursive, philosophical, improving, and if possible, moderate in price."

And it was in precisely that fashion that the following retrospective paper chanced to be written.

New York's social progress during the past three decades or so can arbitrarily be divided into four periods which, for want of a better classification, might be called (1) The First, or Rustic Period; (2) The Pompous, or Snobbish Period; (3) The Boom, or Bonanza Period; and (4) The War, or Jazz Period.

The First, or Rustic Period, lasted from 1888 to 1892. Society, in those early days — the late eighties — was a small, snug, indolent, almost a family affair. Two or three hundred people composed it. They were well-bred, carefree, and easy to amuse. Their entertainments were, for the most part, on the informal side. Men did not dress for dinner on Sunday evening; everybody, more or less, knew everybody else; flunkeys in knee-breeches were not dreamed of; the Dutch strain was still a good deal in evidence in society; one met Van Rensselaers, Van Cortlandts, de Peysters, and Stuyvesants, who boasted of nearly two hundred years of American ancestry, going all the way back to the Knickerbocker days in New Amsterdam. The country was really the fashionable centre of the day. Social life in certain country colonies flourished extraordinarily.

Smart people kept out of New York as much as they could, a life made possible by the existence of a very considerable group of young men of leisure. The really smart thing for young men

WARD MC ALLISTER

Brown Brothers

102 [1913 – 1923]

THE SLOCUM-CAMPBELL TENNIS MATCH
FOR THE CHAMPIONSHIP,
NEWPORT, 1890

Newport, R. I., Historical Association

then was to forswear forever the vulgar marts of trade. Men and women were both a good deal more addicted to hunting and to country sports than are their children today. This passion for outdoor life very naturally led to the formation of a number of wholly delightful country clubs: the Meadowbrook Club at Hempstead, the Rockaway Hunt at Cedarhurst, the Tuxedo Club at Tuxedo, the Club at Aiken, the Club at Morris Park, the Coaching Club — a successor to the famous Four-in-Hand Club — and the Casino at Newport.

Picnics, indeed, and outdoor lunches, became the really chic functions of the day. They seemed to reach their highest point at Newport, perhaps because of Mr. Ward McAllister's avowed predilection for them. Those people bidden to one of his famous picnics usually met on Narragansett Avenue, dressed in flannels and country clothes, and proceeded to Mr. McAllister's farm. The men were armed with bottles of Chambertin — sometimes even with a bottle or two of champagne — and boxes of Havana cigars; the women with sandwiches, pâtés, cold chicken, and salads.

A small band of music, a cook or two, a fire boy, a platform for dancing, a four-in-hand, a dozen riding-horses, a claret punch, and a little yellow sponge-cake: such were the simple ingredients needed, in those happy Arcadian days, to delight the simple-hearted belles and beaux of New York.

Horses, dogs, steeplechasing, coaching, riding, polo, racing, and hunting! Aiken, Hempstead, Rockaway, Newport, Tuxedo! Those were the chief pleasures of that period and the chief scenes in which they were enacted.

It was only in the second, or Snobbish Period (1892-1901) that an urban formality and a greater gravity of deportment stepped in to usurp the place of an almost country simplicity.

New York was now growing apace, both in numbers and in riches. One was either *in* society or out. Society, being a unit with a strong clan spirit, was in reality much too small to contain all the worthy aspirants who sought admission to it. The fun for those inside came from keeping the others out. Entertainments became more and more formal; three men — Theodore Havemeyer, William C. Whitney, and W. K. Vanderbilt — began to entertain on a lavish scale; footmen in knee-breeches appeared and multiplied; a hundred more families descended upon Newport; dinners of forty, with changes of gold plates, became the order of the day.

It was during the first few years of this period that fashionable people began to build iron walls around their country houses, to blackball the less known candidates at their clubs, and to band together in every possible way in order to keep the threatening invaders out. This dread of outside encroachments upon the part of society made the way easy for a famous and picturesque figure in New York life, the redoubtable Ward McAllister, whose inspired and happy task it was to keep the insiders in and the outsiders out, a task that occupied him until his death in 1895.

In 1892 people began to take society very seriously. Mrs. William Astor, the most portentous figure in the social history of America, became its undisputed sovereign, and was able, with the aid of the indefatigable Ward McAllister, definitely to organize it and make it do her slightest bidding.

At her annual ball at 840 Fifth Avenue, one saw what one never saw elsewhere in New York: masses of austere and elderly people who, because of fading powers or wasted incomes, had completely dropped out of the sight of the world, but who, by reason of their unquestioned breeding and previous prestige, were made to answer the great lady's annual roll call. Mrs. Astor had very little use for newcomers. Only old families, old names, old lace, old operas, and old traditions appealed to her; her loyalty to old friends was proverbial.

It was Mrs. Astor who, in 1892, turned to Mr. McAllister and said, "I am beginning to think about my annual dance, and, as my ballroom is only large enough for four hundred people, I want you to help me cut down my invitations to approximately that number." After the invitations had been dispatched Mr. McAllister chanced to remark to some friends of his at the Union Club that only four hundred

[1913 – 1923] 103

THEODORE AUGUSTUS HAVEMEYER

WILLIAM K. VANDERBILT, SR.

Brown Brothers

WILLIAM C. WHITNEY

people had been invited to the great lady's dance. His remark was repeated and subsequently found its way into the pages of the *New York World*, which printed the names and pen-and-ink portraits of the fortunate mortals bidden to the sacred festival. Thus arose the term "Four Hundred" to describe those in society's rarefied altitudes.

Typical entertainments of that snobbish epoch were the large and formal dinners dedicated to ceremonials and salaams which were given in the dozen great houses on Fifth Avenue.

Imagine a company of exactly forty people: twenty men and twenty women. The engraved invitations have been issued for at least three weeks and have been accepted, or refused, promptly and in writing. Gold plates are at every place. Half of the women are wearing tiaras — some of them surmounted by an upper deck and turret. Nobody, *mirabile dictu*, has been more than ten minutes late. No cocktails are served. Ten flunkeys, obsequious and doleful, hover around in knee-breeches and paste buckles, prepared to do the butler's imperious will. No motor-car has conveyed the guests to the dinner, for no guests have ever seen a motor-car, or wireless telegraph, a motorcycle, a submarine, a moving-picture, or cabaret. Nobody discusses golf because, in all America, there are as yet but two nine-hole golf courses. Bridge is totally unknown. Nobody at the table is divorced because divorce is virtually unknown. The women have not rouged their faces, or reddened their lips. They do not smoke after the dinner, or during the dinner, because such an effrontery would not only make them ill, but would bring down a summary social ostracism upon them. No lady present is even remotely connected with a profession, because women painters, decorators, and singers are contraband and taboo. Even the women who write — Mrs. Edward Wharton, Mrs. Burton Harrison, and Mrs. Rensselaer Cruger — are looked upon with a lifted eyebrow and a little tinge of suspicion.

The guests, as soon as they sit down, begin talking about a variety of absorbing banalities: Harry McVickar's illustrations in *Vogue*; Marie Tempest's songs in *The Fencing Master*; Mrs. Grover Cleveland's good looks; Loie Fuller's suggestive skirt dancing; Mrs. W. C. Whitney's dinner-dance; the startling news that Charley Macdonald, the wonderful Chicagoan, has returned from Scotland with six whole sets of golf clubs, including lofters; and other matters of equal pith and consequence.

The dinner lasts exactly two hours, during which time all the guests comport themselves with the utmost decorum. Four sets of knives, three of spoons, and five of forks are at every place. A string orchestra of four pieces makes mournful music in the adjoining drawing-room. The feast begins with a clear turtle soup, with forcemeat balls. Then follow, in stately sequence, terrapin; *filet de boeuf à la jardinière*, with truffles; and three hot vegetables; a *pâté de foie gras* encased in jelly; hot artichokes with Barigoule sauce; a *sorbet à la surprise* (so called because, being essentially ice cream, the guests believed the dinner to be over as soon as they saw it). After the sorbet comes the most gustful and delectable dish of all, canvasback duck — served very hot and very rare, with plenty of currant jelly, celery salad, and hominy; then a suger-cured ham with a *sauce Maintenon*, Camembert cheese (as an excuse for the Burgundy or Johannisberger); coffee, hothouse grapes, *marrons glacés*, and cigars.

As for wines: first came champagne — the vintages of 1880 or 1884, never of course the inferior '83 or '85 — from the fish to the roast; your *vin ordinaire* throughout the dinner; your very best claret with the roast; your Romanée Conti Burgundy with the cheese; your port and Madeira when the ladies have left. After that, you are at liberty to light your cigar and sniff your chartreuse or your glass of Napoléon brandy.

After the men have finished smoking, they are driven into the rose and gold drawing-room, where the long-suffering ladies have somnolently been awaiting them. Then, for what seems an interminable half-hour, the men talk to the women — tête-à-tête, never in

104 [1913 – 1923]

groups — and at last, thanks be to Allah and all his angels, the carriages are called and the whole grisly business is over.

That, my friends, was a formal dinner in New York society thirty years ago. Yes, the smart thing in those days was to be dull, to be opulent, to be stuffed, to be bored.

Almost as terrifying and spirit-blighting as the dinners were the formal dances. A ball, in those days, meant a cotillion. A cotillion lasted two hours and was burdened with a heavy ritual. Every woman was obliged to have a partner, not only for the cotillion itself, but another for the supper. The latter was a "sit-down" affair. The lady's cotillion partner was obliged to send her, on the day of the dance, a considerable bouquet of roses; he could not hope to get off with a mere bunch of violets or a spray of gardenias. No girl ever went to a cotillion without a female escort — her mother, an aunt, or a maid. The management of the cotillion rested absolutely in the hands of the leader, a long-suffering creature who originated the figures, gave out — according to his likes and dislikes — the numbers for the absurd little gilt chairs upon which the doomed dancers were to sit, directed the distribution of the favours — parasols, bouquets, hat-boxes, lace scarfs, powder boxes, cigarette-cases, and bonbons. The leader also controlled the matter of the music, introduced unselfish and unsuspecting young men to the more devastating wall-flowers, and assumed, in general, the role of a Christian martyr at the stake.

Two of the cotillion leaders of that period were extraordinarily endowed with tact and aplomb — Elisha Dyer, a bachelor who had come to New York from Providence; and Worthington Whitehouse, a bachelor from Irvington on the Hudson — autocrats in their reigns. They were both so well-liked, so fair-minded, so generally known, and so genuinely bent upon making a dance "go" that it is small wonder they ruled so absolutely the ballrooms of New York for a period of fifteen years.

In those days only half a dozen hostesses, Mrs. Whitelaw Reid, Mrs. Wil-

MRS. WILLIAM ASTOR'S BALLROOM *New York Historical Society*

MRS. WILLIAM ASTOR

[1913 – 1923]

liam D. Sloane, Mrs. Ogden Mills, Mrs. Elbridge T. Gerry, Mrs. Cornelius Vanderbilt, and Mrs. John Jacob Astor, habitually gave dances in their own houses. These, by the way, were the great and gracious ladies who, on the retirement of Mrs. William Astor, inherited her emblems of power and divided them amicably among them.

But the majority of dances — the

MRS. WILLIAM GROSVENOR AND HER DAUGHTER ROSE IN NEWPORT

Campbell Studio

Assemblies and the Patriarchs — were held either in the beautiful Assembly Room which Stanford White had just built in the Madison Square Garden, or else at Delmonico's. The etiquette that surrounded these dances was uncompromising in its nature. For a mere man it was particularly terrifying. Exchanging cards, writing letters, applying for a pair of numbered gilt chairs, securing a partner — for both the dance and the supper — thanking the hostess, dancing with the richly upholstered matrons in attendance, collecting one's partner's favours (sometimes a work of great magnitude, as a belle of that period frequently received as many as thirty favours), finding her maid, summoning her carriage — it all appears to us now, in these days of helter-skelter entertaining, as part of a futile and preposterous ritual.

Two other soul-blighting forms of entertainment were popular in those days: the gigantic afternoon tea and the evening reception, with music. The hooded figure of Justice, carrying her neatly balanced scales, would be needed to decide which of these abominations of desolation was the more desolate or the more abominable.

The real reason why society was then so austere and so deficient in gaiety was that everybody took it so frightfully seriously. Ward McAllister was, of course, the worst offender. Beyond the horizon of fashionable society he could not see at all.

The brightest spot in the dreary social life of the nineties were the two smart New York social clubs. They were alive with likeable young men who were wholly divorced from business, who inevitably wanted a bet on a horse-race or a pigeon-match; who liked a good game of polo, a contest at billiards, or a ride to hounds. They were kindly, tolerant, indolent, well-bred, and probably held women in twice the reverence and esteem now accorded to them by most of the young men who muck about in society today. All in all it is to be doubted if a more generous, idle, incorrigible, or attractive set of men ever graced the society of America.

This was the period when taste in New York — which had never been particularly good with respect to decoration and architecture — received an immense stimulus from Stanford White, an outstanding social figure of the time, who was then at the height of his fame as an architect, designer, collector, and connoisseur. In this same epoch Miss Elsie de Wolfe, a young American actress of breeding and position, exhibited such a flair for interior decoration that she abandoned the stage and gave her attention, with great success, to the furnishing and decoration of houses.

Society, then, did not change appreciably from season to season; in fact, it is quite conceivable that a woman who entertained a good deal in the early nineties knew practically everybody in society. There were only ten theatres in New York which were attended by smart people. Few men had fortunes of more than two or three millions. No lady ever dined in evening dress at a restaurant. Divorce, by agreement or collusion, was unknown. Champagne — the famous and incomparable vintage of 1884 — sold for as low as thirty-nine dollars a case; a good seven-room apartment near Fifth Avenue rented for a hundred dollars a month; a butler's monthly wages hovered around sixty dollars; the Virginia reel was a feature of every smart ball.

But a third, or Bonanza Period, was at hand, a period that lasted from 1901 to 1914 and was ushered in by the sale of the Carnegie Steel Company to Mr. J. P. Morgan and his associates for approximately half a billion dollars (a tenth of the national wealth). A group of six or eight steel merchants from Pittsburgh had divided those five hundred millions and had proceeded to invade New York. Others followed. It was estimated, during that period, that more than a thousand men in America amassed a million dollars between the years 1898 and 1907, and that three hundred of these captains of industry gravitated to New York.

At the beginning of this third period, boom times were certainly at hand. New theatres, art galleries, concert-halls, jewellery shops, dress-making establishments, hotels, restaurants, cafés, social clubs, golf-links, and costly city houses sprang into existence almost overnight. The hordes waiting to be admitted to society, whether in New York, Newport, Long Island, Aiken, Tuxedo, or Lenox, were so numerous, so insistent, so rich, and, on the whole, so agreeable in appearance and so aboveboard in character that there was nothing to do but throw down the top bars that guarded the privacy of what was, after all, a somewhat light-headed little band.

Thereafter, the tempo of life in New York became more accelerated, the spirit of it more and more buoyant. It would be a serious injustice at this point if I failed to make admiring mention of Mrs. Stuyvesant Fish, who, stepping in at this juncture, sensed the necessity for a brisker, livelier, and more informal code of social procedure, less austerity and more democracy. Being by nature the gayest, wittiest, most energetic, and most enlivening lady imaginable, she grasped society by the hand and proceeded to lead it such a dance as it had never imagined. She knocked what was left of Mr. McAllister's ceremonials into a cocked hat and discarded all his fopperies and flummeries without scruple or ado. She said exactly what she meant and injected candour where before she had found cant.

Just before the breaking out of the war she gave a large dinner at "The Crossways," her enchanting house in Newport. Among the guests of the evening were Bishop Darlington and Count Von Bernstorff. She put the Bishop on her right, the Ambassador on her left. After the dinner two great ladies hurried to her side, gasping with surprise. "How, in Heaven's name," they asked, "did you dare put the Ambassador on your left? Don't you know that Count Von Bernstorff represents the Kaiser and all the German people?" "Perfectly," said Mrs Fish, "but please don't forget that Bishop Darlington represents God and all the angels."

Laughter in society, thanks to Mrs. Fish (ably abetted by Mr. Harry Lehr, an original, eccentric, good-hearted and diverting young bachelor from Baltimore), soon replaced an owlish gravity of demeanour.

It was Mrs. Fish who first introduced society to the fifty-minute dinner, who decreed that one wine should take the place of five, who replaced string orchestras with jazz bands, who injected wit and good-natured raillery where, before, there had been too many, far too many, evidences of pretension and pose.

But the most devastating and astounding changes that ever swept over society in America appeared during the Period of Jazz (1914-1922).

Those sudden and terrifying changes included (1) a growingly anarchic attitude toward authority in whatever form; (2) the liberation of youth to its own whims and devices; (3) the removal of every ritual of escort or chaperonage; (4) the scant attention paid to older people; (5) a blinking at supposed, or open, liaisons; (6) the sudden growth of drinking, smoking, dancing, and card-playing among women; (7) an increased neuroticism; and (8) a fantastic increase in the number of divorces among people of fashion. These phenomena, naturally enough, completely disorganized the social life of New York.

And that, apparently, would seem to bring us to the end of our review of New York's social progress. But, for the benefit of those who come after, we must describe a festival that was general from 1919 to 1922, a dance in a Broadway cabaret, a social custom looked upon with forgiveness even by the children of those stuffy old people who graced that gold-plated dinner in the nineties.

Picture, then, a party of ladies and gentlemen sitting in a cabaret which has become popular probably because of its noise and vulgarity. Blasts from the saxophone and explosions from the drums partially drown the screams of those at the supper tables. Bootleggers are admiringly pointed out to the young men of fashion, demi-mondaines to the débutantes. Hawaiian cabaret performers, relying upon beaded breastplates for protection from the police, execute hula-hulas with abandon, flasks are in every pocket, intoxication — if not in too advanced a stage — counts not at all against one.

The unrest of the dancers is stimulated by the perfume of women's bodices, kerchiefs, and hair, by the teasing music of the viols, and by the plaintive and moaning songs of the Negro singers. On the dancing-floor old men of position and breeding are partnered with young girls without either; while dotted about the smoke-laden room, groups of well-bred and fashionable women smile out their contented and benevolent approval.

What a memory! What a target for future generations of ministers and moralizers to shoot at!

LEFT: J. P. MORGAN, SR.; J. P. MORGAN, JR.; MRS. HERBERT SATTERLEE, DAUGHTER OF J. P. MORGAN, SR.

MR. ANDREW CARNEGIE PRESENTS ST. ALBANS WITH A LIBRARY. LEFT TO RIGHT: MRS. WHITELAW REID, MR. CARNEGIE, THE MAYOR OF ST. ALBANS; CENTER BACK, MR. WHITELAW REID

[1913 – 1923]

PORTRAITS

BY BARON DE MEYER

BILLIE BURKE

OPPOSITE: LILLIAN GISH IN "BROKEN BLOSSOMS"

JANE COWL

GRACE GEORGE

DOROTHY GISH

BY BARON DE MEYER

OPPOSITE: JOHN BARRYMORE

CHARLIE CHAPLIN

GEORGE ARLISS

AMELITA GALLI-CURCI

Baron de Meyer — MELBA AS MARGUERITE IN "FAUST"

[1913 – 1923]

LA DUSE

BY KENNETH MACGOWAN

The four hundred of fashion, the four hundred of art, and forty hundred other human beings — jamming the great golden shell of New York's Metropolitan Opera House and shaking it with expectancy. The greatest audience ever assembled in an American theatre. Ten minutes of tense waiting after the curtain rises; ten minutes of Ibsen's *Lady from the Sea* in Italian; ten minutes crammed with such intensity of expectation as I have never known in a theatre. Then, a little noise off-stage. The players turn. The whole audience turns. This is the moment for which the American theatre has been waiting.

Enter Duse!

I think I have never known a higher moment or felt a lovelier realization. Grey mist off a blue sea; the long lines of snow mountains on a Japanese screen; milky veils that hang for a moment in sharp, uplifting curves, then sway through the indefinite into another pattern of evanescent beauty.

Before she has spoken, here is Duse, greatest tragedienne of her age. When the voice sings — for it sings in the simplest speech, sings with an easy vibrancy more eloquent than music of studied tone and pitch — here is the actress that could lift the realism of nineteenth-century drama and place it beside the poetry of d'Annunzio, almost beside the poetry of Shakespeare. To-day, the voice weakens, perhaps; yet, a vocal beauty rises to match the lovely significance of face and movement which this frail woman of sixty-four distils from a life that seems passing away even as you watch.

Duse went through the motions of Ibsen's heroine, and went through them beautifully in spite of all the weight of the years pressing down upon her; she spoke the lines that night with a rightness that only death could silence. 1923

ELEONORA DUSE

ISADORA DUNCAN
ON THE STEPS OF THE PARTHENON,
PHOTOGRAPHED BY
EDWARD STEICHEN

THE MARRYING AGE

BY PAUL GERALDY

One never reaches an age so discreet as to assure one against a marital misalliance. Were I, however, asked to express an opinion or try to lay down a rule, I should say that the wife should be very young and the husband — well, hardly young at all. I do not mean that he must be old; only that he should have outlived the age of indecision and come to the age of practical realities. Nor do I imagine that this is an original idea. It is mere agreement with an ancient and accepted standard.

Time was when a young woman was expected to marry young, and a young man equally expected to wait. But it is with some scepticism that we contemplate an idea so stereotyped. We feel that we must reopen the matter to discussion, verify its wisdom, and search out its basic principles.

These basic principles can be reduced to just one, which a while ago would have been accepted as self-evident, but which will today, I am afraid, arouse great indignation. *Tant pis!* I give it for what it is worth, though I bring upon my head the wrath of that terrifying battalion of modern young suffragists.

Women should marry young, because woman is at her best in youth. It is an absolute fact that life, knowledge, and education do not enhance a woman's charm. Quite the contrary! Man, on the other hand, is before all a tool of society, and in order to adapt himself gradually to this society in which he must play so active a role it is essential that he should know life in all its phases. Life lends him importance, while it diminishes woman's charm. Naturally, it is impossible to form a perfect match unless each party brings to the union his highest worth. If man's worth is made up of his strength and knowledge, I have no hesitance in asserting that woman's is made up of her weakness and her ignorance. Let me explain. As life increases man's value by slowly adapting him to the needs of society, it also destroys or diminishes in him the attributes of youth that are not also contributions to utility. It makes of him a specialist, a little cog in a great social wheel, and gradually, he grows further from nature, losing day by day a little of his ability to feel. I might almost say that in growing old he becomes more and more inhuman. In proportion as this process goes on within him, so is his value to society increased; but in like proportion also are his natural propensities for enjoyment, so indispensable in life, decreased.

Woman is a creature of instinct. She brings to society a freshness without which it would die of stagnation and boredom. She rejuvenates society as the breeze from the forest restores the inhabitants of a village when stifling for want of air. She is the voice of nature in the midst of civilization. She is a savage, or, if it shocks you less, a primitive full of vigour, purity, ingenuity, and charm. She says to man, "Work if you want to, build cities since it amuses you, establish your authority and spread your rule throughout the land, but do not lose sight of what awaits you ultimately, after all your labour — to return to that primitive love of life of which I am the living image. The joy of childhood — that is what you will have to find again. Without us, you would have too great a tendency to allow yourself to become boresome pedants. You would have accumulated wealth for the sole pleasure of accumulation. You would have lost the divine faculty of enjoyment. You would have lost sight of the true end of life. But we women are here, we bring to you from nature — that you have left so far behind — the odour of the sap fresh from the trees. We are the substance of life, the world's taste of youth, the bath of resurrection."

This, then, is woman's message, or rather what her message should be. Unfortunately, she says it less and less, she even tends not to say it at all. Suffering from some strange aberration, she is trying to cast aside this charming role, refusing with increasing vehemence to be a woman. It is man's role which attracts her. She wants to be wise, strong, and free. She wishes to go and come as she pleases. She does not realize that woman's flesh is weak. She repudiates the marvellous instinct with which she has been endowed by nature. She wants to pick and choose. Once upon a time, man was the savant,

DOUGLAS FAIRBANKS and MARY PICKFORD, most famous couple in Hollywood, photographed by Edward Steichen. His new film, "The Thief of Bagdad," and hers, "Dorothy Vernon of Haddon Hall," have just had successful premières.

woman the poet; this partnership is no longer agreeable to her. The other day, a young girl of sixteen said to me, "I am striving to rid myself of my emotions." Good Lord, what will be left of her?

I admit that woman would make herself ridiculous were she content always to play the role of ingénue. I do not ask so much. I only ask her to keep intact her feminine conception of love and not to kill it as she seems to be deliberately trying to do by setting up as her ideal a mannish mode of life. If only she would marry young, before she knows life, and would be content to play the part of youth, gaiety, spontaneity, and grace in life, man would take care of all else.

Now it remains for me to make you understand what I mean by youth. Mr. Ford, for instance, thinks that the young girls of today marry too early. Do I disagree with him? Not at all. Not many years ago, a girl of sixteen was a young girl. At sixteen, today, a girl is a mere child. Likewise, a woman used to be old at thirty-five, but today, a woman of forty is refulgent. It is no longer possible to draw a definite line between youth and age. So I can agree with tradition and say that girls should marry young and add that I agree with Mr. Ford that there is no need of going to extremes. It was not against the principles of young marriage that Mr. Ford raised his voice, but against the interpretation of the word "youth." He demanded only that youth and infancy should not be confounded. And, of course, he is right. A girl who is really a young girl, when faced with the problem of love, is guided by a sort of divination, an extremely suitable instinct which is of much more value to her than any knowledge of life could possibly be. If too young, she is like a leaf tossed by every wind that blows; she is easily led along paths that later she would like to retrace.

Of course, my only aim has been to establish a general rule. Like all generalities, it has its exceptions. There are many happy households in which the rule which I have just been defending is not observed. In any case, one can rest assured of two things. First, that an extreme difference in age between husband and wife leads to a kind of uneasiness. And second, that this uneasiness can be borne when it is the husband who is too old, but it is frightfully difficult when it is the woman who is too old.

A most excellent way of verifying truths is to push them to extremes, making caricatures of them, as it were. Many times has my hatter said to me, "It is wise to wear a large hat, and I will tell you why. If your hat is very much too big, you are only partially ridiculous. But if your hat is very much too small you are wholly ridiculous and look like a clown." This excellent gentleman knew whereof he spoke. Similarly, with a couple, if the man is too old and the woman too young, we are annoyed, perhaps we protest. But, if a mere lad is the husband of an old woman, we are scandalized, we refuse to countenance such an alliance.

It is, then, as I have said, woman's youth joined to man's maturity which makes the perfect match.

GEORGE GERSHWIN, photographed by Nickolas Muray. After his sensational symphony, "Rhapsody in Blue," Mr. Gershwin, young dean of modern American music, turned his talents to musical comedy. He wrote the music for "Lady Be Good," and is now completing the score for a new venture to be called "Funny Face," in which the popular brother-sister team, Fred and Adele Astaire, are to be starred.

LOVE IN THE 20s

AS HOLLYWOOD SEES IT

BUDDY ROGERS SURROUNDED BY EXCITED EXTRAS

A SCENE FROM "BEN HUR"

JOAN CRAWFORD AND WILLIE HAINES

Buddy Rogers at left, the handsome, round-faced, all-American matinee idol, is admired by Virginia Bruce, Carole Lombard, Kathryn Crawford, and Josephine Dunn.

Center: A present-day interpretation of love in the days of the Caesars unrolls itself on the screen as Ramon Novarro and Carmel Myers romp through the super-spectacular *Ben-Hur*, maker of box-office history.

Bottom left: Joan Crawford and Willie Haines enjoy a romantic moment at West Point.

Below: Charlie King, in top hat and tails, looks approvingly at Anita Page in *Broadway Melody* the first all-talking, all-singing, all-dancing picture.

Opposite: Rudolph Valentino, whose lusty, hot-sand role opposite Agnes Ayres in *The Sheik* earned him for an entire decade the title of "The Great Lover," is shown here in a portrait by Edward Steichen, one of the last photographs of him.

THE STARS OF "BROADWAY MELODY"

OPPOSITE: RUDOLPH VALENTINO

CHAMPIONS' CHAMPIONS

Tye Sanders

BOBBY JONES, modest, charming and undefeated. Among his other championships, he is the only golfer ever to score the "Grand Slam," winning in one year British Amateur and British Open, United States National Open and National Amateur.

SUZANNE LENGLEN (right), tennis queen, of France, remained undefeated in singles, doubles, and mixed doubles championships in France and at Wimbledon from 1919 to 1926, except for the one year, 1924, when illness prevented her from competing. She has now turned professional.

HELEN WILLS (below) was tennis singles champion of both the United States and Great Britain for three years in a row—1927, 1928, 1929. (Miss Wills, University of California Phi Beta Kappa, has other tennis crowns in her locker, too!)

Steichen

Steichen

MANNEQUINS

BY COLETTE

Two men, five men, ten, twenty men ... I give up trying to count them. They come to this solemn ceremony of the fashion world even more eagerly than to the great social occasion in Paris, a dress rehearsal at a major theatre. They profess to "adore" these processions of dresses and pretty girls, of fabrics which, as less and less yardage is used, are constrained to become ever more gorgeous. Freely and frankly they admit their liking for these sartorial rites that every famous couturier organizes with theatrical and religious pomp. Monsieur accompanies Madame to the dress shows and Madame nods knowingly; "Yes, of course, to have a good look at the mannequins." In which she is frequently wrong. For Monsieur is capable of two or three pure emotions, among which can be reckoned love of colour, movement, form, and, above all, novelty. The male has long since ceased to be as embarrassed at a dress collection as a big boy caught playing marbles or a castaway washed ashore on the Isle of Women.

While his secretly frenzied female companion is having her heart torn to shreds as she renounces a little "creation" at six thousand francs, the blissfully relaxed male is drinking in knowledge. He notes the low waist at X, the drapery at Z, as he might memorize the characteristics of a school of painting. Man appreciates a total effect far better than woman does. He likewise — and in all innocence — realizes better than she how much is due to the mannequin. While a fevered female spectator keeps muttering under her breath, "That's the one, that's it, that's the dress I want," the judicious male is admiring not only a bronze sheath more revealing than a swim-suit but the milky whiteness and the copper hair of the redhead who is wearing it. He knows that the tunic, the colour of absinthe and moonlight, would lose everything if it were sundered from that girl who has the dignity of a greyhound and whose long hair has never been outraged by scissors or curling tongs. He realizes, at last, that a serious mission has devolved on what his wife, between clenched teeth, calls "that creature." Is it criminal of him, if he wants the dress, to long at times to carry it off as the designer conceived it ... in other words on the limbs of the radiant young woman whose voice he never hears?

In short, man, nowadays, feels at home wherever feminine luxury is created and displayed. The latest snobbery puts him entirely at his ease there for, at the dress shows, he will meet the painter of the moment, the smart socialite and her novelist, the politician and his Egeria.

The mannequin glides from one group to another like a slender, glittering boat, casting her nets. She, that final and disturbing collaborator, is the culminating point of a series of efforts whose importance no one belittles. The public of today fully appreciates the value of the work of the weaver, the designer, the cutter, and the *vendeuse*, as well as of the mastermind who directs them; when it comes to the mannequin, it does not commit itself but merely dreams, admires, or suspects.

In the modernized form of the most luxurious of industries the mannequin, survivor of voluptuous barbarism, is like a victim loaded with spoils. She is the prey of shamelessly greedy eyes, the living bait, the passive realization of an idea. Her ambiguous profession confers an equal ambiguity on herself. Verbally, her very sex is dubious. We literally call this charming girl a "little man" (manikin) and her work consists of simulating idleness. A demoralizing occupation keeps her equally remote from her employer and from the ordinary workgirls. Is not all this enough to excuse and justify the mannequin's peculiar temperament and caprices?

"Patience," they tell me; "all that is going to change. The evolution of the mannequin is around the corner. ... We dress-designers are going to make the mannequin into a loyal collaborator, punctual and decently paid, who will be able to make a regular honest living out of her beauty and grace. ..."

Moguls of the dress-world, I should like to believe you. But, if I am not mistaken, you still have a very long way to go. You will actually pay a salary — even up to forty thousand francs a year for the supple shoulders, the noble necks, the royal gait of these girls who glorify the works of your genius more than all other women? So far, so good. You aim to give the mannequin not only enough money, but your respect as well and the confidence that rightly rewards, for example, your head saleswoman. You no longer wish to see your elegant flat-chested Diana wilting and yawning after a night out with the wolfpack. Your aspirations are those of decent and kindhearted men.

But beauty is one thing and bureaucracy another. Beauty thrives on admiration and you arm it so that it may be admired even more! You say to Beauty, arrayed for love and battle, "This is your realm, you must not step outside it. Queen it here in this salon, pace up and down this gallery like a caged wild beast. Go, come back, turn around, come back again. Half naked, you will not feel cold except when, withdrawn from the public gaze, you

[1923 – 1933]

MISS MARIAN MOREHOUSE, CELEBRATED MANNEQUIN, WHO LENDS HER OWN ELEGANCE TO THIS FUR-EDGED, GOLD CHIFFON LAME WRAP AND DRESS. STEICHEN, WHO PHOTOGRAPHED HER HERE, CONSIDERS HER TO BE THE BEST OF MODELS

find yourself shivering without it. Never forget that this year we want you unpadded with soft flesh and hard as a sports champion. But you can not go in for any form of athletics, so eat as little as possible and don't indulge in the pleasure of buying roast chestnuts at street corners. . . ."

Visionaries! You want your agressively beautiful mannequins, prisoners of luxury, saturated with coffee and deprived of manual work that regulates both pulse and impulse, to acquire the souls of bookkeepers. You are by no means at the end of your troubles. But your effort is a praiseworthy effort. While waiting for success to crown it, waiting for the lure of good money and the charm of peace and independence to create you beautiful, calm-browed young women with souls devoid of desire; retain the mannequin and go on recruiting the capricious creature. For longer than anyone can prophesy, you will continue to put up with her neurasthenia, her nervous yawns, her bursts of tears, her sudden listlessness, her momentary brilliance that singles her out for homage, her casual way of trampling superlative luxury underfoot as if it were her native soil. You will, in fact, put up with everything you tolerate, everything you excuse, everything you respect in her greater brother, the artist.

[*Translated by Antonia White.*]

MISS TILLY LOSCH, INTERNATIONALLY KNOWN DANCER, ACTRESS, AND BEAUTY, PHOTOGRAPHED BY CECIL BEATON

1929:

WOMEN ARE ALL EYES
AND LEGS
HATS DOWN, HAIR OFF
SKIRTS TO THE KNEES

1927-1929

In the twenties, the unshaped, knee-length dress, worn with pulled-down cloche, is the sight that meets the eye in Paris, London, New York. Glamorous at night are little strings of dresses stopping just above the knee. Upper left, Cecil Beaton's slightly malicious drawing of the "little nothing dress" for evening.

MISS EDITH HOPE ISELIN

MRS. WILLIAM GASTON

MISS FANNY MOORE

MISS ELIZABETH ALTEMUS AND COUNT ALESSANDRO BETTONI

MRS. CARROLL CARSTAIRS

COUNTESS LUDWIG
SALM-HOOGSTRAETEN

MRS. ROBERT MC ADOO

THE EARLY THIRTIES

Patou of Paris tired of women in those "ridiculously short dresses" and late in 1929 astounded and terrified the fashion world by evening dresses like those sketched by Beaton at left. Day clothes are below mid-calf; after some resistance, longer skirts once more are in.

MISS JOAN BENNETT

MRS. O. J. GUDE

MISS MARY TAYLOR

LONG SKIRT AT PARIS RACES

MISS KATHARINE HEPBURN

MISS DORIS DUKE, MISS BARBARA HUTTON, DEBUTANTES

ON STAGE 1928-1931

"THE BARRETTS OF WIMPOLE STREET"

One of the most emphatic successes of recent years is Rudolf Besier's *The Barretts of Wimpole Street*, with Katharine Cornell playing the sensitive Elizabeth Barrett to Charles Waldron's stern Mr. Barrett. In the photograph with them are Dorothy Mathews (left) and Margaret Barker (second from right.) Another theatrical milestone is Vicki Baum's *Grand Hotel*. In this play the beauty of Madame Leontovich's acting haunted one long after the performance was over. As the dancer who feels tragically that she has lost hold on her public and whom love suddenly rejuvenates, Madame Leontovich (opposite) played with sweeping depth and sympathy. Also on the facing page are: Hope Williams, who played to packed houses in *Holiday*, a vehicle specially written for her by Philip Barry; Elissa Landi as Catherine Barkley in *A Farewell to Arms*, the play based on Ernest Hemingway's great novel; and the principal trio of the all-male cast of R. C. Sherriff's modern masterpiece *Journey's End*, depicting life in the trenches during the Great War.

MADAME LEONTOVICH IN "GRAND HOTEL" — Steichen

HOPE WILLIAMS — Steichen

ELISSA LANDI IN "A FAREWELL TO ARMS"

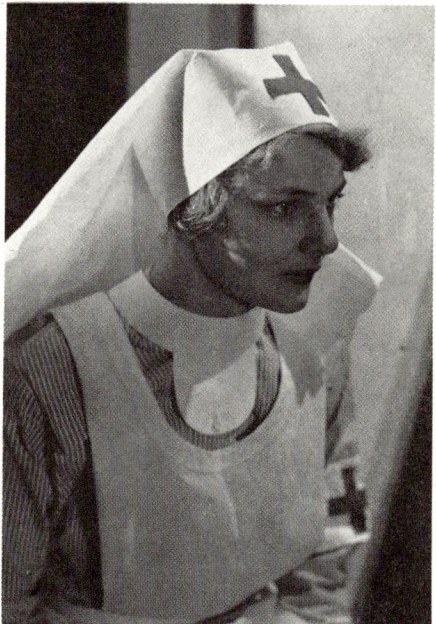

Tony Von Horn

Steichen

LEFT: HENRY WENMAN,
COLIN KEITH-JOHNSTON,
AND LEON QUARTERMAINE IN "JOURNEY'S END"

[1923 – 1933]   129

GERTRUDE LAWRENCE AND NOEL COWARD IN ONE OF THEIR FEW FRIENDLY MOMENTS IN "PRIVATE LIVES," MR. COWARD'S LIVELY AND ULTRA-SOPHISTICATED NEW COMEDY

Vandamm Studio

130 [1923 – 1933]

WHAT MAKES OR BREAKS A PARTY?

BY ELSA MAXWELL

How often have I been asked this poignant, heart-rending question — by sadly disillusioned hostesses of dismal and dreary parties that have been, and by aspiring but fearful hostesses yet unborn, wriggling through the embryonic dream-shell of gallant parties-to-be — robust and rollicking parties that march to a gay finale by the sheer impetus of their own dynamic rhythm.

What a delicate analysis is necessary to dissect the different fluids or vibrations that form the component parts of a really good party! And *who* ever studies a party from that angle? One should — for the making of a successful party is like the baking of a wonderful soufflé — the ingredients and proportions must be weighed and measured by the hand of an artist — should be taken out of the oven at exactly the psychological moment — and served hot.

So many parties begin well, only to die, alas, but too soon, owing to the fact that the hostess has taken her own party so seriously that the guests end by taking it seriously, too — and the cloakroom is stampeded by those certain "bright young people" in a panic to depart for the haunting jungles of Harlem or the mellow marshes of Montmartre, while the plaintive, tearful voice of the hostess is heard remonstrating thus to the unheeding waves of fleeing guests drowning her in their efforts to escape, "Oh, you're *not* going? Just when Olga Petslopsky is about to sing those darling Russian boat songs from the steppes." — "Oh, you can't go before supper. Won't you have just one little egg, please?"

But the brutal, callous guests of the overserious hostess push her aside, still expostulating, and, with grim determination, leave her Pommery and Greno frappéd 1915 champagne — to relax happily in the stuffy, unbelievable atmosphere of a Montmartre night-club, where a blasé octoroon raucously warbles a hackneyed song, one that has been heard interminably for the last five years, and where the band is bad, the drink undrinkable, the people unthinkable, and everybody completely happy.

"What is the use of entertaining?" sobs the unhappy hostess of a most lamentable soirée. "I sent out invitations a month ago. I have spent weeks in preparations and thousands of that which Daddy makes on margin — and not a cat stayed after twelve." This is the epitaph of most parties, carefully arranged and prepared long in advance — when the edge of spontaneity has been rubbed off and the delicate antennae of anticipation have atrophied with so long an interval between desire and fulfilment.

Carefully studied effects must appear just to happen, and the joy of the hostess in her own party must be the first element encountered by a guest. I have often been moved to sudden inward unholy laughter when, upon entering salon or ballroom, I first catch sight of the harassed and anguished face of an unhappy hostess in the doorway, so obviously suffering at being trapped by her own party, and, as the hordes of that vast vacuity known as the "Visiting List" troop in, her last hope dies, and she knows all is lost.

For the "Visiting List" sounds the death-knell of every party where it is employed. How often I have heard a charming, gay, debonair butterfly anxiously demand from her friend the loan of her visiting list when she is about to issue invitations for a party. Poor butterfly! Little does she know she is thereby placing the noose around her neck with her own hands.

One should never have to ask people to a party just because they are on one's list. Guests should be selected with as much care as a new Reboux hat, and should be equally becoming, for a hostess should wear her guests at a party as she wears a hat — with an air! Also, people should not be invited because one dined with them last week — or because you owe them a lunch — or because your father played backgammon with their father at the club — or because a friend asked to bring a friend — or because you feel sorry for those "poor things" next door: "Let's ask them just this once," and the "poor things" instantly became your deadliest enemies on the spot, murdering your party merely by being there. No — the gravest menace to a good party is the

132   [1923–1933]

dangerous, emotional kindness of most hostesses in the extension of their invitations.

Ruthlessness is the first attribute towards the achievement of a perfect party. Also, one should have practically no really established "position" — by that, I mean in the world of finance, religion, or diplomacy. If you are officially associated with any one of these worthy métiers, then give up the idea forever of achieving a party, for official functions should be added to the list of Horrors of the Inquisition.

Snobs, also, are curiously incapable of gaiety, perhaps because gaiety comes from the soul, and snobs only take their soul *à la meunière*. Also, snobs are as busy nicking notches on each rung of the social ladder as the gangster who nicks each kill on his gun. I have always thought that snobs are as cruel as gangsters, anyway — certainly they hold up a party in the same way.

Wealth does not play a large role, either, towards the giving of a good party. Many of the great and glorious artists in that wonderful world of make-believe — without whom no party can be a success — with that true generosity known to them alone, will step immediately into the breach, should a party lag ever so little, and with royal prodigality scatter their genius or their laughter in the face of impending ennui. The party immediately takes on a new lease of life and never ends — that is, if it is the party of a friend. Money can not buy this — it can only be given.

Then there is the deliberately casual hostess who prides herself in letting her guests do as they want. This is a great mistake. No guests want to do what they want — everything must be done for them at a successful party.

Also, guests should be selected for their human attributes. If celebrities, they should be human ones, and never, under any consideration, should one dull person be allowed to darken your door. I have often thought what a wonderful and humane act it would be to rid the world of all its tiresome guests by giving a sumptuous dinner to all the well-known bores, placing them most carefully — for all bores must be well placed at dinner; their position demands it — and, having served them the best of gastronomic efforts, implacably turn on a deadly laughing gas, and they would all die painlessly, laughing gaily for the first time in their lives.

A good party should occur in one room only, and that room should always be too small for the number of guests invited. A party given in a house is generally a failure. Also, the room in which the party is given should be brilliantly illuminated. It is a mistake to have dim and soothing lights.

One should enter a party to sounds of some kind, for the psychology of sound is an important thing to study in the giving of a successful party. I once gave a party in a room too cold and cavernous, where I knew the band would reverberate in hollow cacophony and smite the eardrums too unpleasantly upon entering, so I hastily procured some beehives, and, successfully concealing them in the room, the ears of the guests were assailed by a pleasant buzzing during the lulls in the music.

Never show the slightest anxiety about the ultimate success of your own party. Show, by your attitude, that you are convinced it will be the best party ever given, and your guests will believe it, too, and help to make it so.

Always endeavour to incur the opposition of one or two of the so-called "social-powers-that-be" in whatever place you happen to be giving your party. This will inevitably ensure its complete success. People will violently take sides at once. Feeling will run high; excitement will ensue. Courage will be shown — courage to go to the party or to stay away — particularly if it is based on a new idea. Which brings me back to that poignant query: "What makes or breaks a party?"

A new idea, plus a sense of humour, makes a party — *and the bores break it.*

MISS ELSA MAXWELL AS A BICYCLING GIRL OF THE NINETIES, PHOTOGRAPHED BY HOYNINGEN-HUENE

BEATRICE LILLIE:
HOW TO
RUIN A GOOD DRESS

Steichen

ARE THE ENGLISH HYPOCRITES?

BY HAROLD NICOLSON

I was asked, the other day, to write an article for a German magazine. It was a reputable magazine, but one which deals gladly with topical subjects. I said I would. And then they asked me to take as my subject the problem, "English cant: is it as formidable as ever?"

I was distressed by this mandate. In the first place, I much dislike washing British linen before a foreign public. In the second place, I am not so sure (or rather I was not so sure) what this word "cant" really meant. And in the third place, I did not feel quite certain that the readers of the *Literarische Welt* would appreciate my point of view.

Yet it is not for nothing that I am, or was, a journalist. I pulled towards me my little Remington portable. I inserted a clean sheet of paper. I began to tap. And after the first few words, I was obliged to have recourse to the dictionary. For what, after all, is cant?

The dictionary was not very illuminating. It said that the word was used for thieves' jargon and, by association, for the slang or current language of any particular caste or set. I therefore journeyed to London, and, more specifically to Saint James's Square.

In the upper gallery of the Reading Room of the London Library, I found a larger and better dictionary. The balustrade which runs across this gallery is not a wide balustrade. I am not a narrow man. I was thus much disturbed when a gentleman of no mean proportions wished to pass me on the way to the Dictionary of Islam. I let him pass. And then, having unfolded and propped my own volume against those little lecturns which enliven and mitigate the said balustrade, I turned to the word "cant."

There were many abbreviations and sub-paragraphs, but in the end I reached the point which the *Literarische Welt* desired. I found the definition of that use of the word which (I am glad to observe) is dying out in England, and which (I regret to observe) is employed on the Continent with ever-increasing frequency. "A term," I read, "used to denote the desire to adduce an ethical motive in place of an egoistic motive." That, I felt, was a very apt definition. And it was around that definition that I endeavoured, with laudable patriotism, to defend my countrymen.

I did not, and I do not, deny that there is a special shade of hypocrisy which is more frequenty met with in these Islands than across the Channel or even the Atlantic. Yet I contend that this ill-adjustment between motive and action proceeds, not from any conscious imposition, but from something muddle-headed about the British habit of thought. I developed that thesis. And I flatter myself that I developed it with some conviction.

I took as my axiom the undoubted fact that the average Englishman (I use that dangerous term advisedly) is mentally more indolent than other races. Whereas he will condemn and despise any man or woman who refrains from physical exercise, he will approve and like those who are inert in the brain. At moments he will dub those who depart from the national lethargy of mind as "highbrows" — implying thereby that a taste for general ideas is a snobbish quality, and, as such, apt to provoke resentment and reprisals in those by whom it is not shared. Conversely, he will praise those who, while leaving their minds fallow, will expose their bodies to continuous and quite pointless movement. Such was my axiom. The deductions which I drew from it were logical, and, I trust, patriotic.

I contended that foreign observers underestimated this mental laziness on our part, while overestimating our conscious habits of thought. The average Englishman has no conscious habits of thought; he substitutes two other processes; the first is "good form," which is merely a habit of conduct; the second is "instinct," which is little more than intuition. The Englishman, although devoid of all power of logical reasoning, is, as regards his antennae, extraordinarily alert. I concluded, therefore, that the illusion of British hypocrisy arose from thinking too highly of our intelligence (since they judge by results) and too low of our intuition (since they are too well educated to believe in intuition as a constant element in practical affairs).

[1923 – 1933] 135

Having established myself upon this clever basis, I proceeded to exploit my advantage. I wrote of Palmerston and Salisbury. I talked of Egypt and Belgium. I evolved the interesting, and by no means untenable, theory that the average Englishman was conditioned by two major influences — the first the influence of puritanism, the second the lust for power. I argued that these two influences were constantly in conflict and that, when this conflict arose, the average Englishman was apt to render unto God the things that are Caesar's. I was rather pleased with that phrase — which is one, indeed, which I have frequently employed when considering my own countrymen. And it was on that note that I concluded an article which, though I blush to say it, was both succinct and suggestive.

It was only when I read that article in German that I blushed indeed. Had I been honest and outspoken? I had been neither of these admirable things. I had blinked the facts. And now that I write for men and women of the Anglo-Saxon race (a race peculiarly slow to draw analogies between their own actions and those of others) — now at least I can cease blinking and stare the blinding facts full in the face.

In my article for the *Literarische Welt* I had not mentioned animals. The continuity of British Foreign Policy (the business, for instance, about the Balance of Power) — the magnitude of our Imperial achievement — both these can, without undue jingoism, be explained away. Yet it is difficult to account for that great gulf in logic — that vast abysm between reason and emotion — which gashes our whole attitude towards the animal world. Let me, as I am now writing in the privacy of my own language, refer with sorrowed precision to these particular anomalies.

The Anglo-Saxons, as a race, are fond of animals. Even in London, even in New York, they possess, for instance, dogs. With abundant leniency they allow the dogs of other people to deposit dung upon the pavements, and even upon the doorsteps, of the Englishman's home. Yet it is not to dogs only that they are kind; they are also kind to cats. Many a widow would have died intestate had it not been for the cats. And their kindliness extends, not only to domestic pets, but to other animals, such as bulls, pythons, and such pigeons as are the property of foreigners.

Many an English virgin has struck a Florentine cabman for stimulating, with Latin exuberance, his horse. There have been Members of Parliament who have risen to their feet in that august assembly for the sole purpose of drawing attention to the iniquities practised in Spain (a friendly country) upon bulls. A bishop wrote a long letter to the *Times* about the cruel treatment of cormorants by Chinese fishermen. And the tongues of larks (though not the scalded or still-living flesh of shell-fish) are excluded from our nicer menus.

This protective attitude on our part is invigorating and a source of national pride. Yet it is no exaggeration to say that a Master of the Fox Hounds would, without a blush, severely condemn the laceration of horses in a Spanish bullfight. Nor is it fantastic to suppose that a man who would regard as "sport" the hounding of a tame deer, would regard as iniquitous the shooting of pigeons released from a smaller but not dissimilar trap. The man, moreover, who would positively gloat over the slaughter of reared pheasants would regard as "unsportsmanlike" the Spanish rustic who shoots dead a happy little lark.

Surely, there is some inconsistency in such a point of view? Surely the foreigner, on observing this disparity between theory and practice, is entitled to consider us a nation of hypocrites? Is it logical to suppose that an aged and blindfolded horse in the *corrida* feels more pain and apprehension than the fox, whose agony and incertitude last for "a splendid run of forty minutes"? Is it logical to suppose that a stag, when hounded out to sea, is less aware of his peril and affright than the pigeon who flutters for a few gay moments on the ringing air of Monaco? Is it logical to draw a distinction between the cruelty of rearing pheasants for the guns of sportsmen, and the incidental massacre of sparrows by an Andalusian farmer? I may be obtuse in such matters. Yet when foreigners question me thereon, I can find no excuse for my countrymen. I cannot say that they enjoy inflicting fear and suffering upon dumb animals. That would not be true. Yet I cannot say that many sections of my countrymen do not derive acute pleasure from this infliction. That again would not be true.

All I can say is that Englishmen are not wont to think; that they never apply to themselves the standards which they apply to other people; that they always consider national habits, even when they are bad habits, to be good conduct.

And when I say these things, when I adduce these pitiable defences, the foreigner replies with one word only. And that word is "cant."

CHARLES LAUGHTON in *The Private Life of Henry the Eighth*, the Alexander Korda film that has put the struggling English film industry on the map. Playing with Laughton are his wife, Elsa Lanchester, in a droll interpretation of Anne of Cleves, and a beautiful new star, Merle Oberon, as the ill-fated Anne Boleyn.

AT THE OPERA BALL, 1933,
GIVEN IN AID OF THE METROPOLITAN OPERA HOUSE.
MRS. FRANCIS MC ADOO AS THE DOWAGER COUNTESS
OF MOUNT EDGECUMBE, AND HER DAUGHTER, MISS MARY TAYLOR,
AS THE HON. EMMA LASCELLE.
OPPOSITE: MRS. HARRISON WILLIAMS
AS THE DUCHESS OF WELLINGTON AT THE COURT OF NAPOLEON III

Cecil Beaton

FASHION AND THE FINE ARTS

BY ANDRE MAUROIS

Whether it is a question of chairs, umbrellas, pictures, or books, the tastes of men change with time. What seems admirable today appears ridiculous tomorrow; and our enthusiasms of 1931 will be the absurdities of 1950. Many among us have seen, accepted, and, without doubt, liked the clothes that women wore before the War; now, when we come across photographs of them in Paul Morand's *1900*, we utter cries of horror. Our memory renounces them.

What are the underlying causes of such changes? They are many. To begin with, one of the elements of aesthetic pleasure is the shock of surprise which a new thing gives. This shock must not be too violent, or the pleasure will change into a disagreeable surprise, and that is why fashion evolves slowly. To pass from the short skirt to the long skirt, or from classicism or romanticism, fashion searches for transitional forms. (Nevertheless a shock is necessary. The first time that the bright colours of the Ballets Russes were shown in Paris, there was a cry of delight. Ten years later, the style of Bakst seemed old. When *Hernani* was played a hundred years ago, the play appeared to be in the vanguard of daring modernism. Today it would make young people and even the most sentimental of the older generation smile.)

Suppose that our civilization should be forgotten — obliterated — and that in six thousand years an archaeologist of a new race discovered, digging about the ruins of Harvard, copies of Victor Hugo's plays. It is possible that then *Hernani*, giving a shock of surprise once again, would become "new." Such is the case today with primitive sculpture. It was the fate of the Greek and Latin poets when the scholars of the Renaissance rediscovered their manuscripts. Today, writers who rank among the best, like Dreiser or Hemingway, who speak brutally of matters concerning love, produce the effect of shock. In twenty years, chaste and sentimental writers will produce, by contrast, the same effect, and they will seem new.

Such is the reaction of the public. It is abetted by the conscious effort of the writer. In our day, the "make-up" of literature is of a crude colour, because the number of books is so great; the imitations are so rapid and so numerous that every innovator is soon outdone. The blasé public is quickly bored. It likes a war book; immediately, the word is passed among the editors: "There is a demand for war books." Each editor looks for his own author, each wishes to have the most horrible, the most gruesome, the bloodiest war book. A hundred war books are published — the public gloats for a season and then is saturated. People turn away from them with boredom — there is no longer a demand for war books.

It would be difficult to be insensitive to the charm of the new, but one must keep from confusing what is new with what is really beautiful. Great works of art do not grow old. I have read the romances of Tolstoy, of Balzac, twenty times; the poems of Ronsard, of Keats, a hundred times. I find them quite as beautiful as the day when I made their acquaintance for the first time — more beautiful, perhaps. I do not believe Proust's success to be a success of the moment. Without doubt, because he is in vogue, readers who are not made for him and cannot appreciate him, pretend to read him. These will disappear with his vogue, but Proust's true public will remain faithful to him and will reform itself every generation.

I have always had the most profound contempt for amateurs of music who say to me, "I can no longer listen to Beethoven. I care only for Stravinsky." For my part, I admire Stravinsky enormously, but Beethoven inspires me as greatly as ever. Neither have I much admiration for the amateur of painting who disdains Vermeer or Delacroix under the pretext that he loves Matisse or Derain; or for the literary amateur who says, conscious of his fashionable modernity, "I like Joyce too much not to despise Kipling."

Masterpieces pass always through a period of eclipse, but they take their rightful places again and keep them. On the contrary, the books and the pictures which have been admired only for their novelty fall into profound oblivion. Sometimes they come out of it, because the history of their time begins again. Thus, the Beaux Arts troupe turns round and round, and the moment always comes when the stragglers unexpectedly find themselves in the dazzling yellow limelight of the vanguard.

ANDRE MAUROIS

Hoyningen-Huene

EDITH SITWELL AT BREAKFAST, PHOTOGRAPHED BY CECIL BEATON

SOPHISTICATED LADIES KISS EVERYBODY

BY MARY BORDEN

I am speaking of manners, because I want to leave morals out of this discussion. I say Ladies, because I mean well-bred women of assured social position, and when I use the term "everybody," it signifies any man whom the lady may fancy for a moment that measures exactly sixty seconds.

All this may sound frivolous. I warn the reader that it is, on the contrary, a very serious subject and that I am approaching it in all seriousness, for what, after all, is more seriously interesting in a race or more significant of its culture than the manners of its leisured people? Their amusement and habits stand surely as a sign of what the nation has achieved in the way of a conquest over the world of nature; their social technique is most certainly an art only less important than painting or music. They are, these darlings of fortune, artists in life, good or bad, and their manners paint a living portrait of a civilization.

As for that other word, "sophisticated," I've looked it up in Webster's Dictionary. It comes from "sophist," of course, and refers to the group of ancient Greeks who were masters of specious, captious, fallacious reasoning. Tiresome men, who refined overmuch upon nothing and whose amusement it was to dilute, adulterate, and falsify the truth. And this, Webster tells us, is what sophisticated means. The sophisticated man or woman is the subtly wordly-wise person who is habituated to artificial or false values. And so, when I speak of sophisticated ladies, I mean women of the world to whom such a thing as a kiss is not what it seems, but something quite different. And it is these kisses and only these that interest me just now as signs of the times and evidences of the manners of our generation. Kisses that are given lightly, casually, suddenly, noncommittally, or deliberately, by women who know just what they are doing and who are in complete control of any situation and realize just how much the man chosen to be a victim can bear.

The Englishman can bear a great deal. He can bear more without turning a hair or flickering an eyelid than any man, I think, in the Western Hemisphere. Certainly, it would not be safe for our sophisticated ladies to employ the same technique with a Latin. But I don't think the ladies' free manners are possible in England simply because the man is cold-blooded. I think it is because he went to Eton, Harrow, Winchester, or some other famous English school and learned there how to behave with complete *sang-froid* in any difficult situation. For that is exactly what they do learn, those English boys, instead of lessons from books, and that is why Etonians, Harrovians, and Wychamists still administer justice over half the globe. They can bear solitude, exile, being made love to, or being made fools of without flinching. It is impossible to tell, in the case of one of these, whether he is angry or embarrassed when suddenly kissed in public by an impulsive lady friend.

He shows no sign of embarrassment or temper, and the peculiar little smile on his face when she's finished may mean anything. They understand each other very well, these two, better I think, than almost any man or woman in any other country. For, in this land where men have things their own way, they have decreed that women are to be their companions. Although they own the world and withdraw often and shut themselves up in bits of it, they are always turning up where attractive women are to be found, and they expect their women to be interested in everything that they do. Politics, business, farming, hunting, shooting, games; a good wife must either listen to the afternoon's golf stroke by stroke, or play herself. The fact is that they like

MAURICE CHEVALIER has won the hearts of Paris, London, and New York as an inimitable *chanteur*, and is fast becoming the rage of the musical pictures. *The Big Pond* was an instant success. Soon he will be seen in *The Little Café*.

Steichen

each other, the two sexes, in England, and they like being together, and they always are together, especially in the set that is devoted to pleasure.

And so, when my sophisticated English lady kisses a friend whom she fancies kissing, just like that, on an impulse, she knows that he understands.

The two may be already very old and very good friends. If so, then it is all a friendly joke with again just a dash of something else in it. On the other hand, if he's a new friend, the gesture is time-saving. It's an invitation, but not to a passionate intimacy. It's the beginning, not of a love affair, in ninety-nine cases out of a hundred — oh, not at all — but of an easy, cozy friendship that will last a long time and be just a little sweeter than if they were friends of the same sex.

As for her reputation, she doesn't give it a thought. It doesn't depend on such trifles as an impulsive kiss. It is so established a fact that she can and does entirely ignore it. In other words, she is a free woman and a very privileged one, and of late years she has made such dashing use of her freedom that she has evolved a new social technique, and it is this that interests me.

I was on my way to a party after the theatre, the other night. We were four men and two women. The other woman was an entrancing creature and a very sophisticated lady. Her husband sat beside the chauffeur, two young men were on the strapontins of the car, and one man was on the back seat between us. It was in the middle of the Strand that she kissed this one. Suddenly, she hooked her arm around his sedate neck and planted her mouth firmly, if for only the fraction of an instant on his. Then she gave a little laugh and said, "You're such a darling, I simply had to. You don't mind, do you?" Her voice was very flattering.

He didn't mind, apparently. He was a very nice man and a perfect gentleman, and he patted her hand soothingly. "There, there," he seemed to be saying, "be a good girl."

And then suddenly I remembered a room I had seen, over a year ago, in a big house in the country. It was a circular room, and it was an old house in Ireland. It had no windows and very little furniture, and the smooth grey walls were hung with pastel portraits of ladies. Lovely, demure ladies with ringlets on either side of smooth brows and enormous, strange, liquid eyes. Such gentle ladies, so prim, so modest, with such delicate noses and small, sweetly closed lips. But it was their eyes I remember. I can see them now, looking out from those frail faces, framed in oval frames. Deep, beautiful, wise, witty, and passionate eyes, wells of wisdom and experience, glowing in smooth and placid frames.

Such harmless ladies, they looked, if one didn't watch their eyes; so proud and so meek and docile, so childish and delicate and oh, so fastidious and frail. They were actually the most dashing women of their time, *grandes amoureuses*, who wrecked homes, brought wild happiness to a few and dire unhappiness to many, and figured in the grand, muffled private scandals of Georgian and Early Victorian high society. They had loved much, but not in public. Nothing they ever did was done in public, and little of their doings was ever known. And they have passed, unknown by the public, into oblivion.

"Manners change more rapidly than morals," I reflected, as we whirled down the Strand to our night-club. "And I dare say my impulsive companion is far more moral than they were. It's a question of reserve, or lack of it; of a love for privacy that is out of fashion. The movies have something to do with it." And I remembered reading in a history of modern England how a law had been passed by the House of Commons, forbidding the public to stand outside Lily Langtry's house to stare at her when that famous beauty was in her prime. Beauty is no one's private property nowadays. Women are free, and, being free, are the property of the public.

To show off one's charms and treasures, not to hide and store them up in secret, is the vice of our period. Fame can no longer be attained by whispers, nor beauty by a legend. It is romance that suffers, not morals, if immorality means a life disordered by the passions.

It has become the fashion in English society to assume a complete contempt for conventions, respectability, or grandeur. If you are very privileged and very attractive and very solidly set up with house and husband and children, and if you have a great English clan behind you and are inwardly extremely proud, it is amusing to pretend that you are the most modest and forlorn and humble of women. You are grateful to any one, any dull old woman or frightful bore of a man, who is kind to you. You implore your friends humbly to help you out, to save your life and come to a tiresome lunch or dinner party where they know they'll find the most amusing people in town. You wonder if one of them, the worst-dressed one, could possibly tell you the name of the dressmaker who made her lovely frock, and you hope piously that it wasn't too frightfully expensive, for you are terribly poor.

All this is deliberate deception, but of an extremely clever kind. It is flattery carried to its completest expression, and it is so well done that I swear the frump in the badly made dress goes home a much happier woman, and the crashing bore glows with a feeling of being a great social success as he puts on his coat. The idea is to make everyone happy by making them seem lovelier and more important than you are. And what you get out of it yourself is, well, a sense of duty done, of having oiled the social wheels, of having given happiness and having a little joke all to yourself. For all the time, this English lady that I'm talking about, who humbles herself to all women less lucky than herself, is as proud as Lucifer and knows quite well that she wouldn't change places with anyone on earth for any consideration. Indeed, she is so proud that she is exquisitely polite to upstarts who are rude to her. It is only to her equals that she is rude; to her best friends, and they are usually men with whom she is provokingly and provocatively frank, impulsive, and careless. To the outside world, she is as smooth and as delicious and as harmless as cream.

It may seem strange that solid and stolid and phlegmatic England should have produced such a subtle, artificial creature. Nevertheless, it is so. And, after all, strange as she is, this flower, growing out of the rich, damp, sodden soil of this island, is natural enough, for it is her nature to be incongruous. Smart society in any country is not the normal bloom one would expect the land to produce. Its chief characteristic is always incongruity, and its appearance is no more appropriate at first sight than orchids growing on an apple tree or sprays of peach blossoms springing from the hearts of cabbages. For that is the aim of such people. It amuses them to seem quite different — different from the rest of the nation, first, and then different from what they really are. And what amuses me about these flighty, dashing, exotic English women is that they are really not flighty or exotic at all.

They are really steady and strong, level-headed and loyal and very healthy. Hardy, country-bred girls at bottom, capable of standing any amount of cold, wet, hunger, and fatigue, capable of getting up early and going to bed late, of running big houses and bigger charities; good organizers, hard workers, keen politicians, very knowledgeable as to the problems facing farmers, colliers, or shipbuilders and aware of the British Empire as a part of the show for which they and their husbands have always been responsible. Two lives? They lead half a dozen and switch from one to another with consummate ease. And my lovely lady who kisses any friend she may fancy at night in the Strand has probably motored down that afternoon from a Mothers' Meeting in her village or after high tea in a farmer's kitchen.

I was taken seriously to task just the other day in America by an irate gentleman who sat next to me at luncheon. Something I had said about American women annoyed him. I was very surprised when I learned what it was that made him glare at me, for he was an intelligent man, or at any rate passed as such. I had merely said that American women were, in my opinion, less sophisticated than English or French women. The statement had been reported in the press, and he had read it, and it rankled in his mind. He was, in fact, boiling with resentment, and he began to attack me at once.

I should have realized, for I had heard the word "sophistication" constantly since my arrival in New York. It had been uttered by a hundred lips. Had I read such-and-such a book? It was a very sophisticated story. I would probably like it. Would I lunch at a certain club? Quite sophisticated people, therefore worth my while. Did I know a certain sophisticated writer? Well, I ought to know him. He would prove to me that New York was as sophisticated as Paris. And newspaper reporters had interviewed me on the word. Obviously, I should have known by this time that the question was one of vital interest to my compatriots. But even then, I couldn't understand, and so I cried out at him in bewilderment, "But why do you want us to be sophisticated, and why do you want to prove to me that we American women are? It's not at all a nice word. It simply means the habit of living artificially, and I don't see anything in that to be proud of."

We couldn't understand each other. His pride was injured, and he was beyond reasoning. Indeed, I implored him to recognize that we were, by comparison with the hardened old worldlings across the Atlantic, a fresh, innocent, naïve, and youthful race; that we were bound to be, having recently stepped out of log cabins, and that we ought to be proud of it. But at the word "naïve" he jerked away from me as if I'd pricked him with thorns, and so I gave it up, began trying to soothe him, and it was only under my breath that I murmured, "Surely your violent resentment is a proof that what I say is true."

For that matter, am I not myself a proof of it, since, after ten years of French life and ten years of English, I remain the naïve American, interested enough in the manners of these ladies to write about them, and am even a little shocked?

MISS ILKA CHASE, photographed here by Edward Steichen in an afternoon coat of black caracul with a deep silver-fox collar. The little black felt hat is plumed in pink. Miss Chase, an elegant young figure of the New York stage, has appeared with Leslie Howard in Philip Barry's *The Animal Kingdom*.

[1923 – 1933]

"LES COQUELUCHES DES DAMES"

The movie idols have succeeded the matinée idols,
with this chief difference:
in the new motion-picture era
they have become international idols.

CHARLES BOYER

RONALD COLMAN Hoyningen-Huene

LESLIE HOWARD

Steichen

ERROL FLYNN

HENRY FONDA Weston

TYRONE POWER

JAMES STEWART

JAMES CAGNEY

FREDRIC MARCH Nelson

ROBERT TAYLOR Allan

WILLIAM POWELL Hurrell

DON'T FLATTER YOURSELVES, GIRLS

BY PAUL GALLICO

Some months ago, before departing for England, I wrote an essay dedicated to the premise that ladies in sport simply would have to stop getting sweaty and breathless at their games, especially when competing in public, because I didn't like it and wasn't going to have any more of it. It was published in this valuable magazine, a portion of which is heroically devoted to seeing that the gals don't go around with their back hair scraggly, or wearing the wrong kind of clothes, or climbing into underwear that sticks out at the wrong places — a noble and apparently necessary mission.

The magazine apparently gets around, because the postmen are all bow-legged from lugging up my hill letters of complaint and protest from bilious and irritable females from all over the United States. The letters ran from one to nine pages in length, but they all said the same thing. In effect, the gist of the two questions asked were these:

Do you flatter yourself that girls make themselves attractive just for you men?

Do you think that you men are any bargains all mussed and hot and perspiring and red-faced after violent exercise?

In order to spare the barking dogs of His Majesty's letter-carriers lugging individual replies *down* the hill again, I have decided to answer all these complaints collectively in this erudite composition, and really settle the matter once and for all, at least as far as I am concerned. The girls will know where I stand, and that will be that.

The simple answer to both questions is — yes. Men look most fetching and attractive immediately after violent exercise. At least I do — all manly, and red, and tousled, and full of muscles — sort of a little like Clark Gable and Robert Taylor and Cary Grant with just a touch of George Bancroft, Walter Huston, Fredric March, and Wallace Beery. Remember Beery in *Viva Villa*? I thought it was swell.

I do not wear shorts when I play tennis because I am too smart for that, which is more than I can say for most girls. Not that I haven't got better-looking legs than most females I ever saw with the possible exception of Marlene Dietrich (though I don't think she can sing a lick). If you wear those long woollen golf hose rolled at the knee, you look like a yodeler, which is something that only a Swiss or an Austrian can afford to do. And if you just wear short wool socks, rolled at the ankle, you look as though you had been in a hurry dressing and had come away to the tennis-courts without your pants. The girls haven't solved this one yet. I have — by wearing slacks.

I use a half-sleeved light wool or jersey shirt with a roll collar attached and open at the neck. They say that at the end of four sets of singles I'm a riot, with my hair falling down over my eyes, my face a healthy red, and perspiration dripping from the end of my nose.

Or take me right after I have finished a couple of fencing bouts. Listen, you dopes, don't you think that Bayard and D'Artagnan and Douglas Fairbanks got hot after leaping about and swinging from things? And yet, look at all the dames they always got. You don't think that Romeo got up that balcony without wheezing a little and burbling a trifle from the upper lip, as the English say. And yet you don't see Norma Shearer making a fuss, do you? She was nuts about him. He was a man and a tough cookie even if he did speak in blank verse. A good guy, with hair on his chest. You girls are always pretending to prefer those softies who part their hair in the middle, quote Proust, and tango without looking harassed, but that's because there are only eleven men on a football team, and they go fast. The whole thing is ridiculous.

Men never look better than when they are taking exercise or playing a game. Women never look worse. The woman athlete has yet to be born who is half as graceful at any game as a competent male. Take a look at Frank Shields playing tennis some day, or Craig Wood or Jimmy Thompson hitting a golf-ball, and you'll get what I mean. I've sat at Forest Hills too often, with my field-glasses, watching brother Shields come off the courts, exhausted and dripping after five tough tournament sets, his hair limp, his mouth and shoulders sagging a little. Who was I watching with my glasses? Shields? No, dears, you. You with your doe eyes and compassionate glances and yearning sort of you-poor-tired-boy-come-let-mother-hold-you-a-minute-until-you-get-your-breath expressions. I've been married twice. The more wretched, dishevelled, and messed up a man is, the more you love him. You can't help it, poor things. You get it right from your maternal ancestor, the she-ape, Mrs. Pithe-

FRED ASTAIRE, THE INCOMPARABLE,
PHOTOGRAPHED IN REHEARSAL
BY ANDRE DE DIENES

canthropus, who used to have to gather up her guy after he had been stepped on by a Diplodocus. You saw *King Kong*, didn't you? Well, all right. The chimp falls in love with Fay Wray because she's so beautiful, and, above all, well tailored, and wears the right kind of scent, or *parfum* as we used to call it in our alley. And although she's scared to death of the big monkey, *still* she's attracted to him. You can see that. She takes Bruce Cabot in the end on account of the Wills Hays office — you know how strict they are, but what I mean is, the thing is significant. Who is off his subject? How do *you* know what my subject is?

The original error in my first essay was limiting my demand for tidiness to women in sports. All women should keep themselves in order at all times looking as though they had just stepped out of an automobile or travel ad. Otherwise, there seems to be very little excuse for them that I can see. Well, we'll correct that error. Hereafter, I want *all* of you girls, whether you are athletes or not, to look beautiful, cool, calm, intelligently powdered, and with your hair in order and decently brushed, *all* the time. Get it? Yes, and I'm coming to the little matter of lipstick. For heaven's sake, either find a lipstick that won't come off or quit smearing your kissers with what seems to be a preparation of red lead and tallow. None of you has any idea how many fine kisses you miss out on just because you smear on lipstick with the technique of a house-painter instead of that of an artist.

There are two times in life when a gentleman manages to look inordinately silly. One is when he is pulling on his socks, and the other is just after he has been the recipient of a loving buss from a badly lipsticked lady, and he fishes his handkerchief out of his breast pocket, drags it violently across his mouth, and then helplessly regards the fearful mess of red on the white linen. It kills romance, that's what it does. Why, do you know what happens after Joan Blondell kisses Gary Cooper in a scene? They stop shooting while he goes and takes a shower, changes his clothes, and then gets made up all over again. Well, they've got plenty of money in Hollywood, and they're organized for that. The average guy isn't. He looks at the handkerchief; wonders how a doll can have all that paint on her without some one trying to hang her in the dining-room or art gallery with the modern contemporary portraits; wonders whether he has gotten it all off; takes another wipe; gets more off, but smears some of the first onto his chin; swears; puts the handkerchief back into his breast pocket; snatches it out again, and stuffs it into his pants pocket for fear someone will spot the evidence of it; wonders whether any of it has gotten off onto his collar, and, of course, by that time, the Mood Has Passed.

Do I flatter myself that girls make themselves attractive just for us men? Certainly. For what else? You are not trying to tell me that you spend three hours in a beauty parlour, stifling under mud packs, roasting under driers, and getting tweezed, slapped, prodded, yanked, and waved just because you like it, are you? You girls have acquired a lot of subsidiary interests these days, but Man-Snatching is still Number One.

There is no use sending me letters of protest over this one, because I'm on to you, though I will accept indignant, complaining letters if they contain twenty-five cents in stamps because I use a lot of stamps in my business. Mind you, I'm all for fixing up. But let us just not try to kid ourselves what it's for. It's for us, and as long as it is, why not do it the way we like it, huh?

I realize that all women can not look like Greta Garbo, or Anna Sten, or Mae West, and a very good thing, too. But you can all be neat and tidy and have charm, which comes in bottles, and smell nice and be soft and cuddly and appetizing and mussable and everything else that is dear to the heart of a man, who, after all, seems to be the important member of the human species and the one that matters. Bless me, you don't think that *I* like the arrangement any better than you do, but that's the way it is, and what can any of us do about it? I find it a bore, most of the time, to be superior and muscular and wear pants and be smart and decisive, frank and essentially honest, which women are not, but what can I do about it? I didn't arrange things that way. But I am willing to admit that seems to be the way that nature fixed things up. And if nature did skip you girls when it came to equipping you with brains and stability and all the other things that go to make man the dominant sex, it did give you sex-appeal — for which you all ought to be very grateful, and admit it instead of pretending that you'd rather ride horseback or play squash over at the Women's Club.

So why not stop squawking about why you paint your toenails pink and have little hairs yanked out of your faces by the roots, one by one, or spend billions of dollars annually for goo to put on your faces, and get on with the laudable aim and end of it all — which is to make yourselves just as attractive and adorable and kissable as you possibly can?

I am returning to the United States very shortly, and when I get there I want to see some progress. Keep your noses powdered, your hair neat and shiny — a touch of fine brilliantine if it hasn't a natural shine — but it *will* have a natural shine if you're not too lazy to brush it enough — your nails nicely manicured, your skin soft, the nape of your neck delicately fragrant, and your lips, soft, red, yielding, but not after the manner of a rubber-stamp pad.

Do these things and you too, some day, can have a fine, wonderful man all for yourselves to have and to keep until you get lazy and sloppy again. But don't come around bothering me, thanks. I've had enough.

Collection Mr. and Mrs. Donald S. Stralem

HENRI MATISSE, "THE HINDU POSE"

HELEN HAYES AND VINCENT PRICE IN "VICTORIA REGINA," THE NEW PLAY BY LAURENCE HOUSMAN

THE CLARK'S FORK VALLEY, WYOMING

BY ERNEST HEMINGWAY

ERNEST HEMINGWAY

At the end of summer, the big trout would be out in the centre of the stream; they were leaving the pools along the upper part of the river and dropping down to spend the winter in the deep water of the canyon. It was wonderful fly-fishing then in the first weeks of September. The native trout were sleek, shining, and heavy, and nearly all of them leaped when they took the fly. If you fished two flies, you would often have two big trout on and the need to handle them very delicately in that heavy current.

The nights were cold, and, if you woke in the night, you would hear the coyotes. But you did not want to get out on the stream too early in the day because the nights were so cold they chilled the water, and the sun had to be on the river until almost noon before the trout would start to feed.

You could ride in the morning, or sit in front of the cabin, lazy in the sun, and look across the valley where the hay was cut so the meadows were cropped brown and smooth to the line of quaking aspens along the river, now turning yellow in the fall. And on the hills rising beyond, the sage was silvery grey.

Up the river were the two peaks of Pilot and Index, where we would hunt mountain-sheep later in the month, and you sat in the sun and marvelled at the formal, clean-lined shape mountains can have at a distance, so that you remember them in the shapes they show from far away, and not as the broken rock-slides you crossed, the jagged edges you pulled up by, and the narrow shelves you sweated along, afraid to look down, to round that peak that looked so smooth and geometrical. You climbed around it to come out on a clear space to look down to where an old ram and three young rams were feeding in the juniper bushes in a high, grassy pocket cupped against the broken rock of the peak.

The old ram was purple-grey, his rump was white, and when he raised his head you saw the great heavy curl of his horns. It was the white of his rump that had betrayed him to you in the green of the junipers when you had lain in the lee of a rock, out of the wind, three miles away, looking carefully at every yard of the high country through a pair of good Zeiss glasses.

Now as you sat in front of the cabin, you remembered that down-hill shot and the young rams standing, their heads turned, staring at him, waiting for him to get up. They could not see you on that high ledge, nor wind you, and the shot made no more impression on them than a boulder falling.

You remembered the year we had built a cabin at the head of Timber Creek, and the big grizzly that tore it open every time we were away. The snow came later that year, and this bear would not hibernate, but spent his autumn tearing open cabins and ruining a trap-line. But he was so smart you never saw him in the day. Then you remembered coming on the three grizzlies in the high country at the head of Crandall Creek. You heard a crash of timber and thought it was a cow elk bolting, and then there they were, in the broken shadow, running with an easy, lurching smoothness, the afternoon sun making their coats a soft, bristling silver.

You remembered elk bugling in the fall, the bull so close you could see his chest muscles swell as he lifted his head, and still not see his head in the thick timber; but hear that deep, high mounting whistle and the answer from across another valley. You thought of all the heads you had turned down and refused to shoot, and you were pleased.

You remembered how this country had looked when you first came into it. You could remember all the hunting and all the fishing and the riding in the summer sun and the dust of the pack-train, the silent riding in the hills in the sharp cold of fall going up after the cattle on the high range, finding them wild as deer and as quiet, only bawling noisily when they were all herded together being forced along down into the lower country.

Then there was the winter; the trees bare now, the snow blowing so you could not see, the saddle wet, then frozen as you came downhill, breaking a trail through the snow, trying to keep your legs moving, and the sharp, warming taste of whiskey when you hit the ranch and changed your clothes in front of the big open fireplace. It's a good country.

[1933 – 1943] 153

MARINE LIFE, FROM A TO E: in which, if your eyesight is keen and your perception keener, you can discover in this picture by Constantin Alajalov the pleasures, passions, and privacies of a great liner's enormous human cargo, from the gilded patterns of first class to the more congested *bonhomie* of those deep down in tourist and third class, with a special peep at the crew.

[1933 – 1943] 155

EUGENE O'NEILL

PAULINE LORD SCORED A NOTABLE TRIUMPH IN "ANNA CHRISTIE," O'NEILL'S PULITZER PRIZE WINNING PLAY

George Jean Nathan, who is a best friend as well as the severest critic of Eugene O'Neill, used to call him "Gladstone," which is the middle name of this gloomy, great dramatist. "To say that he was melancholy, even morbid, in his early days, is to put it mildly," wrote Nathan. "Life to him was a serial story consisting mainly of advice from mad dogs, fatal cancers, and undertakers' disappointments in love." But O'Neill's almost psychopathic depression has left unshadowed the Nathan admiration for this extraordinary, sombre talent, lightened, according to Nathan, by plays with an occasional streak of humour. Among these he includes *Marco's Millions, Desire under the Elms,* and *Emperor Jones.* And, unbelievably, *Strange Interlude* has an occasional twisting glint of humour. (But not enough to prevent its being banned in Boston in 1928.) O'Neill has been, always, a dramatist, just as some men are tenors, some develop extraordinary biceps. O'Neill is a dramatist, inevitably. He is, according to Nathan, the hardest of workers among his (Nathan's) writing acquaintances. And to the agony of writing a play, O'Neill himself adds the additional burden of casting. To him, insensitive acting corrupts his plays; he once said that he would like to be rich enough simply to publish them in book form, and not have them spoiled by a performance.

EUGENE O'NEILL, GREATEST AMERICAN DRAMATIST, NOBEL PRIZE WINNER FOR 1936

Steichen

"MOURNING BECOMES ELECTRA," PRODUCED BY THE THEATRE GUILD, STARRED NAZIMOVA, ALICE BRADY, AND LEE BAKER

[1933 – 1943]   157

SHAKESPEARE ON STAGE AND IN THE FILMS

Steichen

NORMA SHEARER IS STARRED WITH LESLIE HOWARD IN "ROMEO AND JULIET"

Wurts

MAURICE EVANS IN "KING RICHARD II"

JOHN GIELGUD WITH JUDITH ANDERSON. HIS IS THE GREATEST "HAMLET" SINCE BARRYMORE'S

Stei

OLD HOME TOWN

BY WILLIAM SAROYAN

Of the unchanging things, the town in which you first met the world is one of the most unchanging and mysterious. It is always a place of monotony and at the same time, as you grow, change, go away, remember, return, and go away again, one of the most inexhaustibly full and rich places. And yet what it is is so nearly nothing, except for the dull, drab, lonely, lost objects of it, that you never know, each time you return to it, what it is that holds you so strongly to it, no matter where you go.

What is it but an ordinary American town, no different from ten thousand others, where thirty million others were once born and where once they knew childhood and youth; and went away or stayed?

What is it more than a place where two or three dozen paused one day of one year and stayed, and others came, and stayed, and others came out of their staying?

What is it more than two depots, one on each side of town, east and west, the city in between, the streets and houses all around, the dwellers never out of hearing of the trains which keep coming and going?

What is it more than the beginning of the world, with winter coming to it, cold and dark and health, gloom and chill and sickness, street corners and walking men, coming and going?

Is it anything more than waking one morning in a stillness out of this world and knowing presence in this place?

Or more than sitting at a desk at school and wishing to learn from the simplest lesson of arithmetic what all of it is, where it is from, where it is going, who all of them are, each alone, each strange, uncommunicable, not speechless but nevertheless dumb?

Is it ever a place more than where, not in dream, the streets occurred and yourself came about in them, walking?

The empty lots where you moved about at games, the ringing of church bells Sunday mornings, the summer noon whistles of packing-houses, the epidemics of disease with fright rising everywhere and humour, too, and the knowledge that in his day any man who lives lives by reason of miracle or accident, at best by anger and impudence?

Is it anything more than vague longing summer and winter that you do not know shall go on till you are dead? Loneliness you do not know shall never end?

Is it anything more than twenty years ago, seeing beauty in the face of a small girl and adoring it and not knowing that never shall the light of that face go out of your sleep, never shall the image of that solemn innocence break away from the other things that visited your sleep?

Is the small town a place, truly, of the world, or is it no more than something out of a boy's dreaming? Out of his foolish love of all the things that are not of death made? All things somewhere beyond the dust and decay, to the eye somewhere undiscoverable beyond what is the top of every object, beyond each of all its sides, beyond bottom, outside, around, over, under, within, beyond every edge of it? Beyond the clear, bright, hard, supple, faraway night, faraway over the levelness of the earth, faraway into the end of the sky, faraway within the clear suddenness of all of night, the swift arrival of a remembrance lithe and without image?

Is it a boy's knowing that, although this is a place of sorrowed trying, or

[1933 – 1943]

sorrowful men trying for the best, it is also a place where in the midst of things seen and men known moves the race that never was born to men and within the crying grief of its streets and structures is the whole towering world which almost came to be? To his nostrils just beyond the stench of sweat and decay and disease and rot, the holy odour of all things with only loveliness in them and no death. To his ears, the multimillion sound of silence staying within and around all things. The soft, listening silence of the continuous and never begun and always beginning.

While the automobile goes over the highway this year seventy miles an hour, my Uncle Melik, remembering everything, says with grief, including himself among those he speaks of, they are alive only because they are not dead. It is not as if they are truly alive. It is only that they are not dead. That is the thing that is awful about it. That they are not truly alive, that they are neither dead nor alive, that they only breathe, that they have been engulfed, swallowed, eaten by its enormity and strangeness, that no one who came here has found the way to live so that his living will be more than momentary absence of death. That is the thing which after all the years bewilders me.

Once again I am back in my home town. I came to see if I could learn something more of the winters of the beginning years. I was here in the spring this year and learned something new of springtime when I was here twenty years ago, and I was here this summer, looking to the vineyards for something I hadn't understood long ago. Last night I learned that a great part of what this town is, wherever I go, is the sky, and the way day comes to its end here, and the night-time sky, faraway, clear, sudden, and full of loneliness.

Early this morning I walked to town down Ventura Avenue over streets I walked twenty years ago. I found nothing changed but a few signs on a few buildings, a few trees lost, a few new ones come, a few grown greater, a house fallen into disrepair but still inhabited, the porch in decay. The silence is the same, and it is broken the same as twenty years ago, by the coming and going of trains.

From Ventura Avenue to Tulare Street I walked on the Santa Fe railroad tracks, and from north going south came the freight train. When it reached me I couldn't believe the years had gone by, and I knew a man will go out of this world without ever finding that largeness and wholeness in the living and in himself which was the cause of all his longing when he was no more than ten years old.

While the train was going by, I knew that a man will go away without ever having reached anywhere, he will die time and again before he stops breathing, and he will be alive only because he is not dead, and never will the image of loveliness just beyond all things, all ends and edges, over and above and within, cease being in his sleep until he is truly one who is no longer alive, and no longer able to dream at all.

QUEEN ELIZABETH, PRINCESS ELIZABETH, AND PRINCESS MARGARET ROSE CROSS THE ANCIENT THRESHOLD OF GLAMIS CASTLE, THE QUEEN'S ANCESTRAL HOME, WHICH IS AS OLD AS SCOTTISH HISTORY, AS OLD AS THE LEGEND OF MACBETH AND DUNCAN

Central Press

THE WEDDING AT CANDE: 1937

BY CECIL BEATON

On the grounds of the Château de Candé, a swan, blindingly white in the sunlight, glides like clockwork over the glassy lake. Cairn terriers bask in the sun, and the greyhound can hardly bother to saunter along the dappled lawns. Inside, the preparations for the wedding reach their final stage.

The conservatory floor is a mountain of imported flowers; women in large picture hats, white piqué overalls, and surgical-looking rubber gloves are trailing bundles of Madonna lilies, syringa, and laurel into the main salon. The butler, assisted by footmen in their shirt-sleeves, is presiding over the setting of the elongated dining-table.

The altar is in the lime-coloured music-room — quite a small but sunny room, with sun-coloured curtains. The Duke himself attends to the positions of the squashed strawberry chairs for the thirty-two guests, and to the candlesticks and the draping of the curtains.

Upstairs, in readiness, hangs the grey-blue wedding dress and slip that Mainbocher made to give the bride-to-be the fluted lines of a Chinese statue of an early century. The bonnet of pale blue feathers and tulle is on a stand by the open thirteenth-century window. Downstairs, the bride-to-be, trim and smiling in yellow, is giving last-minute instructions and the first greetings to the organist. A large white carnation arrives for the Duke's buttonhole, and the final touches have been given to the preparations for this historic wedding for which Edward gave up the English throne.

162 [1933 – 1943]

THE DUKE AND SEVERAL OF THE WEDDING GUESTS

THE DUKE AND DUCHESS OF WINDSOR ON THE CHATEAU BALCONY

MR. CHARLES BEDAUX, HOST OF THE CHATEAU

THE CHATEAU DE CANDE

RIGHT: THE COUPLE AT CANDE BEFORE THE

Photos: Cecil Beaton

HIS MAJESTY'S SMILE. KING GEORGE VI

CONVERSATIONAL KLEPTOMANIA

BY G. B. STERN

It is perfectly possible not to quote. The man, or woman, who adorns his conversation with a rich embroidery of quotation is merrily having his fling; and such self-indulgence is perfectly curable from within or without.

But there is another, more insidious way in which we are enslaved by what we read. Every now and then, some odd, unimportant phrase, chosen and remembered by who knows what random process of selection, leaps from the printed page, gets itself into the household idiom, settles down there, and makes itself forever comfortable. It cannot be flung out again because, however absurd, however trivial, once you have discovered a short cut in speech by allusion, you will never want to trudge the whole distance by the long high road again.

Examples will best show what I mean. We quote from, let us say, *Hamlet:* "Whether 'tis nobler in the mind to suffer," and so forth, but we could just as easily conduct daily conversation with *Hamlet* eliminated, not missing it as we should miss using, for instance, that querulous complaint, "Nobody tells me anything" — a familiar sensation, half aggrieved, half joking, of being kept out of the family secrets, which originated with old James Forsyte, father of Soames, brother of Jolyon, created by Galsworthy.

And when somebody employs loose exaggeration to impress us — "Apple-blossom everywhere!" — how easy to subdue them with Lady Caroline's airy snub: "Surely only on the apple trees?" You recognize Saki, of course. Close all the windows and doors, and it still becomes difficult to keep Saki from trickling in. The great and ponderous masters of literature do not supply these savoury odds and ends; they supply quotation, but that is quite different from the intimate collection now on exhibition. "Uncle John, what do you do when you feel too well in the mornings?" That, I believe came out of *Punch;* used ironically, it is of continual value in the home. The picture showed a small boy bouncing up and down on the bed, kicking his heels in the air; Uncle John was shaving, and you could tell from his expression that the question had not arisen, of feeling too well in the morning. If somebody chatters during breakfast, in what sounds like a mood of unnatural exuberance, you will find much comfort in remarking drily, "Feeling too well in the morning?" Or even, provided your listener can be trusted to seize the point, merely exclaim, "Uncle John!"

Equally in the spirit of irony is the expression, "Sorry for wolves." I think I first met it in a book by Sylvia Townsend Warner: *The True Heart.* The young heroine of the novel (known among country folk as an "innocent"), during a severe winter, and in the very depths of her own and local misfortunes, found time to be unnecessarily sorry for those ravening wolves up in the Arctic regions who perhaps might not be getting enough food in the bitter snowy weather. Here is an indispensable short cut when you wish to intimate that someone is wasting his sympathy for some wholly far-fetched, problematic sorrow, "Oh, God, sorry for wolves *again!*"

Everyone has his own individual list, of course; this is merely to show how the items get picked up and worked in. And not only is it a question of two can play at that game, but two or more *must* play at it, or the swift convenience is obviously lost. The context of a *Hamlet* quotation can be universally recognized; but only your circle of initiates, we imagine, will get the idea of "falsely genial in a knitted coat," which occurred in a short story by Sylvia Lynd: A man was having a bad time in the wrong sort of house-party; he describes how the baby was brought in — "falsely genial in a knitted coat." That is precisely the subtle twist of phrase to hail with a shout of pleasure, and which will remain behind when the rest of a story has dropped from your memory. After a visitor has left the room, pleased, no doubt, at having left a good impression, "She's in her knitted coat," you remark, casual and cruel; and that will be enough to sum up the whole of the last two hours.

My urgent desire, when I seem to have been convinced of something, and cannot take the trouble to go on arguing, but secretly retain my own opinion, is still to murmur, *"Und sie bewegt sich doch,"* which dates from very early childhood. It was my father's favourite quotation: more recognizable, perhaps, translated to the Italian *"Eppur si muove,"* ("And yet it does move"). You will recognize that Galileo said it after he had been forced to recant his discovery that the earth moved round

[1933 – 1943] 165

the sun. In any language, it tersely indicates the inevitable obstinacy of the person who knows he is right after he has had to swear he is wrong.

From a more modern source, yet expressing very much the same thing, we get Thurber's weary reply to an argument: "*All* right, you *heard* a seal bark!" I believe the picture first appeared in *The New Yorker*. A husband and wife arguing in bed, the husband wanting to turn over and go to sleep, the wife who will not let him; some strange, delirious fancy has got into her mind, and nothing he said would remove it. At last he gave in: "All right, have it your way, you heard a seal bark!" (Personally I find it necessary to misquote him slightly to get the right inflection: "All right, have it your *own* way, you *did* hear a seal bark!" But there *was* a seal, you know, incredible as it appears to us and to the lady's husband; and Thurber knew there was a seal; he drew it wistfully hauling itself up onto the bed-post behind her head.

Years ago, Sinclair Lewis told me an anecdote which ended on a fine, simple lesson in contentment: "Take away the cow." That story deserves a place in our collection: A peasant and his family have to sleep in the same room with the hens; he asks the local rabbi for a remedy; but, to his bewilderment, the rabbi suggests that he should first add his goat and furthermore his cow to the already miserably overcrowded room. At the end of a fortnight of this intolerable discomfort, he goes again to the rabbi, still faintly trustful that a remedy can be found for despair. "It is well," said the wise man, "your troubles are at an end. Go home and take away the cow." And it is an undeniable truth that after a fortnight cheek by jowl, so to speak, with a cow, the hens, formerly so obstreperous, will hardly seem to be there any more. "Take away the cow," only takes a few seconds to say, while to expound the creed and psychology underlying the incident would be a matter of hours.

From H. G. Wells' *Kipps*, there remains for us "buttud toce" and "Oh, Ann, I been so mis'bel." And finally, "Oo, I dunno," which is Kipps' final summing-up after a struggle to express himself on the world. "Oo, I dunno" comes as close to it as we can hope from any more fine-sounding philosophy. Galsworthy gives us a snub in typical Soames Forsyte style; his daughter, Fleur, had carried on too enthusiastically over a picture he had given her: "Oh, Dad, how jolly!" But Soames disliked hyperbole and metaphor and symbolism. "It isn't," he said; "it's a monkey eating fruit."

If you have read *1066 and All That*, you will realize that "the Barons should not be tried except by a special jury of other Barons who would understand," illustrates perfectly, with maybe a sly wink towards connivance, our natural, if secret, desire to save time and explanation by letting our acts be judged always and only by our peers, those "other barons who would understand."

From Kenneth Grahame's *Wind in the Willows*, the phrase I find myself using most often, in vehement dispraise of almost anything, is "*horrid* little cart, *common* little cart, *canary-coloured* cart!" And when someone is swaggering and blowing himself up: "Intelligent Mr. Toad!" ("She asked, 'Who is that handsome man,' and they answered, 'Mr. Toad!'")

Rebecca West mentioned in one of her review articles, "Surprise made me look like a goldfish," and that, too, is pretty useful once you have laid hands on it. You are more than just surprised; surprise has made you look like a goldfish.

These items are showing signs of strong wear and tear. "She must have seen something nasty in the woodshed!" That, I should say, with its mockery of the Freudian School when overdoing it, has become fairly universally understood. It originated in Stella Gibbons' *Cold Comfort Farm*, where the old grandmother of ninety was still privileged to have three meals brought up to her bedroom every day because at the age of four she had seen something nasty in the woodshed.

About two months ago, a group of us read *The Sword in the Stone*, by T. H. White. And for a brief while, conversation became so cryptic by its close association with that most delightful, most magical of books as to be really tiresome to the uninitiated. I have left out nearly everyone's inevitable references to *Alice in Wonderland* and *Through the Looking-Glass*, because, as in Hardy's *Jude the Obscure*, they are "to menny" (and this tragic reference is one of those, I fear, which I use constantly and flippantly). *The Sword and the Stone* challenged "Alice" by the number of its intoxicating contributions to our daily talk. Gradually, however, they sifted themselves out; and I will content myself by noting down only one (for me) wholly indispensable fragment: "Come along, Robin Hood," snapped King Pellinore, for once in a temper, "stop leaning on your bow with that look of negligent woodcraft!"

"With that look of negligent woodcraft" ... And how did I manage to do without it, all these years?

166   [1933 – 1943]

A PARTY IN HONOUR OF MR. COLE PORTER. The hostess was Miss Elsa Maxwell. The occasion — a "coming-out" party for Mr. Porter's coming out of the plaster cast in which he'd been encased since fracturing both legs when recently thrown from a horse. The guests — a brilliant mixture of society, stage, beauty, and brains. The place — the Waldorf-Astoria Perroquet Suite. The entertainment — a revue of Broadway stars including Beatrice Lillie, Jack Buchanan, June Sillman, Ethel Merman, Imogene Coca, Jessie Matthews, Mary Jane Walsh, and swing-singer Maxine Sullivan. And, of course, two dance orchestras and plenty of champagne.

MR. COLE PORTER
AND MRS. VINCENT ASTOR

MISS ELSA MAXWELL
(BACK TO CAMERA)
MR. CONDE NAST,
MRS. VALENTIN PARERA (GRACE MOORE),
MR. FREDERICK LONSDALE,
MISS ETHEL MERMAN, MR. JULES GLAENZER,
MRS. GILBERT MILLER,
AND MRS. W. R. HEARST

Karger Pix

FAR LEFT: PRINCE
SERGE OBOLENSKY

MISS GERTRUDE LAWRENCE
AND MR. FULTON CUTTING

PARIS COLLECTIONS

BY BETTINA WILSON

A collection is something that a couturier designs, mannequins show, fashion magazines report, and buyers buy ... which eventually reaches you in the form of "So-and-So's latest model." It sounds like a simple supply-and-demand story, but actually it has a superb theatrical confusion about it that gives it excitement.

Buyers, fashion reporters, and friends crowd to couturiers' openings for much the same reason that theatre-lovers crowd to first nights; because they like to be the first ones to see something new, because the mannequins give their best performance of the season, and because the author-producer is there to see that you get the best show the house can possibly put on.

The salons are invariably hot and smoky, thanks to the person with his

MLLE. CHANEL IN HER FAVOURITE PHOTOGRAPH, TAKEN BY HORST IN 1937

[1933 – 1943] 169

LUCIEN LELONG always sits on a high stool between his two salons, inspecting every dress as it passes.

PATOU's collection is shown in small salons. One *vendeuse* calls numbers; another helps the mannequins.

In PAQUIN's new salon, with mirrored pillars and tall white lamps. Several models are shown at one time.

MAINBOCHER, in his studio just before his opening, gives a black and white tulle dress the final once-over.

SCHIAPARELLI receives congratulations on her collection. SALVADOR DALI (right) and JEAN-MICHEL from Frank.

back to the window who is afraid of a *courant d'air*; the atmosphere is tense, because you can't take in colours, fabrics, lines, and effects in one glance without tying your faculties into knots. The great, calm exception always seems to be Miss Frankau, of Bergdorf Goodman, who looks as if she were sitting in a comfortable chair in her living-room in the country.

What does the couturier do at her own show?

Chanel, in a sweater and skirt, stands on her mirrored stairs and peers intently through her glasses at the models as they appear on the gold stage — as if she were seeing them for the first time. She has lived and worked with them for the last month, and probably felt completely despairing about them at midnight, after the dress rehearsal. But by eleven the next morning she knows, from the tense stillness at her opening, that the collection is a success. An hour later, she is still sitting on the stairs, reviewing a few last-minute models that weren't finished for the first opening. She is too tired and happy to care about lunch.

Schiaparelli stays behind the scenes, looking every mannequin over before she goes out. She has probably not slept more than two hours the night before, and is as nervous as a prima donna making her operatic debut. Her friends have to pull her out of the back hall afterwards to tell her how good her collection is. She is wearing a beautiful new flower clip, and Perugia's high-soled black suede shoes which increase her diminutive height.

Lelong always sits on an uncomfortable high stool in the doorway, buzzing a button to give the next mannequin her entrance cue so that the collection never lags or goes too fast. His buffet, afterwards, is one of the nicest apologies in Paris for asking people to work late.

Vionnet sits very straight on a backless chair in her small salon, adjusting the girl's dresses as they enter. She looks very much like a dignified matron passing on the débutantes at a ball.

Alix stays in the dressing-room, and finishes her most beautiful last-minute dresses on the mannequins. How often collection habitués have heard Annette, with her back to the closed door, saying "Don't go — there are three more beautiful models," sparring for time while Alix pins up a complicated drapery.

Molyneux modestly sits in a corner of his first salon, with friends, and shows remarkable agility in escaping after the collection, before the "too, too divines" can break over him.

Mainbocher never appears at all. Insistent friends can dig him out in his studio, if they can brave the busy *vendeuses* in the inner hall.

Madame Lanvin receives her guests at cocktail time, and stops to speak to every one before she takes her place behind the desk. She interrupts to serve the best possible champagne and sandwiches, which makes it seem much more like a musicale at home than a theatrical performance.

Maggy Rouff gives a late party with everyone in full evening dress, an orchestra in the distance, and bowers of flowers. She herself receives and sits through the show with the air of an interested spectator rather than a nervous creator.

When the couturiers stop working, the buyers begin. They are busy people, with only ten days or two weeks in which to absorb the Paris fashion scene and decide what they will offer you for your next season's wardrobe. To see a collection is pleasurable excitement; to buy from it is concentrated work. Paris, to them, means long hours, terrific responsibility, and little time to relax.

What do the buyers do in their few leisure moments? They have cocktails or lunch at the Ritz — where collection criticism runs high. They see every good play in Paris. They go to the circus, because the Cirque Médrano is the most divine old-fashioned one-ring circus where you can see everything that goes on. They go to Sunday concerts. They go to the Flea Market, the Flower Market, and the Bird Market, but they rarely have time for sight-seeing — that's something they are saving for that Paris trip they are going to take, some day, for pleasure and not for business.

CHANEL watches her own collection from the mirrored stairway in her salon, famous vantage point for specially favoured guests.

MADAME LANVIN, left, takes time out for champagne and a sandwich at her opening, held in the evening.

MAGGY ROUFF's opening. Guests wear full dress, an orchestra plays, and mannequins appear on a stage.

"FANNY—YOU FOOL!" BY MARJORIE KINNAN RAWLINGS

All my life I have watched beautiful women in the manner of a small boy peering in a pastry window. Women were surely intended to be beautiful, and it is a low trick on the part of Creation to make some of them ravishing and to give Phi Beta Kappa keys to the rest of us as a sop. It is only as middle age has moved in that I have discovered the compensations of being born "plain." The greatest of these is that where the glamour girls of my generation have lost all, I and my kind have had nothing to lose. And a great understanding has dawned on me, as well, that the beautiful woman has a certain philosophy that makes her desirable. This philosophy may be had by any woman. My maternal grandmother possessed the quality in the highest degree.

Fanny was not beautiful. She was too small and too impudent. She was pretty, and I think the prettiness itself came largely from the impudence. She was five feet two at most, pleasantly plump, with naturally curly hair and eyes as blue as an April sky and with the peculiar wickedness of a kitten's. But what gave her her charm was what Grandfather called her foolishness.

Many a woman would have lost all charm under the circumstances of her life. She came of Michigan pioneer stock, as did Grandfather. They were married when she was sixteen and he was nineteen. He had his own inherited farm of some two hundred acres, and they set out, a pair of children, by our notions, to make a life. Grandfather, to the day of his death at eighty-odd, was always fatuously enamoured of her. Abe was six feet four, lean and awkward, with no sense of humour with which to defend himself against her super-abundance of it.

As a young mother, she appeared at the back door of the farmhouse one day completely disguised as a tramp. How she evaded her offspring to get into her rig of ragged trousers and shirt, straw hat, and false moustache, I would not know, but there she stood, growling a demand for food. Honest and solemn Abe having warned his young against such predatory folk, they set upon the intruder with broom and shovel. It was only when her shrieks of laughter gave her away that they recognized with horror their vagrant parent.

She played one practical joke with never-failing success on her sober husband. He would drive to the village on business, and returning at dusk, drooped in all his length and brooding earnestness over the reins, would see a white-sheeted apparition jump out from the bushes under the heads of the horses. The horses never became accustomed to Fanny's nonsense, either, and would bolt and run with satisfying regularity. Arrived at the house, the horses at last under control and stabled, Abe would find Fanny rocking placidly and would storm in on her, shouting, "Fanny — you fool!"

She was the only human being who could upset him. She managed this in all ways known to such a female. Being a presumably settled married woman, she wore her lovely chestnut curls piled in a discreet knot on the top of her head. But until her children were full grown, Abe would beg her to come to him where he was at work. There he would take the pins from her hair so that it fell in a whirlpool around her face and shoulders. He would run his long, bony fingers through it, and I have sometimes wondered indiscreet things about the beginnings of some of the seven children.

Typically, Fanny delighted in telling it on him that, for all his Puritan severity, he loved to have her play the hussy. He would watch her by the hour, unaware that his grave face was luminous with his idolatry.

He was not alone in his adoration. Her kitchen, her pantry, her cellar, her dining-table enslaved her grandchildren. She managed her household and her cuisine with casual efficiency. I have never, at any great table, amateur or professional, eaten more delicious food than she served daily as a matter of course. There was always a divine odour in her house, and I finally traced it to the raspberry tarts always in the pantry, to the buckwheat honey in crocks, to the molasses cookies forever on tap, and to the black walnuts and hickory nuts waiting to go into a salad, a cake, or batch of cookies.

The food would account for the devotion of Fanny's grandchildren. But, above all, we loved her for her absurd tricks. Of many of them I dare not tell. But I remember that in her latter years we made excuses to invite strange children into the house, solely to show off one of her accomplishments. She would be sitting innocently and would suddenly and unconcernedly protrude her false teeth and roll her eyes at the visitors. This appalling picture invariably brought shrieks of delight.

The key to Fanny is that she was sublimely herself. She was not indifferent to those who worshipped her, certainly, or she would not have played so to the gallery. But she quite simply went her own way, saucy, ribald — and took admiration for granted. It came to her as a moth flies to the flame. The point of view is natural to a beautiful woman. I recommend it as well to the merely pretty and to the plain.

[1933–1943]

PAUL GAUGUIN
"Still Life with Three Puppies."
Courtesy Museum of Modern Art, New York, Mrs. Simon Guggenheim Fund

John Swope

LAURENCE OLIVIER AND VIVIEN LEIGH IN THE NEWEST STAGE PRODUCTION OF "ROMEO AND JULIET"

Toni Frissell

THERE WAS NO MORE SEA

BY MARY ELLEN CHASE

"And I saw a new heaven and a new earth; for the first heaven and the first earth were passed away; and there was no more sea."

I heard these words as a child sitting beside my father on a Sunday morning in the white church of a Maine coast village. The minister who read them seemed calm and undisturbed enough in the face of such lamentable prophecy. Quite evidently to him, as to the prophet who had seen this inglorious vision, the reaches of blue water, which I could see just beyond the clear windows of the church, were one with the sorrow and the crying, the death and the pain, which also were to be no more. They were all alike undesirable things for which Heaven would have no place.

I looked at my grandfather, old and unconcerned, in the pew opposite our own, at my grandmother beside him. She had sailed with him in his ship to the uttermost parts of the earth, to Shanghai and Martinique, to Madagascar and Bombay. To her, Marseilles and Cadiz were better known than were Boston and New York; the Indian Ocean than Penobscot Bay. Whatever would she and my grandfather talk about, I wondered, in this Heaven where there was to be no sea? With what would my restless grandfather occupy his endless days when there were no tides to watch, no long piers and quays to walk upon, no compasses to teach us, no incoming sails bursting upon a far horizon? There were other sea-captains in other pews, men with still, firm faces whose familiar stories had seemingly been born with me like my hands and my feet. Were they who had known the harbours of

[1933 – 1943] 175

the world going to be content with the great and high wall of the New Jerusalem, with her shining foundations of precious stones and her streets of pure gold? How would the fishermen along our coast, like Peter and James and John along the Sea of Galilee, make out in callings strange to them?

Since none of the quiet faces about me bore any of the disappointment and injustice which I felt, I concluded either that age had dulled their sorrow or that they, having years ago been informed of this monstrous intention on the part of God, had gradually become used to it. "You can get used to anything," my grandmother was always saying. Perhaps this favorite remark of hers was largely the fruit of her own gradual hardening through the years to the knowledge of what irreparable loss awaited her in the world beyond.

God had been partial to the inland people, I thought, those for example who lived in Vermont. Never having known the ocean, they would not care a fig for its banishment. They might conceivably even be relieved, for, as I had already learned from cousins living in the mountains, the sea gains lovers slowly. Vermonters could enjoy to the full the passing away of pain, sorrow, and crying without paying a price for their comfort, whereas all of our large family, our neighbours, and our friends, would have bought their freedom from sadness with the bitter price of another and far more overwhelming grief.

Throughout the long sermon I gazed from the window beyond the green fields which sloped to the rocky ledges at the edge of the incoming tide. If there was to be no more sea, I thought, then there would, of course, be no more shore. The brown ledges would go; the frail sea lavender that grew in the pebbly sand farther up the beach; the matted borders of brown kelp, which with all their possible treasures lay just at the edge of the tide; the sea-urchins and jellyfish at low tide, the snails and the crabs, even the clams who stupidly spurted jets of water on one's bare feet and legs and gave their welcome whereabouts dead away — these, too, would be no more.

In a Heaven of no shore and no quiet harbours there would be no long summer afternoons when one could lie on one's stomach with a book among the purple vetch and sea goldenrod of a quiet cove, the sandpipers scurrying before the tide, a heron asleep in a still inlet, and the drowsy sound of the creeping, slipping water. In a Heaven of no shore and no harbours there could be no wading in the shallows, no building of sand-castles or launching of boats, no sailing with older brothers or sisters in a dory borne by an open umbrella skillfully moved from side to side to catch the wind. With no shore there would be no wharves and no quays, no slapping of blue waves against green-encrusted piers, no entanglement of lines as we perched like a row of pigeons along the worn, silvery timbers above the tossing water.

Since there was to be no more sea, there could be no more harbour islands, to which one could wade over the sucking flats at low tide and which at high tide lay engirdled by shining water. Worst of all, there could be no incoming schooners, loaded far above the gunwales with fragrant logs for the sawmill by the brook. The schoolhouses in Heaven, I thought, would be dreary affairs, set in wide, dull fields. Their windows would open on no sweep of blue water and the children in them could never neglect their lessons to watch the incoming fish-boats. . . . All in all it was a desolating prospect. Summer visitors in Heaven would have no place at all to go; and coast children might just as well give up at once any struggle for virtue since their reward was to be so ironic and so incomplete!

Now that childhood anxieties have passed away, I have no further quarrel with the prophet on theological grounds, yet aesthetically I still feel his vision lacking. Perhaps, since higher criticism has questioned his identity, he may have been one of those ancients who for purely physical reasons, based on sad experience, distrusted and hated the sea. Perhaps, he was a Roman and, like most Romans, in constant terror of seasickness. Like Horace, who, it will be remembered, wondered at the foolishness of men in leaping across the seas when there was dry land which might be traversed to one's desired haven; or like the great Cato, who considered a journey by sea one of the three grave mistakes and misfortunes of his life; or even like Lucretius, who saw pleasure in watching from the land those in peril from the waves. They, like him, would have recognized both common sense and great comfort in that "sea of glass like unto crystal before the throne of God."

In the allegory of the prophet there may be this of truth: that we must forego much for the compensations of any future life. The blue waters of Passamaquoddy; the pounding of surf on the ledges of Marblehead; the long rollers of the Pacific on its yellow sands always suggestive of a sophistication and a finish unknown to the vigour of Atlantic waters; these conceivably may have no place in any reality which we may perchance retain. And if the dreamless sleep of Socrates be our fortune, we are clearly in no better situation. For in that endless night we can hope for no memories of the Dardanelles before the plains of windy Troy, the purple Aegean beyond the white temple of Sunium on its headland, Penobscot Bay with the snipes racing before the wind.

Considering all these things, I am beset by that terror native to all who gladly go down to the sea in ships or look upon it from any one of a thousand headlands from Monhegan to Tintagel. "Seize the day!" cried Horace, that hater of deep water. *Carpe diem.* Shall it be the cliffs of Monhegan or the moors of Nantucket, or an island in Casco Bay? Or shall I wire New York for a passage in any good ship and prayerfully await the hour when I shall slip down Ambrose Channel to the open, unharvested Atlantic?

MISS BRENDA FRAZIER, NEW YORK'S
DEBUTANTE OF THE SEASON.
SHE IS THE DAUGHTER OF MRS. FREDERICK WATRISS
AND THE LATE FRANK DUFF FRAZIER

Horst

1938:

WOMEN ARE
ALL SHOULDERS
JUTTING OVER
NARROW SKIRTS

SKETCHES BY
CHRISTIAN BERARD

BLACK MOIRE AND
BREITSCHWANTZ COAT
MAGGY ROUFF DESIGN

SCHIAPARELLI DESIGNS FOR EVENING

THE DIXIE CLIPPER TAKES OFF ACROSS THE ATLANTIC CARRYING TWENTY-TWO PASSENGERS

AIR HISTORY

Air history was made on June 28, 1939, when the *Dixie Clipper* made its first transatlantic passenger flight. Mrs. Whitney kept a log of the flight for *Vogue*, wrote in part, "We arrived at the Port Washington terminal at 2:10 on the great day and at three in the afternoon Captain R. O. D. Sullivan gave her the gun. The ground crew slipped the cable at the stern, and the Clipper surged forward through the waters of Port Washington Bay. The motors roar, the propellers bite their intolerant way into the air, and the ship comes suddenly alive. Speeding heavily into the wind, she hesitates a fraction of a second, then rises lightly and proudly to her step. Now only the tail on the water restrains her; faster, and then off she gets, and we are one with the sky and gone away. We were twenty-two passengers — sixteen men and six women — with twelve in the crew. Everything is unbelievably comfortable and stable — except for the distant drone of the motors, one might be at home. At seven that night we had a five-course dinner, twelve of us at a time at tables laid with blue-and-white china. The next morning we arrived at Horta in the Azores. Then on to Lisbon, where we saw a plaque unveiled, commemorating this flight."

Toni Frissell

MR. AND MRS. CORNELIUS VANDERBILT WHITNEY crossed on the "Dixie Clipper." Mr. Whitney is chief executive of Pan American Airways.

Toni Frissell

1938

JACQUELINE COCHRAN, the record-breaking flyer. In the past year she broke three United States speed records and a new world speed record, for women; and the non-stop record, New York to Miami. Six years ago she won her licence in a three-week vacation. She has never bailed out, though once her plane caught fire at 12,000 feet.

FAMILY FUGUE: VARIATIONS ON THE JOSEPH KENNEDYS

BY LESLEY BLANCH

During the tautness of the European crisis, the newspapers, the radio, the commentators constantly told of the visits to Neville Chamberlain by the American Ambassador, Joseph Kennedy. In his first season at the Court of St. James's, the American Ambassador found himself in the core of the storm. In the last few months, he and his family have swept upon London, which has lowered its defences and taken them in. The family gained splendour by numbers, but not by numbers alone. In the beginning, it seemed as though the press could harp on no other string but that of the nine children who ranged from six to twenty-two.

Joseph Kennedy's career, the young beauty of his wife, and their sudden entry into the world of high diplomacy — all went for nothing beside the apparently much more sensational fact that, for example, the parents kept a card-index of their children, the better to check upon measles, trips to Europe, and visits to dentists. To England, it was a most unheard-of transatlantic efficiency; big-business methods, which, applied to the personal aspects of life, seemed bewilderingly new, especially in diplomacy's more traditional rut.

The news-ferrets began their search: it was soon established that the family was united, even when divided; that they all doted upon music, and Toscanini in particular; that they had their own talkie-machine installed at the Embassy; that they attended Mass at the Oratory; that the Ambassador rode in the Row, upon which the Embassy windows look; that they golfed passionately; that Mrs. Kennedy often snatched a round at Roehampton, after visiting her daughters' convent-school nearby; that they rose early, and seldom kept late hours; that they had brought a nurse and governess with them from America; that they liked simple American food; that architects did over the gilded Louis-Quinze interior of 14 Prince's Gate; that they were thankful to snatch a few hours of week-end rest at their country house near Ascot; that the social exigencies of their life were all work and no play; that where twenty lunched with them, forty dined, and two hundred danced.

Still, the season waits for no man . . . and the Kennedys went to Court balls, presentation parties, receptions, dinners; an endless corridor of functions, speeches, bouquets, kid gloves, and press photographers stretched ahead. Even the nursery had its share, and Master Bobbie and Master Teddy made their public appearances, cut tapes, and made speeches.

But when the alarums of the press had died away, the impact of Joseph Kennedy's dynamic personality was felt. This wide-grinned, sandy-haired charmer was no mere figurehead. He brought with him new methods, new manners, new members of the Embassy staff, and his own secretary, Edward Moore, whose association with the Ambassador has been lifelong. He brought, too, a special press secretary, which is a rarity if not an innovation in diplomatic circles. There were several big parties for the press, and it was seen that Mr. Kennedy was not inaccessible.

From his first contact with London, the Ambassador agreed that he in no way impaired his ambassadorial prestige by expressing himself with such a national trenchancy, and, when it was seen that he would grasp every nettle firmly, the English began to take serious stock of Mr. Kennedy.

Rawlings

EUNICE, JACK, AND PATRICIA

They have found that his originality of thought and independence of action are tempered by his knowledge and command of the situation; that he is a man of vision and vitality, just, temperate; a man of ideals, of hard facts, witty and occasionally inflexible. No sentimentalist, he, by his own admission, rates his paternal responsibilities as highly as his ambassadorial. He tries to equip his children for their battle with the incalculable future, and believes that a sound knowledge of economics combined with an understanding of people is the best surety for their welfare. He astutely observed during all the ceremonial of a week-end at Windsor Castle as Their Majesties' guest, that the little Princesses were being brought up on similar lines of reality and simplicity.

These views were told to me, early one morning, at the American Embassy in Grosvenor Square, as the cold, skim-milk light of an English summer day fell on the austerity of the Ambassador's room. Pale blue walls, sombre mahogany, a great deal of space; dignity, but no magnificence. Tall windows looking out on the Square's gardens and the few old family mansions still left standing in a changing London. Near the door, a rather Dickensian hat-stand; on it, a silk hat and a white scarf — for Mr. Kennedy was resplendent in tails and white tie at ten a.m., as there was a levée at St. James's Palace that morning.

The ambassadorial residence, 14 Prince's Gate, was presented to the United States Government by Mr. J. P. Morgan. Its windows look over the Row; in back, there are green views over terrace and gardens. Behind its eighteenth-century walls, the furnishing and decorating of the Embassy are French in feeling.

The ballroom has Aubusson carpets, French panel paintings, and Eugénie furniture, blending to make an elegant, spirited *décor*. There are other reception-rooms — the Louis-Seize room, copied from Versailles, has gilded mouldings and marble plaques set in its creamy walls. Opening from it is Mrs. Kennedy's reception-room, known as the Pine Room because of its panelling, and rich with tapestry — an early French one hanging on the wall, and English tapestry for the furniture.

Mrs. Kennedy's beauty and serenity have astonished the more solid English matrons. She is a phenomenon: her lithe grace, her hipless elegance, her calm, unruffled gaiety, her dark Irish hair and absurdly débutante-blue eyes — and her nine children. For Rose Kennedy, time has marked time. Even now, with the harassing routine of an Ambassador's wife, besieged with official duties, Royal commands, charity requests, and all the unceasing round, she is practical. Sharing her husband's life and work, she is a hostess who is first an exacting housekeeper, who supervises her domain vigilantly.

The launching of two débutante daughters is usually considered more than enough for one woman's undertaking, but Mrs. Kennedy takes this easily. She visits her daughters' convent; watches the boys play cricket; finds time to confer with the hairdresser over Kathleen's new coiffure, with Molyneux on Rosemary's white tulle . . . to walk across the park to the Round Pond, applauding Teddy's masterly command of his toy yacht.

So this remarkable woman stands, and London finds her responsible for much of that rare harmony which is both the central theme and the *leitmotif* of the Kennedys. To continue the metaphor, they might be described as a fugal family, since the pattern of their lives is the interweaving of many melodies into one melodic whole; a set of contrapuntal variations upon a centrifugal theme which resolves itself into the common chord of unity.

Rawlings

MRS. KENNEDY WITH TEDDY, BOBBY, KATHLEEN, AND ROSEMARY

THEN AND NOW

THE FIVE SONS OF JOHN D. ROCKEFELLER, JR. On the day in 1921 when the photograph at right was taken the five "Rockefeller boys" were walking up Fifth Avenue. Still serious and dignified, the Rockefellers (below) now in 1940, run Radio City: John is in the real-estate department, Laurance in the operations branch, Nelson is president of Rockefeller Center and the Museum of Modern Art. Winthrop works for Socony-Vacuum Oil Company, and David is studying government in New York City Hall.

Acme

Paul Thompson

INP

Acme

JOAN WHITNEY and JOHN HAY WHITNEY. On the day in 1910 when the photograph at left was taken, the Whitney children were obviously spectators, in their beautifully conspicuous hats. Although the hats have changed, the Whitneys are still famous spectators. Joan Whitney is now Mrs. Charles S. Payson, has four children, and runs a racing stable. Mr. Whitney has become a top-flight sportsman and top angel of Hollywood and Broadway.

Paul Thompson

[1933 – 1943]   185

KIRSTEN FLAGSTAD
IN
"TRISTAN UND ISOLDE"

Horst

THEY PACK THEM IN

BY HOWARD TAUBMAN

If an opera manager had three wishes, he would wish first for productions that would balance in a perfect ensemble, with fine, but preferably not famous, artists. His second wish would be for audiences large enough to make such productions pay. Having used up two wishes, he would discover that the fine artists are almost always famous and that audiences do not pay for artists who are not. With his third wish, he would play safe. He would ask, like Caliban, for a handful of stars. For stars pack them in.

Of all the stars who have been the answer to an opera manager's dream, no one has packed them in more consistently since the days of Caruso and Farrar than Kirsten Flagstad. You have but to hear her and see her as Isolde to understand why. When she sings the "*Liebestod*" at the end of *Tristan und Isolde*, she is no longer an opera singer wearing grease-paint and watching the conductor's beat. She is an Irish princess and a woman. She raises her arms slowly with the gathering momentum of the music, and the great, flexible voice soars over the hundred instruments of the orchestra.

It is almost seventy-five years since the first Isolde sang the "Love-Death" before an audience in Munich. *Tristan und Isolde* is the greatest love story ever sung, and there have been other Isoldes, Lilli Lehmann, Milka Ternina, Lillian Nordica, and Olive Fremstad, who packed them in. But it is thirty years since any Isolde has come along who, like Madame Flagstad, had the power to turn the heart to water and, for the management, the equally important power to make your money burn holes in your pockets.

The figures reveal a modern box-office record. In her five seasons at the Metropolitan Opera, Madame Flagstad has sung Isolde about fifty times, an average of ten a season, in New York and on the road. The Metropolitan takes in about fourteen thousand dollars for a capacity house. Since *Tristan und Isolde* is a capacity draw with Madame Flagstad in the cast, the company has grossed in the neighbourhood of seven hundred thousand dollars on the work in the past five years. No other opera has been done as often by the Metropolitan, and it is no exaggeration to say that, if there had been no Flagstad for *Tristan und Isolde*, the Metropolitan might not have survived its hard times. Only Madame Flagstad sings Isolde these days at the Metropolitan.

Madame Flagstad, naturally, commands the highest fee that the Metropolitan can pay. When the great leveler, the Depression, had come and gone, Metropolitan salaries were stabilized, with a maximum of one thousand dollars a performance. If Madame Flagstad, who had been paid something like five hundred dollars a week her first year in New York, wished to, she could force the Metropolitan to raise her price. It never occurs to her. Madame Flagstad does not sing for the money alone. She can triple and quadruple her fee in recital and radio appearances. But should the Metropolitan ask her to forgo an outside date to do an extra Isolde, she would, I know, very happily consent.

There are no airs about Madame

LAURITZ MELCHIOR IN "SIEGFRIED" Horst

[1933 – 1943] 187

LOTTE LEHMANN
IN "DER ROSENKAVALIER"   Horst

EZIO PINZA
IN "BORIS GODUNOV"   Horst

Flagstad, but she does not undervalue herself. It makes her furious when people say carelessly that her acting has such simplicity because that's the kind of person she happens to be. She recalls the unremitting efforts to master the secrets of the singing-actress's art and the twenty years of knocking around in small theatres in Scandinavia — she even sang in a night-club. Then you recall that moment in *Die Walkure* when Wotan, having sung his farewell, puts his arm around her as Brünnehilde, and leads her to the foot of the tree where she is to slumber until her hero, Siegfried, arrives. Most Brünnehildes walk stolidly beside Wotan, like a *Hausfrau* going to market and wondering how much spinach will cost today. Madame Flagstad inclines her head gently, so that it rests on Wotan's shoulder. It is a natural gesture; yet it reminds you that Brünnehilde is young and brave and womanly. It is the kind of art that conceals art.

Flagstad is unique, but there are others who, in their specialties, exert a continuing fascination on the paying customers. There is that giant of a tenor, Lauritz Melchior, who is Madame Flagstad's partner in love in *Tristan und Isolde*. He is not only a great Tristan, but the finest Siegfried of our time. He packs them in because, in *Siegfried*, he can sing the forging song at the end of the first act with a splendour and an amplitude of voice that thrill his listeners. He packs them in because, after two hours of work in the opera, he can come back in the final duet with Brünnehilde to hit a brace of high C's as if he had been saving himself for that effort alone.

Mr. Melchior is six feet three and weighs two hundred and forty pounds. As Siegfried he wears a short bearskin, and he disports himself lightfootedly, as a boy should; I cannot get out of my head the impression that he looks like the young Pantagruel. He needs his heft and endurance to carry on through the title role of *Siegfried*, probably the longest in opera. Mr. Melchior himself, having a taste for precision and figures, once sat down and worked it out. He found that Siegfried had to be on the stage for two and a half hours. He found that the young hero had more words to sing than any other character in Wagner. He did not stop to count every word. He could not afford the time; that might have meant giving up a game of hearts with his card-playing cronies, Artur Bodanzky, principal Metropolitan conductor, and Friedrich Schorr, incomparable as Wotan and as Hans Sachs.

Mr. Melchior is another one-thousand-dollars-a-performance star. He earns about forty thousand dollars a year at the Metropolitan, and he draws in proportion to his pay. With Flagstad, he sings more often at the opera than any other star, because, like her, he is irreplaceable. When he is finished in New York, he trots off to London for another seige of Siegfrieds, Tristans, and Parsifals. He could find gainful employment fifty-two weeks a year, if he chose, for great *Heldentenors* are almost as rare as benevolent dictators.

It is not only the specialist in heroic roles who stirs the public and fills the opera house. The master of intimate moods, the artist who can universalize the problems and emotions common to all of us, belongs among the elect of the operatic stars. Lotte Lehmann is such an artist. Her *Marschallin* in *Der Rosenkavalier* is such a characterization. As the first act draws to a close, she has allowed her youthful, dear cavalier, Octavian, to go off to deliver the silver rose to young Sophie. The *Marschallin* looks at herself in the mirror. She sees the beginning of wrinkles and a greying strand of hair. She is still a handsome woman, but she fears approaching middle age and the loss of love. Richard Strauss has found the just and affecting melody and accent for the doubts and fears that well up in a woman's breast. But no artist vivifies them as does Lotte Lehmann. What she makes you feel is not this woman's vanity and sorrow, but the ache of all fleeting things.

With Lotte Lehmann in the company, the Metropolitan cannot cast another singer as the *Marschallin* without a serious drop in trade. It happened once last season, and there were patches of empty seats in the house. The public knows what is good, and will not pay for substitutes. The public senses, beneath the paint and the costume, the human being who rings true in her own right. Madame Lehmann is sensitive, perceptive, quick to understand, and far-ranging in her sympathies. An exile from her native Germany by her own choice, she could not endure the indignities heaped upon others because of the accident of birth. Like Arturo Toscanini, who admires her art and personality as much as he does any singer alive, her music has validity and meaning for her in her daily life. She does not merely feel these things, but *thinks* about them, and is even articulate about them. Charm and clarity appear in her book, *Midway in My Song*, which is autobiographical.

It may be more difficult to win the public favour with an intimate rather than a heroic art, but an even knottier task is to become a box-office draw if one is born a basso. In recent years, Chaliapin and Michael Bohnen were the only deep-voiced gentlemen who could translate their activities into a flow of cash for tickets. The Metropolitan is lucky to have one today in Ezio Pinza. The handful of extensive basso roles has been dusted off for him, and recently he assumed the role of Boris Godunov, a part that Chaliapin made so vitally and dramatically his own that only a courageous artist would dare follow in his footsteps.

Mr. Pinza is courageous, and to spare. After all, he was a professional bicycle rider before he turned singer, and you have to possess a steady hand and a steely nerve for that hazardous sport. Being a basso, Mr. Pinza has never been tempted to turn prima donna, as so many tenors do. The basso who wants to work regularly has to take the bad with the good, the lean roles with the fat. Mr. Pinza likes to work regularly, for one thing; for another, he is a good soldier.

The opera management, however, knows when it has a good artist and a public attraction in its midst. Mr. Pinza has received more opportunities than most bassos. He has sung roles like Don Giovanni and Escamillo, which are written for baritones. There is no special favouritism here. Mr. Pinza happens to have a voice of range and beauty, and he can sing the baritone roles as well as, perhaps better than, most baritones. Here is no pot-bellied, waddling Don Giovanni or toreador; his silhouette is straight and tall, and his leg is good. You cannot blame Carmen or the women in the Mozart opera for being attracted to him. Then you see him as Boris, the Czar of all the Russias. He holds the sceptre with a regal ease, his step and his stance suggest the power, dignity, and passion of the man. Such is the versatility of a basso who draws at the opera, and Pinza is the highest paid low voice in the Metropolitan today.

There are others who make the till sing a merry tune. Grace Moore is one of the Metropolitan singers who receive one thousand dollars a performance, and her fee brings the company ample dividends. As Charpentier's Louise, a working girl of Paris who wishes to find love for herself, she has packed them in this season. Five performances of the opera in New York drew close to seventy thousand dollars, whereas in years gone by even Lucrezia Bori could not turn this opera into a money-maker. What is more, Miss Moore made it a seven-dollar show, the highest-priced tickets selling faster than the others, which is contrary to all precedent.

She worked hard to make Louise a success. She went to Paris and studied with Charpentier, the composer. She sang the part at the Paris Opera. She returned to New York, turning down all concert engagements to devote weeks to further preparation for *Louise*. She could have earned her opera salary three or four times over by singing three or four songs on the radio, but money was a second consideration where there was a job to be done, and done well.

Lawrence Tibbett as Baron Scarpia, Lily Pons as Lucia di Lammermoor, John Charles Thomas as Figaro, the barber of Seville — they are also potent box-office attractions. As they draw, so do they receive. They, too, are at the top in artistic prestige and in earning power among the stars of the lyric stage. They, too, sacrifice time and higher fees to prepare their roles and to sing at the Metropolitan. For opera offers gratifications that the concert stage and radio cannot parallel or equal. To wear the sock and buskin, to live another life on the stage for an hour and to sing at the same time with the tongue of sinners and angels — these are compelling factors in an opera singer's career. If the fee is good and the public and management shout for joy, what matter the sacrifice?

There was, for instance, a sacrifice of a tenor at the Metropolitan, a box-office draw of some magnitude in his own right. He was singing Rodolfo to a famous prima donna's Mimi in *La Bohème* some time ago. He thought he detected signs of a cold in the leading lady's head when she appeared on the stage in the first act. He himself came down with a cold the next day, and he blamed it all on her.

"I see she has a cold," he explained to his friends as he rested in his bed of pain. "But we are in love — in the opera. I get seven hundred dollars a performance. She has a cold but for seven hundred dollars, I cannot help it. I moost keess her!"

GRACE MOORE
IN "L'AMORE DEI TRE RE"

Rawlings

[1933 – 1943] 189

PICASSO

FOUR EARLY SKETCHES OF A TRIP TO PARIS (1902) AND A RECENT OIL PAINTING (1937)

ON THE BARCELONA-PARIS TRAIN; PICASSO WITH BERET, SEBASTIA JUNYER WITH MOUSTACHE

CROSSING THE BORDER: "AT ONE O'CLOCK THEY ARRIVE AND THEY SAY, 'PRIME!'"

"AT NINE IN THE MORNING THEY FINALLY ARRIVE IN PARIS"
(THE UPPER LINE IS IN CATALAN, THE LOWER IN SPANISH)

"DURAND-RUEL ASKS HIM TO COME IN, THEN GIVES HIM MUCH DOUGH"

Drawings owned by the Junyer family

"SEATED WOMAN." ONE OF THE EXHIBITS IN THE GREAT RETROSPECTIVE PICASSO SHOW AT THE MUSEUM OF MODERN ART, NEW YORK

THE HOUSE OF VANDERBILT

BY FRANK CROWNINSHIELD

The doom of the old Vanderbilt mansion has been sealed.

What in 1881 was the habitat of the richest man in the world and for twenty-five years has remained the last stronghold of ceremonial society in America will soon — like the fated House of Usher, or the supposedly imperishable monument of Ozymandias — vanish into impalpable air.

For those of us who remember the agreeable gamut of the eighties, it is certain that — when the house has become a mass of mortar and mortuary stone — sounds, sights, and memories of a most haunting order will issue from its dust.

If the stars are propitious and the witches benign, we may hear, emerging from the ruins, an old mazurka in 3-4 time; an air from Offenbach; a waltz by Waldteufel; or the sighing, sorrowing voice of Christine Nilsson. It would be pleasant, too, to catch the mingled scents of orris and Jacqueminot roses and truly ancient Madeiras.

But pleasantest of all — in such a shadowy parade — to review those lovely, vanished ladies who, in their great *calèches*, circled the ramble in Central Park; trooped on a Sunday from St. George's into Stuyvesant Square; danced at Delmonico's, in their intriguing bustles and ruffled trains; stood before their cheval-glasses, practising the Grecian bend; or, in their parures of diamonds, rubies, and emeralds, graced the musty loges at the Academy of Music.

And if those ladies should chance to be escorted by masculine shades — as they most certainly will — a goodly number of them will bear the name of Vanderbilt, for everywhere, in those departed days, the Vanderbilts — the men, in particular — in a very special way imparted to the fabric of their time much of its richness, gaiety, and design.

With the razing of the mansion at Fifty-first Street the ancient rivalry between the Vanderbilts and the Astors, whether in railroads or the arena of society, takes on a new turn. For it is Lord Astor of Cliveden, the great-great-grandson of the original, fur-trading John Jacob, who now buys the old house from Brigadier-General Cornelius Vanderbilt, who was the grandson of William H. Vanderbilt, who built the mansion, and the great-grandson of the Commodore, the prodigious figure who, on Staten Island, with a hollow scow or two and a pair of strong hands, founded the Vanderbilt dominion.

When, in 1881, William H. Vanderbilt first erected the house, it was twice its present size and occupied the entire block from Fifty-first to Fifty-second Street. In 1926, however, their half of the house was sold to make way for what is now the De Pinna building.

On the construction and decoration, old Mr. Vanderbilt spent a little over two million dollars. On his collection of paintings he expended another million and a half. In the task of decorating its interiors, a mission which, viewed aesthetically, proved a major disaster, for a year and a half he employed six hundred men, while sixty sculptors were imported from Europe and, for the same period, these "artisans" were kept at their really appalling manual tasks.

The house, at the time of its début, was a terrifying conglomeration of cornices, attics, dwarf pilasters, entablatures, and arched openings. With respect to its furniture and decorations, it was also a masterpiece of poor taste. It was really William H. Vanderbilt himself who was primarily at fault, for he had merely, in the manner of rich and busy men, given his decorators *carte blanche* to roam the world and create, at their own sweet will, what to them might seem the most beautiful habitation in New York.

But, wherever the fault, the result was such that nearly sixty years later, when the Selznick cinema forces — at work on *Gone with the Wind* — were looking over a mass of photographs to find a sufficiently spirit-blighting interior in which Clark Gable as Rhett Butler could enjoy his seances of drinking, they decided that the mansion was exactly the jewel they were after.

Nyholm

THE FIFTH AVENUE MANSION, LAST OF SEVEN VANDERBILT HOUSES THAT ONCE DOTTED THE AVENUE

MRS. CORNELIUS VANDERBILT PHOTOGRAPHED BY CECIL BEATON AGAINST A CLASSIC LOUIS XVI BACKGROUND IN HER FIFTH AVENUE HOUSE

[1933–1943] 193

MRS. VANDERBILT GIVES ONE OF HER CEREMONIAL DINNERS

The photograph shows a typical formal dinner at the Vanderbilt house. From the centre of one side, Mrs. Vanderbilt (wearing one of her famous bandeaux) presides over the long, glittering table. Forty-one of the forty-six guests at this dinner are listed below:

NEAR SIDE OF THE TABLE, LEFT TO RIGHT:

MRS. GRAFTON H. PYNE
MR. J. NORMAN DE R. WHITEHOUSE
MISS JULIA A. BERWIND
DR. HAMILTON RICE
MRS. TRUXTUN BEALE
THE HON. ALFRED ANSON
MRS. J. BORDEN HARRIMAN
MR. FRANK LYON POLK
MRS. JAMES W. GERARD
THE HON. OGDEN H. HAMMOND
MRS. GODFREY HAGGARD
BARON HUBERT LEJEUNE
MRS. PARMELY W. HERRICK
MR. WILLIAMS BURDEN
MRS. FREDERICK FRELINGHUYSEN
MR. LOUIS BRUGUIERE
MRS. JOSEPH CLARK BALDWIN
MR. WILLIAM M. CHADBOURNE
MRS. J. NORMAN DE R. WHITEHOUSE
MR. FREDERICK FRELINGHUYSEN

FAR SIDE OF THE TABLE LEFT TO RIGHT:

MISS VALERIE MOORE
LIEUT. JOHN G. MUNROE
MR. KENNETH W. PENDAR
MRS. ALEXANDER BIDDLE
MR. EDGAR W. LEONARD
MRS. FRANCIS C. BISHOP
THE HON. JOSEPH CLARK BALDWIN
MRS. OGDEN H. HAMMOND
MR. GODFREY HAGGARD, THE BRITISH CONSUL GENERAL
MR. ELMENDORF L. CARR,
WHO LECTURED AFTER DINNER
ON SOUTH AMERICAN AFFAIRS.
MRS. VANDERBILT
THE HON. JAMES W. GERARD
MRS. FRANK LYON POLK
MR. WILLIAM GOADBY LOEW
MRS. ROBERT L. BACON
MR. J. HENRY ALEXANDRE
MRS. EDGAR W. LEONARD
MR. A. CHARLES SCHWARTZ
MRS. J. HENRY ALEXANDRE
MR. JAMES BECK
MRS. W. THORN KISSEL

Carswell

THANKS TO CASEY JONES

BY JOHN MASON BROWN

Some people need to be lured into travel by the threat or promise of Nautch-girls, Hopi snake-dancers, the Taj Mahal, or at least the music of faraway names. I don't. Although I like going places as much as the next member of the Joad family, I also like the mere act of getting there. More particularly I like trains — American trains, regardless of where they are going, so long as they are moving.

In fact, I like them so much that were Mr. Rockefeller to remember me in his will (which, alas, seems unlikely), I would be tempted to exchange my bed in my apartment for a berth, have it draped with heavy green curtains, equip it with a machine to rock me gently while I slept, and ensure my slumber by installing a sound track to release such blessed night-sounds on a train as distant whistles, expiring radiators, clanging road signals, passing freight-cars, and the hum of ties. I would go even further. I would have cinders blown in my face from time to time, just to remind me of the good old days. And at eight o'clock each morning, I would be awakened by having a gnarled black hand shake me firmly by the patella, and by hearing a cheerful voice sing out, "Eight o'clock, Lower Six — only thirty minutes to Wichita."

To my surprise I find myself somewhat lonely in my enthusiasm for railroads. The reason is that most people appear to consider trains as no more than necessary evils. Trains, they argue, are only means of getting someplace. To feel this way about them is, of course, to miss all of their pleasure and at least half of their point. For the real charm of a train is self-contained and has very little to do with its destination.

Far be it from me to deny that trains serve a purpose. Their chief justification no doubt remains as carriers to and from a spot to which people have either wanted or been compelled to go. Granting this—granting also that trains can occasionally win even more of our gratitude by getting us out of a town than by getting us into it — the real joy to be had from them begins where their usefulness ends.

The only happy travellers by rail are those who, knowing they have journeys to make, surrender themselves completely to such comforts as a railroad alone can provide. All of them depend upon one thing — a joyous resignation to the fact that when a time-table says a trip is to last eight, twenty, or forty-eight hours, no amount of looking at watches or squirming in chairs will cut these hours down. The unhappy travellers are the restless ones; the ones who are always trying to go faster than the engineer; the ones who are fond of playing conductor and shake their heads like mourners if they are ten minutes late pulling into Wilmington. They give themselves away in countless fashions, these malcontents who cannot adjust themselves to trains.

They come aboard with enough chewing-gum tucked away in their pockets or bags to supply a stewardess on a transcontinental airliner. In their hands are four local newspapers which they never read beyond the front pages. Their arms bulge with magazines they would never think of looking at at home. They dispose of these quickly, often presenting them to neighbours as a bait for casual conversations about Roosevelt, Hitler, and the weather.

Soon they develop train thirst and keep rushing to the back of the car to consume sufficient water to provision a camel. Or they prowl up and down the aisle looking for friends they never expect to find. Or they insist, as they wander out to have countless smokes, upon accosting the porter with "Say, George, do you think we'll make it up?"

The trouble with these victims of Pullman St. Vitus is that plainly they regard trains as their enemies rather than their friends. Although they ride the Iron Horse, they are thrown by it. They are not in condition for travel because they are not exhausted. They come aboard too healthy for their comfort or anyone else's.

That train travel has its hazards even the staunchest defender of the rails acknowledges. Waiting in a swaying line

KATHARINE HEPBURN, ENCHANTINGLY PORTRAYED HERE BY CECIL BEATON, IS STARRED IN THE THEATRE GUILD'S HIT, "THE PHILADELPHIA STORY," A PLAY BY PHILIP BARRY

[1933–1943] 197

to get into a diner is never fun. Trying to shave when ten other people glower at you for having had the same idea and blow cigarette smoke in your face before you have had your breakfast is likewise a very minor sport. Listening to other people's kidlets as they caterwaul, or making those summer hegiras (*en masse* and decidedly *en famille*) with children of your own when they are young enough to require all the paraphernalia necessitated by the formula, both before and after taking, must be counted as tribulations.

Dressing and undressing in a berth, or even in a single room (especially if you have crawled on the train in evening clothes and have to get out tomorrow's suit and put away your dinner-jacket and repack your bag while thrashing about like an elephant in a shoe-box), can also be somewhat trying. At least it can be until you have evolved a personal routine of slipping into pyjamas, a method of your own for triumphing over space. Soon thereafter the ritual becomes not only second nature, but almost agreeable. Necessity once again goes into a maternity ward to be delivered of invention.

These drawbacks, though challenging, are minor compared to the advantages of a train. The little trips — the ones lasting less than an hour and a half — do not count. They are sissy stuff. Although they can be agreeable, they fall into the category of commuting.

The wise traveller, the self-indulgent and the happy one, is he who never looks at his time-table and hides his watch. Time is the engineer's business, not his. He rejoices in the fact that he is as free from it as he is from the telephone. Unless bad news has summoned him, or worries lie ahead, a train can become for him a place of refuge; a restful pause in life; a sanctuary on wheels which devours space even as it annihilates time.

As one of the drama's Typhoid Marys, I confess travel plays a large part in my life. Year after year, with ever-increasing pride in this great quilt of a country sewed together by steel rails, I have swung down, up, and around the United States on trains of all kinds. Streamlined wonders, expresses, locals, transcontinentals, chromium or plush, air-conditioned or dust-blown, electrified or steam, Rockets or Toonerville Trolleys — I have ridden on more of them than have the delegates to most porters' conventions.

I have fallen onto them at two in the morning at flag-stops during a blizzard, and fallen off of them in strange cities at dawn. During lecture tours, I have slept on them for twenty-five consecutive nights. At least as someone who long ago had to become a contented chain-sleeper, dividing what ought to have been the night between Pullmans and hotels, I have relied on them for rest, and found it.

And I have never lost my fondness for them. I like them not only because of the places to which they have taken me; I like them for themselves. I like them for their comfort, their serenity, their warmth (which is usually adjustable when it becomes too warm). I like them for their efficiency, their impersonality, the darkness and the quiet which one of their rooms can maintain in the broad light of noon, and the illusion they give me of being miraculously becalmed in the midst of motion. I like them because a good train, well used, is among the best of friends. Certainly it is the most excellent restcure a healthy landlubber can find, if he happens to be tired and yet must keep on moving.

There is also the appetite which only a full day's inactivity on a train can whip up. It is the kind of appetite lumberjacks, campers, draftees, and clubwomen at a tea understand. Only it is acquired without effort. It is so lusty an appetite that not only do the steaks, the Idaho baked potatoes, and the bacon and eggs have a miraculous crisp taste, but even the canned vegetables and the overcooked coffee seem viewable, if not palatable.

For the overworked person as much in search of rest as Pirandello's six characters were of an author, the ideal business trip is the solitary one. Particularly when you are talking your way around the country, you want quiet. You want it as surely as the clown dreams of playing Hamlet. You get so sick of the sound of your own voice that you can hardly bear to release it.

There are far better places than a train for talk, but few places are a train's equal for reading. Not magazines or newspapers alone. They are merely canapés to the heavy meal which can follow. The classics you have always meant to read, the new books you have failed to get around to, the fat books which usually are put aside for summer, the volume you could not resist while browsing in the station bookstore, the old books you are anxious to reread to see how you and they have changed — these are the perfect companions on a journey.

Even the six stout volumes of the Sandburg *Lincoln*, that absorbing keystone in the Hernia Library, become manageable when a Redcap is present to tote them for you. Undisturbed, at ease, horizontal in a berth, sitting upright in an observation car, or sharing a day-coach seat with a stranger, you can find few libraries as concentrating as a train. Only a deck-chair, on the first two days out, before you have met any of the other passengers, is its superior. For full comfort, however, for the kind of comfort I have indulged in only twice in moments of complete exhaustion, give me a drawing-room, made down for the night and yet occupied for a full day, with sleep permissible at will, with books littering the bed, and with meals brought in as by a summons from Old King Cole.

Who knows, too, but that when you are travelling by rail these days, you may be so fortunate as to ride on a train that goes through Washington. So long as it does not stop there; so long as it comes from this city to which you never hear of trains going, but from which all of them seem nowadays to leave, you will be a made man for at least a week. Whether you have done no more than take a peek at the scaffolding on the Jefferson Memorial, you will be indistinguishable from Walter Lippmann by the time you get home. For the surest way to become an authority at present is just to have come from Washington.

Horst

THREE LADIES OF THE SCREEN

LORETTA YOUNG (top left), utterly lovely, follows one screen success with another — her next film: *Lady from Cheyenne*. She poses in a huge Lilly Daché picture hat of yellow spun glass.

MYRNA LOY (above), after abandoning her Oriental roles, has become the "dream wife" of the movies, playing opposite William Powell in the "Thin Man" series. The ostrich-feather hat is an exact twin of one with which she raised $30,000 worth of War Bonds at a recent benefit.

BETTE DAVIS (left), is now interpreting Somerset Maugham's *The Letter* as memorably as she did his *Of Human Bondage*. Her silk taffeta dress by Nettie Rosenstein.

Photo: Emelie Dar

THE CHARMED LIFE

BY KATHERINE ANNE PORTER

In 1920 he was nearly eighty years old, and he had lived in Mexico for about forty years. Every day of those years he had devoted exclusively to his one interest in life: discovering and digging up buried Indian cities all over the country. He had come there, an American, a stranger, with this one idea. I had heard of him as a fabulous, ancient eccentric completely wrapped up in his theory of the origins of the Mexican Indian. "He will talk your arm off," I was told.

His shop was on the top floor of a ramshackle old building on a side street in Mexico City, reached by an outside flight of steps, and it had the weathered, open look of a shed rather than a room. The rain came in, and the dust, and the sunlight. A few battered showcases and long rough tables were piled up carelessly with "artifacts," as the Old Man was careful to call them. There were skulls and whole skeletons, bushels of jade beads and obsidian knives and bronze bells and black clay whistles in the shape of birds.

I was immensely attracted by the air of authenticity, hard to define, but easy to breathe. He was tough and lean, and his face was burned to a good wrinkled leather. He greeted me with an air of imperfect recollection as if he must have known me somewhere. We struck up an easy acquaintance at once, and he talked with the fluency of true conviction.

Sure enough, within a quarter of an hour I had his whole theory of the origin of the ancient Mexicans. It was not new or original; it was one of the early theories since rejected by later scientists, but plainly the Old Man believed he had discovered it. It was a religion with him, a poetic, mystical, romantic concept. About the lost continent, and how the original Mexican tribes all came from China or Mongolia in little skiffs, dodging between hundreds of islands now sunk in the sea. He loved believing it and would listen to nothing that threatened to shake his faith.

At once he invited me to go with him on a Sunday to dig in his latest buried city, outside the capital. He explained his system to me. He had unearthed nearly a half-hundred ancient cities in all parts of Mexico. One by one, in his vague phrase, he "turned them over to the government." The government thanked him kindly and sent in a staff of expert scientists to take over, and the Old Man moved on, looking for something new.

Finally, by way of reward, they had given him this small and not very important city for his own, to settle down with. He sold in his shop the objects he found in the city, and with the profits he supported the digging operations on Sunday.

He showed me photographs of himself in the early days, always surrounded by Indian guides and pack-mules against landscapes of cactus or jungle, a fine figure of a man with virile black whiskers and a level, fanatic eye. There were rifles strapped to the bales on the pack-mules, and the guards bristled with firearms. "I never carried a gun," he told me. "I never needed to. I trusted my guides, and they trusted me."

I enjoyed the company of the Old Man, his impassioned singleness of purpose, his fervid opinions on his one topic of conversation, and the curiously appealing unhumanness of his existence. He was the only person I ever saw who really seemed as independent and carefree as a bird on a bough.

He ate carelessly at odd hours, fried beans and tortillas from a basket left for him by the wife of his head digger, or he would broil a scrawny chicken on a stick, offer me half, and walk about directing his men, waving the other half. He had an outdoors sort of cleanliness and freshness; his clothes were clean, but very old and mended. Who washed and mended them I never knew. My own life was full of foolish and unnecessary complications, and I envied him his wholeness. I enjoyed my own sentimental notion of him as a dear, harmless, sweet old man of an appealing sociability, riding his hobby-horse in triumph to the grave, houseless but at home, completely free of family ties and not missing them, a happy, devoted man who had known his own mind, had got what he wanted in life, and was satisfied with it. Besides, he was in perfect health and never bored.

[1933 – 1943]

SALVADOR DALI designed these jewels in collaboration with the Duc di Verdura. Mostly paintings on gold or ivory seen in transparency through a clear semiprecious stone, the tiny masterpieces are set against a background specially painted by Dali for *Vogue*.

Crowds of visitors came and bought things, and he dropped the money in a cigar-box behind a showcase. He invited almost everybody to come out and watch him dig on Sundays, and a great many came, week after week, always a new set. He received a good many letters, most of them with foreign postmarks, and after a few rapid glances he dropped them into the drawer of a long table. "I know a lot of people," he said, shuffling among the heap one day. "I ought to answer these. Big bugs, too, some of them."

One day, among a pile of slant-eyed clay faces, I found a dusty, dog-eared photograph of a young girl, which appeared to have been taken about fifty years before. She was elegant, fashionable, and so astonishingly beautiful I thought such perfection could belong only to a world-famous beauty. The Old Man noticed it in my hand. "My wife," he said in his impersonal, brisk tone. "Just before we were married. She was about eighteen then."

"She is unbelievably beautiful," I said.

"She was the most beautiful woman I ever saw," he said, matter-of-factly. "She is beautiful still." He dropped the photograph in the drawer with the letters and came back talking about something else.

After that, at odd moments, while he was polishing jade beads or brushing the dust off a clay bird, he dropped little phrases about his wife and children. "She was remarkable," he said. "She had five boys in eight years. She was just too proud to have anything but boys, I used to tell her."

Again, later: "She was a perfect wife, perfect. But she wouldn't come to Mexico with me. She said it was no place to bring up children."

One day, counting his money and laying it out in small heaps, one for each workman, he remarked absently, "She's well off, you know — she has means." He poured the heaps into a small sack and left the rest in the cigar-box. "I never wanted more money than I needed from one week to the next," he said. "I don't fool with banks. People say I'll be knocked in the head and robbed some night, but I haven't been, and I won't."

One day we were talking about a plot to overthrow the government which had just been frustrated with a good deal of uproar. "I knew about that months ago," said the Old Man. "One of my politician friends wrote me . . ." He motioned towards the table drawer containing the letters. "You're interested in those things," he said. "Would you like to read some of those letters? They aren't private."

Would I? I spent a long summer afternoon reading the Old Man's letters from his international big bugs, and I learned then and there that hair *can* rise and blood *can* run cold. There was enough political dynamite in those casually written letters to have blown sky-high any number of important diplomatic and financial negotiations then pending between several powerful governments. The writers were of all sorts, from the high-minded and religious to the hearty, horse-trading type to the worldly, the shrewd, the professional adventurer, down to the natural moral imbecile, but they were all written in simple language with almost boyish candour and an indiscretion so complete it seemed a kind of madness.

I asked him if he had ever shown them to any one else. "Why, no," he said, surprised at my excitement.

I tried to tell him that if these letters fell into certain hands, his life would be in danger. "Nonsense," he said vigorously. "Everybody knows what I think of that stuff. I've seen 'em come and go, making history. Bah!"

"Burn these letters," I told him. "Get rid of them. Don't even be caught dead with them."

"I need them," he said. "There's a lot about ancient Mexican culture in them you didn't notice." I gave up. Perhaps the brink of destruction was his natural habitat.

A few days later I went up the dusty stairs and, there, in a broad square of sunlight, the Old Man was sitting in a cowhide chair with a towel around his neck, and a woman was trimming his moustache with a pair of nail scissors. She was as tall as he, attenuated, with white hair, and the beauty of an aged goddess. There was an extraordinary pinched, starved kind of sweetness in her face, and she had perfect simplicity of manner. She removed the towel, and the Old Man leaped up as if she had loosed a spring. Their son, a man in middle age, a masculine reincarnation of his mother, came in from the next room, and we talked a little, and the wife asked me with gentle pride if I did not find the shop improved.

It was indeed in order, clean, bare, with the show-windows and cases set out properly, and tall vases of flowers set about. They were all as polite and agreeable to one another as if they were well-disposed strangers, but I thought the Old Man looked a little hunched and wary, and his wife and son gazed at him almost constantly as if they were absorbed in some fixed thought. They were all very beautiful people, and I liked them, but they filled the room and were not thinking at all about what they were saying, and I went away very soon.

The Old Man told me later they had stayed only a few days; they dropped in every four or five years to see how he was getting on. He never mentioned them again.

Afterwards when I remembered him it was always most clearly in that moment when the tall woman and her tall son searched the face of their mysterious Wild Man with baffled, resigned eyes, trying still to understand him years after words wouldn't work any more, years after everything had been said and done, years after love had worn itself thin with anxieties, without in the least explaining what he was, why he had done what he did. But they had forgiven him, that was clear, and they loved him.

I understood then why the Old Man never carried a gun, never locked up his money, sat on political dynamite and human volcanoes, and never bothered to answer his slanderers. He bore a charmed life. Nothing would ever happen to him.

MRS. FRANKLIN D. ROOSEVELT. No American President's wife has ever been more familiar at home and abroad, more bustlingly busy, or more widely beloved than she — a newspaper columnist, a radio commentator, and, all her life, a tireless and generous philanthropist. Mrs. Roosevelt has set her own precedents of personal benevolence, and broadened the position of a President's wife to fit the measure of her own spirit. She is photographed here by Steichen in her dress for the third inaugural ball.

[1933 – 1943] 203

ON STAGE
1939-1941

Tallulah Bankhead (right) has the part of her career in *The Little Foxes*, Lillian Hellman's distinguished exhibition of playwriting about a family of Southern industrialists, mean with a money hunger. Quick, tense-voiced, beautiful, Miss Bankhead plays Regina Giddens magnificently, with a sweeping wickedness of ambition.

The three people shown below are the backbone of the galloping new musical comedy, *Keep Off the Grass,* set in Central Park, played in the pungent vernacular of New York. The parody, "Rhett, Scarlett, and Ashley," is a rich mixture of Ilka Chase's calmly acid satire, Jimmy Durante's earnest toughness, Ray Bolger's gangling goofiness.

Ethel Merman, the heart of *Du Barry Was a Lady*, is seen (opposite) with Harold Cromer in a version of Van Dyck's famous portrait of the Marchesa Grimaldi, with page. Also on the facing page are Howard Lindsay and Dorothy Stickney, the father and mother of *Life with Father*, photographed with members of their celebrated family, in the stage success by Russel Crouse and Howard Lindsay based on the book by Clarence Day; and a scene from *Lady in the Dark*. Of all the high points of extravaganza, this circus scene is the season's most beautiful. It is part of the year's most complicated tour de force, the peak of Moss Hart's psychoanalytical drama, with its musical-comedy dreams. At the far left is its amazing star, Gertrude Lawrence, in purple and brilliants. Victor Mature is in tights, and Danny Kaye is posed against a horse.

TALLULAH BANKHEAD

Horst

THE HAPPY TRIO OF "KEEP OFF THE GRASS"

Horst

ETHEL MERMAN,
PRINCIPLE OF
"DU BARRY WAS A LADY"

Anton Bruehl

THE STAGE
FAMILY OF
"LIFE WITH FATHER"

Karger Pix

THE FAMOUS CIRCUS
SCENE IN
"LADY IN THE DARK"

Karger Pix

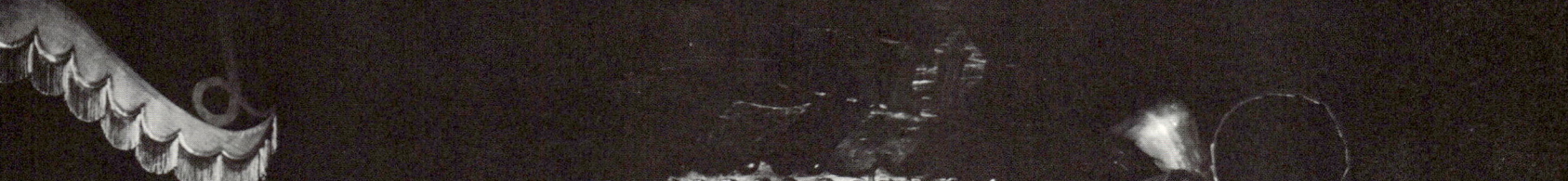

A SONG HISTORY OF IRVING BERLIN

BY ALLENE TALMEY

Toni Frissell

IRVING BERLIN WATCHES A REHEARSAL OF HIS GREAT SOLDIER SHOW, "THIS IS THE ARMY"

Irving Berlin has an extraordinary effect on people. Even those who don't know the man are likely to be memory-swept by the sentimental dynamite of any one of his seven hundred songs. There is no counting the number of people whom he has accompanied in and out of love — from "Always" to "Say It Isn't So." He has made the world's feet twitch to time more often than any other songwriter.

Irving Berlin, the man, is a cosy mass of contradictions. He is modest but never humble, gentle, but tough, agreeable but adamant.

The pattern of Berlin's words and music is usually recognizable, his lyrics inevitably peppered with colloquialisms. He remembers not only that love is often unrequited, but that no one's heart breaks a little. Although Berlin tunes may become dated romantically, they almost never are, musically. Jerome Kern, when he was asked to describe an American citizen, said, "The American is best epitomized in Irving Berlin's music — both have humour, originality, sentiment, pace, and popularity."

Everyone knows that Irving Berlin was born on New York's lower East Side, that he started out as a singing waiter in Nigger Mike's, down in Chinatown. His first song sold for thirty-five cents, his second for twenty-five dollars. "Alexander's Ragtime Band," written four years later in 1911, the first of his great hits, made rag respectable. It translated the hoarse musical croakings played in back rooms of honky-tonks into real rhythm, instead of mere dislocations of sound.

"Alexander's Ragtime Band" was only the beginning. In 1914, shrewd showman Charles Dillingham produced Berlin's *Watch Your Step*, starring the incomparable Castles, dancing with fastidious abandon. The show, a crinkling tissue of gaiety, was a whistling success. For the first time, Irving Berlin provided all the music for a musical comedy and was now an established Broadway figure. His rivals read him like a barometer. When he seemed particularly wan and distressed, they knew that he had written another song hit. In 1916, Berlin wrote *Stop, Look, and Listen*, a kind of syncopated circus to star Gaby Deslys, a long-legged, blonde French music-hall sensation, said to have cost young King Manuel of Portugal his crown. King Alfonso of Spain, it was rumoured, had also shown an interest. Gaby was obviously box-office.

Then came the *Ziegfeld Follies of 1919*. That was the year when William A. Brady, the producer, lashed out: "Theatre managers no longer fear the theatre critics; it's the ticket speculators who make or break our play." In this fabulous thirteenth edition of the Follies, there were Marilyn Miller, smiling with exhausting persistency; Eddie Cantor, who, according to one critic, was "one prolonged scream"; poker-faced, honey-voiced John Steele; a glazed papier-mâché camel; and beautiful, scantily dressed girls posing in Ben Ali Haggin tableaux. It was an aphrodisiac Follies, topped by a persistent Berlin tune called "A Pretty Girl Is Like a Melody."

That was a time of theatrical opulence. At its height, in 1921, Sam Harris and Irving Berlin opened their Music Box Theatre, with the first *Music Box Revue*. This was the year that Lynn Fontanne made her biggest hit in a comedy of bromides called *Dulcy*; the year that Eugene O'Neill's plays were new. It was a year when Irving Berlin seemed to shrink, to grow more nervous and wispish than ever. The *Music Box Revue* opened to an audience that, though callous to extravagance, caught its breath at the most conceitful theatre, the most spangled, sparkling revue. In it appeared a young newcomer to Broadway, with a sweet operatic soprano voice. Her name was Grace Moore, and she sang a simple little song called "What'll I Do?" She and the song were immediate first-night hits.

There was one strange oversight in the reviews of this show. None of the critics had much to say about his song, "Everybody Step." And yet, according to musicians, this is technically Berlin's most brilliant tune. John Alden Carpenter, the composer, tells of sitting on an international jury asked to select the masterpieces of music. That jury included in its final list Bach's "B Minor Mass," Beethoven's "Seventh Symphony," Chopin's "Polonaise," Stravinsky's *Petrouchka*, Gilbert and Sullivan's *Pinafore*, and Irving Berlin's "Everybody Step."

Now, Berlin's private life and his song-writing merged. He was deeply in love with Ellin Mackay, daughter of the late Clarence Mackay. Growing paler and more dyspeptic, Berlin turned out three of his greatest hits, the ballads "All Alone," "Remember," and "Always." They were inspired by Ellin Mackay, according to Broadway legend, and "Always" was her wedding present from Irving Berlin.

By this time the hot breath of Hollywood was singeing Berlin's neck, and *Puttin' on the Ritz* was his first movie success. Harry Richman, sleek, cane-toting, Prohibition pet, made the title song a hoofer's favourite. Like Broadway, Hollywood was in for a long line of Berlinisms. There was *Top Hat*, the first Fred Astaire–Ginger Rogers film. From it came "Cheek to Cheek," Berlin's greatest Hollywood song hit.

Broadway had by now emerged from its chrysalis of sensual extravagance into the half-light of the Depression. And Irving Berlin, in the show *Face the Music*, made a wry, mischievous face at the whole business. For it he wrote the topical, irrepressible song, "Let's Have Another Cup of Coffee."

Later, straddling the disillusionment of the country, Berlin went back to writing syrupy tunes. In 1933 in collaboration with Moss Hart, he wrote *As Thousands Cheer*. Percy Hammond, critic for the *New York Herald-Tribune*, reported on this: "Mr. Berlin, in his tunes and verses, holds sex to be sacred, and then Mr. Moss Hart comes along proving that nothing on this footstool is holy." Two top Berlin tunes came wrapped up in *As Thousands Cheer*. The first one, apparently unforgettable, was "Easter Parade." A musical daguerreotype, it has become an Easter classic. All the reviewers loved "Easter Parade," but most of them slid over another song, which in its way has proved even more of a hit. That song was "Heat Wave," magnificently sung by Ethel Waters, her body weaving, her voice as dark as a thunderstorm.

MRS. IRVING BERLIN   Steichen
(Ellin Mackay)

Undoubtedly, Irving Berlin is the greatest, the most versatile, surely the most prolific songwriter in America. His tunes, not satisfied with catching on, have an insistent way of living on. And so it is no surprise to find the war song of 1917, Irving Berlin's, "Oh, How I Hate to Get Up in the Morning" returning to the ranks in 1942. Prophetically, in 1925 Alexander Woollcott wrote, "This is the only song of the last war that is likely to be carried along the roads by the soldiers of our next war."

[1933 – 1943]   207

1911: "Alexander's Ragtime Band"; Irving Berlin sang it first at the Friar's Frolic. It made music history, by making "rag" respectable.

1913: "International Rag"; Sophie Tucker, big, bold, and raucous, put it in the big-time—sang it in vaudeville throughout the whole country.

1921: "Say It with Music"; Wilda Bennett sang this theme song of the *Music Box Revue*.

1921: "Everybody Step"; The Brox Sisters sang it in the first *Music Box Revue*.

1914: "This Is the Life"; Al Jolson, putting on a black face, launched the song, and with it became one of America's greatest singing comics.

1914: "Syncopated Walk"; Irene and Vernon Castle in *Watch Your Step*.

1924: "What'll I Do?"; Grace Moore made this the hit tune of the *Music Box Revue* of 1924.

1926: "Always"; John McCormack made it popular.

1916: "The Girl on the Magazine Cover"; Gaby Deslys sang it in *Stop, Look, and Listen*.

1917: "Poor Little Me, I'm K.P."; Irving Berlin, doleful as a cocker spaniel pup, sang it in *Yip, Yip, Yaphank*.

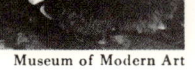

1929: "Puttin' on the Ritz"; Harry Richman, vaudeville star, night-club entertainer, sang this song in the movie of the same name.

1919: "A Pretty Girl Is Like a Melody"; Ziegfeld show girls made this the memory-laden scene of the *Ziegfeld Follies of 1919*.

Photographed by Culver and White St

1932: "Say It Isn't So"; Rudy Vallee, first among radio's breathless crooners, helped make it so popular.

1932: "Let's Have Another Cup of Coffee"; Kay Carrington sang it in *Face the Music*. The social significance of its lyrics made it the theme song of the depression.

1933: "Heat Wave"; Ethel Waters, high-powered, full-voiced, made this a classic in *As Thousands Cheer*.

1933: Marilyn Miller sang "Easter Parade" in *As Thousands Cheer*. With her here — Clifton Webb.

1935: "Cheek to Cheek"; Fred Astaire, with Ginger Rogers, light-footed through this in the movie *Top Hat*.

Anton Bruehl   Vandamm

1936: "Let's Face the Music"; again the team of Astaire and Rogers danced and sang this in *Follow the Fleet*.

1937: "This Year's Kisses"; Alice Faye, baby-faced blonde, made her first hit singing it in the movie *On the Avenue*.

1937: "The Girl on the Police Gazette"; the same girl, same movie. Now, Gypsy Rose Lee sings this in her super-burleycue, *Star and Garter*.

1938: "God Bless America"; Kate Smith was the first to sing it.

1942: "Oh, How I Hate to Get Up in the Morning"; Berlin wrote it for *Yip, Yip, Yaphank* (1917), sings it now in *This Is the Army*.

1942: "White Christmas"; Marjorie Reynolds sings it with Bing Crosby in the movie *Holiday Inn*.

THE FAMOUS FACES OF SWING

Vic Volk

ABOUT BAND LEADERS

BY JAN SPIESS

The immortals of swing are serious specialists who believe that their form of music is as important to the American scene as Gabriel's trumpet will be to the end of the world. They tell you where the "blues was born" down on the levees, on river boats, on the Barbary Coast. They trace the tradition of this form of American folk music from spiritual, to ballad, breakdown, blues, ragtime, jazz, and now sweet jazz or swing.

Paul Whiteman, that great first maestro of mad music, held the first swing concert in Aeolian Hall in 1924 with a roster of names that today are the names of top-flight masters of swing. It was then that Gershwin was introduced to an American audience with his famous "Rhapsody in Blue." Grofé, who had arranged the "Rhapsody," was a viola player, Bing Crosby sang in the quartette, the Dorsey boys were in the band.

The concert was a terrific success. It established swing as a medium of music that even the Bach Society could not ignore. When the critics acclaimed Whiteman, he received their words with becoming modesty. "Toscanini could do it with the right 'get-off men,'" he said generously. Whiteman took swing on the road — he took it east, west, north, and south. In one year he spent $350,000 in railroad fare. He sold two million platters of his record, "Whispering." He endowed the Paul Whiteman Museum of American Music at Williams College. He made America proud of American music. Most important of all, he inspired many of the young men in his band to take the hard, long road to recognition as swing leaders.

The famous names in the bounce bands of today are hard to classify. They vary as much in training, inspiration, and arrangements as they do in the surrealistic solo licks, riffs, jazz, and swing and sway. They don't care, they say, "who is hotter than who" so long as he is not "hair-pin," not "bustle," not a "clover kicker." And that, for readers outside the inner circle of jazz, means "not corny."

Larry Clinton organized his band hastily to make a recording; it was so successful that he took it out on the road. His greatest hit was a swing interpretation of a little-known Debussy melody; the classicists complained bitterly when he made a swing arrangement of "I Dreamt I Dwelt in Marble Halls." They even petitioned the Federal Communications Commission to bar performances of popular interpretations of the classics from the networks.

The best-selling release that Victor-Bluebird has had in nine years is "Begin the Beguine," with Artie Shaw handling the baton. Odd footnote: somewhere in the process of becoming a jitterbug band leader, Artie Shaw felt that the little people weren't getting the fine effect of his swing while they danced (?) ... he wants them to *sit* and listen!

Benny Goodman began his meteoric career in a four-piece combination that included Bix Beiderbecke, that trumpeter who is still remembered with wide-eyed wonder by every horn-blower in the business.

But it is not necessary always to appeal to jitterbugs to be a well-known band leader. Xavier Cugat has proved that. Cugat was brought to this country by Caruso, who heard him in Spain and had immediate faith in his future as a violinist. But Cugat turned away from the concert stage and initiated in Americans the popular desire for Spanish and Argentine music. He made Manhattan tango and rhumba until it was a serious question as to which side of the ocean Spain was on. But fine as the Spanish music is, it isn't American. It may move your feet and stir your pulses ... but it isn't swing.

Tommy Dorsey is a trombonist who is sometimes hailed as Gabriel, while his brother Jimmy is called by the more ardent of his fans "the world's greatest saxophonist." The two brothers had an orchestra together for a while, but after a short but very special civil war they separated, each to form his own band. Jimmy Dorsey was once heard to say, during an erudite moment, that "swing is surrealism in music."

Another famous brother of a famous brother (as Gertrude Stein might put it) is Bing Crosby's brother Bob, whose orchestral selections range from New Orleans Dixieland to streamlined swing and/or boogie-woogie. And boogie-woogie, if they should ask you what it is next time you are on "Information Please," is a repeated pattern of the theme with the left hand, while the right hand improvises like mad.

[1933 – 1943] 211

TEN AMERICANS WITH A SIXTH CLOTHES SENSE

Intentionally or unintentionally, the ten American ladies shown here influence fashion. Numbered among the best dressed, they have an unmistakable clothes sense — call it a sixth sense, call it taste, call it talent. No two achieve results by the same means — their personal convictions are summed up briefly herewith.

THE DUCHESS OF WINDSOR: American born, European trained, the former Wallis Warfield has a worldly sense of clothes and the courage of her convictions. Never undecided, never distracted by passing idiosyncrasies, she knows how she wants to look. She's an unswerving exponent of off-the-face hats, simple dresses, bold jewellery.

LADY MENDL: Her talent for decorating is reflected in her sense of clothes-assembling. She can put together a two-year-old dress, six-month-old-hat, and a new jewel — with magic elegance. She rarely wavers from black and white; often has favourite dresses copied, was first to "blue" her white hair.

COUNTESS HAUGWITZ-REVENTLOW: The former Barbara Hutton chooses clothes with an intuitive sense of the feminine. She can be both pretty and chic — a difficult paradox. Crisp and immaculate as porcelain, she looks at night like a doll, wearing a fantastic Edwardian dog-collar of rubies; and on the tennis-court, like a small boy.

MRS. RONALD B. BALCOM: From her girlhood days as Millicent Rogers, she has had an independent dress sense. Her clothes are undated. She wore dirndls and peasant handkerchiefs when only the Austrians did. She wears her gloves three sizes too large.

MRS. THOMAS H. SHEVLIN: The former Lorraine Rowan has always had an instinctive, spontaneous sense of clothes. She puts things together with effortless flair. She buys few, but good, things; advocates imaginative colors; never wears black or slinky clothes; helped to initiate hair-bows, lapel carnations, topaz jewellery.

MISS INA CLAIRE: The theatre's gifted comedienne has, too, a gifted sense of clothes. She is quick to discern the new, quick to adopt it. At the moment, she has discarded her pompadour for bangs. She likes to experiment, venture the untried. Her hats are invariably whimsies, her clothes young, simple.

MRS. GILBERT MILLER: She is the wife of the well-known theatrical producer. Her cosmopolitan life has developed a sense of the "fitness" of clothes. She abhors overdressing or underdressing; is extremely soignée, a perfectionist about details. She likes the conservative, cares less for a first than for a lasting impression.

MRS. CARROLL CARSTAIRS: She has the sense to stick to her own type. She is American (born Susan Burks Yuille), looks American and encourages it. She wears her brown hair long, skull-caps on the back of her head, schoolgirl cardigans, and short fur jackets. She loves sweaters and was one of the first to wear an evening sweater.

THE DUCHESS OF WINDSOR

MRS. BYRON C. FOY: The former Thelma Chrysler has a figure for clothes and a highly developed sense of the dramatic. She advocates extremes: slinky sheaths or twenty-yard-wide skirts. She usually bares her shoulders at night, emphasizes her waist — one of the smallest extant — and always looks as if she'd stepped out of a bandbox.

MRS. HARRISON WILLIAMS: The blue-eyed, grey-haired Mona Williams has a subtle sense of colour. She likes conservative rather than "latest" fashions. Her clothes are usually designed for her. She seldom wears black, prefers colours to match her eyes or hair. She helped to launch halter necks and wide tulle skirts.

212 [1933 – 1943]

Photographed by Horst P. Horst and John Rawlings

LADY MENDL (ELSIE DE WOLFE)

COUNTESS HAUGWITZ-REVENTLOW

MRS. RONALD B. BALCOM

MRS. THOMAS H. SHEVLIN

MISS INA CLAIRE

MRS. GILBERT MILLER

MRS. CARROLL CARSTAIRS

MRS. BYRON C. FOY

MRS. HARRISON WILLIAMS

ARTURO TOSCANINI, the greatest conductor of his time. The maestro recently amazed his admirers by opening his twelve NBC broadcasts with a spirited performance of Gershwin's *Rhapsody in Blue*, which, as one reviewer put it, "went whooping down the groove."

SERGEI RACHMANINOFF, leader of the music world for the past fifty years. The fabulously gifted Russian-born composer, pianist, and conductor died on March 28, 1943. Destined to live forever: his Second Symphony in E Minor and his piano concertos.

Karger-Pix

Adrian Siegel

MARIAN ANDERSON, famed Philadelphia-born singer, is, in many people's estimation, the world's greatest contralto. At a Salzburg concert in 1935, Toscanini told her, "A voice like yours is heard only once in a hundred years." Here she runs over a score with Eugene Ormandy, conductor of the Philadelphia Orchestra. In 1945 she plans to repeat at New York's Carnegie Hall the recital she gave at her Town Hall debut ten years ago.

YEHUDI MENUHIN (right), to whom, after a concert he gave when he was ten years old, Einstein said, "You have once again proved to me that there is a God in heaven," has long since successfully passed the critical period between childhood and maturity that often defeats the prodigy. At twenty-eight, he is master of the violin. After benefit concerts for war relief in Australia and South America, Menuhin recently returned to the U.S.A.

216 [1933 – 1943]

EXODUS

BY LEE AND CARL ERICKSON

We left Senlis in a ramshackle car, bought that morning, and joined a slowly moving mass of carts, farm wagons, *camions*, and cars piled with bedding and families; refugees on foot, some women with thin shoes worn through, stumbling along on swollen, bleeding feet, pushing perambulators, pulling carts, carrying babies, dragging small exhausted children by the hand. They had come from the north, from Picardy, from Flanders; they had been walking two days, three days, a week; they had eaten little, slept in fields, lain in ditches as the airplanes machine-gunned the road. They didn't know where they were going. This sluggish river of tragedy filled the road as far as the eye could see. It was moving slowly along all the lovely roads of France in the bright sunshine, like slowly flowing blood. I saw only one woman weeping. Set faces, hard and patient. Farmers driving huge hay-carts with grandmother enthroned on mattresses at the head of the wagon and all the family gathered around her — except the young men. The high wagons were jolted up onto the curb time and time again to let pass a swift and imperious car. Grandmother was thrown violently from side to side, but her expression didn't change.

There was a woman hugging a bland-eyed goat; there were four great farm dogs riding in state and barking joyously. There was a lost dog running frantically among the wheels; farther on he found his master, a lone old man wheeling a bicycle, the seat of his pants worn through. Someone gave him a rope, and with trembling hands he tied his dog to the handle-bars to keep him safe. Thank God, we said, thank God.

Near Chantilly, at a crossroad, in a lovely wood, there was an *alerte*. The sirens screamed, the guns boomed, there was the humming drone of German planes. Everything stopped. Like one mass, the refugees scattered under the trees and under the wagons. They knew. At the all-clear signal, they went on as before, their expressions unchanged. I looked at the pitiful attempts at camouflage, branches of trees, long since dried, and useless anyway.

Here was a *roulotte*, one of those house-wagons one sees on the roads of France, with lace curtains at the windows. At the windows were the smiling faces of the present aristocrats of the road. They, at least, are at home.

Farther on, we moved for a time with a small convoy of soldiers. Where they came from we didn't know. But I have never seen such complete exhaustion. Blackened faces, eyes red with blood, hardly able to lift their fingers to take a cigarette. We were held up at a railroad crossing before a café. A girl was sent over with beer for the soldiers. One looked up with a cracked smile and said: "*O, la belle blonde.*"

A few hours after we left Senlis, a bomb fell thirty yards from our house and blasted our doors and windows across the rooms. The wife, mother, and daughter of our butcher were killed. The butcher has gone mad. All our tradesmen are homeless.

THE COUNTESS OF PEMBROKE AND HER SON,
LORD DAVID HERBERT, AT WILTON,
WITH CHILDREN EVACUATED FROM LONDON

Beaton

ERICKSON DRAWS REFUGEES STREAMING DOWN THE ROADS OF FRANCE

WAR

EUROPEAN FRONT: D-DAY LANDING OF ALLIED FORCES, OMAHA BEACH, JUNE 6, 1944   INP

BUCHENWALD CONCENTRATION CAMP AT WEIMAR; A PILE OF STARVED BODIES

Lee Miller

[1933–1943]

OPPOSITE: PACIFIC FRONT:
AMERICAN MARINES ON SAIPAN, 1944

W. Eugene Smith

ROOSEVELT

When Franklin Delano Roosevelt, thirty-first president of the United States, died on April 12, 1945, America and the mourning world felt deeply the loss of this one man. The war, though drawing to a close, was not yet won, but when victory came at last for the Allies, Roosevelt's words in his last inaugural address were well remembered in the forging of the difficult peace: "We have learned that we cannot live alone, at peace; that our own well-being is dependent upon the well-being of nations far away ... We have learned to be members of the human community."

CHURCHILL

Embattled and invincible, with courage and true statesmanship, Winston Churchill led England through five years of war. Before America entered the conflict, Britain fought alone, her spirit reflected in Churchill's epic words: "... we shall not flag or fail, we shall go on to the end, we shall fight in France, and we shall fight on the seas and the oceans ... we shall defend our island whatever the cost may be, we shall fight on the beaches, we shall fight on the landing-grounds, we shall fight in the fields and in the streets, we shall fight in the hills; we shall never surrender."

V.E. DAY 1945

PRAYERS OF THANKSGIVING IN ST. PATRICK'S CATHEDRAL, NEW YORK

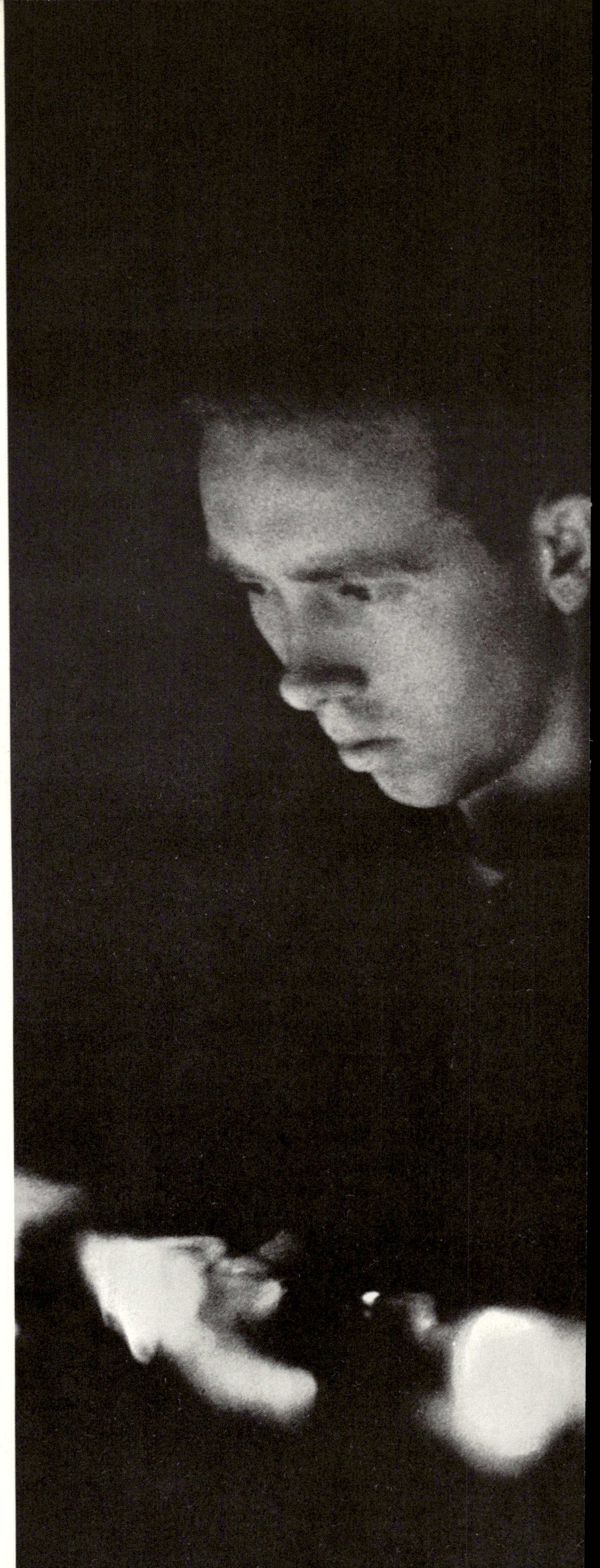

Lofman Photo

UPI photos

THE LIGHTS GO ON AGAIN IN LONDON

UPI photos

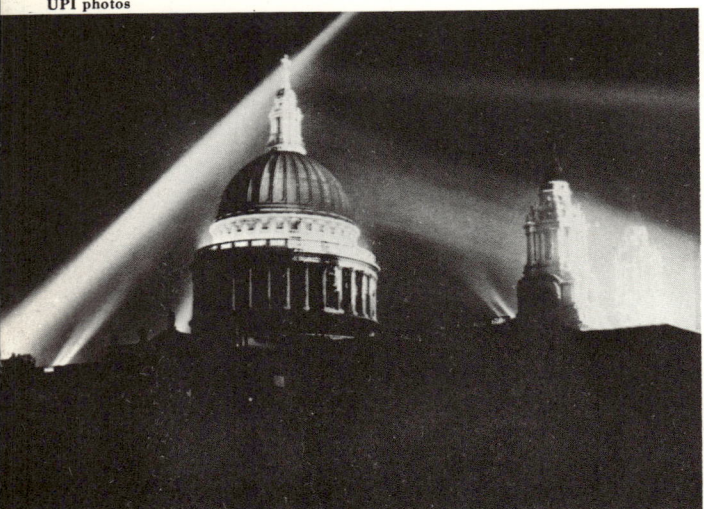

DE GAULLE JOINS A JOYFUL PARIS CROWD

Radio-Photo, Sovphoto

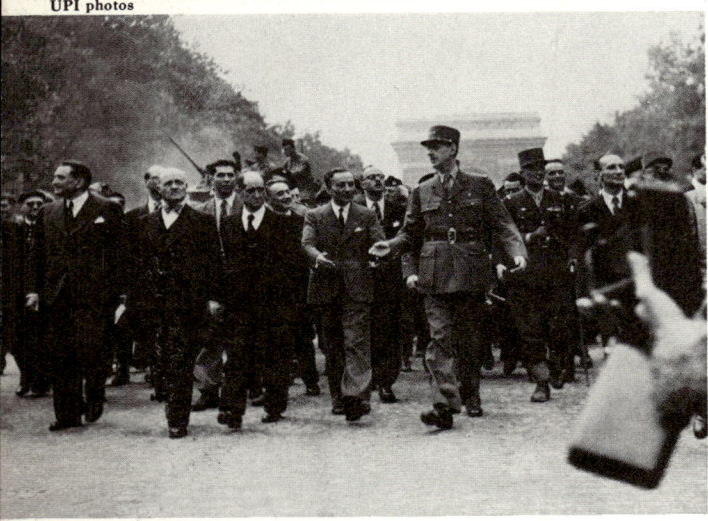

STREAMERS OF LIGHT, V.E. DAY IN MOSCOW

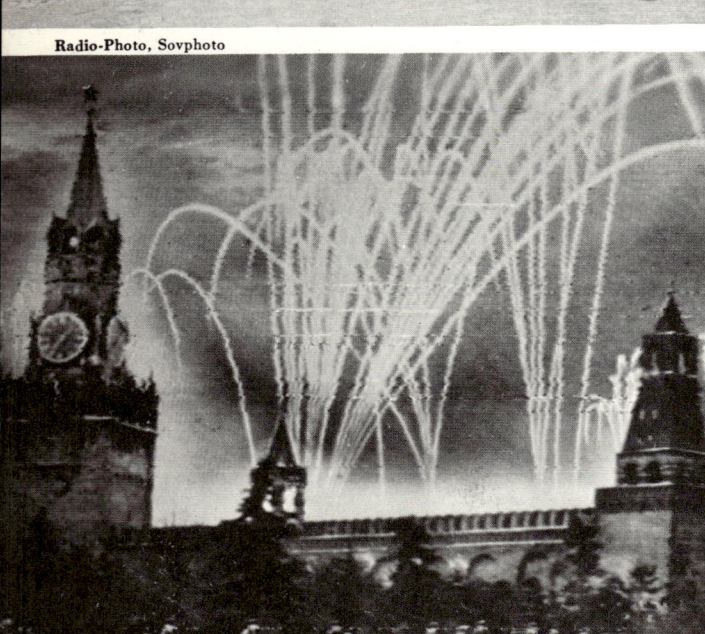

THE CRISIS OF MAN

BY ALBERT CAMUS

Camus is a philosopher, lecturer, playwright, and novelist, one of the most important of the French existentialist writers. During the War he was an editor of the Resistance paper, *Combat*. Although in his new book *The Stranger* he stresses the absurdity of man's predicament, Camus is far from despair, saying in effect that in the present crisis of man fear is the great enemy.

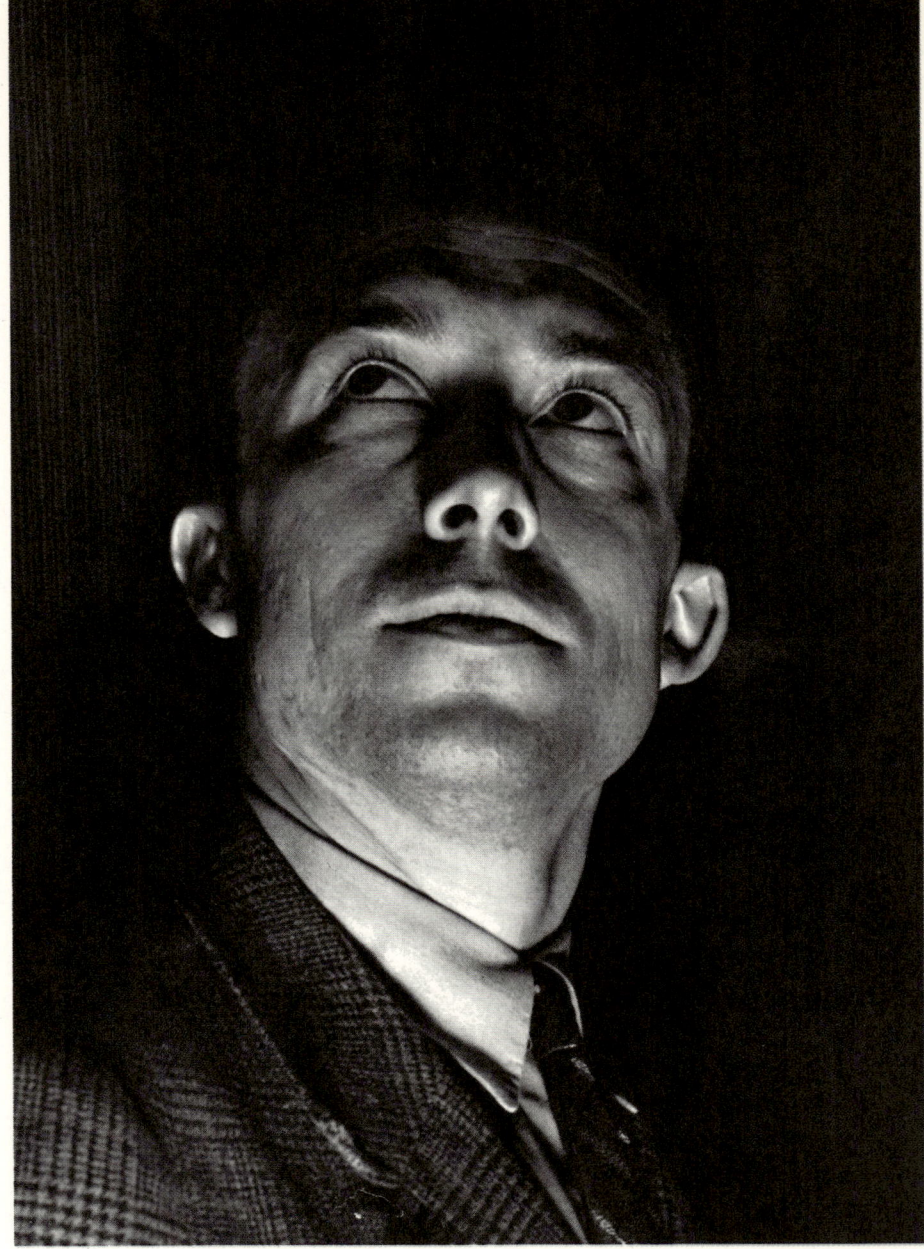
Cecil Beaton

When a European has formulated the idea that life is tragic, he judges that he has become as intelligent as possible. Naturally this is stupidity. But it seems to me that when an American has persuaded himself that life is a good thing and pain does not exist he judges that he has shown himself as reasonable as possible. This, of course, is a grievous error. Face to face with a similar condition, Europe and America suffer from contradictory ills. It seems to me as unreasonable to say that we must not be pessimistic as it is to say that we must not be optimistic.

The ancient Greeks knew that life was made up of darkness and light, that man must keep his eyes set simultaneously on the day and the night in order to remain true to his condition. Civilization is judged by the way it overcomes this fundamental contradiction. Whatever the thought of America or Europe, we are all marching toward that momentous contradiction. Admittedly there are many things in this greatest adventure of the Occidental spirit that do not rest with us. But one thing always rests with us, the ability to declare, to maintain and never betray what we believe to be the truth. And the truth is that the world is neither one of joy nor of sorrow. It is a closed field lying between the need for happiness which is in every heart and the historic fatality at which the crisis of man reaches its peak. We must, therefore, have on one hand an accurate concept of the crisis, on the other hand a precise knowledge of that degree of happiness which each man desires. We must be clear in our minds.

The crisis of man is made up of equal parts of inertia and the fatigue of people faced by the accumulation of stupid principles and evil actions. The strongest temptation of man is the temptation of inertia. And because the world is no longer inhabited by the cry of victims, many think that things will somehow rock along for a few more generations to come. Because it is easier to do one's daily work and wait in

226 [1943 – 1953]

peace for death to come one day, people believe that they have done their share for the good of mankind by not committing murder and by trying to lie as little as possible. But the truth remains that no man can die in peace if he has not at least once questioned his life and the lives of others — if he has not done what he can for the possible peace of mankind.

That is why people who do not want to think too long or too hard on human misery prefer to speak of it in a general way. Such people have asked me whether I was "quite sure that there was a crisis of man and if, after all, such a crisis was not of all ages." All this is at the same time true and false. It is, however, the kind of truth not to be fed to former boarders of concentration camps. I think it must have been impossible for those who were tortured to say to themselves, while their captors were busy at the job, that "after all, such things have taken place in the world through the ages." I think for them there was a crisis of man. And for all men of my generation that crisis still exists. I know that for a long time already, we humans have been ill at ease in our skins, have been unsure of the future, which is not a normal state for supposedly civilized men.

Rightly or wrongly that is what we call the crisis of man. A crisis which exists because there is fear. Fear exists because people are convinced that nothing makes sense, or else that only historical success makes sense, because human values have been replaced by the value of efficiency, the will to liberty replaced by the will to dominate. People are convinced that one is no longer right because justice is on one's side; one is right because one succeeds. And the more one succeeds the more one is right. In the long run this is justification of murder. That is the reason why men can well be afraid, because in such a world it is only by chance or arbitrary good fortune that their lives and those of their children are spared. It is why men can well be ashamed, for those who live in such a world without condemning it from the rooftops are in their way murderers like the rest.

We must be sure not to overlook another force, the will of man as applied to happiness and justice. And here again it is essential to know what we want. What we want is never again to let might be right, never again to bow before the power of arms and money. Naturally this is the kind of statement that makes the realists laugh. Because the realists know that this is an endless job, and subsequently see no reason to prolong it. Realists only undertake jobs that succeed, therefore they will never undertake anything that is truly important or humane. Without meaning to do so the realists condemn the world to murder by failing to see that, though the job is endless, the reason for our being is to assume its responsibilities.

I do not believe in guaranteed progress, or in any philosophy of history, but I think that, at least, man has never ceased to advance in the awareness of his destiny. We have not overcome our conditions but at least we understand them better. Our task as men is to find the formula. We must make justice reasonable in an unjust world and happiness significant in a world poisoned by the sorrow of the century. It is a superhuman task. But call all tasks superhuman that have taken man a long time to accomplish. Seen in this light there is nothing superhuman in the condition of man.

Is this pessimism? No, this is an honest effort to determine what is wanted, what unwanted. When one is sick it is first important to determine the type of disease before attempting a cure. We who are suffering from abstraction and fear might as well know it in order to determine what to do. We young Frenchmen label as pessimists those that say that "all is well and nothing changes human nature." We call them pessimists because they are among those from whom nothing can be expected. It will be their fault if the world never changes. But there are among us enough men of decision pledged to do all that is within their power to cure themselves and the world of its present sickness.

I am often asked, here in America, what the youth of Europe is like today.

The youth I know live without illusions, which somehow has only served to strengthen their decision and their courage. When I am asked if it is good for youth to live without illusion, I can only say that it isn't a matter of what is to be desired but what is true. That is the question, truth. And the truth is that this youth forced to live in direct contact with the most frightful realities of existence has done so without perishing, since today this same youth not only ask the questions that concern the world but retain the strength and determination to answer them. This is as great a key to the future of our civilization as the latest scientific inventions or the ingenious right of veto.

We know the kind of civilization we want and the horror of what we don't want. But what can we expect? We can expect for a while that the world will continue in the hands of those who have no imagination; of those who want to preserve that which can no longer be preserved, who want to destroy that which can never be destroyed. In the hands of those who lie and those who force others to lie, in the hands of the bureaucrats and policemen. And if this continues, someday all these will be swept away by those who kill and find it easy to be killers. That is logic. But it is also logic for us to continue to defend, against the onslaughts of the blind and of the covetous, those things worthy of man's defence. We will continue to do so because we have agreed that it is not necessary to succeed in order to persevere, and because we know that it is the long obstinacy of certain men that alone has ended by changing the world. The early Christians called the great movement that sustained them "the folly of the Cross."

Today what we need is a folly of man. A great, far-thinking, sound folly built on the immense hope, the silent determination which has sustained in the past and will continue to sustain some European minds in a world they have faced without benefit of illusion. When one knows this, perhaps it is easier to answer the question, "Are we pessimists?"

[1943 – 1953] 227

PIERRE BALMAIN

BY GERTRUDE STEIN

There were dark days when we first knew Pierre Balmain. We met his mother in '39 at Aix-les-Bains and she said she had a son up there in the army in the snows of Savoy and he read my books, would I dedicate him one, naturally I was pleased and then came '40 and the defeat, and we wondered about Pierre Balmain whom we had never seen but who was up there in the snows, and then at last we heard he was safe and then he was back and then we met him. He used to come over on his bicycle, we were many miles away but nobody minded that and the winter was cold and we were cold and he made us some nice warm suits and a nice warm coat and Alice Toklas insists that one of her suits was as wonderful as any he was showing at his opening and there was no reason why not, after all didn't he design it and didn't he come over on his bicycle to oversee and was it not as it all just is in dark days, there are bright spots. Well we got to know him better and better, some children played some of my plays and he showed us the chic of making a very tall girl taller by putting her on a footstool. These were nice days in those dark days and then Pierre used to go to and fro from Paris, and he brought us back a breath of our dear Paris and also darning cotton to darn our stockings and our linen, that was Pierre, and then he kept moving around as young men had to do in those days, not to be sent away into Germany and then there was the liberation and then in Paris here we all were and Pierre just full of what he was going to do and we were sure he would do it and he has. I suppose there at the opening, we were the only ones who had been clothed in all those long years in Pierre Balmain's clothes, we were proud of it. It is nice to know the young man when he is just a young man and nobody knows, and now well I guess very soon now anybody will know. And we were so pleased and proud. Yes we were.

ALICE B. TOKLAS

GERTRUDE STEIN
Drawings by Eric

228 [1943 – 1953]

PICASSO, WITH HIS PET OWL
AND ITS PORTRAIT,
PHOTOGRAPHED BY MICHAEL SIMA

MAIL GOSSIPINGS

BY ALEXANDER WOOLLCOTT

To Thornton Wilder: While Ruth Gordon and Ethel Barrymore and Neysa are out on the terrace having high Coca-Cola, I might as well tell you about my experience in Paris the other night. I chanced to be in the topmost gallery of the Théâtre Français when King George came in incog and alone and sat beside me. He pinched my ear a good deal, and we became rather pals, and I agreed to go to a party with him.

I backed out when this proved to be a program of interpretive dancing held, oddly enough, in a commodious aluminum trailer. I did put my head in long enough to explain to Queen Elizabeth that I really couldn't stay. "Oh, you must stay," she said. "After this dance, we're going to read aloud the new four-act play by Thornton Wilder." And what delighted me so much and what — even in the midst of my *dream* — I made a note to impress you with the next time we should meet, was the fact that I had the exquisite social tact *not* to let her know that I had already read it.

In bed with a touch of the flu since the night I got back from Washington, I have been haunted in advance by a legend I am sure will take form. I have written to Mrs. Roosevelt to deny categorically that as soon as she and the President left the premises, I quartered a regiment of Marines at the White House. What I did, as you know, was to seek lodging for the night for one small, measly Second Lieutenant. At the White House, I found that even the ushers had all vanished, so I decided that I was in charge and, on my own authority, tucked him in that huge bed in the Pink Room, where all night he slept the sleep of the just.

I have got myself into a position where I must do a brief piece (750 words) on *The Skin of Our Teeth*. You must brace yourself for my report that Gilbert Miller does *not* like the play. He compares it unfavourably with *Cyrano de Bergerac*, which it seems he understood when he was twelve. With Gus Eckstein, on the other hand, the case is different. He went last night and has been beside himself ever since. In his excitement he woke me out of a sound sleep at midnight and has telephoned me three times since about the play.

I have been reading with strong pleasure the galley proofs of Gus Eckstein's book about the Japanese. From time to time he tried to be severe with them. The effect is a little jolting. It is as if he said, "See that dear family. See what goodness there is under this humble roof. How spartan they are! How passionately loyal! How deeply good! Of course, we must kill them all."

To Beatrice Kaufman: I have just been weekending with the Cazalets in Kent. I admired a large paper-cutter (nearly a yard long), and it was given me on my departure. I also admired the famous Cazalet orchids and received a spray. But thus far nothing has come of my raptures over several Augustus Johns, an extraordinary Epstein, a black Cocker named Tiny, Mrs. Peter Cazalet, and an avenue of limes. I suppose these will be sent on to the hotel. I got back here late last night. As my car drew up at the curb, a drunken member of the lower classes cried out, "Make way for Lord Kitchener!" It is not known why, but it attracted enough attention for quite a group to be watching when I emerged from the car carrying a spray of orchids in one hand and a large dirk in the other. They scattered in every direction.

To Alfred Lunt: I don't deserve a letter as I haven't had the strength to write one. I am saving all my energy for the English edition of *While Rome Burns*. The solicitors of the English publisher retired into the Middle Temple with the American text and sent out word that virtually every chapter was libelous. They were particularly disturbed by the suggestion in one paragraph that Lady Robert Peel had had the hiccups. They seemed to think this would convey to the reader the suggestion that Bea Lillie was occasionally guilty of intemperance.

Don't think for one moment that these old eyes escaped the rotogravure glimpse of you and the little woman being peasantish at brekker. The subject is an embittering one. A celebrated amateur photographer has just come out with one of me. The print sent here for my approval was on a scale which would make it a suitable mural for the Pennsylvania Depot. I think it should be reduced somewhat, turned into a lithograph, and sold widely under the caption, "Somebody's Grandmother."

GARY COOPER and INGRID BERGMAN in *For Whom the Bell Tolls*: Although the Spanish Franco government has certain worries about it, Ernest Hemingway's novel has finally been turned into a movie, strong and beautiful, with Miss Bergman as Maria and Gary Cooper as the American idealist, fighting for the Spanish Loyalists.

1947

WOMEN WEAR A NEW LOOK,
CINCHED-IN WAIST, SOFT SHOULDERS,
PADDED HIPS, SKIRTS TO
MID-CALF — ALL BECAUSE
OF THE IDEAS OF
PARIS DESIGNER CHRISTIAN DIOR

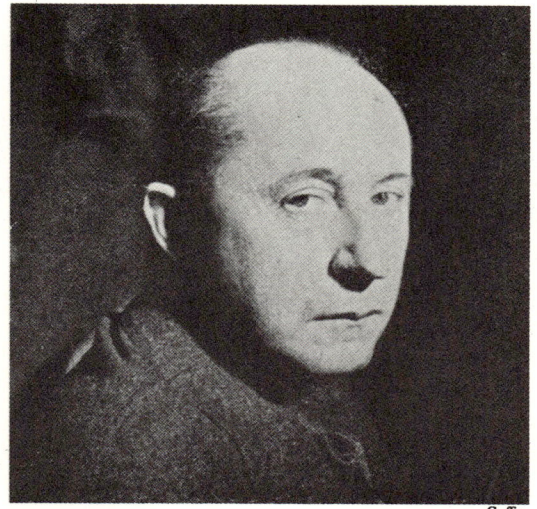

DIOR, MOST INFLUENTIAL PARIS DESIGNER

Coffin

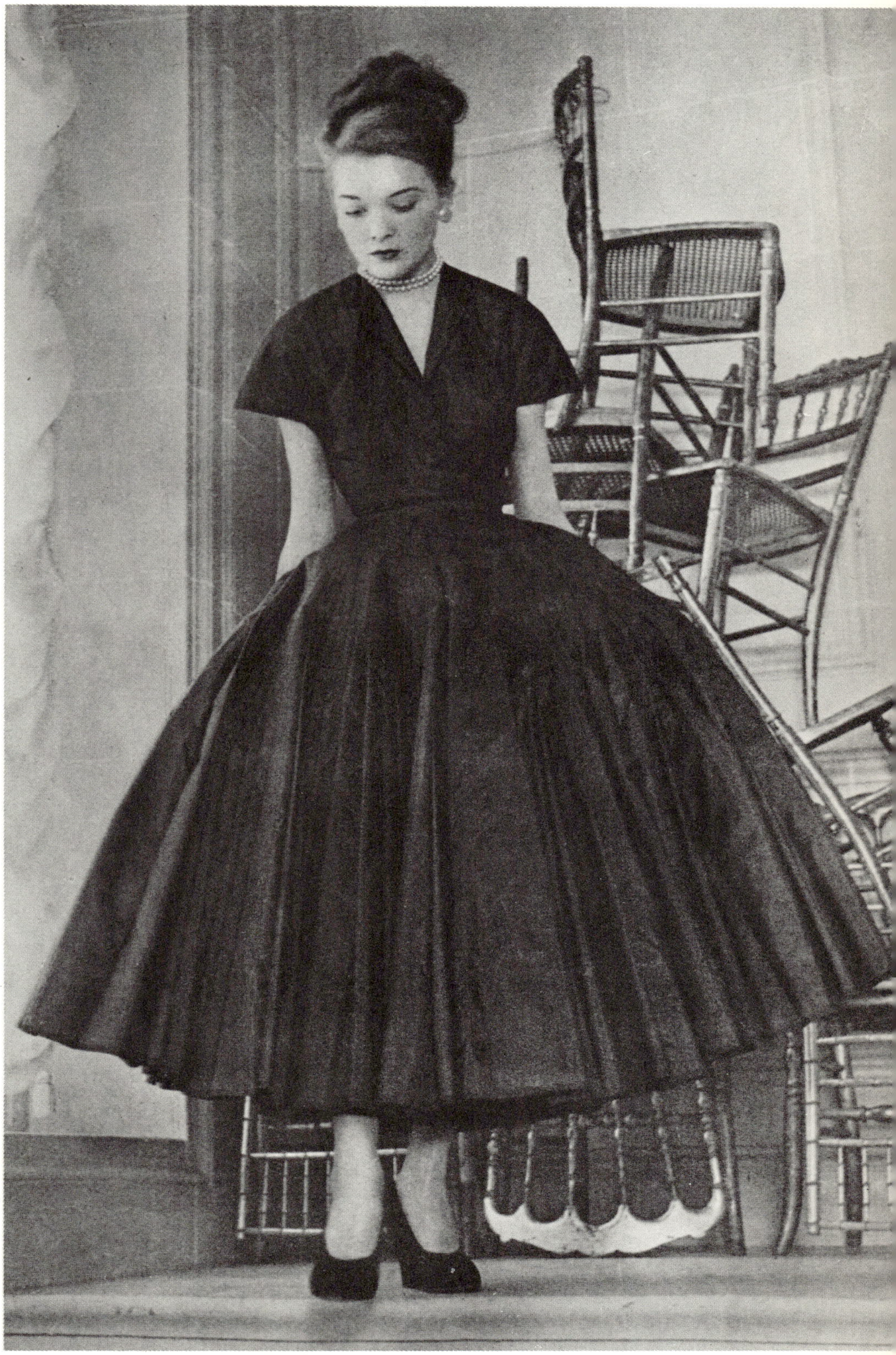

TWENTY-FIVE YARDS OF PLEATED CHIFFON

PALE TUSSORE JACKET
PLEATED JERSEY SKIRT
Balkin

A YOUNG ACTOR AND A YOUNG PLAYWRIGHT

MARLON BRANDO, found two seasons ago on Broadway, is twenty-one, and very good indeed. His first big part was in *I Remember Mama*. He then gave a superb performance as the war-shocked murderer in the Maxwell Anderson play *Truckline Café*, and is currently a stormy Marchbanks to Katharine Cornell's Candida. He has a chaos of hair, and a wilful theatrical talent.

PETER USTINOV, grandson of the famous Alexandre Benois of the Diaghilev Ballet, is one of the few young playwrights worth watching. His fresh experimental plays include *The Banbury Nose*, *Squaring the Circle*, *Blow Your Own Trumpet*, and *The House of Regrets* (a sad story of very old Russian émigrés — at twenty-three Ustinov is obsessed with old age). With Eric Ambler, he wrote one of Britain's most stirring war movies, *The Way Ahead*.

236   [1943 – 1953]

1946

OPERA ADDICT

BY W. H. AUDEN

No one is dispassionate on the subject of opera. Either he thinks it the most ridiculous and boring entertainment ever devised by man or he becomes an addict who will cheerfully sacrifice his health, his fortune, and his friends to gratify his craving. What makes an opera addict? To answer that question, one must, I believe, first ask another. What is opera about? Just as art in general can only deal with a portion of our total experience, so each of the arts has its special field with which it can deal better than any rival medium can, and its special limitations which it transgresses at its peril.

Thus, the essence of literature is reflection; there can be poetry and prose because we can stop to consider ourselves and the words. Drama depends upon the fact that we can be deceived, about character or identity or time. Ballet is based on ritual, that is, on an acknowledgement that there are relationships which are obligatory and independent of our personalities; its most characteristic gestures are those of courtesy, homage, and command.

And opera? One can, of course, only draw conclusions from the past, and the history of opera is very odd. The two greatest outbursts of creative activity in a dramatic medium which the world has seen so far were the succession of plays produced by Athenians during the fifth and fourth centuries B.C., and the succession of operas produced by Europeans, most of them Italians or Germans, in the eighteenth and nineteenth centuries A.D. Only one hundred and twenty-five years separate Gluck's *Orpheus* (1762) from Verdi's *Othello* (1887) but the list of operas produced in that period occupies 452 closely written pages in Loewenberg's *Annals of Opera*.

Hundreds of these have, of course, been deservedly forgotten, but there remain many more works of great value than the combined opera houses of the world have time or talent to produce. Every opera fan builds his daydream house in which with his daydream cast he stages his daydream repertoire of seldom performed operas by, say, Bellini or Rossini or Weber or Meyerbeer or Gounod or the young Verdi, which he longs to hear and fears he never will. That is one reason why, as a rule, he is a conservative who does not welcome new opera; there are too many from the Golden Age which he has still to hear. That age is over; after Verdi and Wagner come Puccini and Strauss, but one cannot listen to either without being conscious that this is the end of something. From Gluck until them the development of the form is continuous and organic, but there it stops. New operas, let us hope, will be written, but their composers cannot carry on from where their predecessors left off, but must start anew from the beginning.

What, then, is opera, as we know it so far, *about*? It is about *wilful* feeling. There could be no opera if we did not, in addition to simply having emotions, insist upon having them at whatever inconvenience to ourselves and others. The ideal operatic hero and heroine are people who make life very difficult indeed; they fall in love with the most unsuitable person they can find, an enemy, a social inferior, the consort of a friend, a criminal, a nun; they keep appearing at the most embarrassing and improbable times and places possible; they persistently and shamelessly make scenes in public; they expire in a prodigious explosion of defiance and *folie de grandeur*. All the great operatic characters, Don Giovanni (who is wilfulness incarnate), Norma, Lucia, Brünnhilde, Aïda, Carmen, etc., conform to this type, and, indeed, it is risky for an opera to attempt to use any other variety. The passivity of Mimi, for example, almost wrecks *La Bohème,* and *Figaro* is, in my opinion, the least satisfactory of the great Mozart operas because its hero is too sensible; he is ingenious and practical

[1943 – 1953]   237

rather than wilful, which has the effect of making me more interested in secondary characters like the Count than in him. The Figaro of the "Barber" is more operatic because he is more of a busybody who interferes for the sake of interfering.

Whether or not you will like opera will depend, then, I think, upon how characteristic of human nature, and how important to understanding it properly, you believe wilfulness to be. If you think that, normally, emotions just happen to people and that only a few hysterics try to make them happen, or that most human conduct is dictated by the demands either of natural appetites and aversions or of reason, then you will find opera artificial and insincere. If, on the other hand, you believe that human beings are most characteristically human, as contrasted with any other creature, when they are doing something just for the hell of it, or that all men are constantly adopting some emotion and defending it with the same intense energy as that with which the characters in a Shavian play adopt and defend some point of view (incidentally, Shaw, on his own admission, learned his trade by studying opera), then all the usual objections of the opera-hater — the unromantic physical appearance of the lovers, the improbability of the plots, the suspension of critical action, while the singers get things off their chests, the palpably sham scenery, will seem to you not objections but positive advantages of the medium.

"But how true to life," you will reply, "that out of two mountains of corseted flesh should issue such difficult and wonderful expressions of undying passion; that is what any really human love always is — and what a medium like the movies, which make love seem a natural effect caused by animal beauty, conceals — a triumph of Spirit over Nature. What psychological insight to construct so many plots around one or the other of two most uniquely human acts, laying down one's life for one's friend and cutting off one's nose to spite one's face. How realistic to show that, whatever it may be in between, life at its best and at its worst is a *performance* that defies common sense."

Opera can show these aspects of life better than any other medium, for drama is already to some degree reflective literature. That is why, though *verismo* is fatal to both, it only makes drama dull but reduces opera to comic bathos; a naturalistic music drama seems much more absurd, more "artificial" than a formal opera like *Alceste* or *Così fan Tutte*.

Yes, opera is a performance like drama, only more so, and this has one unfortunate consequence. We opera-addicts are a quiet, inoffensive people until singers are discussed; then we become socially intolerable. Among our contemporaries we suddenly turn into choleric maniacs who will publicly insult a perfect stranger for daring to express an opinion that differs from our own, and among our juniors we turn into merciless bores. The fact that I have suffered acutely from the Melba and Tetrazzini generations is not for a moment going to stop me inflicting the same punishment in my turn.

I can see myself thirty years hence, when the young are raving over some new performance of *Götterdämmerung* or *Walküre* or *Don Pasquale* or *Ballo in Maschera* or *Il Trovatore*, ignoring the glazed stare on their faces as I thump the table and croak, "What do you know about opera who never heard Flagstad, Lehmann, Sayao, Milanov, Bjoerling?" And, wilful as the art I love, I shall refuse to believe that their successors are any good. I shan't even listen. Let the young, though, be patient; soon enough my senile head will droop and they will be able to escape and still arrive in time for the overture.

For we are natural beings who must eat, sleep, and forget as well as spiritual beings who are always on the go; we are the anonymous faces accidentally caught by the newsreel camera as well as the wilful hero or heroine of our private operas, and we must straddle these two worlds as best we can. If the straddle makes our lives often hard and at times horrible, at least it ensures that they are never dull.

ALFRED LUNT AND LYNN FONTANNE ARE THE STARS OF THE PLAY "O MISTRESS MINE," A ROMP AS GAY AS THIS LAUGHING PHOTOGRAPH BY CECIL BEATON

[1943 – 1953]   239

MAUGHAM EPIGRAMS

A SELECTION FROM MAJOR WORKS

W. Somerset Maugham approved this choice by Karl Pfeiffer, but pointed out that his characters said some of these things and he may not have agreed with them.

You can't expect marriage to be amusing. If it were, the law wouldn't protect it and the church wouldn't sanctify it.

People always think they could put up with the faults we haven't got. Somehow or other it's always those we have that stick in their throats.

Heroism is all very well, but at a party it's not nearly so useful as a faculty for small talk.

What exactly is one's reaction to a great work of art? What does one feel when, for instance, one looks at Titian's *Entombment* in the Louvre or listens to the quintet in the *Meistersinger*? I know what mine is. It is an excitement that gives me a sense of exhilaration, intellectual but suffused with sensuality, a feeling of well-being in which I seem to discern a sense of power and liberation from human ties: at the same time I feel in myself a tenderness which is rich with human sympathy; I feel rested, at peace and yet spiritually aloof.

To do one's duty sounds a rather cold and cheerless business, but somehow in the end it does give one a queer sort of satisfaction.

Whatever the learned say about a book, however unanimous they are in praise of it, unless it interests you it is no business of yours.

The worst of having so much tact is that you never quite know whether other people are acting naturally or being tactful, too.

I think it a pity that Christianity has laid so much stress on sin. We assert in church that we're miserable sinners, but I don't think we mean it, and what's more, I don't think we are.

A virtue which causes havoc and unhappiness is worth nothing. I call it cowardice.

It is dangerous to let the public behind the scenes. They are easily disillusioned and then they are angry with you, for it was the illusion they loved.

The good are difficult to get on with, but fortunately they're so few it's not often they seriously inconvenience the rest of us.

I wonder if it has ever occurred to the young how tiresome is their conversation to the middle-aged. Chatter, chatter, chatter about nothing at all. Just to hear yourselves speak. And you take yourselves with such appalling seriousness. You know nothing, and you haven't the sense to hold your tongues. You utter the most obvious commonplace with the air of having made a world-shaking discovery. You're so solemn. You're so self-satisfied. You're so dogmatic. You're inane. The only excuse for you is that you're very young. One tries to have patience with you. But, my God, don't think we find you amusing. We find you quite incredibly dull.

I have little sense of reverence. There is a great deal too much of it in the world. It is claimed for many objects that do not deserve it. It is often no more than the conventional homage we pay to things in which we are not willing to take an active interest.

If women were ridiculous because their husbands are unfaithful to them, there would surely be a great deal more merriment in the world than there is.

GOUACHE PAINTED BY JOAN MIRO DURING THE SOLITUDE OF THE WAR YEARS IN SPAIN

Penn
MARGARET SULLAVAN

ORSON WELLES

PORTRAITS WITH SYMBOLS

JUST IDLING ALONG

BY DAPHNE DU MAURIER

DAPHNE DU MAURIER   Coffin

The other day, on a brief visit to London, I met a woman I had not seen for many years. We discussed family and friends, and just before parting she said to me, "Tell me, when you are not actually writing a book, what exactly do you do in Cornwall? Are you frightfully busy in the country? Do you know heaps of people?"

"I never go anywhere," I answered, "and I scarcely know a soul."

"Are you very house-proud?" she said. "And a slave to the children?"

"No," I said, "the house looks after itself, and so do the children." She stared, incredulous. "Well, then — what on earth do you do?"

"Nothing," I said, "nothing at all..."

She did not believe me, but it was true. I do nothing. I hope I shall continue doing nothing to the end of my days. But the delights of monotony are not for everyone. One must have at the basis of one's character a fundamental streak of dullness, a sort of apathy to pleasure and to excitement. And few people will admit to being dull. It is the ultimate deadly sin, which I glory in with complacency. Yes, but let's get down to facts, someone will say. There are twelve hours to the normal day. How then are they filled, if nothing is accomplished?

Let us imagine a warm spring day. The sky is blue. The sun tops the trees in the garden. I am called at nine, with tea and toast, and as I rub my eyes, and stretch my arms, I remember with a feeling of zest that as usual I have no engagements before me, the day is blank, and the only mark on the white page of the monthly calendar is for the half-hour at the dentist's, Tuesday fortnight. I munch my toast with relish. The children appear to say good morning, and disappear to lessons. What a relief that the youngest is now five, and is an individual. I think back to the wartime routine. That endless pinning and unpinning of napkins, the angry baby roar, the dreary walk, come sun, come rain, up a hill with a back-breaking pram until the motion had lulled him off to sleep. The bliss of twenty minutes' silence and then — a roar — he was awake again. And after that the impossibility of settling to anything, because to take one's eyes off a toddling baby, for even a brief moment, spells disaster.

By this time I have had my bath, and am dressing, and am composing a letter to the *Times*, never published, on the subject of birth-control. The birth-rate is falling and I know why, and so do all the other women of my generation. It has nothing to do with insecurity or atom bombs or wishing to go to the movies. It is because we don't want a lot of children, and had the women of past generations known how to limit their families they would have done so.

My post arrives. A cheque from France. Enough francs to keep a family in France for six months. And the Treasury will not allow me to send one miserable centime to a dear friend in Paris who is on the verge of starva-

244   [1943 – 1953]

tion. I don't need the money. She does. And nothing can be done about it. If this is world economics, I don't understand it. I make my bed and dust the room. I wander out into the garden with a basket and a pair of secateurs, and cut camellias for my library. This, I think to myself, is what ladies of leisure did a hundred years ago, but they wore gloves and shady hats, not corduroy pants and polo jerseys. I spend twenty minutes gazing at the camellias, the soft rose petals, the waxen leaves, and I wonder which is the more trying, the woman of today who sits on brain-trusts and committees and "runs things," or her Victorian predecessor whose world was bounded by what her husband said, and whose sole relaxation was tittle-tattle.

The camellias are picked and put in vases. I fetch my saw and cut some lengths of old laurel into logs for the fire. Surely, I say to myself, the trouble with the mines is much the same as the trouble with the birth-rate. Women don't want to have babies. Men don't want to be miners. And all the pit-head baths and canteens in the world won't make them miners. The work is too hard, too rough, too ill-paid. The young men prefer to be clerks, or shopkeepers. Who then is to do the manual work of the world? I saw away at my logs and think that a little manual labour is good for everyone. But only a little.

My back is aching as I go in to lunch. Corned beef again. And boiled potatoes. Irony to receive a cable in the middle of lunch from America saying the millionth copy of my last book has just come off the press. I look down at my jumper. It is pre-war, and full of moth-holes. I have twelve coupons left in my clothing book. Enough for two jumpers, or one summer coat. I think of all the lovely goods I might buy on Fifth Avenue, and remember that not one cent can be spent across the Atlantic, but must be brought back here to be turned into pounds. And when the pounds have been taxed a few shillings will remain. Which is, no doubt, very good for one's sense of proportion but hardly a stimulant to further effort.

The corned beef has been washed down with a cup of lukewarm coffee. But the sun is shining still. I saunter out to my favourite seat that overlooks the sea. Who could wish for more than this? I don't wish to venture further than the Dodman yonder, that headland some ten miles out to sea. Does travel really broaden the mind? I wonder. Who more boring than the globe-trotter who says, "I remember when I was in Bagdad in '21"? What was I doing in '21? I was fourteen, and sick with love for the actor Basil Rathbone, who, in a gent's straw boater and grey flannel suiting, came up to Hampstead to play tennis with my father.

Do we change every seven years, or is it a fallacy? I think it is true. I see a whole procession of selves go dancing past me in the sun — the shy child, the moody adolescent, the cynical two-and-twenty, the eager-to-please young married woman, the bewildered, slightly baffled mother; and now? Ah, well, the middle years have a goodly smack about them. No more puzzling "What am I to become?" No more questing for adventure. "Wait till you come to forty years," said my father, twenty years ago, "you'll find it's not so easy then." One year to go.

My daughters run races in the field below. My son approaches, holding in his hand a minute clockwork monkey in a red jacket that lifts a large white tankard to its mouth with a stiff clockwork gesture. "Who's this?" I ask. "God," answers my son, without hesitation, as the monkey hops along the seat, drinking as it goes.

Why are the churches empty? Because, with modern warfare, hellfire holds no terror for us. And was it only fear of the hereafter that made my lady in her crinoline go to church three times of a Sunday? No, it was boredom. Church was the social function of the week, and rich and poor went gladly because there was nothing else for them to do. Also, the parson gave advice to troubled minds. Today we go to a psychoanalyst.

Will there ever be a return to organized religion? No, not as past generations knew it. The churches will be museums for the historian, and the Bible escapist literature for scholars. Only one message may survive into the Atomic Age and adapt itself to the future; the Kingdom of Heaven is within you. Perhaps this is the message that the Almighty intended should survive....

Now the sun has gone beyond the trees. Tea draws us to the house. And after tea the ritual of "reading the books."... My sister and I are changed into white frocks, and sit in the drawing room with Mummy. Security is about us. We shall never be grown-up. And in a flash I am grown-up, I am climbing the broken staircase of that same house in Regent's Park, blitzed beyond recognition, the paper torn in strips from the nursery walls, the rain seeping through the broken windows. ... What if my children return to their nursery in thirty years' time and find dust and ashes?

"Go on," urges my daughter, "what are you stopping for?"

Tonight is bath night, and by the time the children are in bed and tucked away I am ready for supper, and readier still for my glass of gin-and-lime. Supper consists of soup (from a tin) and water biscuits. Statistics prove that we are healthier for eating less, but as I swallow my soup I think of the suppers of yesteryear.

On what shall I feed my husband when he returns from Singapore? He tells me he has a dinner party every night. The problems of our time. The soldier husband who returns, not to an empty house but rather to an empty larder.

I read my *Times*, I switch on the news. No longer "Three hundred Lancasters of Bomber Command today attacked the targets of . . ." That, thank God, is over. Over for how long? We, of the middle years, have no illusions. So, off with the news, and on with a Sibelius symphony. The wood fire sinks, the music simmers in my head. A sense of well-being pervades me. This is my home. I am content. Another day has come and gone. And I have done nothing. Nothing at all.

[1943 – 1953]

MEN
OF
LETTERS

Bernice Abbott JAMES JOYCE

T. S. ELIOT Lee M

Rutledge JACQUES BARZUN JEAN-PAUL SARTRE Cecil B

JOHN P. MARQUAND Pix Inc.

ALDOUS HUXLEY G. P. Lynn

MEDITATION ON SIMPLICITY

BY RUMER GODDEN

I am not thinking of bast sandals, or of eating nuts and apples and raw oats; or of spinning wheels, and homespun clothes and digging and candlelight.

I, personally, like all these, except the oats, but one of the dangerous things about simplicity is that it can mean artlessness, credulity, silliness, folly, and posing — and it often does. I want to think of it together with freedom and power, the two wings of living.

When anyone has anything really important to do, all other considerations have to give way before it, otherwise it will not be done; a thread of singleness immediately comes into the day — and singleness is one of the meanings of simplicity. A degree of singleness is necessary or we will not do what we can, because each person, like the horse or like the engine, has only a degree of power.

> ". . . late and soon,
> Getting and spending we lay waste our powers."

Life at Alfoxden, at Grasmere, in Dove Cottage, flowed evenly, but it was life. William's, of course, was conditioned by poetry: "William added a little to his ode"; "William tired himself out with hammering at a passage"; "In the evening William began to write 'The Tinker'"; it is not of William I am thinking, but of his sister, Dorothy.

Dorothy Wordsworth had the quality of simplicity and she escaped its danger; she was not artless, she was an artist; she was not credulous, she was a thinker and questioner; she was not silly or given to folly, she had all her five native wits; she ordered her life well and, for a woman of her time, it was a life that was remarkably and startlingly full.

As far as I know, she wrote only one poem herself, but much of William came out of Dorothy. She made infinite time for him; walking, reading, copying, travelling abroad, listening, writing, and yet she had time for all the doings of his household and their relations; for friendships with Coleridge, Southey, De Quincey, the Lambs, Scott, Shelley; time to know vividly the peasant life of Westmorland; time to see the details of flowers and trees, birds and beasts, mountains and lakes; to see the changes of the season and the progress of the years; time for everything, for the whole of life.

In my copy of her journal the editor says, in his introduction, "There is no need to record all the cases in which the sister wrote, 'Today I mended William's shirts,' 'William gathered sticks,' or 'I went in search of eggs.'" For me there is. I want to know how much power she spent, late and soon, how much she had left, how she arranged it as well as she did, because I, too, in my modern equivalent have to mend shirts, fetch sticks, find eggs.

I think her secret is that she did all she did in the most straightforward way possible, plainly, without complication, with no excess of adornment, which are other meanings of simplicity. Whether it was a walking tour in Scotland with a visit to Lasswade and Sir Walter Scott; or going to France to see William's ex-mistress and bastard child; or sowing scarlet beans and shelling peas; or copying a poem, it was all done with the same straightforward calmness.

This was not a pose, it was necessity; she was too busy living to be anyone but herself, and sincerity is the last, and deepest, meaning of simplicity.

In Roman days, pottery, when it came from the kiln blemished, had wax sealed into its cracks. A flawless piece was sold in the shops "*sine cera,*" without wax. It is sometimes said that our word "sincere" comes from that. When rung, it gives out a whole true note, William's note; Dorothy had that same straightforward truth. It is powerful and free and it has beauty:

". . . villages enbosomed in the trees."

". . . purple waves, brighter than precious stones, melting away on the sands."

". . . after tea, we walked upon our own path . . . we talked sweetly together about the disposal of our riches. The sky to the North was of a chastened yet rich yellow . . . fading into pale blue . . . with steady islands of purple . . . it was like a vision to me."

Yes. Simplicity leaves time for vision. Life can spread its wings.

This part of Dorothy's journal ends on the evening before she and William went to fetch William's bride, for a marriage that was to break the complete intimacy of brother and sister. It must have been sad for Dorothy, but she met it simply.

She writes, "The hour is come. I must prepare to go. I must leave them, the swallows, the garden, roses, all. Well. I must go. Farewell."

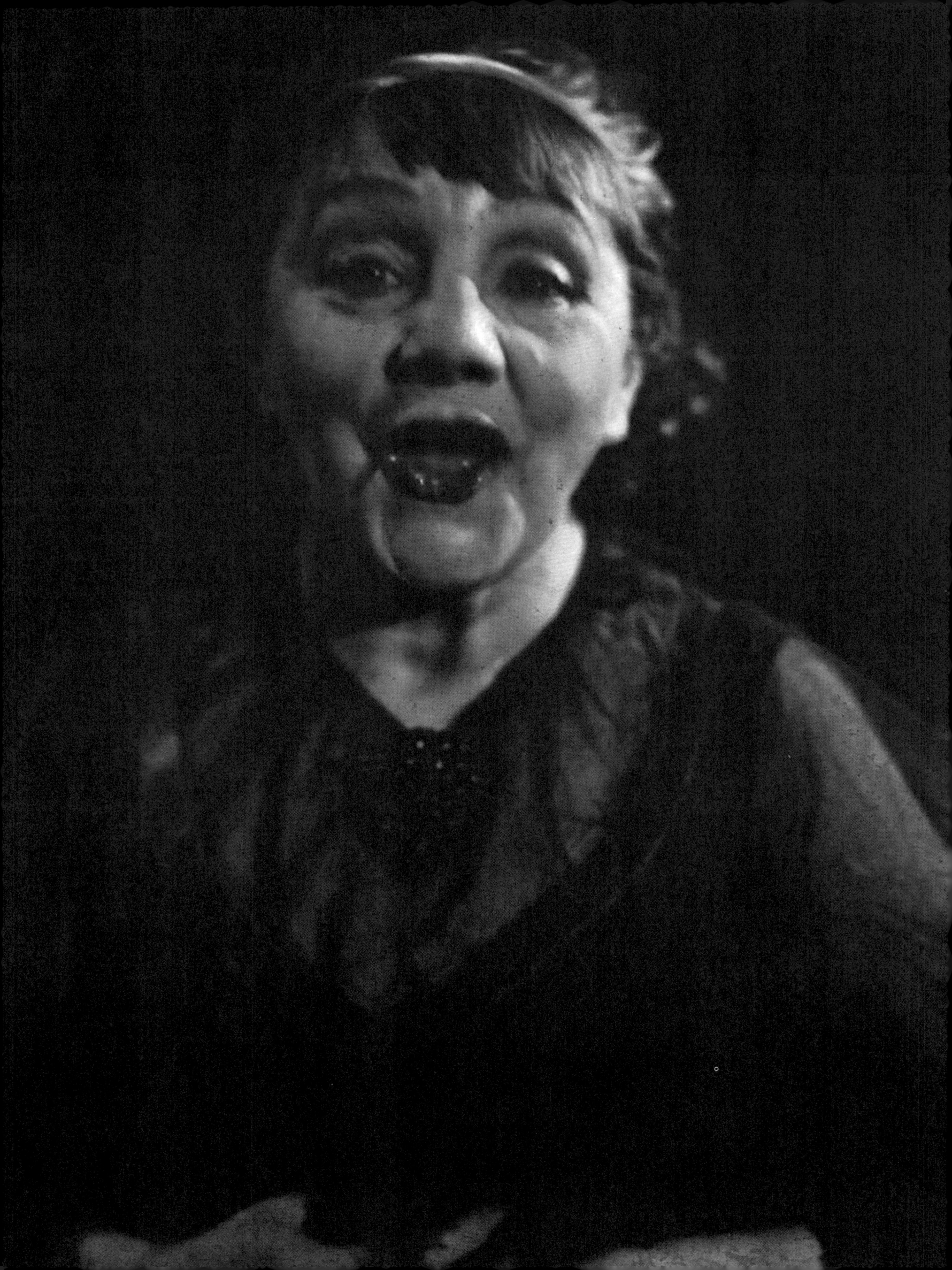

THREE DRAMAS
WITH FAMILIAR AMERICAN SETTINGS

In *The Glass Menagerie* (1945) Laurette Taylor was the star of the year in Tennessee Williams' first full-length play in New York — a distinguished, hard-hitting play that weaves in and out of tragic sensibility, a play that is a man's memory of his mother and sister in a St. Louis flat that is like a dark trap.

Below: *The Heiress*. The notable drama of 1947, with its Henry James origin and Washington Square setting, tells the story of a father who, in saving his daughter from a ne'er-do-well, succeeds in breaking her heart. Miss Hiller played with enormous range against Mr. Rathbone's father, cool, unforgivingly protective.

Right: *Death of a Salesman*, Arthur Miller's harrowing, nervous, cumulatively disturbing plea against pipe dreams, is the most powerful non-historical drama of 1949. It has the force of Mr. Miller's writing, distinguished acting, screw-tight direction by Elia Kazan, and Jo Mielziner's emotional, skeletonized set — a house in Brooklyn with lowering apartments pushing in.

LEE J. COBB, MILDRED DUNNOCK, AND ARTHUR KENNEDY IN "DEATH OF A SALESMAN"
Beaton

BASIL RATHBONE AND WENDY HILLER IN "THE HEIRESS"
Blumenfeld

OPPOSITE: LAURETTE TAYLOR IN "THE GLASS MENAGERIE"
Blumenfeld

[1943 – 1953]   249

MAN'S BURDEN

THEME WITH SLIGHT VARIATIONS, BY STEINBERG, AN ARTIST GENTLY LETHAL

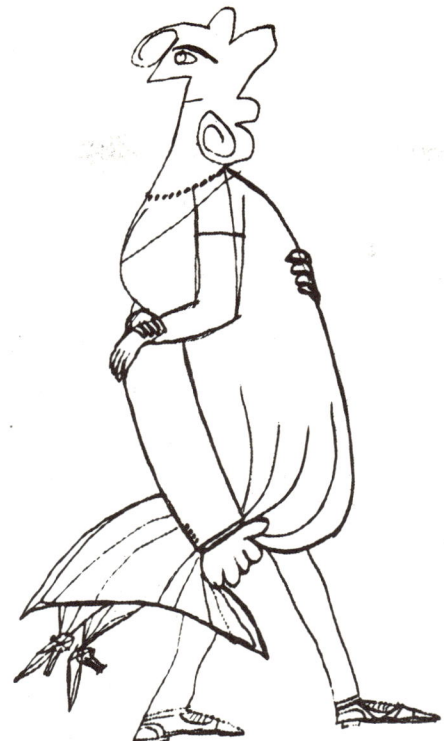

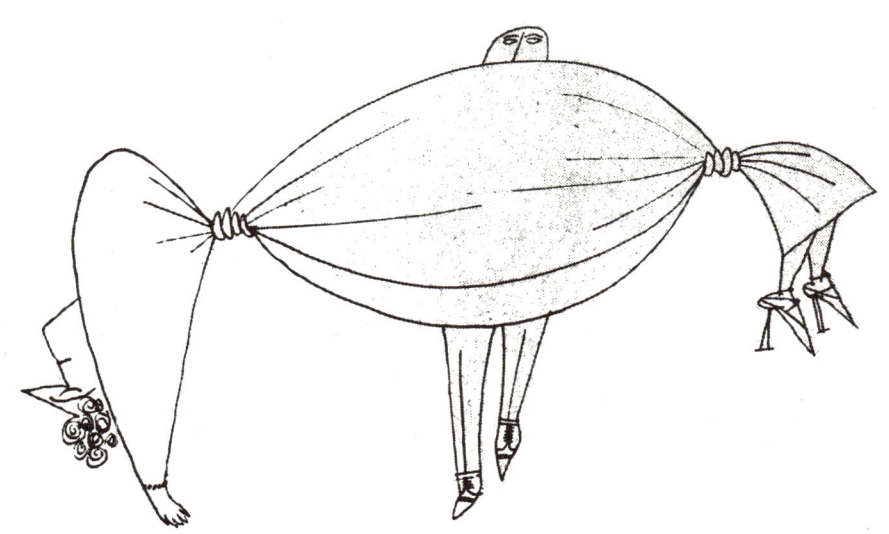

[1943 – 1953]

FOOD, ARTISTS, AND THE BARONESS

BY ALICE B. TOKLAS

What is the first food you remember, remember seeing it if not eating it? The first food — after breakfast foods which in my early childhood in the late seventies were cracked wheat with sugar and cream, corn meal with molasses, and farina with honey. Well, the first food that I saw and remember was soufflé fritters, which of course were not included in a diet prescribed for a child. Nora was my mother's cook and she fortunately stayed on long enough for me to taste her fritters.

Before coming to live in Paris I was interested in food but not in doing any cooking. When in 1909 I went to live with Gertrude Stein at the Rue de Fleurus she said we would have American food for Sunday evening suppers; she had had enough French and Italian cooking, the servant would be out and I would have the kitchen to myself. So I commenced to cook the simple dishes I had eaten in the homes of the San Joaquin Valley, fricasséed chicken, corn bread, apple and lemon pie. Then when the pie crust received Gertrude Stein's critical approval I made mincemeat and at Thanksgiving we had a turkey that Hélène, the cook, roasted but for which I prepared the dressing. Gertrude Stein not being able to decide whether she preferred mushrooms, chestnuts, or oysters in the dressing, all three were included.

Once when Picasso was coming to lunch I decorated a fish in a way that I thought would amuse him. I chose a fine striped bass and cooked it according to a theory of my grandmother, who had no experience in cooking and who rarely saw her kitchen but who had endless theories about cooking, as well as about many other things. She contended that a fish, having lived its life in water, once caught should have no further contact with the element in which it had been born and raised. She recommended that it be roasted or poached in wine or butter, or cream. So I made a court bouillon of dry white wine with whole peppers, salt, a laurel leaf, a sprig of thyme, a blade of mace, an onion with a clove stuck in it, a carrot, a leek, and a bouquet of *fines herbes*. This was gently boiled for half an hour and then put aside to cool, until it was put in the fish kettle and the fish was then placed on the rack, the kettle, covered, placed on the fire and slowly brought to boil, and poached for twenty minutes (for a fish weighing four pounds). Taken from the fire it was left to cool in the court bouillon. It was then carefully drained, dried, and placed on the fish platter. A short time before serving I covered the fish with an ordinary mayonnaise, and, with a pastry bag, decorated it with a red mayonnaise, not made with catsup, horror of horrors, but with concentrated tomato juice. Then I made a design with sieved hard-boiled eggs, the whites and the yolks apart, with truffles and with finely chopped *fines herbes*. I was proud of my *chef-d'oeuvre* when it was served and Picasso exclaimed at its beauty. "But," said he, "should it not rather have been made in honour of Matisse than of me?"

Picasso was for many years on a strict diet, in fact he managed somehow to continue it all through the war and the occupation and characteristically only relaxed after the liberation. Red meat was proscribed but that presented no difficulties for in those days beef was rarely served by the French except the inevitable roast filet of beef with *sauce Madère*. Chicken, too, was not well considered, a roast leg of mutton was viewed with more favour. We would have a tenderloin of veal preceded by a spinach soufflé, spinach having been highly recommended by Picasso's doctor and a soufflé being the least objectionable way of preparing it. But could it not be made more interesting by adding a sauce? But what sauce would Picasso's diet permit? I would give him a choice. The soufflé would be cooked in a well-buttered mould placed in boiling water and when sufficiently cooked, turned into a hollow dish around which, in equal divisions, would be placed a Hollandaise sauce, a cream sauce, and a tomato sauce. It was my hope that the sauces would make the spinach soufflé look less nourishing. "Cruel enigma," said Picasso when the soufflé was served to him.

When the Germans in '40 were advancing we had no precise information concerning their progress through France. Could one believe the radio? We didn't. We heard cannon fire. Then it grew louder. The next morning, dressing at the window I saw not more than two miles away, and quite low, German planes firing on French planes. This decided me to act in the way I felt any forethoughted housekeeper should act.

We would take the car into Belley and make provision for any eventuality as I had done in San Francisco that April morning of '07 when the fire had commenced. Then I had been able to secure two hams and my father had brought back four hundred cigarettes. With these one could, he said, not only exist but one could be hospitable. So at Belley we bought two hams and hundreds of cigarettes and some groceries. The garden at Bilignin would provide fruit and vegetables. The main road was filled with refugees, just as it had been in '14 and '17. Everything that was happening had already been experienced, a half awakening from a nightmare. The firing grew louder and the first armoured cars flew past. Crushed, we took the little dust road back to Bilignin.

The widow Roux, who had been for many summers our devoted servant and later during the occupation proved to be our loyal friend, opened the big iron gates to let the car through, and we unloaded the provisions. What were we to do with the two enormous uncooked hams? In what could we boil them so that they would keep indefinitely? We decided upon *eau de vie de marc* for which, throughout France, the Bugey is famous. It seemed madly extravagant but we lived on those two hams during the long, lean winter that followed and well into the spring and the *eau de vie de marc* in which they were cooked, carefully bottled and corked, toned up winter vegetables. One throws nothing, but absolutely *nothing,* away, living through a war in an occupied country.

The Baronne Pierlot was our neighbour, châtelaine at Béon, some ten miles away. One day, before the war we had drvien over to a *goûter* to which she had bidden us. It was being served in the summer dining room whose windows and door gave on a vast terrace. In the foreground was the marsh of the Rhône lately reclaimed by the planting of Lombardy poplars, to the south the mountains of the Grande Chartreuse, to the left in the distance the French Alps, and above it all the Tiepolo blue sky. The table in the dining-room, set for twenty or more, was elaborately decorated with pink roses. Madame Pierlot's observant eye passed quickly and lightly over each object on the table. I heard her tell the *valet de chambre* to ask the cook for the *pièce de résistance* and to place it in the centre of the table.

But Marc did not leave the room, he merely took a cake from the serving table and put it in the empty space. There was evidently a contretemps. I was enlightened when I caught knowing looks passing between Gertrude Stein and one of the daughters-in-law of the house. It was Gertrude Stein's white poodle, Basket, a very neat thief, who had done away with whatever had been in the centre of the table. Later when Madame Pierlot, to show that she had forgiven the dog, threw him a piece of cake we could not protest that it was against our principles to reward a misdeed.

Madame Pierlot told me that when she had engaged her cook Perrine she had asked her if she knew how to prepare several complicated dishes which she mentioned. She saw that Perrine had had a large experience. "As she was well recommended, I decided," Madame Pierlot told me, "to engage her, but I told her that it was on the condition that she would forget everything she knew and follow the recipes and instructions I would give her."

Our enchanting old friend was as original in her housekeeping as in everything else. Long ago the *Figaro* which was then the newspaper read by the fashionable world asked well-known society women to contribute a recipe which they were to print in a special column. When Madame Pierlot was asked to be one of them she sent the recipe for *gigot de la clinique*. A surgeon living in the province, as fond of good cheer as he was learned, invented this recipe, which we acquired by bribing his cook. No leg of venison can compare with a simple leg of mutton prepared in the following manner.

GIGOT DE LA CLINIQUE

Eight days in advance you will cover the leg of mutton with the marinade called Samaritan Balm, composed of wine and oil: old Burgundy, Beaune, or Chambertin; and virgin olive oil. Into this balm add salt, pepper, bay leaf, thyme, beside an atom of ginger root, a pinch of cayenne, a nutmeg cut in small pieces, a handful of crushed juniper berries, and lastly a dessert spoonful of powdered sugar (effective as musk in perfumery) which serves to fix the different aromas. Twice a day you will turn the gigot. Now we come to the main point of the preparation. After you have placed the gigot in the marinade, arm yourself with a surgical syringe, holding half a pint, which you fill with half a cupful of cognac and half a cupful of orange juice. Inject the contents of the syringe into the fleshy part of the gigot in three different spots. Refill the syringe with the same contents and inject into the gigot twice more. Note: each day you will fill the syringe with the marinade and inject its contents into the gigot. This you will repeat twice. At the end of the week the leg of mutton is ready to be roasted; perfumed with the condiments and spices, completely permeated by the various flavours, it has been transformed into a strange and exquisite venison. Roast and serve with the usual venison sauce to which has been added, just before serving, two tablespoonfuls of the blood of a hare.

Everyone thought that the syringe was a whimsy, that Madame Pierlot was making mock of them. Not at all. Years later I found it in the great collection of French recipes, Bertrand Guegain's *Le Cuisinier Français*. The Baronne Pierlot's recipe is classical, it has entered into the Grande Cuisine Française.

[1943 – 1953]

FAMOUS MODELS

The most photographed fashion models of the decade posed for this group picture by Penn. They are:

1. MEG MUNDY
2. MARILYN AMBROSE
3. HELEN BENNETT
4. DANA JENNEY
5. BETTY MC LAUCHLEN
6. LISA FONSSAGRIVES
7. LILY CARLSON
8. ELIZABETH GIBBONS
9. MURIEL MAXWELL
10. KAY HERNAN
11. ANDREA JOHNSON
12. DORIAN LEIGH

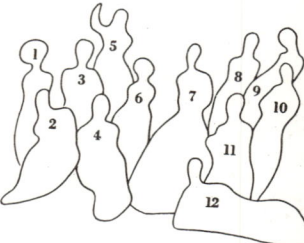

254   [1943 – 1953]

MY GRANDMOTHER AND MR. GLADSTONE

BY BERTRAND RUSSELL

My childhood and early youth were dominated by my two grandmothers, Lady Russell and Lady Stanley. Lady Russell, in whose house I lived, was Scotch, gentle and shy, but inflexible when a moral principle seemed to be involved. She had lived all her life in the great world — her grandfather was Governor General of India, her father was an Ambassador, her husband was twice Prime Minister. Nevertheless, she remained completely unworldly; she became a Unitarian at the age of seventy, and would have been glad if I had entered the Unitarian ministry.

She was the epitome of Puritan courage and Victorian propriety. She decided all political questions on the loftiest moral principles, without regard to political expediency. Often her influence caused my grandfather to change his opinions, so that his colleagues called her "deadly nightshade." She spoke always in a low voice; she was easily pained, but never angry. It was not she, but my other grandmother, whom I found alarming.

My other grandmother, Lady Stanley, whom I saw only occasionally, was a complete contrast, at once baffling and frightening to my young mind. Whereas my Grandmother Russell was dark and short and thin, my Grandmother Stanley was fair and tall and fat. Her family, the Dillons, had been Irish Jacobites, and had fled to the Court of the King of France after the battle of the Boyne.

It was French policy to make much of the Jacobites, and the Dillons rose to eminence in France; they even had a proprietary regiment in the French Army. During the French Revolution, however, they were proscribed along with other aristocrats, and had to fly once more. But this flight was less painful than the former. The head of the family, after consulting Louis XV, had become Protestant in order to be able to hold the family estates in Ireland, remarking that if anyone found fault with him, he would say he had followed the advice of the Most Christian King.

My grandmother was brought up in Florence, where she visited once a week the widow of Bonnie Prince Charlie (the young Pretender who, it will be remembered, flourished in 1745). My grandmother belonged mentally rather to the eighteenth century than to the nineteenth, but to the eighteenth century of the Enlightenment. She was intensely nationalistic, with a contempt for "nonsense"; on her birthday she always had a dinner-party of thirteen, and made the most superstitious of the guests go out first.

When she was eighty, she still read popular science, such as Huxley and Tyndall, in bed for two hours every night. She promoted the cause of women's education, and was one of the founders of Girton College at Cambridge. But most reform movements seemed to her silly, and for silliness she had no faintest vestige of toleration.

When I first knew her, she was already a widow; I never saw her without the widow's cap, which in those days was customary. It was said that her husband who, on account of his sharp tongue, was generally known as Sir Benjamin Backbite, had oppressed her; I found this incredible, but from letters recently published I have learned that it was true, although to me she had seemed a woman whom nobody could oppress. She was clever, caustic, and contemptuous.

In her vast drawing-room at 40 Dover Street (now the Arts Club), immovable in an enormous armchair, she used to receive guests at tea-time. All the leading literary men of the time used to come, sitting in a circle and carrying on a general conversation, in the hope (often vain) of escaping an assault of withering criticism from her tongue. When one of them went away, she would sigh and remark, "Fools are so fatiguin'."

I was appallingly shy, and she did nothing to make me less so. On one occasion, before a room full of distinguished guests, she put to me a series of scientific questions. When it appeared that I did not know the answers, she turned to the company and remarked sadly, "I have no intelligent grandchildren." I did not venture until many years later to doubt the truth of this verdict.

As a child, I was always filled with trepidation when I was taken to visit

---

CLARK GABLE is probably the world's most famous male screen star. At forty-eight he puts up with no nonsense about his age. He is exactly what he is — middle-aged, solid, with definite crow's feet — and audiences respond happily to his rogue male magic, and call him simply "the King."
Ernest F. Stein

her. The only mitigation was that the food was much better than at home. She thought me too goody-goody, and set to work to make me less of a prig; the only time I ever pleased her was when I asked for *Tristram Shandy* as a birthday present. (Perhaps, if she were alive now, she would regret her success.)

She used to say, "No one could say anything against me, but I always think it is not so bad to break the Seventh Commandment as the Sixth, because at any rate it requires the consent of the other party." On one occasion when she had a new doctor, she wrote out her complete medical history, including her very numerous confinements and some miscarriages and read it to the assembled company (of whom I was one), to obtain their opinion as to whether anything was omitted. Everybody feared her, and she feared nobody, with one single exception: and that was Mr. Gladstone.

To those who only know of Mr. Gladstone from books, his career must appear unintelligible. In books he seems a sanctimonious humbug, to whose authority people submitted for no discoverable reason. In real life he was different. His hawk's eye was terrible as an army in battle, his deep bass voice inspired awe, and his rounded, inexorable periods produced a sense of doom. It is said that once, at a large public meeting, he was disturbed by a drunken man, no doubt introduced by his political opponents in the hope of putting him off his stride. At first he paid no attention; then he fixed his eye upon the man, and pronounced these awful words: "May I request that gentleman, who has not once, but repeatedly, interrupted the flow of my remarks, to extend to me that large measure of courtesy which, were I in his place and he in mine, I should most unhesitatingly extend to him." The drunken man became sober, and spoke no more.

My two grandmothers differed as to Mr. Gladstone's Irish policy. Lady Russell supported Home Rule; Lady Stanley (the formidable one) opposed it. I remember an occasion when I was staying at Dover Street, and it was announced that Mr. Gladstone was coming to tea. My grandmother told us in considerable detail how she was going to put him in his place about the folly of making friends with the Irish; it appeared, in fact, that she was going to give him an elementary lesson in the art of politics. I looked forward to the occasion with pleasurable tremors.

At last the great man arrived. I was present, as a silent spectator, throughout his visit, but not one word did my grandmother utter of the marvellous speeches she had led us to expect. Instead, she was all honey and sweetness, as submissive as a young girl while he laid down the law in mellifluous sentences of involved but faultless syntax. From this moment I was persuaded he was indeed a great man.

I had not always the good fortune to be a mere inactive onlooker in his presence. When I was seventeen, and had just acquired my first evening clothes, he came for the week-end to visit my other grandmother, Lady Russell. When my grandfather was Prime Minister, Mr. Gladstone had served under him; to my grandmother, his visit was nothing out of the ordinary. She invited no one to meet him, and after dinner, when she and her unmarried daughter retired, I was left tête-à-tête with him to play host while he sipped his port. I can see the scene still in my mind's eye as vividly as if it were yesterday.

We lived in a house in Richmond Park, given to my grandparents for their lives by Queen Victoria. The dining-room had an odd wallpaper, representing trelliswork and landscapes adorned with birds of various imaginary species. Two vast, ornate edifices of Dresden china (a present from the King of Saxony) were posed on two cabinets that stood against the wall. The middle of the room was occupied by the large, round dinner-table, in one small sector of which Mr. Gladstone and I sat, while I prayed that the earth would open and swallow me up.

I knew it was my duty as host to make conversation, but try as I would no remark occurred to me. Nor did he do anything to make things better. After a silence which to me was agonizing, his great voice boomed out one sentence: "This is very good port they've given me, but why have they given it me in a claret glass?" I had not the vaguest idea of the difference between a port glass and a claret glass, and I could only stammer out a few incoherent noises.

Since that awful moment, I have felt that nothing equally terrifying could ever happen to me again. I have known six subsequent Prime Ministers, but none of them inspired me with awe; I have conversed tête-à-tête with Lenin, and felt him a mere mortal. But if hereafter I should meet Mr. Gladstone in the Elysian Fields, I should become once more the frightened, tongue-tied boy of that evening fifty-four years ago. Is the breed of great men extinct, or have I lost the faculty of new reverence? I do not know.

MARY MARTIN is the "cockeyed optimist" of *South Pacific*. As Knucklehead Nellie the Navy Nurse, she is fresh, gay, comic and unself-conscious. This new Rodgers and Hammerstein musical, based on James A. Michener's *Tales of the South Pacific*, has bawdy roughness, wisdom and fun, at least ten superb songs, and more comedy and love than usual.

Blumenfeld

NEW YORK

BY TRUMAN CAPOTE

It is a myth, the city, the rooms and windows, the steam-spitting streets; for anyone, everyone, a different myth, an idol-head with traffic-light eyes winking a tender green, a cynical red. This island, floating in river water like a diamond iceberg, call it New York, name it whatever you like; the name hardly matters because, entering from the greater reality of elsewhere, one is only in search of a city, a place to hide, to lose or discover oneself, to make a dream wherein you prove that perhaps after all you are not an ugly duckling, but wonderful and worthy of love, as you thought sitting on the stoop where the Fords went by; as you thought planning your search for a city.

Have seen Garbo twice in the last week, once at the theatre, where she sat in the next seat, and again at a Third Avenue antique shop. When I was twelve I had a tiresome series of mishaps, and so stayed a good deal in bed, spending most of my time in the writing of a play that was to star the most beautiful woman in the world, which is how I described Miss Garbo in the letter accompanying my script. But neither play nor letter was ever acknowledged, and for a long time I bore a desperate grudge, one which was indeed not dispelled until the other night when, with an absolute turning over of the heart, I identified the woman in the adjoining seat. It was surprising to find her so small, and so vividly coloured; as Loren MacIver pointed out, along with those lines one scarcely expects colour, too.

Lunch today with M. Whatever is one to do about her? She says the money is gone finally and, unless she goes home, her family refuse absolutely to help. Cruel, I suppose, but I told her I did not see the alternative. She belongs to that sect most swiftly, irrevocably trapped by New York, the talented untalented; too acute to accept a more provincial climate, yet not quite acute enough to breathe freely within the one so desired, they go along neurotically feeding upon the fringes of the New York scene.

Only success, and that at a perilous peak, can give relief, but, for artists without an art, it is always tension without release, irritation with no resulting pearl. They feel compelled to prove something, because middle-class America, from which they mostly spring, has withering words for its men of feeling, for its young of experimental intelligence, who do not show immediately that these endeavours pay off on a cash basis. But if a civilization falls, is it cash the inheritors find among the ruins? Or is it a statue, a poem, a play?

Down the street there is a radio-repair shop run by an elderly Italian, Joe Vitale. Early in the summer there appeared across the front of his store a strange sign: "The Black Wido." And in smaller lettering: "Watch This Window for News of the Black Wido." So our neighbourhood wondered, waited. A few days later two yellowed photographs were added to the display; these, taken some twenty years before, showed Mr. Vitale as a husky man dressed in a black, knee-length bathing-suit, a black swimming-cap, and a mask. Typed captions below the pictures explained that Joe Vitale, whom we'd all known only as a stoop-shouldered radio-repair man, had once been, in a more supreme incarnation, a champion swimmer and a lifeguard at Rockaway Beach.

We were warned to continue watching the windows; our reward came the following week. In a bold streamer Mr. Vitale announced that the Black Wido was about to resume his career. There was a poem in the window, and the poem was called "The Dream of Joe Vitale"; it told of how he'd dreamed of again breasting the waves, conquering the sea. It was an invitation, really, one which said we were all welcome to come to Rockaway on August 20, for this day he planned to swim from that beach to Jones Beach, a far piece.

Then one morning the world woke up and laughed at the dream of Joe Vitale. His story was in every paper, the tabloids put his picture on the front pages, standing on the beach at Rockaway with policemen on either side. The lifeguards had seen him out swimming too far; they put to their boats and brought him to shore.

The proper thing to do would be to go and tell Joe Vitale how sorry you are, how brave you think him, and say, well, whatever you can; the death of a dream is no less sad than death, and, indeed, demands of those who have lost as deep a mourning. But his radio store is closed; it has been for a long time; there is no sign of him anywhere, and his form has slipped from place, has fallen beyond view.

H.H. THE MAHARAJA OF JAIPUR. ONE OF THE DAZZLING PICTURES IN COLOR TAKEN BY CONSTANTIN JOFFE ON A RECENT TRIP TO INDIA

[1943 – 1953] · 261

ITALIAN FILMS
BY RICHARD WINNINGTON

"THE BICYCLE THIEF," DIRECTED BY VITTORIO DE SICA

It is in the nature of the cinema that its source of inspiration should have shifted from country to country. Hollywood, Germany, Russia, Britain, France have in turn held custodianship. And it is clear that the cinema has best flourished when it has not been at the mercy of an organized and streamlined industry; when in fact there have been elements of financial uncertainty. Thus before the war, when the French screen dominated the world, Renoir, Carné, Prévert, Vigo, and the others made their films from hand to mouth, insecure, insolvent, but artistically fulfilled. And the British documentary school was made up of probably the worst-paid film outfits in the world who were the masters of their genre.

But in Italy other factors besides poverty and insecurity have aided the maturing of such men as de Sica, Rossellini, and Lattuada. There was the "friendly" occupation, utterly repressive to men of their temperaments; there was the war itself; there were the preceding restrictions of the Fascist regime; there were political chaos and a terrible heart-rending poverty. And there were few facilities for making films.

Yet, with begged and borrowed equipment, boiling over with the suppressions of years, they made films which announced Italy as the new centre of the cinema. *Shoe-Shine* (de Sica), *Open City* and *The Miracle* (Rossellini), *Without Pity* (Lattuada) dazzlingly succeeded, as the actress Valentina Cortese put it, in "taking life by surprise."

OPPOSITE: "THE MIRACLE," PRODUCED AND DIRECTED BY ROBERTO ROSSELLINI, STARRING ANNA MAGNANI

THE BEST OF TALK

BY JEAN COCTEAU

Jean Cocteau has had a long and spectacular run as a kind of international battery, charging up ideas in plays, poetry, music, films, ballets, stage decor. He has had published almost forty volumes of poetry, eight novels, and seven volumes of drawings; has had produced seventeen plays and ballets, and ten films.

It has often been said that to miss my conversation is to miss a large part of my work. Nothing could be less exact. It is through conversation that a man is stimulated to think quickly and to write. Conversation is often the contrary of an exchange. Certain persons (I should say the vibrations certain persons throw out) stimulate you. Then occurs what Baudelaire expressed amusingly the first time he met Victor Hugo in Belgium: "He plunges," he said "into one of those monologues which he calls conversation." That is a tribute to Baudelaire. I imagine that it was enough to find oneself in his presence for all one's intellectual faculties to start scintillating.

I have known few people whose conversation dazzled me. I can only remember that of two which was really astonishing, and they were poles apart — the Comtesse Anna de Noailles and Marcel Proust. Anna de Noailles was a virtuoso of conversation. She was invited to be listened to.

I was at that time very young.

I was to know Madame Simone before I knew the Comtesse de Noailles, which was logical. No one could better prepare my meeting with the poet than the actress who had served her so well and recited her poems. Besides, Simone shared with the Comtesse the privilege of the spoken word. In a warm clear voice, hurrying the delivery or dragging out certain consonants, precise as a sewing machine, and deep as a viola, the great interpreter of Bernstein's works excelled in narrating, describing, in making one see what she had seen. She possessed, like all those who know how to see, and whose listeners think they are embroidering, the genius of exactitude, so dear to all really imaginative people. You will hear it said that Madame de Noailles never listened. That is false. She and Simone were marvelous listeners. They handled divinely that royal politeness of the ear. Always prepared to take up the song again and the pyrotechnics, why should they bother to rehearse them mentally while their partner is talking? They could be all ears, the Comtesse affecting deafness, with her hand as an ear trumpet lifting her black hair, Simone punctuating her silences with "No? — Impossible! — It can't be true!" that broke into your recital, encouraging you and furnishing the proof of a sustained attention.

The beauty of the Comtesse de Noailles, of this little person, the charm of the timbre of her voice at the service of an extraordinarily droll descriptive gift, overcame everything else, and I understood, once and for all, that all those snifflings, tossings, crossings, those pauses, those little open hands shot out as from a sling, all those gestures scattering veils, scarfs, necklaces, Arab rosaries, muffs, handkerchiefs, Tom-Thumb umbrellas, belts, and safety pins, constituted her stage setting, her mechanism and, in a way, the props belonging to her act.

I confess that when I felt developing one of those friendships that goes beyond the grave, I began taking every imaginable precaution. At table she wanted the guests to listen to her and to be silent. I have already quoted Baudelaire's remark: "Hugo plunges into one of those monologues he calls a conversation." The Comtesse, even before going to table, would seize upon such a conversation and never let it go. With her right hand she held her glass, with her left she made a sign for the others not to interrupt her. And she was obeyed. Hostesses "offered" her, repeating, "Oh, that Anna, she is marvellous! Simply marvellous!"

The Comtesse talked on and on. From her chambermaid to George Sand, from her valet to Shakespeare, she juggled, she walked the tightrope, swung from trapeze to trapeze, performed sleight-of-hand tricks. Let us admit, and this is where my precautions began, that she sometimes cheated; the weights she lifted were only cardboard, sometimes she lost her balance. Some people would notice this, some laughed at her behind her back, others suffered. I was one of the latter, I felt sorry for her, I could see her getting embroiled, floundering, going off at a tangent. Anything rather than to have recourse to silence! A sort of speech madness, a verbal vertigo prevented her from being conscious of her lapses. After several experiences of this kind I decided never to meet her in public, to see her only alone.

And yet ... and yet! Since I am letting myself go, and I prove my fraternal affection in refusing to follow the detestable practice of incense burning which does so much harm when the incense burner is swung too vigorously, let me recall one profoundly successful evening. It was at the Princesse de Polignac's. I liked the Princesse; I liked her sly way of handing down irrevocable verdicts, accompanying these verdicts with a little smile half hidden in her tulle, while she swung her head with the movement of a malicious young elephant; I liked her magnificent profile like a cliff worn by the sea. ... It was probably to the fact that it was the end of the evening that we owed the good fortune of an Anna de Noailles in full possession of her gifts.

The evening was almost over. On the pale *Savonnerie* carpet the musicians' stands and the listeners' chairs were left stranded in disorder. All at once, among the musical wreckage, I caught sight of the Comtesse de Noailles seated in the midst of a circle of ladies. She was engaged in the most singular exercises. Before a nightingale begins his song, he practices. He croaks and caws and bellows and squeaks, and anyone standing at the foot of the nocturnal tree, who is not familiar with his methods, is amazed. The Comtesse went through the same prelude. I watched her from a distance. She sniffled, she sneezed, she burst out laughing, she sighed as though her heart would break, she dropped her Turkish rosaries and scarfs. She took a deep breath and then, swiftly working her lips in and out, she began.

What did she talk about? I no longer remember. I know that she talked, talked, talked, and that a great crowd gradually filled the vast room, and that the young people sat on the floor and the older ones on chairs in a circle around her. I know that the Princesse de Polignac and the Princesse de Caraman-Chimay (her friend and sister), standing at the right and at the left, seemed like the acolytes in a prize ring. I know that the footmen in black and the powdered valets in knee-breeches approached through the half-open doorways. I know that through the June windows, like the waltz in the Lubitsch film or as in the film where Liszt played, the words of the Comtesse bewitched the trees, the flowers, the stars — that they penetrated the neighbouring apartment houses causing quarrels to cease, embellishing the sleepers, and that everything, from the star to the tree and from the tree to the chauffeurs of the waiting limousines, murmured, "The Comtesse is talking ... the Comtesse is talking ... the Comtesse is talking ..."

It is glory that she idolizes. Glory, her *idée fixe!* "You admire only failures!" she reproaches me. In vain I show her that the privilege of France is precisely to possess secret glories, illustrious men whose existence the crowd does not suspect. Rimbaud, barely. Verlaine, scarcely more. But Hugo! Glory is the number of squares, streets, and avenues. For the Comtesse the proof of God's existence would be His celebrity, Rome, and the number of His temples. "Anna," I say to her, "you would like to be your bust in your own lifetime, but with legs to run about everywhere." Our disputes always ended by my flight. I would leave the table. The Princesse de Polignac remembers having gone to look for me and found me with Anne-Jules, the Comtesse's son, playing checkers. One evening (the dispute was caused by my letter to Jacques Maritain) the Comtesse in her long nightgown, brandishing a chair, chased me to the landing. She leaned over the stairs holding on to the banisters and cried, "Besides, you know, if God existed, I should be the first to be informed!"

At the window of the room of the chintzes, a box of hyacinths was an obstacle the Comtesse never jumped over. I believe that (except when she was smelling Amphion's heliotrope) she imagined gardens, corollas, the hairy bumblebee like the eye of a Persian princess, through the box of hyacinths, through those perfumed sentinels watching, erect, over her light and scant repose. She slept badly, she stuffed herself with soporifics, suffered and rarely spoke of her sufferings. She was considered a hypochondriac. Marcel Proust too was regarded as a *malade imaginaire*. To say "I am dead" instead of "I am tired," that is imagination. Poets, imaginary invalids. And they die. What a surprise! How shocking! They thought we were made of steel.

Anna received a thousand doctors. She never wanted them to treat her. She wanted to treat the doctors. ...

She is dead. Life is dead. She is dead, the one of whom Maurice Barrès said, "This is the most sensitive point of the universe."

When I am dead, I shall go to see Anna de Noailles. I shall cross the hall of clouds, I shall open the door, and I shall hear the voice of our disputes: "My dear, you see for yourself, there is nothing, nothing afterwards. You remember ... I always told you!" ... and to my eternal joy, it all begins again. The Comtesse talks.
[*Translated by Louise Varèse.*]

Ernst Haas

G.B.S.

George Bernard Shaw died at ninety-four on November 2, 1950. "I have had no heroic adventures," he once wrote. "Things have not happened to me; on the contrary it is I who have happened to them; and all my happenings have taken the form of books and plays. Read them, or spectate them; and you have my whole story." He was tender to strangers and friends, courageous to the world's victims. His life was a series of dramatic gestures, culminating in a terrifying common sense. It can be said of G.B.S., as he said when William Morris died, "You can lose a man like that by your own death, but not by his."

YOUNGER AND CHARMINGER, I

BY FRANKLIN P. ADAMS

Many years ago, I was young and charming, as some of you may know. I am now, not to put too fine a point on it, old and far more charming than I was in my receding adolescence.

For one (what one means is *this* one) can recall the unjoyous, tragic schooldays with more accuracy than I can remember what I had for dinner night before last. The days of adolescence were filled with daily terror, as I am sure they must be to all my sons, and, yes, my darling daughter.

When my eldest son was four — more than nineteen years ago — I was reading a picture book to him about George Washington. "Did you know him?" he asked. This is another proof — I shall have more — that the gap between parents and children is wide. On the other hand, in 1943, my second son, fifteen, called up one day and asked what I was doing. I told him I was reading *So Little Time*, and I was at the point when a father is embarrassed in the presence of his son, and his son's friends. "That isn't your trouble, Papa. Your trouble is talking to older people."

And one day that year I was passing by the room of one of my boys — all of them are good-looking, which they get from their handsome mother — who was gazing in the mirror, and I heard him observe to himself, "Oh, oh, I am terrible looking!" It was untrue. I, also, looked in the mirror when I was a year or two younger than he, when girls mattered to me, and I felt with truth that I was the facial inferior of such fine-looking fellows as Clarence Schofield, Reginald Miles, George Carpenter, and Jack Buhrer, all good-lookers who would be chummy with girls like Laura Matthews and Bessie Knight and Hester Ridlon.

I had two daily tragedies when I was in the seventh and eighth grades at Douglas School. They all concerned a girl named Corrinne Zimmerman. Corrinne left for school morning and afternoon about the same time I did, and I used to walk behind her for a block or two, and then I'd overtake and pass her, and kept hoping that she'd say, "Hey!" or equally endearing words to that effect. In dreams we walked to school arm-in-arm. But she never spoke to me, and I, who knew myself for no beauty, was desolate. All this was many, many years ago, long before I found out that it didn't matter as much as I thought it did then.

It was when a young woman — I was crowding eighteen then — said to me, "You know, I get tired of those fine-looking boys. I think it's better to look the way you do, and you don't have to think all the time how handsome you are, and what a lady-killer you are." I took this kindly, for I still feel it was said to put me at my ease. I left college on her account, so that I could earn enough money to marry her. P.S. I didn't earn enough, and she didn't wait until I was financially competent. I have four children; she has none.

There are tragedies that must be common to girls, too. The first I recall was the singing, on my first day at school — Room 22, Miss Werkmeister — and I didn't know the words or the tune, as the kids who had older brothers and sisters knew them. So I kept still until they became familiar with daily repetition. I can still sing that song about "My little lamb with his nimble feet. His eyes are so bright, his wool is so white. Oh, he is my darling, my heart's delight."

And even then, with the virility of an eight-year-old boy, I thought the song was effeminate, or sissy, as I used to call the books my sisters read — *Little Men*, *Little Women,* and the Little Prudy and Flaxie Frizzle Books. And speaking of virility, even before I went to school, I had to wear a Lord Fauntleroy suit — white shirtwaist, red Windsor tie, and a black velvet suit. Wearing that uniform was a tragedy that my parents didn't know about. For no parent can understand children, and no children can understand parents.

Parental problems are not the same as those of the kids. And the problems that were mine in the nineties are not the same that confront children like mine, born between 1926 and 1932. Yet my boys would say — still do — "I'd like to discuss a P. of L. with you." (P. of L. is a Problem of Life.) And I'd say, "And then I'll tell you a P. of L. of mine." And we'd exchange. It was a fairish give and take, as I'd even tell them what mine were at their ages; and now and then they'd be the same, owing to what I remembered.

I remember, for example, in 1896, the night before I was to have an examination in plane geometry, my father took me to see *Robin Hood*, and I thought to myself what a wonderful time the Bostonians (they acted in it) were having, and would have tomorrow, for they had no plane geometry to worry about. Matter of fact, I wasn't worried about passing; I was worried about getting an A. (I got it, and if you doubt it, look up the records in what was then Armour Institute and now is Illinois Institute of Technology.)

This I never told the kids. I know there is nothing worse for children than to begin with "When I was your age." When the average parent was their ages, he or she was young, but it

BLACK AND WHITE,
A STRIKING NEW FASHION
PORTRAIT BY PENN

[1943 – 1953]

was twenty-five to fifty years ago. And when the entire world, let alone one's children, may change overnight, it is ridiculous to say, "When I was your age." You might as well say that because Benjamin Franklin, a greater man than any of us ever are likely to see, walked from Boston to Philadelphia we should do likewise, or because I boated to Southampton in 1925, I should do it in 1945, when we planed to and from Paris in a night.

I read Scott and George Eliot; my children can't read them—I doubt that I could now. My daughter's literary heroine is Virginia Woolf; she reads E. A. Robinson and Robert Frost. My sons read T. S. Eliot and Sandburg, but they read aloud from Mr. Dooley, R. C. Benchley, and Ring Lardner. The poems I read were those of Austin Dobson and other formal poets: Hardy and Bret Harte. But I don't ask the kids to read Dobson.

Reading was well enough, but there were other matters of moment. There was bicycle riding in the flat Chicago and vicinity. Not only was I young and far from charming in those days, but also I was a well-garbed boy. I remember riding a wheel — we had "wheels," as opposed to the "bikes" my boys rode. I rode a Barnes White Flyer, and never without a cap, a shirt and high collar, and a bicycle suit, which was a coat, and short pants caught at the knee with a buckle, and plaid stockings, not to add bicycle shoes, for wheels were equipped with rat-trap pedals. I now and then ride the boys' bikes, and they are wonderful with their coaster brakes and lots of pleasant contraptions we in the dim days didn't have.

We didn't have movies, and of course no radio and no television, and I have a notion that I am far younger, though I was born in 1881, and charminger than my father ever was, who never got over his Boston accent with his Vanilla Rice Cream locution. So o. and c. though I am, and have been in the East since 1904, I cannot say, as they say in most parts of New York and Brooklyn, *D*etrert and Tchicahgo.

I play tennis, and never hope to get to the age when I give it up for golf. ...I am old and uncharming enough to hate "like" used as a conjunction, as the baseball radioteers use it, like, "It looks like he was safe." That doesn't grate on the modern ear so much as it does on mine, schooled as I was in the decencies of English.... My eldest boy is a satirist. He said, "Pa, you act like you would stop an avalanche."

And that reminds me that satire is no good. When I was young, I came to New York from Chicago. I had a furnished room on West Nineteenth Street, opposite Siegel Cooper's department store. I would be waked by the horse-drawn trucks. I was lonely; New York is a tough town when you don't know anybody, and to the first person I met, I said that I lived across the street, it was noisy, and one of us had to move. "It'll be you," she said. "Siegel, Cooper, and Co. have been there for years and years."

When I was longhanding my daily column for the *New York Evening Mail*, two feet from where I was working a carpenter was hammering at a window. "Does the scratching of my pen bother you?" I asked. "No," he said, "keep right on. I can't even hear it." Last winter I was asleep when I was waked by a loud radio speaker. I knocked on the door of the offender and said, "Does my sleeping in the next room interfere with your radio?" He didn't answer but my bitter satirical charm worked. He turned it off. So I got up at six-thirty anyway.

Yes — which I apologize for, as radio commercials usually begin with that rhetorical affirmative — I am old and charming; as opposed to the mother of my dear children (and I never was one to flatter) who is still Young and Charming.

P.S. A gambler I, I will give you a Tidy Bet that, No Reader She, she will read the end of this serious essay, written with my Heart's Blood, and will tell me that she loved my Cute Little Article.

"DANCING IS NOT STEPS"   Ernst Haas

Opposite: MRS. WINSTON GUEST is so beautiful that it is easy to forget how much more than beautiful she is. She is an excellent horsewoman, Horse Show blue-ribbon winner; a good shot, has hunted big game with her husband in India; captains many a committee devoted to money-raising for good works, runs a New York apartment and her Long Island, Palm Beach, and Virginia houses with an invisible efficiency. On the internationally best-dressed list, she walks through it all like a slender, blonde, imperturbable *déesse*. In this photograph by Cecil Beaton she wears a polo shirt, and a haircut given her by Mr. Beaton with a studio razor blade minutes before he took the picture.

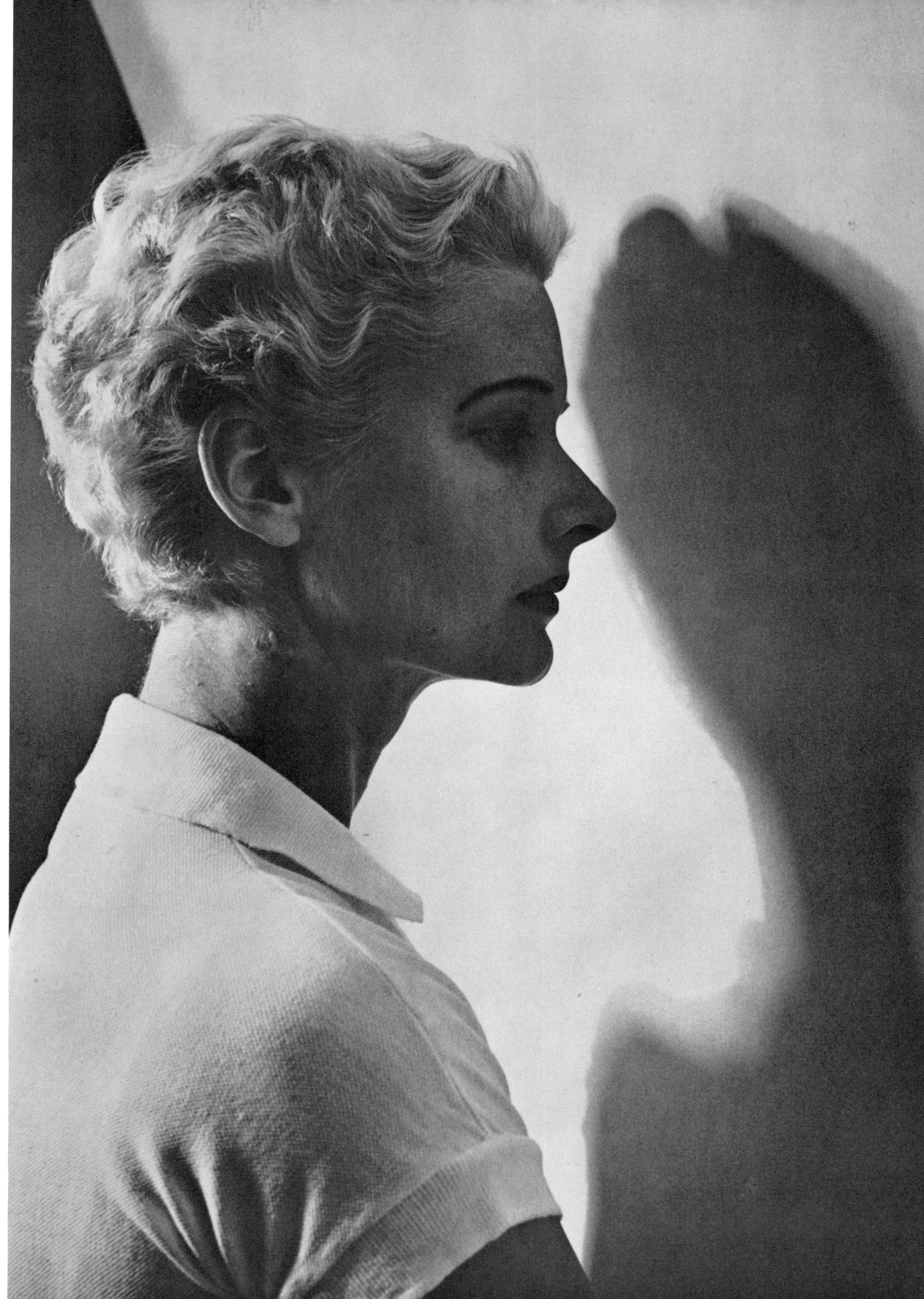

Henri Cartier-Bresson

WILLIAM FAULKNER'S NOBEL PRIZE ACCEPTANCE SPEECH

DELIVERED IN 1950

Walker Evans

Familiar to Faulkner's readers are the gutted Greek-Revival plantation house and the lonely cabin, such as this one, set in the middle of the ecru earth, its tin roof blazing like rhinestones in the sun.

I feel that this award was not made to me as a man but to my work — a life's work in the agony and sweat of the human spirit, not for glory and least of all for profit, but to create out of the materials of the human spirit something which did not exist before. So this award is only mine in trust. It will not be difficult to find a dedication for the money part of it commensurate with the purpose and significance of its origin. But I would like to do the same with the acclaim too, by using this moment as a pinnacle from which I might be listened to by the young men and women already dedicated to the same anguish and travail, among whom is already that one who will some day stand here where I am standing.

Our tragedy today is a general and universal physical fear so long sustained by now that we can even bear it. There are no longer problems of the spirit. There is only the question: When will I be blown up? Because of this, the young man or woman writing today has forgotten the problems of the human heart in conflict with itself which alone can make good writing because only that is worth writing about, worth the agony and the sweat.

He must learn them again. He must teach himself that the basest of all things is to be afraid; and, teaching himself that, forget it forever, leaving no room in his workshop for anything but the old verities and truths of the heart, the old universal truths lacking which any story is ephemeral and doomed — love and honour and pity and pride and compassion and sacrifice. Until he does so, he labours under a curse. He writes not of love but of lust, of defeats in which nobody loses anything of value, of victories without hope and, worst of all, without pity or compassion. His griefs grieve on no universal bones, leaving no scars. He writes not of the heart but of the glands.

Until he relearns these things, he will write as though he stood among and watched the end of man. I decline to accept the end of man. It is easy enough to say that man is immortal simply because he will endure; that when the last ding-dong of doom has clanged and faded from the last worthless rock hanging tideless in the last red and dying evening, that even then there will still be one more sound: that of his puny inexhaustible voice, still talking. I refuse to accept this. I believe that man will not merely endure: he will prevail. He is immortal, not because he alone among creatures has an inexhaustible voice but because he has a soul, a spirit capable of compassion and sacrifice and endurance. The poet's, the writer's, duty is to write about these things. It is his privilege to help man endure by lifting his heart, by reminding him of the courage and honour and hope and pride and compassion and pity and sacrifice which have been the glory of his past. The poet's voice need not merely be the record of man, it can be one of the props, the pillars to help him endure and prevail.

When William Faulkner received the Nobel Prize in Stockholm in 1950, Dr. Gustaf Hellström said of him, at the ceremony, "He grieves, and because he is a poet, he exaggerates the dimensions of a certain way of life ... his sense of justice and humanity ... make his regionalism universal."

"BETWEEN THE BIRDS AND THE POETS"

BY VINCENT SHEEAN

A MILLAY MEMOIR

In one of her wise and sensitive stories about opera singers, Willa Cather advances the hypothesis that the Americans' love for legend about living characters (and the American talent for creating such legends) is based upon the desire to make a substitute "royal family" for the nation. It may be so. At all events there has never been a time in the present century when there were not a dozen or more real living people who had somehow or other become the centre of innumerable stories circulated from one end of the country to the other. It seems to have nothing to do with fame or fortune or even that slippery yardstick called "success."

Edna St. Vincent Millay was one of these persons, and must have learned quite early in her life that the only means of continuing existence on terms bearable to herself was by ignoring her legend. For this purpose her house called Steepletop, near the village of Austerlitz in New York state, must have been, from 1925 when she bought it until 1950 when she died there, a refuge, as well as her own solid and enduring place. She did not live there all the time by any means, but she always returned there for a good part of the year, sometimes for the whole year. She loved life and the world, travelled a good deal, was fond of the sun, enjoyed very much the company of men and women who had nothing to do with literature, and probably in her youth derived a certain amount of amusement and perhaps even pleasure of a kind, at the buzzing and humming of talk that surrounded her wherever she went. She could not have been unaware of the existence of a national legend about her; she was too intelligent. It happened to her very early.

It had been happening ever since she first began to write verses and play the

Culver

EDNA ST. VINCENT MILLAY

piano, as Mrs. Millay's eldest daughter ("the one with red hair and green eyes," they probably said, although her sisters had similar colouring), in Camden, Maine, or earlier at Rockport or Union, Maine. Perhaps, therefore, she may not have fully realized what an explosion she caused in 1920 by the publication of *A Few Figs from Thistles*, her second volume of verses. (*Renascence* was published in 1917.) The "First Fig" in the 1920 book became a sort of motto or epigraph for the whole decade that followed: it is the quatrain which begins "My candle burns at both ends." These lines were caught up and quoted, or more usually misquoted, by every jejune hedonist of the rebellious era, every girl or boy who wanted to experiment with the recently discovered benefits of alcohol, sexual experience, or simply late hours and wild talk. Scott Fitzgerald's stories bestowed a self-consciousness upon the young people of the 1920's, a self-consciousness they did not really need, but Edna in that one quatrain supplied them with a *point d'appui*, an aesthetic justification for kicking over the traces.

And the immediate, inevitable consequence was that Edna herself became a symbol, legend, almost standard-bearer, for a social upheaval which was in reality outside her interest. All her purest work is quite timeless, and it was only the rise of Fascism that aroused her to some poems (such as those written in 1940) which are clearly of a certain hour. In the 1920s, for which she has been said to be in some respects historically responsible, she hardly seems to have noticed the social environment; her responsibility, if it exists, is the same as that of the sea gull for that oceanic wind upon which he rides.

Edna St. Vincent Millay, rare woman and poet, rare poet and woman, spent the secret hours of dawn with birds for many years. The kinship she acknowledged by her habitual action towards them was, it appeared to me, amply confessed by the birds themselves in their behaviour towards her, although Edna laughed at the idea. According to her, they would have behaved in the same way towards anybody who fed them. This I took leave to doubt then as I do now, on the simple ground of probability. What I actually saw myself, and many others have seen, between Edna and the birds (although much was never seen) was improbable enough; that it should occur with any frequency, or to "anybody who feeds them," is beyond credence.

Edna Millay could vary exceedingly. At times she was so afflicted with self-consciousness and dislike for the external world that she could hardly utter a word; I have seen her cringe — this was in New York, in a crowd — actually physically cringe, when she felt herself being observed. She felt free at Steepletop, where every blade of grass was familiar, and there was not the slightest danger that anybody would come near the door. There was no telephone in the house. (When it became necessary to telephone, somebody — usually Eugen Boissevain, her husband — made an excursion to the general store in Austerlitz.) Her dislike for company was so well understood, both among the neighbours and among her distant friends, that nobody would have thought of going to Steepletop at all without an invitation or at least a permission given in advance. But on a memorable visit which Esther Adams and I paid at Steepletop, Edna was in good health, good temper, good spirits, and good form.

She met us at the door with a cheerful welcome and led us into the long room with the big plain window at the end. Her preferred chair, where she most often sat, was beside this big square window and so placed in the corner that she could at all times see what was going on outside the window as well as in the room. This was in the late afternoon and there was still light of a rather damp and subdued nature. Very soon after we had come into the room, almost before we had finished the first flurry of welcome and arrival chatter, I saw a small bird of the most dazzling blue alight on the window sill and depart.

"What in the world is that?" I asked. "Did you see?"

"Of course," said Edna in that deep, serious voice which was characteristic throughout the time I knew her. "Don't you know him? That is the indigo bunting."

"Indigo bunting?"

"He is on his way to the north. He had been in Central America, or perhaps in South America. Do you mean to say that you have never seen an indigo bunting?"

I was abashed a little, as we always are at exhibitions of our own ignorance, but thought I might as well confess at once and get it over. I told her about the scarlet tanager on the farm in Vermont.

"The scarlet tanager should be about the most easily recognized of all migratory birds," she said not too censoriously. "He comes here fairly often. He isn't here just at the moment."

"Why do they come here?"

"Because I feed them, of course," she said.

Eugen was giving us a drink, his huge and friendly and ever-remembered form moving about the room from Esther Adams to Edna to me. He laughed.

"She feeds them!" he said. "She runs a hotel for birds. She's up and at it every morning before dawn."

It became evident to my rather slow perceptions why a big square window of plate glass had been put at the end of the long room: so that the birds could look in at Edna and Edna could look out at the birds. This established the daylong interest of that end of the room; the fireplace was in the middle on the left, and we needed it that day; two grand pianos stood at the other end, near the door which led to hall, dining room, and kitchen. Edna saw me watching at the window with, no doubt, some element of the astonishment I felt. The comings and goings, the general activity, were indeed considerable and I had never seen anything of the kind before.

"Those are only finches," she said. "They aren't remarkable but they're pretty. Various kinds."

And then, as conversation shifted again and the finches disappeared, for one blinding moment the indigo bunting came back. He took a peck or two at the window sill, seemed to glance once penetratingly into the room, and was off in a blue rush. The swiftness of this took my breath away.

"He doesn't like a great crowd of people standing around staring at him," she said. "There is something to be said for his point of view. He lives not far off, you see, up there in that nearest tree, and it's quite easy for him to come back when there aren't so many observers."

We had dinner quite late that night. In the first place, there seemed no end to the extension — forward, backward, and in all directions — to which any conversation with Miss Millay might be subject. I had never fallen upon this particular mood with her before, in our few meetings. She had seemed reluctant to talk much, or for long at a time, or to engage in any very animated discussion, or to pursue a subject with the particular animosity of dispute which engenders lively response and long consideration. Now we fell, by what accident I cannot remember, upon Keats and Shelley, by way of some chance remark about the happiness or unhappiness of poets. Edna asked me which of the two I regarded as more unhappy, and I said Keats.

This was the signal for her to take the opposite point of view with such vigour, wit, and beauty of language as I have seldom heard. Her memory for poetry was, as is well known, phenomenal, and she had also cultivated it — she memorized poetry deliberately when she was sick abed, or alone in a train, the way other people read magazines or play patience — and as the result she could command page after page of Keats and Shelley at will. Since her voice, so deep and clear and filled with melody, was peculiarly suited to the recalling of poetic lines, the quotations with which she filled her talk had never sounded quite like that to me before. I did not surrender my point of view, nor do I now; in so far as I understand them Shelley was not capable of the deep human unhappiness of Keats, nor had he any reason to feel, as Keats did, the gratuitous insults of fate. But Edna's command of the poetry of both, and her multitude of reasons for suffering — by which Shelley's ethereal flight itself became a kind of unhappiness — left me vanquished in the immediate argument.

When she wished to give enough power to her voice it was as thrilling as the voice of the very greatest actress or singer. It was a visceral experience. Then she recited the "Ode to the West Wind" in its entirety. The range of expression, within severe limits (for she did not "act" at all), was astonishing. With the voice alone, without gesture or movement or expression of the face, she remembered the poem and gave it to us anew as if we had never heard it before in our lives. And this extraordinary re-creation had nothing whatever to do with the arts of the theatre, dramatic reading, or anything else of a factitious kind. It was for poetry alone. One could hear precisely where the lines broke and rose and fell, like the sea, and where the mood itself grew faint or strong with the flow of sense and feeling.

"Come with me. I'll show you my poets. We'll look at Petrarch. We'll look at Dante."

She led me across the hall and up the stairs to a small room just at the top where there were, in every conceivable sort of binding and state of repair, all the good poets that have ever written in English, French, German, Italian, Latin, and Greek. They did not take up much space, since there are so few good poets. Some editions were old, and no doubt some were valuable, others valueless; but all had been read and re-read by a poet's eyes. We found Petrarch's sonnet to the nightingale and she read it. We found Dante. We even found Racine. The love of poetry, when it is deep and true as it was with her, is sometimes partisan and exclusive; those who dwell in Shakespeare cannot abide Racine, and those who live by Goethe will have nothing to do with Heinrich Heine. To Edna, each was good and true and beautiful in a particular way, so that she excluded nothing, and condemned nobody, but took it all to herself as she took the sea and the birds. Even in her garden she did not exclude the so-called weeds, and readers of her poems know how they dwell there.

This was the poetry room, as it was called, and I understood afterwards that very few persons were ever allowed to enter it. Even then I knew that I was singularly honoured.

Edna died at Steepletop, at the foot of the stairs leading to the poetry room, at or near dawn on October 19, 1950. I think she had been feeding the birds and was on her way to bed. Mr. Pinney did not find her till many hours later, but the doctors knew. In the year between Eugen's death and hers I had never dared to go near her, for I had heard, and understood, that she wanted only solitude. It did not in the least surprise me, however, that she died between the birds and the poets, for that is where she had lived, and what are life and death but forms of one another?

I was a little surprised, just the same, to learn only the other day, long after I had begun to write these notes, that one of the last fragments of poetry she wrote was about the flight of blue birds, or about blueness. Her sister Norma, reading the last notebook, found it, obviously the beginning and the end of a projected sonnet, and considers that it is one of her last, possibly the last. The couplets, published here for the first time, are:

> Never before, perhaps, was such a sight —
> Only one sky (*my breath*) and that all blue —
> Lapis, and Sèvres, and borage — every hue
> Of blue-jay — indigo bunting — bluebird's flight.

There are three lines underneath, with a circle drawn round them and marked "another poem." They are:

> I will control myself, or go inside.
> I will not flaw perfection with my grief.
> Handsome, this day; no matter who has died.

"STILL LIFE WITH WATERMELON AND BEE" BY IRVING PENN

TRIBESMEN IN A FURIOUS EXHIBITION OF HORSEMANSHIP AT A MOROCCAN "FANTASIA"

Penn

REVISITATION

BY ANNE MORROW LINDBERGH

CUZCO PORTERS — part of an album of Penn photographs, made in a Peruvian photographer's studio. The surrealist quality of the woollen masks, worn by the Indians at fiestas, is heightened by the uncompromising clarity of Penn's photography. The ropes are the marks of their trade.

You have been dead for months; the daylight mind
Has noted in its record the exact
Moment of dying, has transferred the fact
To its dream-counterpart — the shadowy pool
Where all events are mirrored upside down,
Distorted but more vivid than by day —
That nowhere on this earth can you be found;
Not here, not there, nor on a journey bound
From which you'll soon be back. Not just away,
But gone "for good," you are.
    Even though I know,
And grief is past and life goes on — even so,
Still I must make a faithful pilgrimage
To those particular landmarks that were yours,
Or intimately haunted by your sight;
Not in the hope of finding you again,
Not in obeisance to your memory,
Nor self-indulgently in search of pain.
No, I must go
Back to the places where you put your hand,
To see them now without you, gutted, bare,
Swept hollow of your presence. I must stand
Alone and in their empty faces stare,
To find another truth I do not know;
To balance those unequal shifted planes
Of our existence, yours and mine; to fix
The whirling landscapes of the heart in which
I walk a stranger both to space and time.

I must go back;
In each familiar corner wait until
I witness once again the flesh turn cold,
The spirit parting from the body's hold;
And let it go, and love the landscape still;
But now on only for itself alone,
As you once loved it when, in flesh and bone,
You walked it first, naked of memories,
And sharp with life, you loved its flesh and bone.
For I must meet and marry in myself
The truth of what has ended, what is new;
The past and future; death and life. And when
At last the two conflicting pairs are met;
The planes are balanced and the landscapes set;
The strands of past and future tied in one
Tough, weather-beaten, salted twist of hemp,
The present — then
I shall be able to refind myself,
And also, you.

[1943 – 1953] 281

LAUGHTER

BY CHRISTOPHER FRY

A friend once told me that when he was under the influence of ether he dreamed he was turning over the pages of a great book, in which he knew he would find, on the last page, the meaning of life. The pages of the book were alternately tragic and comic, and he turned page after page, his excitement growing, not only because he was approaching the answer but because he

couldn't know, until he arrived, on which side of the book the final page would be. At last it came: the universe opened up to him in a hundred words, and they were uproariously funny. He came back to consciousness crying with laughter, remembering everything. He opened his lips to speak. It was then that the great and comic answer plunged back out of his reach.

If I had to draw a picture of the person of Comedy, it is so I should like to draw it: the tears of laughter running down the face, one hand still lying on the tragic page which so nearly contained the answer, the lips about to frame the great revelation, only to find it had gone as disconcertingly as a chair twitched away when we want to sit down. Comedy is an escape, not from truth but from despair: a narrow escape into faith. It believes in a universal cause for delight, even though knowledge of the cause is always twitched away from under us, which leaves us to rest on our own buoyancy. In tragedy every moment is eternity; in comedy eternity is a moment. In tragedy we suffer pain; in comedy pain is a fool, suffered gladly.

Charles Williams once said to me, indeed it was the last thing he said to me (he died not long after), and it was shouted from the tailboard of a moving bus, over the heads of pedestrians and bicyclists outside the Midland Station, Oxford: "When we're dead we shall have the sensation of having enjoyed life altogether, whatever has happened to us." The distance between us widened, and he leaned out into the space so that his voice should reach me: "Even if we've been murdered, what a pleasure to have been capable of it!"; and, having spoken the words for comedy, away he went like the revelation which almost came out of the ether.

He was not at all saying that everything is for the best in the best of all possible worlds. He was saying — or so it seems to me — that there is an angle of experience where the dark is distilled into light: either here or hereafter, in or out of time: where our tragic fate finds itself with perfect pitch, and goes straight to the key which creation was composed in. And comedy senses and reaches out to this experience. It says, in effect, that, groaning as we may be, we move in the figure of a dance, and, so moving, we trace the outline of the mystery. Laughter did not come by chance, but how or why it came is beyond comprehension, unless we think of it as a kind of perception. The human animal, beginning to feel his spiritual inches, broke in onto an unfamiliar tension of life, where laughter became inevitable. But how? Could he, in his first unlaughing condition, have contrived a comic view of life and then developed the strange rib-shaking response?

Or is it not more likely that when he was able to grasp the tragic nature of time he was of a stature to sense its comic nature also; and, by the experience of tragedy and the intuition of comedy, to make his difficult way. The difference between tragedy and comedy is the difference between experience and intuition. In the experience we strive against every condition of our animal life: against death, against the frustration of ambition, against the instability of human love. In the intuition we trust the arduous eccentricities we're born to, and see the oddness of a creature who has never got acclimatized to being created. Laughter inclines me to know that man is essential spirit; his body, with its functions and accidents and frustrations, is endlessly quaint and remarkable to him; and though comedy accepts our position in time, it barely accepts our posture in space.

The bridge by which we cross from tragedy to comedy and back again is precarious and narrow. We find ourselves in one or the other by the turn of a thought; a turn such as we make when we turn from speaking to listening. I know that when I set about writing a comedy the idea presents itself to me first of all as tragedy. The characters press on to the theme with all their divisions and perplexities heavy about them; they are already entered for the race to doom, and good and evil are an infernal tangle skinning the fingers that try to unravel them. If the characters were not qualified for tragedy there would be no comedy, and to some extent I have to cross the one before I can light on the other. In a century less flayed and quivering we might reach it more directly; but not now, unless every word we write is going to mock us. A bridge has to be crossed, a thought has to be turned. Somehow the characters have to unmortify themselves: to affirm life and assimilate death and persevere in joy. Their hearts must be as determined as the phoenix; what burns must also light and renew: not by a vulnerable optimism but by a hard-won maturity of delight, by the intuition of comedy, an active patience declaring the solvency of good. The Book of Job is the great reservoir of comedy. "But there is a spirit in man. . . . Fair weather cometh out of the north. . . . The blessing of him that was ready to perish came upon me: and I caused the widow's heart to sing for joy."

I have come, you may think, to the verge of saying that comedy is greater than tragedy. On the verge I stand and go no further. Tragedy's experience hammers against the mystery to make a breach which would admit the whole triumphant answer. Intuition has no such potential. But there are times in the state of man when comedy has a special worth, and the present is one of them: a time when the loudest faith has been faith in a trampling materialism, when literature has been thought unrealistic which did not mark and remark our poverty and doom. Joy (of a kind) has been all on the devil's side, and one of the necessities of our time is to redeem it. If not, we are in poor sort to meet the circumstances, the circumstances being the contention of death with life, which is to say evil with good, which is to say desolation with delight. Laughter may only seem to be like an exhalation of air, but out of that air we came; in the beginning we inhaled it; it is a truth, not a fantasy, a truth voluble of good which comedy stoutly maintains.

The music of Christopher Fry's poetry, the luxuriance of his imagery, and the clarity of his wit are the joy of the London and New York stages in such recent plays as *The Lady's Not for Burning*, and his translation of Anouilh's *Ring Around the Moon*.

ROMANTIC AND REMOTE, "THE KING AND I," THE NEW RODGERS
AND HAMMERSTEIN MUSICAL PLAY,
HAS CREATED ANOTHER STAR,
YUL BRYNNER, SWAGGER-SHOULDERED
AND HANDSOME,
WHO HOLDS THE STAGE AGAINST
ALL THE CRAFTS AND ARTS OF
GERTRUDE LAWRENCE

Golby

THE TWENTY YEARS...

BY RUSSELL LYNES

To some of those who look at the United States from abroad — who do not understand the American temperament, American politics, our delight in throwing pop bottles at the umpire, and our horse-trading — the recent election was cause for alarm. We know better. We may squabble but we do not turn back. What America wants and has always wanted, whether it is machines or entertainments or arts or politics or clothes or even ideas and ideals, is not yesterday. It is today and tomorrow. It is good old modern.

This last phrase was thrown at me recently when my twelve-year-old daughter proclaimed the end of an era. She had been to a country fair with some contemporaries and by tossing nickels into a ring filled with glittering glassware she had won a small plate with scalloped edges. She brought it home and presented it to her mother with a slightly scornful "Do you want this?"

"I don't think that's so bad," her mother said, "it has a sort of pleasant Victorian look."

"Not for me," the child said. "Give me good old modern."

So that was what had become of the fight that the Museum of Modern Art had been waging for a little over two decades with such intensity. The struggle, it seemed, was over. Modern was no longer a fighting word: it was merely a period style, comfortably ensconced in the twelve-year-old way of looking at the world. It was less than two decades ago that two friends and I (they were both architects) ordered a shipment of Aalto furniture from Finland. It was bent plywood and very modern and also very inexpensive, and we all felt very advanced. Now most of it is in the cellar, not because it isn't still handsome, but because most of it was uncomfortable. The discomfort seemed unimportant at the time. It was the idea that was important. "Give me good old modern," indeed! It was a cause — then.

Since 1933 causes have risen like water-spouts in a troubled sea and swept on until they collapsed in the crosscurrents of political, economic, literary, artistic, and scientific winds. The sea was indeed troubled in 1933, but the skies were not completely overcast. The "noble experiment" at least was over. The day after Roosevelt's election *The New York Times* proclaimed, "Wets in control of both houses." So much for bathtub gin and applejack cocktails and Al Capone. It scarcely seemed possible. Why, it even meant legitimate jobs for some of the fourteen million unemployed, and legal hangovers for a great many others. But other clouds had just begun to gather on a far horizon. In late January of 1933 Adolf Hitler, after two unsuccessful tries, was made chancellor of Germany. While we were wondering what the new administration might do to help us pull ourselves up by our boot-

THE INAUGURATION, 1933,
DRAWN BY COVARRUBIAS.
LEFT TO RIGHT, OUTGOING VICE-PRESIDENT,
CHARLES CURTIS;
EX-PRESIDENT HERBERT C. HOOVER
AND MRS. HOOVER;
INCOMING VICE-PRESIDENT
JOHN N. GARNER;
THE NEW PRESIDENT AND
MRS. FRANKLIN D. ROOSEVELT;
CHIEF JUSTICE CHARLES EVANS HUGHES

straps, Germany seemed a very long way off and Hitler looked like a comic-opera version of Mussolini. We found out soon enough that the face that supported the silly little moustache also contained eyes that burned with hatred and ambition. Or perhaps we found out too late.

But the Big Cause then was at home. There were breadlines. There was the bank holiday, when many Americans suddenly discovered that they could charge a hamburger and a cup of coffee at the corner drugstore. That summer I got a job driving a car for a company called Europe on Wheels: the publishing firm where I worked was glad to be rid of me for the slack months. I paid my own way to Europe (about $150 round trip in student third class) and when I got back the office stationery had a blue eagle and the initials "NRA" printed on it. Another noble experiment. The Supreme Court called it off.

In the early thirties "class" had a new sound to Americans. Those were the days when the novel of social significance, James T. Farrell's *Studs Lonigan* and John Dos Passos' *U.S.A.* and John Steinbeck's *In Dubious Battle*, seemed to come to grips with the problems of the famous "third of a nation." It was about to be the day of the WPA theatre project, and WPA guidebooks, and WPA post-office murals by the dozens. Never has art been produced in America in such wholesale lots, probably never so much good, so much bad. The cause was the cause of the common man.

But Americans can take their causes seriously and still laugh at them. The ILGWU in the mid-thirties staged a revue which was good enough to go on the road (I saw it in Philadelphia) called *Pins and Needles*, and the hit tune was a spoof named "Sing Me a Song of Social Significance." The Gershwins rode roughshod over the political scene with their satire on elections, politicians, and especially vice-presidents in *Of Thee I Sing*, starring Victor Moore, Lois Moran, and William Gaxton. A great many more people were reading *Anthony Adverse* and *Gone with the Wind* than were reading the novels of social problems. Less sophisticated and probably more agile Americans were learning a new dance called "The Big Apple."

From the time Spain exploded in 1936, war has never been out of the air. The New York World's Fair with its tremendous Trylon and Perisphere flew its flags and shot its sky rockets over Flushing Meadows in an atmosphere that was superficially gay but basically ominous. The fair was scarcely a symbol of world amity, although its theme was peace, but it was certainly a symbol of a new kind of architecture. Modern had landed with both feet on the reclaimed dump that was the fair's site. It was also a symbol of at least partial economic recovery. Millions of people were still unemployed in 1937 in America, but the most famous case of unemployment of the decade was not American at all. It was Edward VIII of England, who voluntarily in 1936 gave up his job "at long last" to marry Mrs. Warfield Simpson of Baltimore. Only two broadcasts in that decade caused more of a stir than Edward's abdication. One was the night Orson Welles horrified thousands with a mock newscast that Martians had landed in New Jersey. The other was the news, about a year later, that Germany had marched on Poland.

Americans had a new cause, but it took two diametrically opposed points of view. Both points of view stressed the necessity of preserving our principles and standing by our responsibilities. One group worked day and night to help "the Fight for Freedom" by all-out aid to England. It was they who made the famous destroyer deal a reality. The other group rallied thousands to the cause of "America First." But no one was indifferent, and no one, I believe, thought that the war could be settled without us. The moment of decision was forced on us, you may recall, during a Sunday-afternoon broadcast of the New York Philharmonic.

The bombs on Pearl Harbor swept away all causes but one. It was America First, all right, but America was in the far Pacific and in North Africa and deep in Europe. America was anywhere in the world — in Burma jungles and on frozen airfields in Iceland, in Murmansk harbour, and New Delhi, and on islands few of us had ever heard of before — the Gilberts and Solomons, Iwo Jima and Okinawa, and Guadalcanal. Americans had a geography lesson that they will never forget.

But already they have nearly forgotten what went with it at home — "Mairzy Doats" and gadgets to make your own cigarettes, recapped tires, and coupons for shoes, taxis with the doors falling off, Bundles for Britain, and the "dim-out" along the Eastern Seaboard. Every man was his own military strategist, but there was only one goal and the spirit of the nation was infrangible.

In the 1910 edition of *Webster's Collegiate Dictionary* "infrangible" is defined as "not capable of being broken or separated into parts; as infrangible atoms." The bomb that blew the atom apart blew apart the infrangible spirit with it. The war was won. The cause was not. We had learned things about how men behave that shocked us; we had learned about gas chambers and 180,000 killed by a single blow, and we had learned something about power and its responsibilities. We began to turn our eyes inward to look at ourselves, our culture and our motives.

Introspection took many forms. To the novelist it meant examination of the roots of behaviour, and the pseudo-Marxian symbolism of the novels of social significance was replaced by the pseudo-Freudian symbolism of the novels of self-analysis. To the politicians it meant investigation of everything from the Pearl Harbor fiasco to "five-percenters," to our policy in China. At times it almost seemed as though America had decided that if it could dig out the past, it could get rid of the future.

We looked back in other ways, especially at our own culture, for as a world power our culture had become of more than passing interest abroad. We revived Henry James and Herman Melville. We began re-reading F. Scott Fitzgerald, for the twenties seemed to have a special affinity to our new post-

[1943 – 1953] 287

war era. Our young writers, as they had after the first war, lit out for Europe, but it was less fashionable for them to go to Paris than to Rome and to the islands in the Bay of Naples — Ischia and Capri. *Pal Joey* came out of moth balls to be a hit, and *The Male Animal* and, but it seemed too remote, *Of Thee I Sing*. Last year was not a good one for kidding about politics.

After the war everything, not just clothes, had a "new look." Campuses were filled with grown-up young men; many of them had wives and small children, and it seemed late to be getting started. Foreign cars and boxed-in jeeps became familiar sights on the highways, and motels of unparalleled splendour sprang up all across the continent to give shelter to a traditionally restless population again able to travel. For those who had travelled too much there were Levittowns and television sets. It was the ranch house that captured the imagination of adults as Hopalong and space cadets caught the fancy of children. Inflation became the bugbear of everyone; it cost a fortune to fill one's basket at the tremendous new supermarkets.

"They tell me a dime is only worth a nickel these days," a New York taxi driver said about a year ago. "But I've got the dime now and I didn't use to have the nickel." It was a far cry from 1933. In a world filled with "have not" nations, we were now a "have" nation, and our new cause was to keep free peoples from becoming enslaved by poverty and overrun by communism. Our determination had plunged us into war again, and our geography lesson rang with still more strange names — Seoul and Inchon and the Yalu River. A good many of us took to looking under the bed for the enemy while others fought him face to face on frozen rice paddies half a world away.

Nevertheless, peace is not a lost cause; we fervently believe that it is merely mislaid. In fact, in the period between the inauguration of Roosevelt in March 1933 and the inauguration of Eisenhower, in this era of causes, the surprising thing is that so few of the causes were lost.

THE INAUGURATION, 1953, DRAWN BY HIRSCHFELD. ON THE CAPITOL STEPS ARE, LEFT TO RIGHT: OUTGOING VICE PRESIDENT, ALBEN W. BARKLEY; EX-PRESIDENT HARRY S. TRUMAN AND MRS. TRUMAN; THE INCOMING VICE PRESIDENT, RICHARD M. NIXON; THE NEW PRESIDENT AND MRS. DWIGHT D. EISENHOWER; AND, OFFERING THE LAUREL CROWN, CHIEF JUSTICE FREDERICK M. VINSON

Penn

THE LIGHT IN THE DARK

BY ELIZABETH BOWEN

The idea of Christmas is like a note struck on glass — long ago and forever. For each of us, this is the earliest memory of the soul. Day-to-day existence, as it goes on, drowns so much in its clamour, deadens so many echoes — but never this. Behind our busy thoughts and distracted senses remains a silence in which, again each year, the sweet resounding ring of the note is heard. We have expected Christmas, almost without knowing — wherever we are, wherever we turn, it claims us. The Holy Night links up all childhoods; we return to our own — to the first music, the first pictures, the first innocent and mysterious thrill and stir. Within the folds of the darkness, something has happened; even the cities know it, and the winter country seems to hold its breath. Once more we have the vision of wide night snow, of the shepherds listening and looking up into air rustling with wings of singing angels, and the Star in the blue of the frosty firmament. This is a time when magic joins hands with holiness. The dear, silly, gaudy symbolism of Christmas cards stems from race-myths and ancient midwinter rites. We inherit this feast from out of the dark of time before Christ was born — mankind sought it, from some primitive need.

There is the necessity to keep something burning — yes, and to make it shine afar. December is the year's midnight; only the little flames of the votive candles show man to man. This reaching out, this signalling through the dark, is for something more than the communication of fears and loneliness; man joins man so that, together, they may lift up their hearts. Never has being human — that is, human only — been quite enough; from the first there has been our need for the miracle. As creatures, we are formed to adore, and marvel. In answer we have been given Christmas.

A ray falls on the crèche — on the bowed head of the Madonna, the white locks of St. Joseph, the upraised hands of the Child. Celestially lighted, the group of three is at the same time softly lapped by shadows; they are on earth. Among the straw of the manger, legend says, last summer's little wild flowers flower again. Half in the reflection of this glow, half in warm tawny gloom stand the ox and ass; we feel the rude strength of the stable roof-beams, over which brood angels. Mary's mantle, having gleamed so blue, also spreads its hems on the humble floor. Such is the scene of the miracle — is it not, also, the miracle of the scene that supernatural and natural should so sublimely merge? What is illuminated as we gaze, is the whole of the tender solemnity of life.

From the crèche light travels, resting on all familiar, domestic things; this is one gift of Christmas — a sort of vision. Now, we perceive the especial dearness of what is dear to us — home, faces, belongings, memories, ties. It is as though mists, of fatigue, of habit, cleared from between ourselves and that which we have and love. "On Christmas Eve," I thought, as a child, "even the furniture looks different!" The chests and cupboards, tables and chairs of my nursery shed on me, possibly, no more than the good nature which was in them always; I simply was more open to it that night. Something truer than fancy, less false than sentiment, makes us find rooms and people, around Christmastime, enchantedly kind — flowers smell sweeter; fires burn brighter; harmony appears in the pattern around us; the very taste-nerves quicken; there is a particular spontaneity about laughter. All this is blessed — has been so since the Star first halted over a roof.

Here is a season which sets a time of its own, finds its own language — the imagery of the calendar and the card.

Each of us, probably, has in mind one ideal and absolute of the Christmas card, as received in childhood. My own taste (date around 1910) is this — I behold a cottage gable in deep, dusky silhouette against an expiring gleam of sunset, one window lit; smoke goes up from the chimney. To this, a woodman returning, footprint by footprint, across the foreground snow; all around stretch white wastes, the bare trees are dark. How it glows and glows through that one small window — core of the world, magnet to man, the home! Towards it, the coach lurches among the drifts, the cravatted rider whips up his horse, the red-mittened children drag their laden sledge, the spotted dog lollops, the cat leads her train of kittens, the crinolined lady picks her delicate way. All Christmas-card-land creatures have the same destination. My woodman's cottage, crouched in smouldering evening, remains for me forever the symbol-scene — no better picture, before or since, has so fixed for me that light in the falling dark; or, by contrast, the elemental and daunting loneliness of the Elsewhere.

That sense of the Elsewhere, and of those straying in it, can but encircle Christmas, if one has any heart.

There are those whom Christmas touches only by its bitter meaninglessness to them — for this is a season to which natural indifference is impossible; those who dread or hate it shrink from its power. And — multiplied by the catastrophes of the world there are

Norman Parkinson

THE EARL OF UXBRIDGE
WITH HIS SISTER
LADY HENRIETTE PAGET,
CHILDREN OF THE MARQUIS
AND MARCHIONESS OF ANGLESEY

the derelict, the placeless; those who are where they are under duress, or who are where they find themselves by sheer bleak fortuity, without ties or love. Of these many, how few can be comforted — at least concretely; the practical reach and scope of our giving, in view of this trouble, can but seem poor and small. We *can*, only, humbly, keep these unknown in mind — which is to say, in imagination. The Child was born of his travel-wearied Mother, in a stable because there was no room at the inn. Is not this a time to remember the crowded-out ones? Now is it, at Christmas, when we feel to the full the happiest implication of being human, that the sense of all other humanity most insistently presses against our doors and windows. To meet it, we send out into the dark some thought — however groping, vague, and unformulated. Who is to say, at this season, what mystic circuit may set itself up between man and man?

At Christmas, no house is childless. Up to the surface wells a forgotten capacity for simplicity, an aptitude and eagerness for delight. The most elderly fingers tremble with expectation as they pluck at knots of tinsel ribbon; wrappings disclose "surprises" which send a flush up cheeks. The real children wake earlier — that is the only difference! Otherwise, as the Day goes on, we old and young find ourselves all made equal, elated and solemn by ceremonial; this, in the home, it is which serves to lift the day up and shape its unique course. We celebrate, dazzled and drawn together; somehow more than ourselves. Who, what has joined our company? Today, tonight, the hours are deep and sounding, charged with the whole of time — with eternity. For indeed the truth of the Story appears most in that it has no end.

MICHAEL ASTOR WITH
HIS SISTER STELLA,
CHILDREN OF THE HONORABLE
JOHN JACOB ASTOR AND
MRS. ASTOR,
PHOTOGRAPHED AT HATLEY PARK

Toni Frissell

THE ART OF SCEPTICISM

BY REBECCA WEST

Scepticism is a pompous name for a simple and necessary process which is seen in its purest form in the kitchen.

When making an omelet one does not break the eggs straight into the basin in which they are going to be mixed. One cracks each egg separately into a cup, sniffs it to see if it is good, then adds it to the others. There is really no more to it. It is a useful precaution, and that is all.

But in life and in art alike it is dangerous to over-value scepticism. Nobody ever made himself a circle of friends simply by refusing to make acquaintances who were not beyond reproach. Nobody ever wrote a good book simply by collecting a number of accurate facts and valid ideas. Nobody ever made a good omelet simply by ascertaining that certain eggs were fresh. There has to be the solid pan that will not burn or stick, the stove that comes to the right degree of heat, the exact amount of butter; the cook must have a golden conception of what an omelet ought to be and the cunning hand which can make the fine compulsive movement which at the crucial moment will force her material to realize her conception.

In both art and life it is important to remember that scepticism does not mean the practice of disbelieving everything one hears. It means accepting no person, no fact, no idea, with which one is going to start something new, without informing oneself of their true nature.

Scepticism is an art and does not have to be practised all over the place, any more than painting has to cover all flat surfaces in the world. The painter restricts himself to a canvas of a size suitable to a composition he has in mind, or to a particular part of a wall or ceiling which needs decoration. One needs a person as a friend who will fulfill certain needs in life, as a partner, as an employer, as an employee, and so finds out what these persons are. Otherwise one suspends judgment on them, and in the meantime gives them the benefit of any doubt and is polite.

The most perfect exponent of scepticism in life that I have ever known was Marie Belloc Lowndes, who died a few years ago as a very old lady. She was half French and half English, and her French part was prudent and logical, her English side romantic and poetic. She lived in England all her life and never ceased to examine with French detachment and patience the wild English creatures that lived around her. People approached her trustfully, for she was a little woman with a short, spreading body and a deprecating style of dress, and a face which must have been softly pretty in her youth and was lit by blue eyes. But she could have made a magnificent criminal lawyer, and at a certain stage she would get each acquaintance to tell her his story and cross-examine him on it; and at the end she knew the truth. Then either that person saw no more of her, or was always her friend, defended by her loyalty, encouraged by her praise, brought together with people of like mind who would otherwise have remained strangers.

Marie Belloc Lowndes' approval of her friends did not depend on their capacity to satisfy the conventional standards of morality, though she was a devout Roman Catholic who followed in all respects the prescriptions of her Church. But though she was in a sense a very worldly woman, who was happy in society and enjoyed its protocol as other people enjoyed bridge, she was following some exalted principle in creating her circle of friends.

But she could not have put such trust in her friends, she could not have made the bonds of friendship carry the strain that circumstances often put on them, had she not exercised her powers of scepticism on her acquaintances before she promoted them to closer intimacy. Her great achievement of forming a circle of friends who thought well of each other and therefore would act in concert as people of good will was done with tested material.

In the sphere of art the process is more difficult to follow. It is carried on differently by creative artists of different sorts, and critics have to use scepticism differently again.

Authors who write works not of the imagination, who deal with hard fact, have soon to realize that very few facts indeed are hard, and have to use the sceptical process overtime. It is a great pity that every human being does not, at an early stage of his life, have to write a historical work. He would then realize that the human race is in quite a jam about truth. It is absolutely necessary to bring up children in the belief that there is such a thing as easily ascertainable objective truth, but it is actually very hard indeed to find out the real facts about anything outside our immediate surroundings. Facts do not lie around in neat heaps waiting for inspection. They get mislaid and confused by time; and every incident sufficiently important to seem a good subject for a book must have exposed the participants to a certain amount of criticism, so that they may have, consciously or unconsciously, lied about it. But nobody wants to admit this, because man is in a dangerous and undignified plight if he cannot control his environment, and it is hard for him to do that if the facts about his environment are hidden from him.

There is, therefore, an inherent difficulty in the production of what is called non-fiction, a not very pretty name which nevertheless contains a germ of historical truth. It suggests that fiction came first, and so, bless it, it did. First there were the bragging songs about victories in battle and genealogies showing descent from gods and heroes, howled round the campfire; then the sober recording of fact came afterwards, and to many authors it must seem that it has never caught up. Just how difficult it is to write biography can be reckoned by anybody who sits down and considers just how many people know the real truth about his or her love affairs.

As for history, the enterprise is hideously uncertain, whether the subject matter is remote or recent. If it is sited far away in the centuries, then the truth has to be traced in documents, which may quite well be written by liars; and one cannot tell by looking at a man's grave whether he was a liar or not. When the subject lies nearer at hand, in time, one can at least have better opportunities for judging whether people responsible for certain statements are liars; but then the libel laws intervene. One can say that a monk who died in 1399 indulged in a weakness for forgery. One cannot say that a contemporary who writes on Balkan politics may not be reliable because he has been in the pay of every government in a certain Balkan country for the last twenty years.

As for travel books . . . but there the thing is monstrous. Human fallibility and the unpredictability of life conspire against the writer. I once wrote a book on Yugoslavia, and while I was preparing it and reading the books other people had written on the country, I became interested in the many allusions they had made to a delightful monastery on a lake in Macedonia. This, I gathered, was a restful place where a number of monks indulged in mystic contemplation. I made arrangements to go there, and at once discovered that the place was really a lunatic asylum. What earlier travellers had regarded as crowds of peasants, whose wild air was accounted for by their remoteness from any centre of civilization, were in fact lunatics who had come to be treated by the monks.

But when I had grasped the true state of affairs, the possibility of error was not exhausted. I took it for granted that these monks were treating these lunatics by some form of magical mumbo-jumbo. I made arrangements to come back and stay there so that I could observe it, tying it up in my mind with a repulsive superstitious rite I had seen in another part of Macedonia, in which a lamb was sacrificed on a stone as an offering to a God that liked blood.

Only because there was a monk who was patient enough to submit to my questioning over many days, in a horrible linguistic mosaic composed of his bad French, my bad Serbo-Croat, our terrible German, did I discover that I was wholly wrong. The work in this monastery was following a path which ran parallel to the main avenues laid out by Western psychiatry. There was a very high rate of insanity in Macedonia. This was due partly to the fact that owing to the disturbed conditions of the district many people had known the fear of sudden death, had seen members of their family killed while they were children, and had known torture or the threat of torture. It was also due, so far as the women were concerned, to the cruel overwork which is the lot of the peasant's wife and daughter in all primitive communities. The monks took these people in for periods of forty days, gave them plenty of food and rest, encouraged them to pour out their miseries, and made them the centre of church ceremonies; a lunatic would be taken up to the golden gate in front of the altar, would have the great book of the Gospel held against his head, would be chanted over by priests in glittering robes, and the maimed and disregarded ego was rehabilitated.

The monks had even noticed that there was a difference in the chances of curing two separate kinds of lunatics. They were, indeed, in agreement with Western psychiatrists in thinking that there was much more hope for the neurotic, the man who is at war with himself but accepts the universe, than for the psychotic, who accepts himself but is at war with society and rejects the universe.

I do not know whether that interested my readers, but I know it interested me; and my scepticism long ago led me to the belief that writers write for themselves and not for their readers, and that art has nothing to do with communication between person and person, only with communication between different parts of a person's mind. A writer composes a book in order to put down what the warring elements in him think on some subject which interests them all, and to arbitrate between them. But how often those warring elements must be wrongly informed, how wildly in error I was over this monastery, how probable it is that I was as wildly in error about other points in my book! That is why down-to-earth reviewing is much more important than it seems. A jog-trot review which questions facts is, if its questioning is on a proper basis, part of a scheme for stripping the earth of its wrapping of deceptive mists, which stripping can never be entirely successful but which should be made without cease lest those mists should one day choke the human race.

More ambitious criticism, which concerns itself with the creative artists who produce works of imagination, often fails because it applies its scepticism at the wrong stage. It should apply itself simply to the results of the artistic effort, but too often it begins at the point where the creative artist himself is applying his scepticism. Bending over the raw eggs it sniffs and says, "But you could not make an omelet with these eggs, they are bad," or "This must be a good omelet, the eggs are good." This is the permanent danger besetting criticism: that it tends to judge a work of art by the conscious intention of the artist, by the ideas he thought he held when he initiated it.

Heaven knows that criticism is always difficult. Ideas are not eggs, and the mind has never developed any detective device as efficient as the nose, and facts and ideas do not advertise their corruption by a strong smell of sulphur. Indeed, by a most inconvenient coincidence, new facts and ideas often give off a distinctive odour which is mistaken by those with a dull intellectual sense of smell for the stink of rottenness. But it is adding to those inherent difficulties to look at the artist's material before he has treated it. It is to be remembered that an artist is something more than a cook; he is a magician. A cook cannot make an omelet out of bad eggs. But there is something in an artist wiser than himself, which can work miracles, even on his own foolishness.

Very often the effect of an artist's work runs far faster than his conscious mind can follow, and it may drag his conscious mind after him in a direction he never meant to go. Many Europeans and Americans have been brought to Catholicism or to a comprehension of Catholic ideas by the writings of Charles Péguy and Simone Weil, neither of whom felt able to be Catholic communicants. Dostoevsky wanted to believe in the Tsardom, he would have liked to suppose that autocracy was justified because it saved the masses from the burden of freedom, of a responsibility which they could not discharge and which would oppress them. But his genius led him to write "The Inquisitor's Dream" in *The Brothers Karamazov*, in which he proved that whether it makes man miserable or not, he can only attain an eternal value if he accepts the responsibility for deciding his temporal condition.

The artistic process is still a mystery. It is inherently improbable that a man holding certain political and social ideas should create valid works of art. For these depend on a sense of sacredness in human beings and their experience. A poem is a great thing because it reverences sensations and emotions enough to commemorate them beautifully. A novel must first regard its characters as having established an inherent claim to importance, whether they are good or bad. It is therefore unlikely that a person who believes in a political system which treats people as things and does violence to them should be capable of producing a work of art. But we cannot be sure of this. It is perfectly possible, in the present state of the world, that we might be faced with a masterpiece written by an artist who appears to hold such a belief. He might be constrained to it because his upbringing had allowed him no vision of an alternative, he might be suffering from an infatuation with some person or group, he might be partially conquered by evil. But if we apply our scepticism to his work, and it tells us that it is a masterpiece, we have to accept its findings, or we and not he will be failing civilization.

Opposite: MARLENE DIETRICH, the eternally alluring, the woman of glamour, dares alternately to tear down the public's glamorous notions and then to rebuild them. She showed herself in a movie washing her teeth, arrived at the front lines during the war in slacks and a shirt, and changed to a beaded sheath when she sang. Recently, she wheeled her grandchildren to the park, and then, at a circus benefit at New York's Madison Square Garden, startled the audience by appearing as the ringmaster. In this costume, which she designed, she appeared in the dark immensity of the ring and, taking the microphone, said to the entranced audience in a dark, warm, cavernous voice, "Hel-looo," adding affectionately, "Are you having any fun?" While Dynamite, "the only horse in the world able to gallop backwards," galloped backwards, some thirty photographers concentrated entirely on the lure of Miss Dietrich.

Milton Greene

IN BRAQUE'S HOUSE

One of a remarkable series of photographs taken by Alexander Liberman, representing famous artists and their studios. This corner of Braque's living room shows an antique Norman chest. On it are: a head, "Hesperis," which Braque chiselled out of stone from the Varengeville cliffs; a pewter teapot that often appears in his lithographs; and an oil and vinegar set he made of two mineral-water bottles. On the wall: Spanish roasting forks. Coming from small windows, intense shafts of concentrated light strike sharply on the rich variety of objects and textures.

MRS. WILLIAM PALEY, photographed by John Rawlings. She is youngest of three famous Cushing sisters, daughters of Dr. Harvey Cushing, the great brain surgeon. Her sisters are Mrs. James Fosburgh and Mrs. John Hay Whitney. On the walls of the drawing room at Kiluna Farm are paintings by Cézanne, Rousseau, Toulouse-Lautrec, and Matisse. Mrs. Paley's dress is by Charles James.

PEOPLE I WISH I HAD KNOWN

BY JACQUELINE LEE BOUVIER

THE WINNING ESSAY WRITTEN FOR
VOGUE'S PRIX DE PARIS, 1951

Putting them in chronological order, I would say that the three men I should most like to have known were Charles Baudelaire, Oscar Wilde, and Sergei Diaghilev. They followed close upon each other in the three quarters of a century from 1850 to 1925. They came from three different countries and specialized in three different fields: poetry, playwriting, and ballet, yet I think a common theory runs through their work, a certain concept of the interrelation of the arts.

Baudelaire and Wilde were both rich men's sons who lived like dandies, ran through what they had, and died in extreme poverty. Both were poets and idealists who could paint sinfulness with honesty and still believe in something higher. The Frenchman, an isolated genius who could have lived at any time, used as his weapons venom and despair. Wilde, who typified the late Victorian era, could, with the flash of an epigram, bring about what serious reformers had for years been trying to accomplish.

Baudelaire in his sonnet "*Correspondances*" developed the theory of synesthesia, a tendency to associate the impressions given by one of the senses with those of another. He speaks of perfumes, "green as prairies, sweet as the music of oboes, and others, corrupted, rich and triumphant." Wilde did not intend it, but I find the same interaction in his poetry; the musk and gold heat that emanates from a vase of flowers in "The Music Room." What a pleasure to set either's poems to music or to paint.

Sergei Diaghilev dealt not with the interaction of the senses but with an interaction of the arts, an interaction of the cultures of East and West. Though not an artist himself, he possessed what is rarer than artistic genius in any one field, the sensitivity to take the best of each man and incorporate it into a masterpiece all the more precious because it lives only in the minds of those who have seen it and disintegrates as soon as he is gone. What he did with the music of a Rimski-Korsakov, the settings of a Bakst or a Benois, the choreography of a Fokine, the dancing of a Nijinsky, make him for me an alchemist unique in art history.

It is because I love the works of these three men that I wish I had known them. If I could be a sort of Over-all Art Director of the Twentieth Century, watching everything from a chair hanging in space, it is their theories of art that I would apply to my period, their poems that I would have music and paintings and ballets composed to. And they would make such good stepping stones if we thought we could climb any higher.

[1943 – 1953]

FUNNY BONES

JACK BENNY: THE CLASSIC CHARACTER, STINGY, SORE, SELF-PITYING, TIMID AS A RAILROAD MAN'S WATCH

ED WYNN: GENTLEST WIT, WITH NO VICTIM BUT HIMSELF

PHIL SILVERS: A STEW OF TIMED TRICKS

BOBBY CLARK: THE INTIMATE ASIDE; SPECTACLES PAINTED ON

SID CAESAR: THE HUMOUR OF EXAGGERATED PANTOMIME — DOUBLE-TALK IN ANY LANGUAGE

LUCILLE BALL: A TOO-HELPFUL-WIFE CHARACTER

EDDIE CANTOR: PRESSURED MUGGING AND NOSTALGIA

Although too much humour of the comics is packaged, repetitious, and, in a way, private jokes for other comics, the public appetite for fun has never been more craving. Here are some of the comics who are twisting it out like saltwater-taffy machines. Nearly all of them show up on television. After ritual beginnings of gratitude and thank-you's, the rhythm of most comic turns begins: the straight line, then the joke, the straight line, then the joke, until audiences, mesmerized by the moving ball of humour, laugh even when the rhythmic line breaks down. There is the same inevitability in Bob Hope's insults about Bing Crosby's fortune, in the gags about Martha Raye's mouth, and in the Seltzer slapstick of Martin and Lewis. The good part of it is that most of it is inevitably funny.

Penn

BERT LAHR: FUNNY FACES AND TRADE-MARK PHRASES, "THIS IS A PRETTY HOW'VE YOU BEEN."

FRED ALLEN (BELOW): "YOU ONLY LIVE ONCE, BUT IF YOU WORK IT RIGHT, ONCE IS ENOUGH"

...IS AND DEAN MARTIN: A MADDENED BURLESQUE

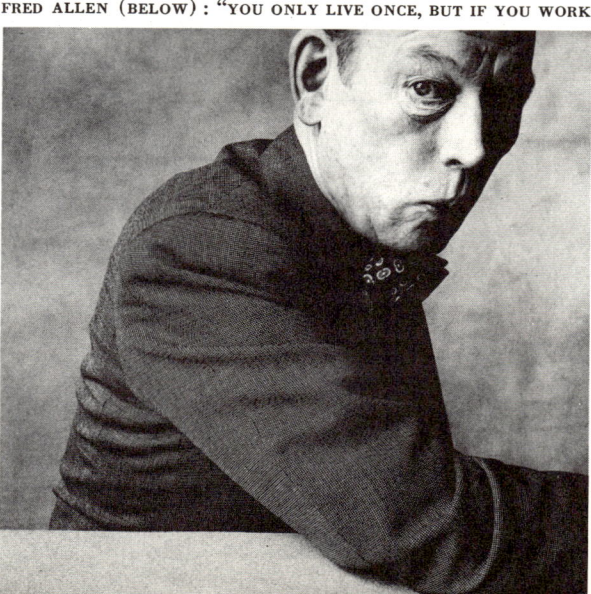

RED SKELTON: "WHAT DO YOU THINK OF THE TAFT-HARTLEY BILL?"
— "I SAY, PAY IT."

ONE MAN'S MONEY

THE ROCKEFELLER PHILANTHROPY

John D. Rockefeller magnificently practised his own premise: that a man "should make all he can and give all he can." As the architect of his philanthropy he had Frederick T. Gates, a flaming Baptist preacher with the instincts of a business man.

Moved by a vein of iron religion, Rockefeller gave seventy-five cents of his first mite-size wages to the Mite Society. Later, using the same orderly business practices by which he evolved the great Standard Oil complex and the largest personal fortune in America, he embarked on "scientific giving."

Rockefeller was a man of deep astuteness, which he largely shuttered, allowing his acquaintances only occasional, almost shocking peeps at his intelligence. Since he was also "taciturn . . . almost stoic in his repression," Gates with his evangelical furor counterpointed him nicely. He orotundly told Rockefeller that if he did not give away his fortune faster than it grew, "it will crush you and your children and your children's children." So passionately did he feel Rockefeller's interest that at his last Rockefeller Foundation meeting in 1923 he banged out to the other trustees, "When you die and come to approach the judgment of Almighty God what do you think he will demand of you? . . . He will ask just one question: *What did you do as a Trustee of the Rockefeller Foundation?*"

Rockefeller's first bold venture in or-

JOHN D. ROCKEFELLER
AT TWENTY-SIX

ganized philanthropy was the University of Chicago. All through the 1880s he had been under strong pressure from Baptist friends in Chicago to found there a great centre of learning for the West. He hesitated because he saw no evidence that the influential citizens of Chicago would reach into their own pockets to support such an institution. Rockefeller realized then that no private fortune (however vast) could shoulder all the world's burdens; that its greatest value was its power as a forcing wedge, inspiring other men of wealth or conscience or both to contribute time, effort — and money. His doubts about founding the university were dispelled in 1889, chiefly because of his meeting the year before with the dynamic Frederick T. Gates, then head of the American Baptist Education Society.

Through the years, as the splendid Gothic buildings rose, many of them copied from buildings at Oxford and Cambridge, Rockefeller gave the university thirty-five million dollars in direct personal grants. He refused to interfere in any way with its management or policies, and only twice visited the campus, when convinced that it would be ungracious to decline.

After this first collaboration, Gates, in 1891, took over the management of all Rockefeller philanthropies. A man whose passion for ideas flamed without intermission, Gates, in 1897, selected for his vacation reading a brilliant thousand-page volume by Osler on the *Principles and Practice of Medicine.* Gates immediately wrote Rockefeller a memorandum, deploring the low state of medical education in the United States, and proposing the establishment of a research institute similar to the Pasteur Institute in France and the Koch Institute in Germany. Rockefeller was deeply interested in the idea; so was his son, John D. Rockefeller, Jr. In 1901, in a loft off Lexington Avenue, the Rockefeller Institute for Medical Research began its first tentative projects, with Rockefeller's pledge of twenty thousand dollars a year for ten years. Eventually, his gifts to the Institute amounted to close to sixty million dollars.

It was also in 1901 that the younger Rockefeller made a trip through the South which crystallized his own and his father's interest in the problem of Negro education. Preliminary studies convinced them, as the younger Rockefeller said later, "that Negro education could not be successfully promoted in the South except as education for the whites was also promoted." In 1903, the General Education Board was incorporated, with an initial pledge from Rockefeller of one million dollars to be used "without distinction of sex, race, or creed." This Board was to carry through fifty years of furious, far-reaching activity, to spend over three hundred million dollars of Rockefeller money, and to prove one of the most far-reaching philanthropic enterprises of the century. The Board found that it had first to teach better farming methods and to fight hookworm, which was devitalizing part of the population (from this campaign sprang the Rockefeller Sanitary Commission).

The classic giant of the charitable trusts, the Rockefeller Foundation, was established in 1913 "to promote the well-being of mankind through the world . . . in the acquisition and dissemination of knowledge, in the prevention and relief of suffering, and in the promotion of any and all of the elements of human progress." Under this sweeping charter the Foundation has spent, prodigiously, a half-billion dollars. Its grants have financed a bewildering variety of projects and enterprises (of which a small sampling is illustrated here). In every year, the financial reports — read perhaps by one per cent of the United States population — have presented startling summaries of the world's most advanced thinking, investigating, and creating, with subheads ranging from "brain chemistry" to "language, logic, and symbolism."

Assessing the end result of this unparalleled spending, Allan Nevins wrote, "It would have been easy to make a random, fumbling, stupid use of these hundreds of millions. But [Rockefeller] employed his wealth with much the same sagacity shown in his business career. Conceivably, the money *might* have been spent to better advantage; but certainly no similar sums ever *have* been better spent."

A PAGE OF LEDGER "A" SHOWING GIFTS MADE BY J.D.R. IN THE FIRST MONTHS IN WHICH HE WAS EMPLOYED

ROCKEFELLER AT NINETY-SEVEN, A YEAR BEFORE HIS DEATH IN 1937

FREDERICK T. GATES, MASTER BUILDER OF THE GREAT CHARITABLE TRUSTS

Mexican Agriculture: a $250,000 foundation and Mexican program for better wheat, corn, beans.

The United Nations glassily overlooks New York's East River from a six-block $8,500,000 chunk of Manhattan island. The land was given by J. D. Rockefeller, Jr.

H. Bagby

Williamsburg, Virginia's restored Colonial capital — a $60,000,000 Rockefeller, Jr., project.

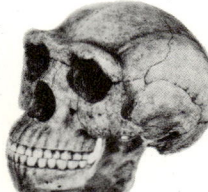
Pekin Woman, an early specimen of femina sapiens, was reconstructed from bones found by diggers financed by Rockefeller.

American Museum of Natural History

Above: Free Hookworm Cures took a million Rockefeller dollars to regenerate thousands.

Blakeslee-Lane

Left: the John Hopkins School of Public Health, fathered and fostered by the Foundation and General Education Board.

Below: the Shakespeare Theatre at Stratford on Avon received $500,000 from Rockefeller, Jr.

New York Botanical Garden, a 280-acre collection of plants for beauty and for research, received some $500,000 from the Rockefellers.

Wide World

The Metropolitan Museum acquired from the Rockefellers over $1,000,000 plus valuable gifts of art. One tangible asset is the classical "Wounded Amazon" reproduced above.

SEXUAL BEHAVIOR IN THE HUMAN FEMALE

The Kinsey Reports qualify as a Foundation by-product. About $150,000 went to Kinsey.

Left: The Cloisters, $20,000,000 treasury of mediaeval art presented to New York by Rockefeller, included the Unicorn tapestries.

Alexis Carrel became first Nobel Prize U.S. scientist, fulfilling a J.D.R. "dream."

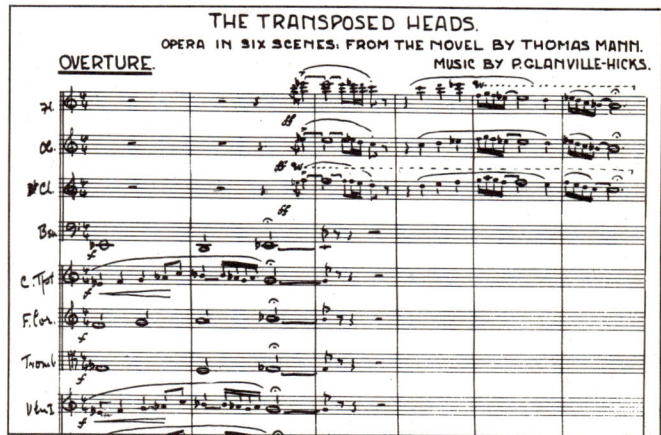

The Louisville Philharmonic Society, aided by its $100,000 Rockefeller grant, commissions and plays contemporary music. Reproduced here: a new opera score by Peggy Glanville-Hicks.

Right: The Museum of Modern Art was founded in 1929, largely through the influence of the late Mrs. John D. Rockefeller, Jr. Family gifts exceed $5,000,000 to date.

Below: The giant Cyclotron, built at the University of California with $1,150,000 from the Foundation (plus University funds), was an early tool in A-bomb research.

[1953–1963]   307

THE MAN WHO PLANTED HOPE

BY JEAN GIONO

For a human character to reveal truly exceptional qualities, one must have the good fortune to be able to observe its performance over many years. If this performance is devoid of all egoism, if its guiding motive is unparalleled generosity, if it is absolutely certain that there is no thought of recompense and if, in addition, it has left its visible mark upon the earth, then there can be no mistake.

About forty years ago I was taking a long trip on foot over mountain heights quite unknown to tourists, in that ancient region where the Alps thrust down into Provence. All this, at the time I embarked upon my long walk through these deserted regions, was barren and colourless land. Nothing grew there but wild lavender.

I was crossing the area at its widest point, and after three days' walking found myself in the midst of unparalleled desolation. I passed the vestiges of an abandoned village, whose five or six houses, roofless, gnawed by wind and rain, the tiny chapel with its crumbling steeple, stood about like houses and chapels in a living village, but all life had vanished.

It was a fine June day, brilliant with sunlight, but over this unsheltered land, high in the sky, the wind blew with unendurable ferocity. I had run out of water the day before, and had to find some. All about me was the same dryness, the same coarse grasses. I thought I glimpsed in the distance a small black silhouette, upright, and took it for the trunk of a solitary tree. It was a shepherd. Thirty sheep lay about him on the baking earth.

He gave me a drink from his water-gourd and, a little later, took me to his cottage in a fold of the plain. He drew his water — excellent water — from a deep natural well above which he had constructed a primitive winch.

The man spoke little. This is the way of those who live alone, but one felt that he was sure of himself. He lived, not in a cabin, but in a real house built of stone that bore plain evidence of how his own efforts had reclaimed the ruin he had found there. The wind on his roof tiles made the sound of the sea upon its shores.

The place was in order, the dishes washed, the floor swept, his rifle oiled; his soup was boiling over the fire. I noticed then that he was cleanly shaved, that all his buttons were firmly sewed on, that his clothing had been mended with meticulous care that makes the mending invisible. He shared his soup with me and afterwards, when I offered my tobacco pouch, he told me that he did not smoke. His dog, as silent as the master himself, was friendly without being servile.

It was understood from the first that I should spend the night there; the nearest village was still more than a day and a half away. Besides, I was perfectly familiar with the nature of the rare villages in that region. There were four or five of them scattered well apart from each other on these mountain slopes. They were inhabited by charcoal burners, and the living was bad. Families, crowded together in a climate that is excessively harsh both in winter and in summer, found no escape from the unceasing conflict of personalities. The men took their wagonloads of charcoal to the town, then returned. The women nursed their grievances. The soundest characters broke under the perpetual grind. There was rivalry in everything, over the price of charcoal as over a pew in the church, over warring virtues as over warring vices, as well as over the ceaseless combat between virtue and vice. And over all there was the wind, also ceaseless, to rasp upon the nerves. There were epidemics of suicide and frequent cases of insanity.

The shepherd went to fetch a small sack and poured out a heap of acorns on the table. He began to inspect them, one by one, with great concentration, separating the good from the bad. When I offered to help him, he told me that it was his job. And, seeing the care he devoted to the task, I did not insist. When he had set aside a large enough pile of good acorns he counted them out by tens, meanwhile eliminating the small ones or those which were slightly cracked, for now he examined them more closely. When he had thus selected one hundred perfect acorns he stopped and we went to bed.

There was peace in being with this

man. The next day I asked if I might rest here for a day. I was interested and wished to know more about him. He opened the pen and led his flock to the pasture. Before leaving, he plunged his sack of carefully selected and counted acorns into a pail of water.

I noticed that he carried for a stick an iron rod as thick as my thumb and about a yard and a half long. He left the little flock in charge of the dog and climbed to the top of the ridge, about a hundred yards away.

There he began thrusting his iron rod into the earth, making a hole in which he planted an acorn; then he refilled the hole. He was planting oak trees. I asked him if the land belonged to him. He answered no. Did he know whose it was? He did not, nor was he interested in finding out whose it was. He planted his hundred acorns with the greatest care. For three years he had been planting trees in this wilderness. He had planted one hundred thousand. Of the hundred thousand, twenty thousand had sprouted. Of these twenty thousand he still expected to lose about half, to rodents or to the unpredictable designs of Providence. There remained ten thousand oak trees to grow where nothing had grown before.

That was when I began to wonder about the age of this man. He was obviously over fifty. Fifty-five, he told me. His name was Elzéard Bouffier. He had once had a farm in the lowlands. There he had had his life. He had lost his only son, then his wife. He had withdrawn into this solitude, where his pleasure was to live leisurely with his lambs and his dog. It was his opinion that this land was dying for want of trees. He added that, having no very pressing business of his own, he had resolved to remedy this state of affairs.

Since I was at that time, in spite of my youth, leading a solitary life, I understood how to deal gently with solitary spirits. But my very youth forced me to consider the future in relation to myself and to a certain quest for happiness. I told him that in thirty years his ten thousand oaks would be magnificent. He answered quite simply that if God granted him life, in thirty years he would have planted so many more that these ten thousand would be like a drop of water in the ocean.

Besides, he was now studying the reproduction of beech trees and had a nursery of seedlings grown from beechnuts near his cottage. The seedlings, which he had protected from his sheep with a wire fence, were very beautiful. He was also considering birches for the valleys where, he told me, there was a certain amount of moisture a few yards below the surface of the soil.

The next day we parted.

The following year came the War of 1914, in which I was involved for the next five years. An infantry man hardly had time for reflecting upon trees. But when, the war over, I found myself possessed of a tiny demobilization bonus and a huge desire to breathe fresh air for a while, I again took the road to the barren lands.

I had seen too many men die during those five years not to imagine easily that Elzéard Bouffier was dead, especially since, at twenty, one regards men of fifty as old men with nothing left to do but die. He was not dead. As a matter of fact, he was extremely spry. Now he had only four sheep but, instead, a hundred beehives. He had got rid of the sheep because they threatened his young trees. For, he told me (and I saw for myself), the war had disturbed him not at all. He had imperturbably continued to plant.

The oaks of 1910 were then ten years old and taller than either of us. We spent the whole day walking in silence through his forest. He had pursued his plan, and beech trees as high as my shoulder, spreading out as far as the eye could reach, confirmed it. He showed me handsome clumps of birch planted five years before — that is, in 1915, when I had been fighting at Verdun. He had set them out in all the valleys where he had guessed — and rightly — that there was moisture almost at the surface of the ground.

Creation seemed to come about in a sort of chain reaction. He did not worry about it; he was determinedly pursuing his task in all its simplicity; but as we went back toward the village I saw water flowing in brooks that had been dry since the memory of man. Some of the dreary villages had been built on the sites of ancient Roman settlements, traces of which still remained; and archaeologists had found fishhooks where, in the twentieth century, cisterns were needed to assure a small supply of water.

The wind, too, scattered seeds. As the water reappeared, so there reappeared willows, rushes, meadows, gardens, flowers, and a certain purpose in being alive. But the transformation took place so gradually that it became part of the pattern without causing any astonishment. Hunters, climbing into the wilderness in pursuit of hares or wild boar, had of course noticed the sudden growth of little trees, but had attributed it to some natural caprice of the earth. That is why no one meddled with Elzéard Bouffier's work.

In 1933 — he was then seventy-five — he received a visit from a forest ranger who notified him of an order against lighting fires out of doors for fear of endangering the growth of this *natural* forest. It was the first time, the man told him naïvely, that he had ever heard of a forest growing of its own accord.

In 1935 a whole delegation came from the government to examine the "natural forest." There was a high official from the Forest Service, a deputy, technicians. It was decided that something must be done and, fortunately, nothing was done except the only helpful thing: the whole forest was placed under the protection of the state, and charcoal burning prohibited. For it was impossible not to be captivated by the beauty of those young trees in the fullness of health, and they cast their spell over the deputy himself.

A friend of mine was among the forestry officers of the delegation. To him I explained the mystery. One day the following week we went together to see Elzéard Bouffier. We found him hard at work, some ten kilometres from the spot where the inspection had taken place.

This forester was not my friend for nothing. He was aware of values. He knew how to keep silent. I delivered the

[1953 – 1963] 309

eggs I had brought as a present. We shared our lunch among the three of us and spent several hours in wordless contemplation of the countryside.

It was thanks to this officer that not only the forest but also the happiness of the man was protected. He delegated three rangers to the task, and so terrorized them that they were proof against all the bottles of wine the charcoal burners could offer.

I saw Elzéard Bouffier for the last time in June 1945. He was then eighty-seven. I had started back along the route through the wastelands; but now, in spite of the disorder in which the war had left the country, there was a car running between the Durance Valley and the mountain. It seemed to me that the route took me through new territory. It took the name of a village to convince me that I was actually in that region that had been all ruins and desolation. On the lower slopes of the mountain I saw little fields of barley and of rye; deep in the narrow valleys the meadows were turning green. The car put me down at Vergons. In 1913 this hamlet of ten or twelve houses had had three inhabitants. They had been savage creatures, hating one another, living by trapping game, little removed, both physically and morally, from the conditions of prehistoric man. All about them the nettles had fed upon the remains of abandoned houses. Their condition had been beyond hope.

Everything was changed. Even the air. Instead of the harsh dry winds that used to attack me, a gentle breeze was blowing, laden with scents. A sound like water came from the mountains: it was the wind in the forest. Most amazing of all, I heard the actual sound of water falling into a pool, I saw that a fountain had been built, that it flowed freely and — what touched me most — that someone had planted a linden beside it, a linden that must have been four years old, already in full leaf, the incontestable symbol of resurrection.

Besides, Vergons bore evidence of labour at the sort of undertaking for which hope is required. Ruins had been cleared away, dilapidated walls torn down, and five houses restored. Now there were twenty-eight inhabitants, four of them young married couples. The new houses, freshly plastered, were surrounded by gardens where vegetables and flowers grew in orderly confusion, cabbages and roses, leeks and snapdragons, celery and anemones. It was now a village where one would like to live. Lazarus was out of the tomb.

It has taken only the eight years since then for the whole countryside to glow with health and prosperity. On the site of ruins I had seen in 1913 now stand neat farmhouses, cleanly plastered, testifying to a happy, comfortable life. Old streams, fed by the rains and snows that the forest conserves, are flowing again. On each farm, in groves of maples, fountain pools overflow onto carpets of fresh mint. Little by little the villages have been rebuilt. People from the plains, where land is costly, have settled here. Along the roads you meet hearty men and women, boys and girls who understand laughter and have recovered a taste for picnics. Counting the former population, unrecognizable now that they live in comfort, more than ten thousand people owe their happiness to Elzéard Bouffier.

When I reflect that one man, armed only with his own physical and moral resources, was able to cause this land of Canaan to spring from the wasteland, I am convinced that in spite of everything, humanity is admirable. But when I compute the unfailing greatness of spirit and tenacity of benevolence that it must have taken to achieve this result, I am taken with an immense respect for that old and unlearned peasant who was able to complete a work worthy of God.

Elzéard Bouffier died peacefully in 1947 at the hospice in Banon.

ALBERT EINSTEIN: INTELLECTUAL ADVENTURER

Professor Albert Einstein, originator of the theory of relativity, occupies a unique place in modern life. His epochal discoveries are understood only by top-ranking scientists, yet he is a towering figure in the imaginations of millions of the ordinary, unscientific people in the world — and oddly beloved. His effect on the public is the reverse of what might be expected; instead of leaving us far behind him in his daring intellectual plunges into the mysteries of time and space, matter and energy, the very secrets of the universe, he seems to raise all of us to a higher level. To understand his work is forever out of reach of most of us; yet most of us feel a curious, fierce flicker of pride that his work has been done in our time.

He has had all the honours that could come to him — the Nobel Prize, the offered Presidency of Israel, degrees from every major university in the Western world, an American medical school rising in his name. Yet he remains utterly innocent of pride or pretension.

Ernst Haas

MRS. HENRY R. LUCE

Clare Boothe Luce, ambassador-designate to Italy, is the first United States woman ever chosen as ambassador to a major country. She has achieved the ability to turn the usual feminine day-dreams into reality by a combination of brains, wit, and beauty plus an indomitable compulsion to work hard. An extremely active internationalist, she served on the House Military Affairs Committee and on the Joint Committee on Atomic Energy during her four years in Congress. Six years before her political career, she married Henry R. Luce, head of *Life*, *Time*, and *Fortune*. Later she wrote three plays, one war book, several movies. She began her many-faceted career by writing for *Vogue*.

NANCY, LADY ASTOR

She was the first woman to sit in Britain's House of Commons. Famous since girlhood for her beauty, gaiety, wit, and political flair, Nancy, Viscountess Astor, in the House of Commons from 1919 until 1945 was a rod around whom political lightning streaked — and she still is. An American, born in Virginia in the 1880s, she was one of the Langhorne Sisters, a famous four that included Mrs. Charles Dana Gibson. She married Waldorf Astor, the second Viscount, in 1906, and to the Astor country house, Cliveden, she has always drawn "the most amusing people of the fashionable world," the political men of power, statesmen, generals and admirals, noted writers — and pretty women.

Cecil Beaton

Drawing by Bouché

REVOLUTION OF THE WOMEN

BY JOYCE CARY

Thirty years ago, college girls were told by various women's leaders that their first duty was to their sex. They had won the vote, but the women's revolution was not complete. They must now fight their way into men's careers. To have a husband, a home, and children was treachery to the cause, a piece of self-indulgence. The age that followed, the twenties — an age we're just beginning to see as a whole — has been described as one of decadence, neurosis, and futility. Scott Fitzgerald expressed the futility, D. H. Lawrence and Aldous Huxley different forms of the neurosis. Evelyn Waugh rattled the bones of his pessimism like the castanets of some death dance. Civilization, we were told, was done for, and women's revolt against the home and against marriage had played the chief part in its destruction. Even in fashion she denied her nature, cut her hair like a boy and dressed like an immature child.

Now we find women in all careers, and these women have homes and children. Fashions have never been more feminine or emphasized more strongly the woman's difference. Yet there has been no great revival of religion, no Savonarola has denounced wicked books and wicked customs, and the cries of ruin and degeneracy which we still hear from some pulpits are either taken as a matter of course or regarded with mild derision. A Rip Van Winkle who went to sleep about 1914 and woke up now would be astonished, not so much by the independence of women as by their competence and their sense of duty. That is to say, more is expected of women than ever before.

The young women and the young mothers of today not only accept the position — they choose it. Whereas thirty years ago the girl of social conscience would almost apologize for having a baby, the same girl now, more often than not, will be anxiously inquiring how many babies she can afford, and if it is possible for her to do her duty by them and her husband while keeping her job. This problem too is one which urgently concerns the family, for a young couple may need the wife's earnings to give the children what they both agree children should have.

For this renascence of the family and family conscience has taken place in the teeth of economics. If we chose to call it dialectical, we would have to decide that it was as far removed from a materialistic dialectic as it well could be. Thirty years ago, prices were low, houses were cheap, good nurses and maids were always to be had. Now on both sides of the Atlantic housing and baby-minding mean an endless struggle with every kind of perverse circumstance.

Such a phenomenon, altogether apart from its affirmation of faith, is exciting to the social historian because it raises the question, What is behind history, what makes it tick, what is the connection between revolt against the family and the little-boy fashions of the middle twenties? What is the mysterious power which, itself unseen and unsuspected, sets in motion these vast complex movements in society?

We are perhaps too near the revolution of the women — probably the greatest social revolution, in the true sense, that the world has seen — to understand all its implications. But we can begin to see some of the factors at work. The age of the twenties seems to us now not so much a time of decadence and futility as of confusion. Every major revolution is followed by confusion and bewilderment for the simple reason that revolutionary slogans which are always used and probably must be used to smash the frame of

314   [1953 – 1963]

any organized situation are useless to construct a new one. So women who had fought for the vote with the battle cry of freedom from domestic slavery — from the old Germanic laws of church, kitchen, and children — found, when they had the vote and when careers were open to them on all sides, that the slogans of their leaders did not answer any of their urgent personal problems. In fact, they prevented an answer. The girl who fell in love no longer found a course of life laid down for her. On the contrary, she was perplexed by a new conflict between her inclinations, her conscience, and her ambition. She was told both by her own leaders and the old conservatives that she must choose between a family and her job, that it was impossible to do justice by both.

As for the ethics of sexual love, the new psychology interpreted them in equally extreme terms. The school of D. H. Lawrence told her that nothing mattered but the crudest sex experience, that men and women must always be secret and deadly enemies, that marriage was an everlasting battle; and that of Aldous Huxley was trying to convince her that men and women alike were victims of a nature only less lewd than it was stupid. She was tempted to doubt even her own affections. She was encouraged to look upon the most profound and common human sympathies as tricks played by a cunning nature, whose only aim was to continue the race. If, after all this questioning, she married and had children, or at least one child, she was even ready to deny the child any show of affection because according to the new psychology, as interpreted to her, sentiment was not only a weakness of the flesh, it was dangerous. It produced complexes which might destroy the child's character for life and turn it into a neurotic or a criminal.

What is surprising about the twenties is not that there was frustration but that thousands of women made a success of their marriages and brought up families which have made a success of life. But that, I suspect, is a tribute chiefly to nature itself, which convinced them in spite of the theorists that love is not all selfishness or appetite, and that children needed it.

A young woman who has a very good position in business, as well as a family of three, and thinks nothing of an achievement which can now be paralleled in any street, said to me the other day that she could never understand why the last generation made such a fuss about the vote. She asked what difference it had made; women, she said, had been breaking into jobs anyhow, and French women, without the vote, had also opened for themselves men's careers. She considered that the suffragette leaders were a "lot of Victorian hysterics due to a silly season" in history.

Such a judgment is, of course, an abominable injustice to the women who gave their lives to a revolution which, whatever she may think, brought to this young wife the greater part of her freedom; but it is an injustice so common to history between one generation and another that we needn't wonder at it. What I found interesting was the sense of security, the moral poise which enabled the judgment to be made. For the speaker was quite confident of her own position. She was perfectly accustomed to judging for herself what was owed to her family or to her job. She faced cheerfully as a matter of course the most complicated problems of management and economy. I may say that also she was a very affectionate mother and did not hesitate to show her affection. By Victorian standards, still more by those of the twenties, she was spoiling three young children, who appear to thrive under the treatment.

But she was only amused when I began to compare ideologies — to ask her where she got her new ideas from. She said that she had no use for ideas about family life. Any woman with the least sense knew how to manage a family. One had only to do "the natural thing." I pointed out that to the Victorian it was the natural thing for a woman to have ten children, to leave them to be brought up by nurses under threat of hell fire and to see themselves barred out on all sides from any careers excepting motherhood and teaching. To her modern mind the Victorians were frumps whose lives were idiotic.

This is not a defensible view. (Malinowski in his work on the Pacific Islanders tells us of many forms of marriage and family life which also seem to their practitioners the only natural thing.) But it is evidence of a new stability, a new ideal setup. The age of confusion is past. Women are essentially free. They know what they want, and they can decide for themselves how to get it. No one says to them "either a career or a family," for the dilemma is seen to be false. Each decides for herself.

And so we return to the question, How did this new situation arise? Why have women found for themselves, apparently without any positive lead, a stable place in a new integrated society? A first clue lies in the changes of fashion. I suggest that the fashions of the twenties were an aberration, an attempt to put off nature, which was itself a symptom of moral confusion. Women tried to seem not so much like boys as asexual; and since this was impossible, the effect was epicene and trivial. They returned to their natural shape precisely as the age of confusion, the revolutionary fog, was blown away, and the new real situation was disclosed, or rather felt, in process of development. And this development, this renaissance, which had been proceeding by itself, under the fog, all the time — where did that come from? The source, like that of the new fashions, seems to me to lie far deeper than any propaganda of ideas. It is in the nature of things; in the very form of what we may call primal society. Nothing can destroy those affections and sympathies which bring about the essential family relation, whatever its local form. Father, mother, and children (even among those Trobrianders, where the direct paternal connection is not acknowledged) are a natural and primitive unit, a miniature civilization in which love, tolerance, and unselfish duty are reborn from generation to generation. Against such immense natural forces any ideal man-made decadence is as temporary a phenomenon as the shell blast which lays a garden waste. The seed remains, to grow again.

As for what we may call, in a large sense, the social and political circumstance, for women — their careers — that has, as with men, adjusted itself to the central position. A man has always been able to decide between family and career, and though there are some in each age who have, for one reason or another, sacrificed family life, civilization has proceeded on its way.

Women are now in the same place as the men. They have achieved the power of independent choice. But such a power carries with it a compulsion. Since woman *can* choose, she *must* choose. Since she has alternatives to marriage, if she marries, she *chooses* marriage, as she might choose a profession; she is deliberately undertaking to make a home. If she wants children, she *chooses* to have them, and by that fact, accepts a quite different responsibility from that of mothers in the past, to whom motherhood was something that happened as a matter of course. Her life, in short, has become infinitely more complex than any lived by women in the past. It is full of difficult choice, and decisions which cannot look to any convention for support. She has discovered, if she has any time over from the daily turmoil to think about such matters, that freedom is a burden and a responsibility, and any doctor can tell you what that means in nervous pressure. But you don't find any woman who would change places with her grandmother. For the fact seems to be that people do not seek peace or happiness in life, but fulfillment, and to get fulfillment, they are ready for any kind of hardship.

Keystone Photo

THE KING'S FAREWELL to Princess Elizabeth as she and the Duke of Edinburgh leave on January 31, 1952, for Australia and New Zealand. The King, Queen, and Princess Margaret stand on the London Airport roof while their Prime Minister stands vigilant below. Six days later, King George died. In her accession speech, a sorrowing daughter referred to the "heavy task . . . laid upon me so early in my life."

ELIZABETH II (opposite) by the Grace of God, of the United Kingdom of Great Britain and Northern Ireland and her other Realms and Territories, Queen, Head of the Commonwealth, Defender of the Faith — with her consort, H.R.H. the Duke of Edinburgh, who after the crowning on June 2, 1953, was first to do homage.

OPPOSITE: PAGES TO THE DUKE OF NORFOLK; THE HONORABLE
JAMES DRUMMOND AND MASTER DUNCAN DAVIDSON

THE GARTER PRINCIPAL KING OF ARMS;
THE HON. SIR GEORGE BELLEW, C.V.O.

Beaton

THE ARCHBISHOP OF CANTERBURY — THE MOST REV. AND
RIGHT HON. DR. GEOFFREY FRANCIS FISHER

Beaton

LADY CHURCHILL
WITH HER GRANDDAUGHTER

Toni Frissell

ROSEMARY

BY MARIANNE MOORE

Beauty and Beauty's son and rosemary —
Venus and Love, her son, to speak plainly —
born of the sea supposedly,
at Christmas each, in company,
braids a garland of festivity.
    Not always rosemary —

since the flight to Egypt blooming differently.
With lancelike leaf, green but silver underneath,
its flowers — white originally —
turned blue. The herb of memory,
imitating the blue robe of Mary,
    is not too legendary

to flower both as symbol and as pungency.
Springing from stones beside the sea,
the height of Christ when thirty-three —
no higher — it feeds on dew and to the bee
"hath a dumb language"; is in reality
    a kind of Christmas tree.

Marianne Moore is one of America's great poets. These are her own footnotes for this Christmas poem: The rosemary of Europe grows four to eight feet high, and according to Eleanour Sinclair Rohde "never grows higher than the height of Christ when He was a man on earth.". . . A Spanish legend explains that the flowers of rosemary turned from white to blue when the Virgin threw her cloak over a rosemary bush while she rested on the Flight into Egypt.

LEFT: SIR WINSTON CHURCHILL in the state robes he wore at the Coronation. Over his uniform as Lord Warden of the Cinque Ports was the blue velvet mantle of the Most Noble Order of the Garter: around his neck, the long golden Collar, from which hung the George, a richly-chased gold figure of St. George and the Dragon. This particular George was presented by Queen Anne to Sir Winston's ancestor, the first Duke of Marlborough; like all Garter insignia, it reverted to the Crown on his death. Later, King George IV presented it to the first Duke of Wellington, with the command that his family should hold it permanently. Sir Winston, because of his own great services to England, was asked to wear it on June 2. Around his neck also hung the Cross of the Order of Merit, rigidly restricted to twenty-four members.

Toni Frissell

SENATOR JOHN F. KENNEDY, AND HIS WIFE, THE FORMER JACQUELINE BOUVIER, AT THE RECEPTION FOLLOWING THE WEDDING OF HIS SISTER, PATRICIA KENNEDY, AND PETER LAWFORD

"BROTHERS, I PRESUME?"

BY SENATOR JOHN F. KENNEDY

The time has come for peace missions from those two great armies, the authors and the politicians of America, to hold a meeting at the summit, to persuade their comrades to put aside those horrible weapons of modern internecine warfare: the barbed thrust, the acid pen, and most sinister of all — the rhetorical blast. For the current hostility between the political and literary worlds has been helpful to neither camp.

The politician and his government make no military secret of their disdain for the author and the scholar. In Washington, our Fortress on the Potomac, we award medals and memorials to distinguished civil servants, to famous military men, to outstanding scientists, and, of course, to retiring politicians — but nothing to distinguished authors. I have serious doubts that a national poet laureate could ever get Senate confirmation. We subsidize beet growers, silver miners, fertilizer spreaders, and even honeybees — but not authors.

The disdain of the author and the scholar for the politician and his government, on the other hand, is equally apparent. My desk is flooded with books, articles, and pamphlets, criticizing Congress. But rarely, if ever, have I seen any writer bestow praise upon either the political profession or any political body for its accomplishments, its ability, or its integrity — much less for its intelligence. Fictitious politicians — whether members of Parliament in the time of Charles Dickens or mayors of Gibbsville in the time of John O'Hara — are inevitably shabby, slippery, or selfish. Many of today's intellectuals and authors share the views of Henry Adams, who in 1869 was told impatiently by a Cabinet member, "You can't use tact with a Congressman! A Congressman is a hog! You must take a stick and hit him on the snout." And in quiet derision Adams replied, "If a Congressman is a hog, what is a Senator?"

Real-life politicians, to much of the literary world today, represent nothing but censors, investigators, and perpetrators of what has been called "the swinish cult of anti-intellectualism" — a cult, I might add, which is matched in the current clash by what might be termed "the snobbish cult of anti-politicalism."

But peace between these long-time enemies will be achieved not by an accentuation of our differences but by a recognition of our similarities, of all we have in common, of all we share and should share.

The American politician of today and the American author of today are descended from a common ancestry. For our nation's first great politicians — those who presided at its birth in 1776 and at its christening in 1787 — included among their ranks most of the nation's first great writers and scholars. The founders of the American Constitution were also the founders of American scholarship. The works of Jefferson, Madison, Hamilton, Franklin, Paine, John Adams, and Samuel Adams — to name but a few — influenced the literature of the world as well as its geography. Books were their tools, not their enemies. Locke, Milton, Sidney, Montesquieu, Priestly, Coke, Bolingbroke, Harrington, and Bentham were among those widely read in political circles and frequently quoted in political pamphlets. Our political leaders traded in the free commerce of ideas with lasting results both here and abroad.

For more than a century this link between the American literary and political worlds was maintained unbroken. Presidents, Senators, and Congressmen were not only political philosophers but biographers, historians, essayists, humourists, and, in some instances, writers of poetry and fiction. Consider, for example, this poem to a young girl:

Remember thee?
Yes, lovely girl.
While faithful memory holds its seat,
Till this warm heart in dust is laid,
And this wild pulse shall cease to beat,
No matter where my bark be tost
On life's tumultous stormy sea:
My anchor gone, my rudder lost,
Still, cousin, I will think of thee.

The author was not Christina Rossetti, nor Robert Browning, but a rugged senator from Texas — Sam Houston.

Literary men, when not directly active in politics themselves, maintained a strong influence on political events. The gifted abolitionists of New England — Ralph Waldo Emerson and John Greenleaf Whittier among others — influenced strongly the years before the Civil War. And Henry Adams' education was involved even more with political matters than with the symmetries of Chartres Cathedral and Mont St.-Michel.

Today this link is all but gone. Where are the scholar-statesmen? The American politician of today is fearful, if not scornful, of entering the literary world with the courage of a Beveridge. And the American author and scholar of today is reluctant, if not disdainful, about entering the political world with the enthusiasm of a Woodrow Wilson.

The modern politician — although not all, I should make clear — knows well that what he says but never writes can almost always be denied; but that what he writes and never remembers may some day come back to haunt him. The thought of Job's lament, "O, that mine adversary had written a book," has dried up many a politician's pen. Political memoirs and diaries, published at the end of one's career, and with the incalculable advantage of hindsight, are considered to be relatively safe. But even this type of publication is increasingly rare. The only fiction to which many modern politicians turn their hand is the party platform; the only muse which they invoke is their party leader. As for the works of Locke, Milton, Coke, and Bolingbroke — the only Locke in which they are interested is on the Treasury door. Milton is on television Tuesday nights, Coke they drink, and Bolingbroke they have never even heard of at all.

At the same time, too many American authors and scholars — forgetting that their forefathers were politicians too — are fearful that the rough and tumble of politics will damage the fine hand by which they spin out carefully conceived works. "All literary men," wrote John Galsworthy, "can tell people what they *oughtn't to be;* that's literature. But to tell them what they *ought to do* is politics." Many literary men *will* tell us what we ought to do — to that extent they will enter politics. But few will put themselves into the open arena, exposed to the pressures of public calumny and to the humiliation of the ballot box. They prefer to remain on the marksman's end of the rifle of political criticism and not on the bull's-eye. This is indeed unfortunate — for our political life would be refreshed if our literary men of today would assume the positions of leadership they have held so decisively in past years.

The American politician and the American literary man operate within a common framework — the framework of liberty. Freedom of expression is not divisible into political expression and literary expression. The lock on the door of the Legislature, the Parliament, or the Assembly Hall — by order of the King, the Commissar, or the Führer — has historically been followed or preceded by a lock on the door of the printer's, the publisher's, or the bookseller's. And if the first blow for freedom in any subjugated land is struck by a political leader, the second is struck by a book, a newspaper, or a pamphlet.

Unfortunately, in more recent times, politicians and intellectuals have quarrelled bitterly — too bitterly in some cases — over how each group has met the modern challenge to freedom both at home and abroad. Politicians have questioned the discernment with which intellectuals have reacted to the siren call of the extreme left; and intellectuals have tended to accuse politicians of not always being aware, especially here at home, of the toxic effects of freedom restrained.

While differences in judgment where freedom is endangered are perhaps inevitable, there should nevertheless be more basic agreement on fundamentals. In this field we should be natural allies, working more closely together for the common cause, against the common enemy.

Politics, politicians, and government have — since man first carved out his thoughts on the walls of caves — ranked second only to romance as a subject for literary plots. The relationship of a Solomon with the Queen of Sheba, the conquests of a Charlemagne, the tragedy of a Lear — these are the tales of politicians, their governments, their laws, their battles. It took politics to hang the witches at Salem, to plunge the knife into Duncan at Inverness, and to quarrel over the remains of Caesar at Rome. It was politics that sent Joan of Arc to die in the city square at Rouen, that sent De Bonnivard to the Chillon dungeons, that sent Davy Crockett to the Alamo. Without politics and governments, there would be no spies, no court intrigues, no revolutions, no prisons, no poorhouses.

Politics and government have touched the lives and works of all the authors and poets we have ever honoured. They ordered Lawrence to Arabia, sent Byron to die in the rain at Missolonghi, dismissed Poe from West Point, and sent Rupert Brooke to die on an island in the Aegean.

Nor is this a one-way street. The influence of literature upon the course of our political life has been equally vast and immeasurable. Time and again, great works of literature such as Rousseau's *Social Contract* have caused great political struggles — and time and again, great political struggles have given birth to great works of literature.

Modern politicians, whatever they may say, could no more get along without authors than authors could get along without politicians. It is partly from books and articles — whether fictitious (like *Uncle Tom's Cabin* and Upton Sinclair's *The Jungle*) or factual (like the memoirs of generals) or philosophical (like Lippmann's *Public Opinion*) — that those of us in the political arena obtain our ideas, our ideals, our issues, and our inspiration.

"Poets," wrote Shelley at the conclusion of his *Defence of Poetry*, "are the unacknowledged legislators of the world." This is truer than most legislators are willing to admit. The causes, the crusades — even the criticisms — of authors and journalists stimulate us and help to guide us. Much as we chafe under the biting comments of our intellectual critics, whether liberal or conservative, there are few members of the Congress who would put themselves above reproach, who would want all their conclusions — right or wrong, wise or dangerous — to go unchallenged and uncorrected.

The politician and the author are motivated by a common incentive — public approval. "How many books will I sell?" asks the author. "How many votes will I get?" asks the politician. The problem, of course, is to prevent the natural desire of both groups for public approbation from becoming dominant.

Certainly this is a real problem in political life, where the number of temptations and pressures to take the primrose path of never-ending compromise is perhaps greater than in any other profession. Torn between his obligations to his constituency, his concern for the welfare of his family, his gratitude to his supporters, his loyalty to his party, his personal ambitions, his sense of public duty, and his awareness that right and wrong on most issues are almost inextricably mixed, the politician stumbles along, seeking shelter from his critics — only a few of whom are disinterested. In few professions other than politics is it expected that a man will sacrifice honours, prestige, and his chosen career on a single issue. I do not say that authors, teachers, and others do not face difficult decisions involving their integrity — but few face them as does the politician in the spotlight of publicity.

It is no wonder that we do not have more men of political courage, willing to go out on a limb for what they believe. It is no wonder that a famous Senator half a century ago had become so accustomed to political caution and guarded opinions that when he went to see the Siamese Twins he warily asked the guard at the exhibit, "Brothers, I presume?"

And it is no wonder that it was said of a similarly inclined and similarly cautious senator of a generation ago, William B. Allison of Iowa, that if a piano were constructed reaching from the Senate Chamber to Des Moines, Allison could run all the way on the keys without ever striking a note.

Unfortunately, there are few groups where the problems of the politician are given as little genuine comprehension as they are among writers and authors who seem to possess that talent for finding the right and wrong on all questions with none of the difficulties that face the politician. It is this extraordinary faculty of so many literary figures that prompted Lord Melbourne's statement that he would like to be as sure of anything as the youthful historian T. B. Macaulay seemed to be of everything.

I do not wish to minimize the difficulty that the author faces in being faithful to his talent. Nor do I wish to defend the art of the politician if it results in situations which are in Shaw's words "smirched with compromise, rotted with opportunism, and mildewed by expedience." Certainly I do not seek any cessation of critical faculties in their application to my profession.

For it is one of the hallmarks of totalitarianism that criticism is directed only against the enemies of the state, rather than against the state itself. And certainly all too frequently it has been the writer and not the politician who has been the truer friend of liberty. But I do suggest the need for a greater comprehension of the very real and difficult problems involved in the successful governing of a democratic state.

And I shall conclude this plea for unity by calling again for recognition of how inextricably entwined are the professions and the fates of our politicians and writers. In this way the synthesis of our efforts and talents may provide a greater service to the cause of freedom — a bulwark to meet the challenge of the future.

COSTUME BALL IN BIARRITZ

THE MARQUIS DE CUEVAS WITH HIS DAUGHTER, MME. HUBERT FAURE (LEFT), DONNA MARELLA CARACCIOLO, AND COUNT CHARLES DE GANAY

An extravaganza of the eighteenth century — the costume ball given by the Marquis de Cuevas. There were two thousand guests, two ballets, two orchestras, and a rather grumpy camel. After the ballet entertainment, guests danced till 6 a.m.

RENEE JEANMAIRE, WHO DANCED IN ONE OF THE BALLETS, ENTERS ON CAMEL-BACK

Sabine Weiss

THE ART OF BALLET

BY AGNES DE MILLE

All ballet dancers need to work with is an even floor, something to hold on to, slippers, and if possible a mirror. They don't even need space. Just the floor, slippers, the *barre*, and — patience.

This is the way each practice begins. This is the way each practice has begun for two hundred and fifty years. Just this way, never any other. In Paris, Milan, Leningrad, London, New York, Tokyo. It is part of the inviolable ritual handed down by rote from teacher to pupil.

Ballet is an ancient art whose technique has stood like the rules of harmony. It represents the oldest unbroken tradition in the Western theatre — more perfectly preserved than any technique in singing, instrumental performance, or acting. And since the time it started developing, from country dances to court dances, about three hundred years ago, ballet has never been out of style. Today it is more popular than ever before in its history. There are in the United States alone more than five million ballet pupils.

The characteristics of classic ballet dancing as opposed to other forms of dancing are: the posture, the co-ordination of head and arms (or *port de bras*), and the turned-out feet. The achievements of ballet as opposed to other forms of dancing are brilliance and strength of footwork and elevation. Elevation is the ability to rise vertically in the air and dance off the earth. The posture is based on a quiet spine and level hips. The hips may not lift, thrust out, or rotate as in other forms of dancing.

The shoulders must also be quiet. We know that all forms of emotion and tension are ordinarily shown first in the shoulders and neck — this is never true with a ballet dancer. A dancer may express all kinds of emotion, but always with relaxed shoulders.

When you or I hate, our hackles rise; but never a ballet dancer's. She hates serenely, with majesty. And this is not so surprising when one considers that the entire style was based on majesty — in particular, one majesty, the French king who built Versailles, the Sun King, Louis XIV. Only royalty and nobility danced in the early ballets. The ballets were, in fact, prolonged, magnificent, expensive royal charades.

The posture of ballet is not an easy one to maintain. It is particularly not easy when one is performing feats of enormous athletic difficulty. It is possible to win a track meet; but to win a track meet and to look at the same moment as though one were far away, reading a book, takes some doing.

The ballet dancer stands with the legs rotated outward at forty-five degrees from the hip. Why do what is so difficult, so arbitrary, so formal? Simply because the first ballet dancers were swordsmen, and swordsmen turned out their feet to provide a broad base for balance so that they could move in any direction instantly. Every courtier was an able swordsman. If he was not a good swordsman, he was not a courtier for very long. Every courtier could dance, and, naturally, he danced as he was used to moving.

Gradually acrobats and dancing masters were recruited to help out and vary the tedium of those early dances, which were basically simple, because the dancers were amateurs.

The ballets involved no technique except floor pattern and stage effects. What with the complicated protocol involved in choreographing for horses, mechanical effects, the upper and lower branches of royalty, and acrobats, matters began to get out of hand, and in 1680 Louis XIV asked his ballet master, Beauchamp, to lay down some rules. It was his task to codify, classify, and name the style and all the acceptable steps. To this day they are known by their seventeenth-century French names, and that is why all ballet language is in French.

All ballet technique is built on five principal positions for arms and feet. The gestures are symmetrical, harmonious, circular, all opening from a central axis. In the two hundred years that followed Beauchamp, enormous expansion and enlargements took place. Each innovation was the invention of some one dancer, most of them anonymous and remembered today only by the turn of the wrist, by the grace and speed of the feet, or by the lightness and brilliance of whirls — some one lovely thing representing a life's effort and bequeathed to the dancers who came after. So the body of technique grew like coral.

Most of the performers are forgotten, but we remember a few. There was Marie Camargo, the most beloved of the eighteenth century. She was a great jumper, credited with having invented the *entrechat* or beaten jump. So that her feet might be seen, she shortened her skirts to midleg. Critics howled and so did moralists, but the skirts stayed up. It took a hundred years to get them to the knees and another hundred to get them off.

We can read her dances from eighteenth-century graphs. But they must be watched with the eyes of her contemporaries. Come back with me to her time, to the eighteenth century when a wagon wheel could be heard a quarter of a mile away, or children calling. Sounds were simpler then, and music was simpler and purer. None who saw Camargo had ever heard a full symphony as we know it, or even a piano. Strings were still plucked as in the harpsichord. Eyes saw farther then. Men who watched Camargo had never seen electric lights, arc beams, or even gas. One could see the stars from any city street, and when one came in from the luminous dark, candlelight made all things gentle and forgiving.

The French Revolution put an end to this pastoral quality. The century which began so graciously went out in blood and cannonades. The new century brought great changes; the eighteenth-century dancer was expected to be robust, charming, and voluptuous; the nineteenth-century dancer was ethereal. She was also, for the first time in the Western theatre, an artist.

Maria Taglioni was the greatest dancer of the century, and one of the greatest of all time. Her father boasted that any gentleman could bring his wife to see her without blushing. The professional artist had at last appeared — dedicated in childhood and cloistered throughout youth in the practice room. Each royal opera house now had a ballet company, and ballet stars were sometimes as famous as the singers. Maria Taglioni was the first Sylphide — all gauze and air.

By the nineteenth century, ballet technique had developed very nearly to what every dancer uses today. Because we have inherited the eyes of our ancestors, along with their language and manners, we find long unbroken lines to be the most exciting a dancer's body can produce. The dancer's leg is turned out so that the front of the knee and the flat unbroken line of the leg are presented to view — never the lax, droopy aspect of the side of the knee.

The ideal ballet body is long-limbed — long arms and legs with a short,

Penn

NORA KAYE, ALICIA ALONSO, ANDRE EGLEVSKY

compact torso. But genius makes its own rules. Some of the finest dancers of history have been short and stocky women. A dancer's legs do not grow naturally. She makes them. It takes her about eight years to make a leg. It took dancing two hundred years to learn how. The well-trained leg is never lumpy with muscles.

The ballet foot neither feels nor searches the ground like the palm of the foot in primitive dancing; it neither taps nor stamps as in folk dancing. It uses the ground as a base for pushing, as a surface for patterns. It springs to attention whenever it is released. This alert and tense arching gives every ballet position a sense of enormous vitality. It also, of course, prolongs the line of the leg. The ballet hand is relaxed, simple; any affectations are considered out of style. The ballet face is quiet, alert, disciplined, and serene; all emotion has been driven from the countenance into the complete dance gesture.

These are the tools; and now we consider devices. One of the most brilliant devices is the pirouette or turn. In turning it is important to maintain balance on a straight spine, and to spot. Spotting is snapping the head around as you turn. The eyes are not permitted to travel with the body, or the vision would swim and the dancer would grow too dizzy to continue. The eyes focus on one spot always, even when the dancer moves across the room. Since the invention of the *fouetté* — or whipped turn — no girl has had any peace. It is the great double dare; it is the four-minute mile, the goal being sixty-four done in one spot. Rather too many.

There are some techniques that women specialize in, and some that men specialize in. The women's most beautiful trick is dancing on the ends of their toes — point work. Maria Taglioni is credited with having perfected this technique. Her slippers were made of light strips of silk ribbon and weighed nothing. They were as light as pieces of paper. She had support only from the darning of the toes and the binding of the ribbons around the

OPPOSITE:
ALICIA MARKOVA

Penn

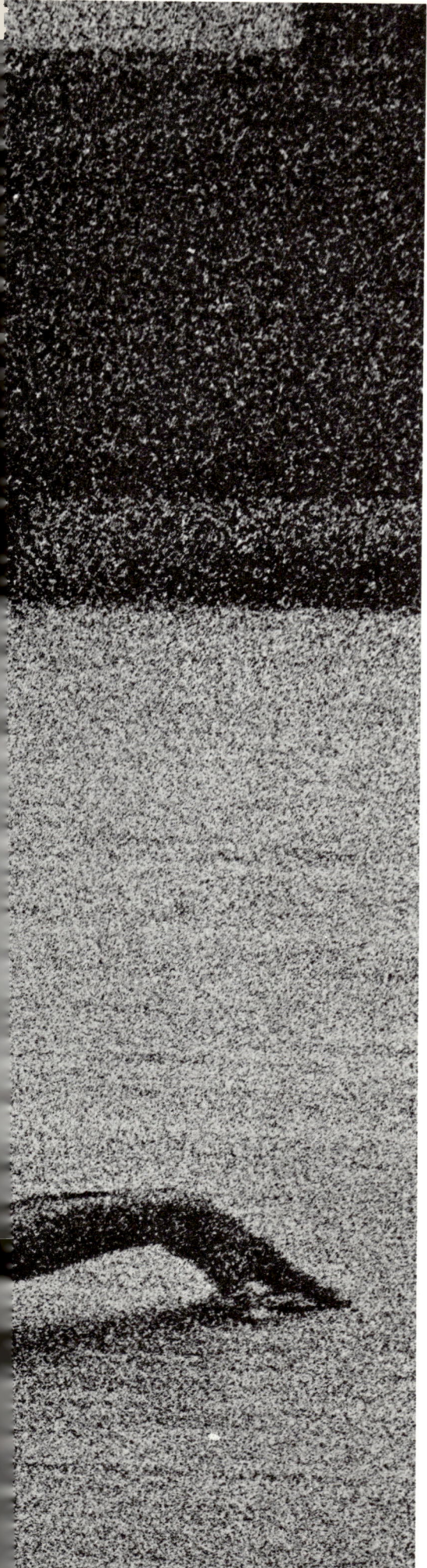

JEROME ROBBINS

ankles. She made none of the grinding virtuoso demands most women today ask of their feet.

The modern American shoe is heavy. The canvas is stiffened with glue and must be broken in. The ends are darned to prevent floor friction from tearing the satin. Maria Taglioni's shoes cost only a few sous, and she had a new pair for every ballet. American shoes cost seven dollars and the dancer hopes that, with care, they will last a week. The foot is swathed in lamb's wool to prevent chafing; and if there is a wrinkle in the stocking, it may rub the flesh off one's toe. Tying the shoe is crucial. If a ribbon slips in performance, the dancer may break an ankle. In a perfect point, the arch has been developed to support the weight of the body. There is no weight on the knuckles of the feet or on the knees or on the hips. It is transferred to the high arch and the spine. There should be no pain. The sensation is of floating, as though walking in water, or on air.

Do not allow your child to go on point until she is eight or nine years old and has had at least a year's training. Her bones are soft, and she can permanently injure her back and spine.

The technique in which men excel is jumping. It is not enough just to jump high as an athlete does. Height is ex-

MARGOT FONTEYN IN "GISELLE"

Parkinson

[1953 – 1963] 333

citing, but the body must at all moments maintain beauty of line. The postures and attitudes practised so carefully at the *barre* are now lifted bodily into the air. You will notice that heads and arms move in slower tempo than feet. This is what gives the sense of effortless ease and flight. The feet must obey gravity; arms can take their time.

What is a ballerina? Her technical virtuosity is extraordinary, but it takes more than this or she would be nothing but a circus performer. She must have style. She must have personality. She must have more; and it is this which lifts her above the ranks. She must have *nobility*. She must divest herself of all pettiness, all personal mannerisms. She becomes, in a manner, selfless.

The term ballerina is regularly misused. It does not mean any girl who takes ballet lessons. It is an exact term and its equivalent in the Army is a five-star general. Below the ballerina in descending order come stars, first soloists, second soloists, coryphees, and members of the *corps de ballet* — or privates no grade. It takes a rookie six years of strenuous training to become a private no grade in this outfit. When a little girl begins to study, she does not see what you see, but the promise.

In old ballets the pantomime or story-telling part was always separate from the dance proper and was performed in acting as artificial as sign language. This may seem arbitrary and even ludicrous until we realize the importance of preserving style. If in grand opera the characters were suddenly to break into normal broken speech the ear would be insulted, and so we have intoned speech or recitative. In like manner the eye would be insulted if we interspersed these highly artificial and formal dances with natural acting; therefore in classic ballet we have stylized pantomime.

Today all dance has been considerably broadened and freed, and so the acting can afford to be natural. It is incorporated into the dance; the dancer's feet are on the earth, the ground is part of the gesture, and she behaves like a human woman. The Swan Queen permitted no familiarity, emotional or physical. The Prince might touch only her hand or her waist. But the girl in the *Oklahoma pas de deux* seems to be motivated by all the normal inclinations, and her sweetheart is happy to oblige. What brought about this relaxation of decorum — this simplicity and directness? At the turn of the century, a California girl named Isadora Duncan, believing that dancing in its artificiality was heading up a blind alley, threw off her corsets and her shoes and danced barefoot across Europe. She was probably the greatest revolutionary the theatre has ever known. Her effect on contemporary artists was overwhelming. Under her inspiration, a part of the Russian ballet left home and came West, bringing such a galaxy of genius as had never been seen before, and inaugurating an era of musical, dramatic, and pictorial creativity without parallel. I am referring, of course, to the Diaghilev Ballet. Dance and passion — dance and drama were forever fused.

And so, back to the ballet *barre*. Practice before rehearsal. Practice before performance. This is it, star or pupil. They are bound to this wheel for life. They gave up their childhood and games. They gave up adolescence, they gave up fooling around and wasting time. Now they are grown — there is no respite. What makes this sacrifice worthwhile? Neither fame nor money can pay for a lost childhood. Is it worth it? Well, we think it is.

To take the air. To challenge space. To move into space with patterns of shining splendour. To be at once stronger and freer than any time in life. To lift up the hearts of those who watch. To be carried on their response. And to walk once more in majesty. An ancient glory breathes around us and the spirit of the dedicated dead. The veils tear. It is enough.

334   [1953 – 1963]

IRVING PENN'S "BULLFIGHT IN BARCELONA" IS
ONE OF HIS EARLY IMPRESSIONIST
PHOTOGRAPHS WITH THE DRAMATIC USE OF COLOUR
WHICH MIGHT HAVE COME FROM A FAUVE PALETTE

THE NEW VAMP

BY ANITA LOOS

The Vamp returns in '58.... This spring the dress designers seem to have in mind a carefree look such as the look of those carefree days of the twenties, before huge taxes had turned gentlemen into money grubbers... when their gifts took the delightful form of stocks, bonds, and real estate, and the intercontinental missile was merely science to be swallowed with a grain of salt, and not a grain of cyanide.

It will really be quite a great service if the new clothes can make girls forget practically everything that has happened to us since the twenties. For today the gifts that gentlemen can afford have degenerated into mere tokens of sentiment, in which there is nothing to gain except the spirit in which they are given. And, as a consequence, girls now prefer jobs to gentlemen. So the fifties will go down in history as the era when girls in the aggregate all went to work, just as the twenties was the era of the Vamp. And for the benefit of those who never learned the meaning of the term, a Vamp is a girl who is intrigued by a member of the opposite sex, to a point where she will make an effort to please him.

It was during the twenties that the technique of Vamping reached its highest perfection. Before those days, a Vamp was depicted by girls of the Theda Bara type, who wore "robes" instead of dresses and put on heavy white face powder. But today this specimen of Vamp has been shown up by Mr. Charles Addams, whose pictures of girls only cause gentlemen to shudder.

The twenties also disclosed that gentlemen respond with the greatest amount of sentiment to the type of Vamps who remind them of the girls they used to play hookey with from high school. And because this discovery is basically solid, it still holds up. And I feel that today, if a gentleman were asked to choose between Maria Callas and Brigitte Bardot for sex appeal, his choice would not send him scurrying to the opera house.

It was during the twenties that the costume best suited to the Vamping of gentlemen was evolved, and turned out to be the chemise dress. For a chemise has the advantage of quite often concealing the female form and as a consequence it supplies girls with an added dimension of mystery. I mean, no gentleman is ever going to puzzle his brains over the form of a girl in a Bikini bathing suit. And it is a significant fact that when gentlemen no longer puzzle their brains over the form of a girl, genuine diamonds might as well go so far underground that the De Beers Corporation might simply prefer to leave them where they find them.

And now that chemise styles are in, the girls of 1958 will require a few hints on how to wear them. For the chemise dress evokes a unique type of behaviour. For instance, the chemise-Vamp shows a provocative manner of walking which never would have been tolerated by Queen Victoria, while walking, during the fifties, has become a mere effort to rush to a job, without a tendency to stop and loiter.

But it is a discouraging fact that every time some benefactor tries to do something for humanity, a feeling of resistance crops up. And, just as there was a hue and cry against the vaccine of Dr. Salk, there has now developed a certain resistance against the chemise dress, even on the part of the girls they are going to do the most for.

So I think that every girl should study the advantages of a chemise.

Seeing that the chemise follows the line of the pinafore, it also tends to make girls look younger than the stark reality.

And, the chemise being casual, gentlemen can fail to realize that girls are on display, which allays their inhibitions. For there are very few gentlemen who wish to coddle a girl garbed in a *robe de style*.

To sum all this up, I believe it will be delightfully nostalgic if girls can forget that the pleasing of gentlemen has become a nonpaying occupation. And that, with the return of the chemise, we may be able to take our minds off jobs and become sentimental over gentlemen once again.

"EYE" BY PENN

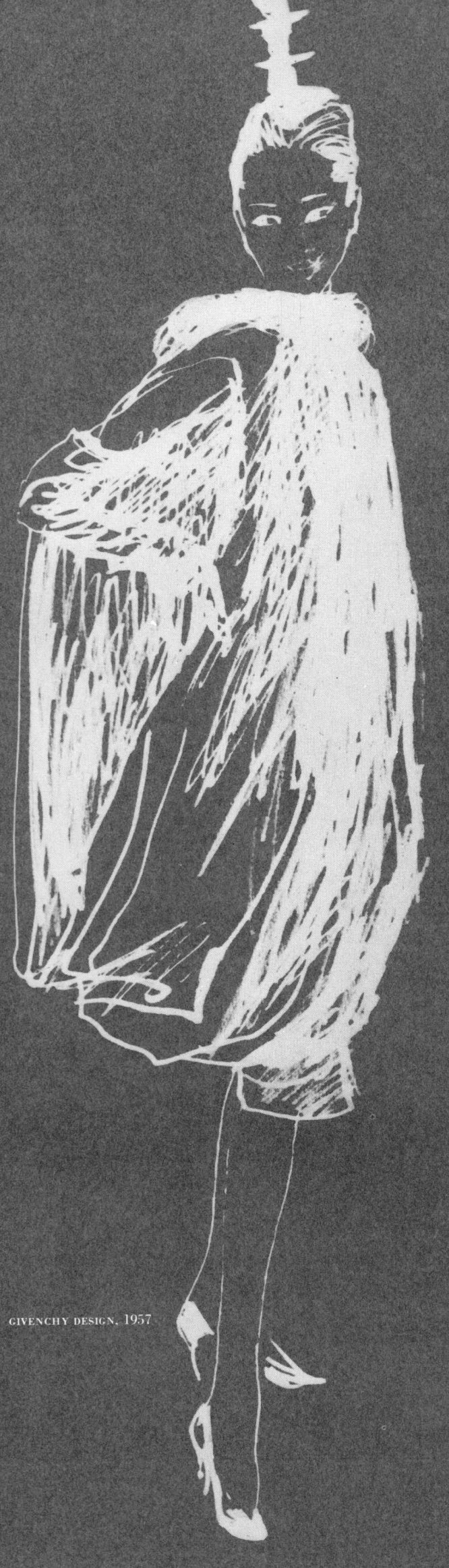

GIVENCHY DESIGN, 1957

1957-1958:

WOMEN WEAR
UNWAISTED,
NO-SHAPE DRESSES,
SHOWING THE LEG FROM
THE KNEE DOWN

TRAINA-NORELL DESIGN, 1958

GIVENCHY DESIGN, 1957

ON STAGE

The pleasure of T. S. Eliot's *The Confidential Clerk* lies partly in the cast, partly in the comic invention of the relaxed but exact verse, and partly in the international game of guessing what Eliot means by his geometric puzzle on illegitimacy. Without too much difficulty, it is fairly obvious that Eliot is saying that it is dangerous to wish for anything if you do not know yourself, and that you can know yourself only through the sympathy and understanding given to and received from others.

BELOW: INA CLAIRE, JOAN GREENWOOD, AND CLAUDE RAINS IN THE NEW T. S. ELIOT COMEDY

Prigent

G.B.S.
ON WOMEN

"... if women were as fastidious as men, morally or physically, there would be an end of the race."

"Home is the girl's prison and the woman's workhouse."

"In Shakespeare's plays the woman always takes the initiative. In his problem plays and his popular plays alike the love interest is the interest of seeing the woman hunt the man down."

"It is assumed that the woman must wait, motionless, until she is wooed. Nay, she often does wait motionless. That is how the spider waits for the fly."

"She had humour; she had intellect; she could cook to perfection; and her highly strung temperament made her uncertain, incalculable, variable, capricious, cruel, in a word, enchanting."

"... domestic pressure may be slow; but it's sure."

"... I found that when I had touched a woman's imagination, she would allow me to persuade myself that she loved me; but when my suit was granted she never said, 'I am happy: my love is satisfied': she always said, first, 'At last, the barriers are down,' and second, 'When will you come again?'"

"In my childhood I demurred to the description of a certain young lady as 'the pretty Miss So and So.' My aunt rebuked me by saying, 'Remember always that the least homely sister is the family beauty.'"

RIGHT: REX HARRISON AS PROFESSOR HIGGINS AND JULIE ANDREWS AS ELIZA DOOLITTLE IN THE HUGELY SUCCESSFUL LERNER AND LOEWE MUSICAL "MY FAIR LADY," BASED ON GEORGE BERNARD SHAW'S "PYGMALION"

PEOPLE AND SPORTS

SKIING EXPERT EMILE ALLAIS, WITH MRS. A. CASEY, AT SQUAW VALLEY

SIGNORA GIANNI AGNELLI, PRINCESS PIGNATELLI, AT BEAULIEU-SUR-MER

Henry Clarke

Joffe

GOLFER SAM SNEAD TROUT FISHING AT GREENBRIER

TOUCH FOOTBALL IN MIDLAND, TEXAS

Frances McLaughlin

Nick De Morgoli   Nick De Morgoli

WINSTON GUEST AND MRS. JAMES VAN ALEN (LEFT) AT A SYNDICATE PHEASANT SHOOT IN NEW YORK

Erwitt

MRS. OTIS CHANDLER SURF-RIDING IN CALIFORNIA

Neneyman

MRS. JOHN FELL GOLFING IN SCOTLAND

MRS. MURRAY VANDERBILT RIDING SIDE-SADDLE

Henry Clarke

Marshall P. Hawkins

Parkinson

PRINCESS RADZIWILL IN LONDON

MRS. ROBERT WINMILL AT A VIRGINIA HUNT

Nick De Morgoli

MR. AND MRS. NEWELL WARD AT MIDDLEBURG, VIRGINIA

TENNIS AT NEWPORT'S CASINO; SEDGMAN VS. MCGREGOR IN FINALS

MRS. HOWARD SERRELL, DRESSAGE EXPERT

Graphic Arts Photo Service

Rawlings

TENNIS CHAMPION WILLIAM TALBERT WITH MRS. TALBERT

BOWLING AT THE BLOOMFIELD HILLS COUNTRY CLUB, MICHIGAN

GIAN-CARLO MENOTTI

His *Saint of Bleecker Street*, a full length opera, recently gave the world of music its most talked-of production. The pro-Menottis call it the greatest modern opera; the "antis" point out its Puccini chord. Almost everyone agrees that it shows his mature genius for the theatre. After years in the United States, Menotti, thin, skeptical, high-tempered, with nerve ends close to the surface, controlled by an almost visible charm, has remained indelibly Italian and at the same time an American phenomenon. He is the only contemporary composer whose operas are almost always in performance somewhere — *The Medium, The Consul, Amahl and the Night Visitors*. His enormous talent lies primarily in his projection of sound to rouse, to play on human feelings, for in the best sense he is a demagogue in music.

LEONARD BERNSTEIN

An intense, vividly energetic man, Bernstein shot into the public eye when he substituted, unexpectedly and brilliantly, for Bruno Walter as conductor of the New York Philharmonic orchestra in 1943. Since then he has conducted everywhere from London to Israel. As a serious symphonic composer, he wrote "Jeremiah," then switched to his flip and rakish rhythms for the ballet "Fancy Free," which led in turn to the musical comedy *On The Town*, and then back to a symphony with "The Age of Anxiety." Later he wrote the scores for *Wonderful Town, Candide*, and *West Side Story*. "When I am with composers," he says, "I say I am a conductor. When I am with conductors, I say I am a composer." When anyone asks his secretary, she says, "He is busy."

Drawings by Bouché

WHAT IS AN ENGLISHMAN? BY PIERRE DANINOS

One of the most difficult things in London is to meet an Englishman.

The difficulty is even greater in English history, where so many peoples have collaborated; there are times when you have to wait six hundred years before coming across a king who was not born in Osnabrück, Hanover, or Blois. The Canutes were Danish, the Plantagenets French, the Tudors Welsh, the Stuarts Scottish, and finally, having got rid of a Scot in order to replace him with a Dutchman on the throne, the English got themselves a German king who did not speak a word of English.

"Good heavens, what of it?" Major Marmaduke Thompson, red as his own flag, retorted. "A Turk can be king of England, for that matter. If we put him in Buckingham Palace it's because we like the fellow, that's all."

So I shall leave kings out of it. But without going back to William the Conqueror, the driver of my first London taxi was waging incessant war against the English in a curious foreign accent. He snarled at every red light, chewing on a bit of the *Daily Worker*.

As we passed Buckingham Palace he asked, "Have you ever thought how many taxi drivers could live in there?"

I told him no; I had never considered Buckingham Palace from that angle. Surprised by such irreverence, I asked him if, like most English people, he didn't feel more affection for the crown.

"*British* I am, but not English," he said. "I'm Welsh."

I thought that I would have more luck at finding a really authentic Englishman at the hotel, but the manager was Swiss, the desk clerk French, the elevator operator Chinese, the chambermaids Irish, the headwaiter French as was the chef, and the waiters Italian.

The evening of the second day, no Englishman having yet crossed my path, I disclosed my perplexity to Mr. Wenger Stücki, the manager.

"I suppose the owner is English?" I asked.

"Mr. MacNamara, the distinguished proprieter of the Elizabethan Hotel chain, is Scottish."

It is a serious error to believe that since 1066 England has never been occupied. She still is — by the Scots. In 1707 they crossed the frontier of the union and never went back. The Scots are people who feel really at home only when they are someplace else — preferably in England. A quick tour of Mr. Wenger Stücki's horizon demonstrated that 72.5 per cent of the key positions in the hotel industry, like those in the ministries, the coal mines, the textiles industry, and the railroads, are in Scottish hands.

The only corner of Great Britain where you almost never run across a Scot is Soho, in London, where you can spend a whole day without hearing any other languages than Italian, French, Spanish, Chinese, German, or Javanese, and where you see people loitering on their doorsteps just like vulgar Continentals.

There are, however, Englishmen in London, even though it may not seem so. One of them overtook me in Piccadilly — a man of about forty, severely elegant, his scarlet face partly obliterated by a thick reddish moustache, wearing on his head a narrow-brimmed black bowler, like half a melon, set straight on and well forward over the brow, his figure impeccable in a dark blue jacket with side vents, his trousers falling straight to gleaming shoes, a red carnation in his buttonhole, and carrying in one hand a small flat leather suitcase, in the other an umbrella sharp-pointed as a rapier. What most impressed me about this man was his walk. He had a firm step, an athletic stride, and at each step his umbrella, raised to forehead height with a crisp flick of the wrist, quivered for an instant in his hand, then dropped back to the pavement, which it struck with an almost unvarying rhythm. Fascinated by the rhythmic step punctuated with measured raps of the staff, I tried to follow but I had almost to run, and running after a gentleman you do not know is one of the things that is not done in London. So I was despondent over having lost my Englishman when suddenly, in the Haymarket, the same man appeared, going the other way this time. Ten times during the day I was to meet this extraordinary gentleman, this supreme ubiquity. And each time I started eagerly toward him, quite prepared to call out, "Hello there, Major!"

But no: it was not Major Thompson. It was one of his five or six million brothers. London is a city in which hundreds of thousands of bowlers, all planted on the same head, advance to the conquest of the same invisible goal. No forest of Île-de-France is more impressive than this forest of melons and umbrellas, eternally on the march. You cannot imagine these men strolling as Latins do. Marching is their lot. There are no other men in the world who march as the man of London, impassive and secure in his right, marches toward his destiny.

And what is this destiny? For a long time I kept wondering.

All these Edens with their big feet, what state secrets, what top-secret documents were in their attaché cases?

One day, in spite of the Major's disapproval, I decided to follow one of them to the end. Leaving the Foreign Office, the black bowler crossed Whitehall, went up the Mall and entered the tube at St. James's Park. Thanks to my having boarded the same car I was in contact when the train plunged into its concrete burrow. The man began by reading the *Times*, but as we left the centre of town and he still had his seat to himself, he folded his paper, placed his precious case on his lap, and cautiously opened it. At last I was to know the secret of one Foreign Office attaché case.

The dispatches of Empire, that day, consisted of a cake of soap, a small white towel, the *Cricket Almanack* for 1955 which I recognized by its cover, and a ham sandwich which the gentleman proceeded to eat as if he had been riding between Angoulême and Poitiers. To be truthful, he ate very daintily. But the fact remains, he ate.

RONALD SEARLE, THE BRITISH CARTOONIST, R OF "THE BELLES OF ST. TRINIAN'S" AND MOLESWORTH, GIVES SHAPE TO PARISIAN PIERRE DANINOS' CREATION, MAJOR THOMPSON

A. THE EMBRYONIC MAJOR, WITH BOWLER

B. THE MAJOR IN FULL EQUIPMENT

That same evening I imparted my discovery to the Major.

"You confounded Frenchman!" he said. "Now I suppose you're convinced that no Foreign Office dispatch case contains anything but snacks —"

No, of course I am not. And yet nothing so resembles an Englishman in a bowler as another Englishman in a bowler. The philosopher James Russell Lowell himself wrote, "Never do I bless Providence more than on the day it introduces me to an Englishman who is not like all the others."

Why this resemblance?

The English can be explained by Saxon heredity and the influence of the Methodists. I prefer to explain them by tea, roast beef, and rain. Above all, a nation is what it eats, what it drinks, and what falls on its head. People continually swept by wind and rain and subjected to perpetual fog eventually turn into waterproofs off which criticism slides like water off rubber. People who drink tea seven times a day and eat the same vegetables and meat all year round must eventually all develop the same complexion. There is roast beef in the Englishman, as there is rice in the Chinese.

"This time I agree," the Major conceded regretfully. "The thing that makes Frenchmen so different from one another is that one likes his snails while another eats his meat pie and the third one's wife cooks him up a stew — her *own personal* little stew, which is quite different from her neighbour's. My colour is never so high as yours by three o'clock closing time, and, my goodness, the British flag isn't the same colour at Saumur as at Nuits-Saint-Georges. Your Côtes-du-Rhône, your Clos-Vougeot, and your Muscadet give the French an infinite variety in colouration. Tea and whiskey condemn the English to greater uniformity. Besides which, you are incapable of understanding us."

How is one to understand them, after all?

How to define people who make it their duty never to ask a personal question about their neighbours' private lives, yet keep informed about their Queen's most inconsequential comings and goings and purchases, as if they were doorkeepers at Buckingham Palace; who vehemently champion individual liberty yet take away your glass of wine at one minute past three; who do not like to talk but adore orators; who detest heat but cherish a passion for fire; who have an innate sense of grandeur but, from their houses to their railroad engines — and including their peonies — are addicted to the worship of the small; who speak of insignificant matters when sober and begin to discuss serious issues when they drink; who, without raising an eyebrow, will watch their children caned by their schoolmasters yet cannot bear the sight of any cripple; who despise all that is not English yet derive their national beverage from a shrub of Indo-China; who never embrace in front of people in the street but do it in Hyde Park in front of even more people; who have a horror of crossbreeding but are themselves a mixture of Celt, Saxon, Scandinavian, and Norman; who accuse the French of living to eat yet spend all their time nibbling; who persist as the most rigid cradle of conservatism yet have taken Karl Marx and Lenin under a protective wing; who practise austerity on Sunday yet, on that day, send the circulation of a weekly scandal sheet up to eight million copies; who like to drive slowly while alive but are driven at breakneck speed in Rolls-Royces when they are dead; who carry an umbrella in fine weather and wear a waterproof when it rains; who are forever talking about home but are delighted to settle down abroad; who never insult anyone without first assuring that person of their respect; who are reputed to have the manners of kings yet walk into restaurants ahead of their wives? . . .

"Nonsense!" the Major said. "Ass! That's respect for feminine modesty — to protect the defenceless female against vulgar contacts."

"Very well. But will you deny — you are supposed to be the best-mannered folk in the world — that your Cabinet ministers at Westminster put their feet on the council table?"

"That is privilege, my dear Daninos, not boorishness."

Major Thompson is always right. Especially when everything seems to give him the lie. Here again is another of the Englishman's strengths; he instantly finds a sound explanation for his compatriot's inconsistencies which I, for my part, refuse to attempt to define except by saying that of all their famous textiles the most indestructible is still the tissue of their contradictions.

"You only confuse yourself, old chap, with this mania of yours for explaining everything. We English are far too intelligent or far too stupid to try to understand ourselves. Every year for the past thousand years some foreigner has gone home from England to write a book designed to explain the English to his countrymen. An Englishman can not be explained, he can merely be stated. Englishmen are like electricity; it exists, but no one can explain it. One small difference, perhaps, I grant you; people use electricity. Englishmen use people."

[*Translated by Charlotte Underwood.*]

BERTRAND RUSSELL, sketched by Feliks Topolski. The protean Earl, philosopher, mathematician, educator, and wit, unhampered by controversy or age, has now one important bee in his Nobel Prize bonnet: "The important thing in the present world . . . is not to have a great war. And that outweighs all the other considerations." The grandson of a British Prime Minister, Bertrand Russell is the author of some fifty books. At eleven he found Euclid "as dazzling as first love."

348 [1953 – 1963]

PORTRAITS BY PENN

PAUL CLAUDEL

Through his work on the staff of *Vogue*, Irving Penn has been able to photograph the great men and women of our time. On these four pages are examples of his photographs. His portraits are not idealizations, and he is never over-impressed by the sitter. He tries to state clearly and tellingly what he sees. There is no deceit in his pictures; his camera does not lie. He cannot and will not compromise with flattery. When Penn searchingly scans a face with his camera, recording the infinite humble details of life, he manages, by a dramatic reversal, to make us feel the significance of the seemingly unimportant. A new ideal image is born, not a sterile ideal of beauty, but a revelation of the true beauty that comes from the portrayal of the real and sometimes tragic aspects of the human condition. — A.L.

COLETTE

350   [1953 – 1963]

SENATOR ROBERT H. TAFT

WALTER LIPPMANN

RODGERS AND HAMMERSTEIN

ALFRED HITCHCOCK

PHILIP WYLIE

JUDGE LEARNED HAND

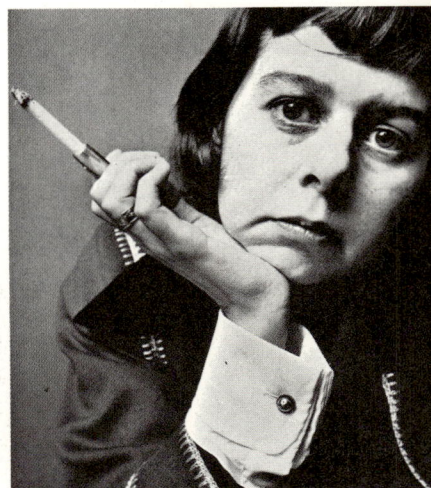
CARSON MC CULLERS

ROBERT SHERWOOD

MARIA CALLAS AND GIOVANNI BATTISTA MENEG

352 [1953 – 1963]

PERE COUTURIER

GREER GARSON

GROUCHO MARX

DANNY KAYE

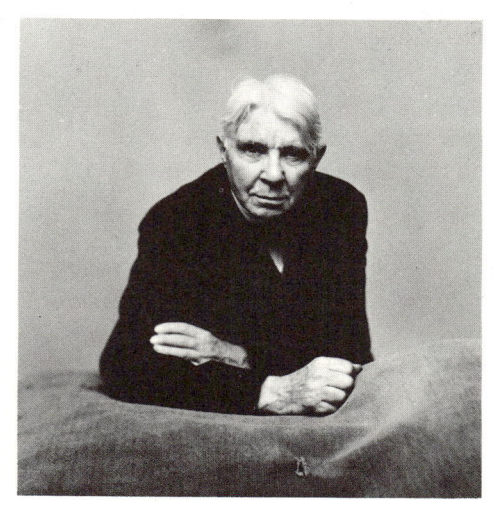
CARL SANDBURG

MR. AND MRS. JOHN GUNTHER

SPENCER TRACY

GEORGE JEAN NATHAN AND H. L. MENCKEN

THORNTON WILDER

[1953 – 1963] 353

Penn

YOU AND THE QUEEN OF SHEBA:

BY HARLOW SHAPLEY

I like numbers, in a playful way. I like counting. The number of sheep that may induce sleep. Or the number of deadly sins — seven of them, I believe. They are as soporific as a hundred sheep; each one leads down drowsy avenues of retrospection.

To indulge ourselves in numbers in a big way we need to enter the realm of celestial distances, or go down into the microcosmic world of atoms. Why not count the atoms in a single deep breath of the Queen of Sheba, or the thought cells in the forebrain of an Einstein. It can be done. For the queen's breath it would require a thousand men counting one hundred atoms a second eight hours a day not much more than ten billion years.

Our concern here is with only one of the hundred kinds of atoms — the inert atom (and gas) named argon, a Greek word meaning that it is idle, will not work. It will not co-operate in forming compounds, but it does tie us up, in a thought-provoking way, with the dinosaurs and the Queen of Sheba, with Brigitte Bardot and the bombast of Adolf Hitler.

How much of this idle argon is there in our gaseous envelope? An approximate value is one per cent of our whole atmosphere — that is 6×10^{13} tons — 60,000,000,000,000 tons — sixty thousand billion tons — sixty trillion tons — 120 quadrillion pounds — different ways of saying the same thing. The total of argon atoms in the whole atmosphere is the incomprehensible number 10^{42}.

Since one per cent of your next breath is argon we can determine approximately the number of atoms in that argonic intake. The calculations are really rather simple and straightforward, but to some readers this dizzy arithmetic is repulsive and I shall simply state the result. You are, in your next determined effort to get oxygen to your lungs and tissues, that is, in your next breath, you are taking in 30,000,000,000,000,000,000 atoms of argon; in briefer statement it is 3×10^{19} atoms of argon. (Count the zeros!) A few seconds later you exhale those argon atoms along with quintillions of molecules of carbon dioxide. The plants will appreciate those carbon dioxide molecules and make vital use of them when sunlight and chlorophyll do their magic of putting the carbon into the plant tissues and releasing the oxygen into the air where we breathing animals can again use it for our living.

Now let us follow the career of one argon-flavoured breath. We shall call it Breath X. It quickly spreads. Exhaled this morning, by nightfall its argon is all over the neighbourhood. In a week it is distributed all over this country; in a month, in all places where winds blow and gases diffuse. By the end of the year the 3×10^{19} argon atoms of Breath X will be smoothly distributed throughout all the free air of the earth. You will be breathing some of these atoms again. A day's breathing a year from now, wherever you are on the earth's surface, will include fifteen of the argon atoms of your single Breath X.

The argon atoms connect us by an airy bond with the past and the future. For instance, if you are more than twenty years old you have exhaled more than a hundred million breaths, each with its appalling number of argon atoms. You contribute so many to the atmospheric bank on which we all draw, that the first little gasp of every baby born on earth this year contained argon atoms that you have breathed.

Every saint and every sinner of earlier days, and every common man and common beast, has left argon atoms in the general treasury. Your next breath will contain more than 400,000 tokens (argon atoms) that Gandhi breathed in his long life. Atomic tokens are here with us now from the conversations at the Last Supper, from the arguments of diplomats at Yalta, from the songs of the classic poets, from the sighs and pledges of ancient lovers, from the battle cries at Waterloo, even from the argonic output of the writer of these lines, who personally has had more than three hundred million breathing experiments.

There was a time when very little argon existed in the earth's atmosphere, practically no free oxygen at all. That was some billions of years ago. The oxygen has been built up to its present abundance by the breathing of green plants, and the argon has grown over the millennia to its present one per cent as the result of the decay of one kind of potassium of the rocks. That radioactive decay steadily goes on; in five billion years there will be in our atmosphere about twice as much argon as now.

As little as a hundred million years ago (the Age of Reptiles) there was nearly as much argon as at present, and there were thousands of kinds of breathing animals trafficking in air. They, too, spread the inert argon atoms. They left us their atomic tokens. In your forthcoming breaths you will pump in and out untold millions of atoms that were spread by the snorts of fighting dinosaurs, and by the squeaks and squeals of the primitive rat-like mammals. Our air-breathing ancestors are, in a sense, with us now. As to the future — as long as animals

---

SOPHIA LOREN, eyes-on-the-bias, with an Egyptian slant, and their brilliance of white expanse, is a unique beauty; nobody at all looks like her. In the last five years or so, the Italian actress has turned herself from a bulgy Neapolitan girl with an impudent, hip-lilting strut in *The Gold of Naples* to an actress of international réclame.

of any kind roam this planet they will be, by one method or another, inhaling some of our own noble gas.

The discovery of argon and the other inert elements is worth recounting. For more than a century the chemists have known that the earth's envelope of air is composed mostly of just two gases, nitrogen and oxygen. But the research of Lord Rayleigh and Sir William Ramsay indicated that there must be something else. Those gifted British scientists had noted, of course, that in the air there is some water vapour, mostly in the clouds; also a slight amount of carbon dioxide from animal breathing and from the breath of volcanoes; but that pollution did not amount to much in the sum total of the earth's atmosphere. The H_2O (water) and CO_2 (carbon dioxide) could be removed for experimental work. When dry clean air was analysed they found that about one per cent of the whole atmosphere could be attributed to a transparent gas theretofore unknown. Isolating and analysing this residue, they announced that the new element is inert, that its atoms are about forty times as heavy as hydrogen atoms, and that the gas is a part of all air, diffused over the earth's surface and probably up a hundred miles and more to the top of the atmosphere. Of necessity this gas is involved in all animal breaths, along with nitrogen and oxygen.

Ramsay and his colleagues pursued their study of air and eventually found in extremely small quantities the other inert gases — helium, neon, krypton, and xenon. They were called the noble atoms — perhaps because of the traditional aloofness and idleness of the nobility?

Nitrogen is not very active in combining with other kinds of atoms to form compounds, it is semi-inert, but oxygen is tremendously active in atomic associations. It is a most democratic element, joining up in myriads of ways, and indispensable for animal life. It is the oxygen of the air that we seek so desperately in our cyclic breathing. Without our continual intake of oxygen for one phase of our bodily chemistry, we would be finished off in a few minutes. Nitrogen does not help, and the argon is completely useless. With each breath it just goes along for the ride. Eliminate it from the earth's atmosphere and we air-breathing animals would take no notice whatever of its absence.

Thanks to the mobility of gases, the winds at the earth's surface keep the atmosphere thoroughly stirred up and in motion. Here today, gone tomorrow, are the atoms that we are now breathing. The atomic mixture remains uniform with respect to the three main components: nitrogen seventy-five per cent, oxygen twenty-three per cent, argon one per cent.

I am being fair enough, I believe, if I invite you to serious thought about the underworld of atoms, for we are living in the amazing atomic age. We are, or should be, atom-minded. While undergoing experiment, the uranium atom broke down in our laboratories twenty years ago and we now have, as a result of its splitting, the A-bomb, the atom-fuelled submarine, some atom-produced electric current in our light and power lines, and a new exciting era in the course of civilization.

Not long after the *fission* of the uranium atom came the still more horrendous *fusion* of the hydrogen-helium apparatus, and then emerged in consequence the H-bomb and the multi-billion-dollar budgets that seem necessary to defend us against ourselves. Certainly we should be atom conscious, for those tiny chunks with a mighty wallop are writing the future of mankind.

The various kinds of atoms not only have names, many of them familiar names such as tin, gold, sulphur, iron, radium, but we have assigned them specific numbers from 1 to more than 100. The numbering is in order of increasing weight and complexity. Simple hydrogen, of course, is No. 1. Its high distinction is that apparently out of hydrogen fuel the universe has been cooked. The fact that so much hydrogen now remains in stars and space betokens a long radiant future for the sun, and, incidentally, for earthly life.

Argon, the principal subject of this sketch, is No. 18. In its most common form it is composed of eighteen protons, twenty-two neutrons, and eighteen electrons. We might say that electrons are chunks of negative electricity, protons are chunks of positive electricity, and neutrons just chunks. But don't ask what electricity is. The electrons are so compactly distributed in the outer structure of the argon atom that other kinds of atoms cannot make combinations with No. 18. It has no handles which other atoms can grasp and hold, as oxygen can grasp and hold two hydrogen atoms and produce a water molecule. Oxygen is very hungry for atomic association, and so is carbon. Their electron arrangements are wonderfully suited to the making of compounds. Carbon and hydrogen can make methane; carbon, oxygen, and hydrogen combine for various kinds of sugar; oxygen and nitrogen make laughing gas; oxygen and silicon form a compound that constitutes about three-quarters of the earth's crust; and so on, thousands of compounds — but argon remains aloof; it has no compounds.

There ought to be a moral to this story of argon. It tells us of the smallness of the units of matter. It reminds us of the mobility of gases, of the turbulence in that healthy gaseous envelope we call our atmosphere. It associates us with the past and the future.

BRIGITTE BARDOT (opposite) is the darling of the intellectual movie-art theatre. She has a kind of seemingly unaware sensuality of which audiences are completely aware. She has a succulent skin which seems about to burst, and a tiger cub's nose, ready to nuzzle. In fact, she has the contours and textures, superbly exaggerated, of a nursling. Without artifice and without premeditated worldliness, Brigitte Bardot has a maximum of straight animal magnetism. It early caught Roger Vadim, who brought her to the attention of Paris director Marc Allegret. Vadim first insinuated her into lesser roles, then into *And God Created Woman*, thus lighting the fuse for firecrackers that light up the movie sky over France, England and America.

William Klein

THE EYE OF A SOLDIER

BY GEOFFREY HOUSEHOLD

The older I get, the more I see that it is trust between man and man which keeps civilization together. You wondered just now how I stand the strain of commanding on the Syrian frontier. And I must admit that Caesar has graciously given me more responsibility than troops.

Tell him we are alert, but not alarmed. I have the confidence of the Parthian governor across the border, and between the pair of us we settle any frontier incidents. A much more able general than I am, he can do what he likes with his home government. As soon as I realized that, I set myself to win his friendship.

If the fates send you a man worthy of trust, then trust him — that has always been my principle. I will give you a very old instance. It happened years ago. Do you remember Silvanus? Yes, that one — a possible for colour sergeant if only he had been tall enough. Now there's a man who has left a beloved memory behind him.

You were at Caesarea then with the legion, and I was commanding the detachment of instructors which we had lent to Herod Antipas to train his local levies. A delicate job for any centurion, even of my seniority. But it was no use sending Herod a battalion commander. Except for the very few like ourselves, who have come up the hard way, they never know anything about drill.

We made a handy little force of the levies, too — just as fast as the Arab raiders and twice as efficient. Lack of discipline always means so much unnecessary bloodshed.

I often wonder how much it was all due to Silvanus. I should never have persuaded him to come with me, if he hadn't been feeling mutinous because the pay was cut. He was just a loyal, sturdy Italian peasant who might have gone far if only he could have bothered to learn to read and write. As it was, a proper old soldier, wise as an owl and not above feathering his nest. The gods know he needed it. But a man on whom his centurion could utterly rely. You know how fond of them one gets.

Of course, my handful of instructors thought themselves Romans among barbarians when they first arrived, and I saw that Silvanus sweated the wine out of them on an early parade in our own barracks before turning them loose on recruits. Meanwhile, I made it my business to learn Aramaic in order to keep the lot of them out of trouble.

They looked for it sometimes. At Capernaum there was a beautiful little grove with its own stream, set just where the blue spearhead of Lake Tiberias would join the shaft, which they insisted was the perfect site for a temple to Jupiter.

I quite agreed with them. But it could not possibly be allowed. Jews are absurdly sensitive about what they call graven images. You remember all the excitement when Pilate carried the Eagles to Jerusalem — a first-class revolt on his hands in twenty-four hours! Myself, I used to warn the villagers whenever there was a colour party marching up the Damascus road from Caesarea, so that they could look the other way. And they did — all but the small boys, of course.

Well, the main point was that there should be some sort of worship on a site which was made for it, and my fellows were not fussy about the various aspects of Jove. So I asked the headmen of Capernaum if they would take over the services of a temple themselves, and dedicate it to their own Jupiter. Rather like Plato's God, if I understood it. Who must exist, but a simple soul like mine needs an intermediary. They were delighted, and so were my instructors. We had a couple of army surveyors with us, training road foremen, and it was child's play for them to run up a temple from the priest's drawings, though it looked a bit bare to me when it was finished.

After that we were as popular as a foreign military mission can ever hope to be. The local population used to talk to me about their history and religion — which seemed one and the same thing — and take me to visit their schools of wisdom. I made very little of it all, but I did learn to feel the mystery behind the words.

One summer evening several of my friends rowed me over to the east shore of the lake to listen to a philosopher who was making a considerable stir by his healing and his curious doctrines. They were doubtful about his politics, and I think they may have wanted me to question him. He was sitting by the side of a goat track and talking to some fishermen. I listened for half an hour, or more. Once our eyes met, and he smiled at me. But I had no right to speak.

I cannot describe him to you at all. You know what every intelligent man thinks when he worships Caesar as a god — that he could not have arrived where he is unless he were as much above plain mortals as the gods are. So was this philosopher compared to ordinary men. He was divine. But his gold was the dust haze of the road, and his purple the bare hills in the last of the

---

SIR ALEC GUINNESS plays a British colonel whose ludicrous heroics cause tragedy in *The Bridge on the River Kwai*, a new movie, alternately marvelous and exhausting. It is sometimes confusing, partly because Mr. Guinness is often so moving that it is impossible to laugh at him.

John Stewart

sun. He made me believe that law and the sword are only a beginning and that the only virtue in making order is to prepare the way for gentleness and pity. I tell you he was young and lovely as Apollo in the stories of the Golden Age.

Soon after that Silvanus got his last attack of marsh fever. A shocking place for it, the Jordan Valley. I saw that he obeyed the doctor's orders to stay off the low ground, but it made no difference. The disease kept on coming back. And when haemorrhage set in, the doctor said Silvanus had had it. A clever Greek he was, true to his Hippocratic oath and excellent on wounds. Provided you could crawl off the field at all, you had a good chance of recovery.

If Silvanus had just been indispensable, I do not think I could have done what I did. But I loved the man; and that, I felt, gave me the right to call in the Galilean philosopher. When you appealed to him for the right reason he would heal. Never for show, or for money.

Of course, I asked our Greek first. He called the cures harmless witchcraft, which was efficacious when a man felt ill and wasn't, and of no use at all in a case of acute marsh fever.

Sound medical theory, no doubt. Yet I believe that if you feel ill you are, and healing is just as mysterious whether it is marsh fever or a Parthian spear in your liver or thinking you are Cincinnatus at the full moon. Somewhere is a divine law which we do not understand.

I did not like to ask the Galilean to come to my quarters where Silvanus was lying. I had a bust of Grandfather up, and a Homa Dea, and my delightful little bronze Aphrodite from Alexandria. Not that I thought he would have objected. But I hate putting people in a false position.

So I wrote him one of those flowery Oriental letters which all Syrians understand, saying that I was not worthy to receive him but that I should much appreciate a word from him about Silvanus.

And just to be on the safe side, I asked a delegation of my Capernaum friends to carry the letter, as I knew they would tell him all about the temple, and that for a Roman centurion I was a reasonable companion. Myself, I doubted if any of this ceremoniousness was necessary. Apollo would not expect you to carry on like the court jeweller trying to get something on account out of Herod Antipas.

Having made all the proper gestures, I walked down the valley to see him myself. I left my uniform at home. I knew he would not be impressed by it. As a matter of fact, I do not think his own followers had any clear idea who I was. They were not interested in Rome.

And then a second time I looked into his eyes. It was as one soldier to another, as if I were saluting Caesar. You know the feeling. There you are, a very small part of the world and yet in contact with all of it. But, as I have tried to tell you, he had an utterly different kind of greatness. We were not in Caesar's world.

I told him about Silvanus, and how I loved the man.

"You need not go out of your way, sir," I said. "Just — do it."

"What makes you think I can?" he asked.

I am very bad at explaining myself. But I had a sense that what I said would, in some strange way, matter — matter more, I mean, than even words of mine which could now compel life or death on the frontier.

"Because there is a law in life as in the legion," I answered, "and you, sir, know what it is. I give an order. I say to a man go, and he goes; or come, and he comes. I need not be there to see the order carried out. Nor need you."

"Go back," he said. "Your servant is healed."

And then he turned to the crowd which had collected, and told them he had not seen such faith in all the Jews.

I do not understand what he meant to this day. I have no faith at all. I am a professional soldier, not a priest. But I know the power to command when I see it, and who was I to impose any limit on his?

I shall never forget him. I cannot help recognizing that he must have gone to his death willingly as you would or I, provided we knew it our duty to civilization — though, speaking for myself, if I foresaw that pain was going to be as cruel as upon the cross I should think twice about it. Yes, he was crucified by Pilate.

"THE WHITE TABLECLOTH" BY PIERRE BONNARD

Paul Rosenberg

COLLECTOR'S HOUSE

Standing in the sunburned hills above Santa Barbara, California, is the brilliantly conceived and executed house built for the noted art collector, Wright Saltus Ludington. Although Mr. Ludington has spread his collection through the entire house, many of the paintings and some of the sculptures are dazzlingly grouped in this black-walled, black-floored gallery, which is just beyond the dark-green and mustard-yellow main entrance hall. At the far right hang two Picasso paintings; above the Richier figure and French painted clock is a Modigliani portrait. To the left, a small Braque hangs above another Picasso; above the tulips on the chest, a Redon, with a Berman above. The paintings beyond include another large Picasso portrait, another Modigliani portrait, a large Dufy, and, above the white door, a Miró. At the far end of the gallery, a Maillol bronze stands in front of the screen; to the right, a Hartley painting hangs above the Lehmbruck nude; to the left, a Kokoschka painting above the Lipchitz bronze. On the left wall, a Venetian chest hangs high above a Bonnard canvas and a larger Venetian chest. At the far end of the gallery, steps lead to Mr. Ludington's bedroom and to his sitting room, with views spanning the hills, the garden, and the Pacific.

Ezra Stoller

"MERRITT PARKWAY," BY WILLEM DE KOONING, 1959

Collection: Mr. and Mrs. Ira F.

HOW TO GET ALONG WITH A MAN
BY PHYLLIS McGINLEY

Nothing fails like success; nothing is so defeated as yesterday's triumphant Cause. I think often and with pity of those old feminist ghosts who won their battles but lost their war. They must be giddy with spinning in their graves. For their daughters and their granddaughters — freedom secure, their shackles burst — have been the meanest of traitors. They have run merrily back to their chains.

Now that girls need not marry for financial security, they marry younger and more eagerly than before. Now that limiting the size of a family requires no esoteric knowledge, the families get bigger and bigger to the despair of school systems and Margaret Sanger. The New Woman has turned out to be romantically domestic. I know women who grind their own coffee, preserve their own peaches, bake their own bread, grow their own herbs. Almost any day I expect to find certain accomplished friends of mine out in their vineyards, treading their own grapes.

So it's not astonishing that in this age of clear-eyed, emancipated youth, the world is fuller than ever of tracts directed at its distaff section — is brimful of recipes for pleasing gentlemen and ensnaring spouses. Even the most ambitious careerist now admits that a husband is vital to her whole scheme of things; that the proper study of womankind is Men.

But I sometimes think the pundits have got hold of the wrong end of the stick. Capturing male fancy isn't all that difficult. Though it can't be taught by rote any more than absolute pitch, nine-tenths of the girl babies born into the world have the gift perfected by the time they are drinking out of a cup. I recall a demonstration of native talent given by a member of my own household when she was four and out with me for a Sunday call. We must have dropped in at cocktail time, for there were present a large number of grown-ups. And, when the moment came to go, she detached her hand from mine, walked all the way across the room to the tallest and likeliest male stranger and murmured meltingly, "Will you tie my bonnet for me?"

I decided then and there that whatever crumbs of counsel on How to Deal with the Other Sex I'd been hoarding, I'd keep them for my memoirs.

If all girls do not play the music thus by ear, they've usually learned, by eighteen, at least to carry the tune. They've learned from their sisters and schoolmates, by trial and error, from exhortations in their own glossy magazines. Besides being all beautiful as nymphs — hair shining, teeth flashing like pearls or kitchen porcelain, complexions incorrigibly perfect — they have studied how to take an intelligent interest in whatever interests their prey. If need be, they can ski down terrible mountains, reef a sail, or listen interminably to the sound of locomotives on hi-fi. They are abetted, moreover, by the passion for marrying which has infected even men. Never has bachelorhood been so little at a premium. So it's an egregious female nowadays who does not, in due course, acquire a husband. One or several.

Which brings me to the root of my particular matter. Getting along with men isn't what's truly important. The vital knowledge is how to get along with a man, one man. And concerning that I think our mothers and our grandmothers knew a great deal more than we.

For one thing, they recognized their luck. They never stopped preening themselves on having the good fortune to be married women. I fear the feminists have had their little victory after all. They've persuaded us that marriage is a partnership, with inflexible rights and guarantees and that the price of feminine freedom, like that of a republic, is eternal vigilance — on our own behalf. Nonsense! Marriage is a lot of things — an alliance, a sacrament, a comedy, or a mistake; but it is definitely not a partnership because that implies equal gain. And every right-thinking woman knows the profit in matrimony is by all odds hers. Simone de Beauvoir, the French humourist, wrote a very funny book a few years ago. (At least I laughed at it a good bit.) What amused me most was her insistence that men had invented marriage to keep women in their places as the Second Sex. Now why would a man deliberately go out of his way to dream up an institution so hampering to his liberty, so chafing to the wild male spirit, and above all so expensive? The wheel, yes; the moon-bound rocket; even Scotch Tape.

[1953 – 1963]

But marriage was all a woman's idea, and for man's acceptance of the pretty yoke it becomes us to be grateful.

If ever I were intrepid enough to instruct my daughters on the care and taming of husbands, I should put gratitude first on my list.

Perhaps it need be the only comment there. For gratitude is a sincerer form of flattery than imitation; and for its sake a man will endure a great deal — will bear with extravagance, too much marjoram in casseroles, or a tendency to sinus trouble. It is better than charity at covering a multitude of faults.

Faults there are bound to be, marked like towels, plainly His and Hers. But the woman who gets along with a man knows how to get along also with his defects. She is too sensible to try to erase them, so she adopts them. The most successfully married couples I know have, perhaps unconsciously, worked this out; and so I shall remark to my daughters. Is the lord of the manor unpunctual about letters or meeting one at the station? Does he drink too much coffee, clutter ash trays, read late at night in bed, turn on all the lights and leave them burning? Is he a pantry-raider, an ice-tray emptier, careless of calories? Does he tramp in gardening boots across the Saturday carpet and think one's old boarding-school friends are bores? Let it not exacerbate the soul. Be unpunctual together. Let the lights burn and the leaves gather on the rug and the ice melt in the sink. See old cronies at lunch without him or suffer them less gladly. Faults shared are comfortable as bedroom slippers and as easy to slip into. I have a feeling that Darby and his Joan were probably both terrible housekeepers and ramshackle hosts, but that Joan kept a pot of coffee — or was it mead? — ready at all times for the two of them. And I'll wager she laughed heartily at every joke he told while they were tucking it away.

For next to gratitude, and ornamenting it, I should put appreciation. Particularly appreciation of his wit. Husbands expect a certain amount of disillusionment. They know that a helpmate before breakfast is bound to be less picturesque than the *soignée* creature with whom he danced at the Assemblies. He has braced himself for hairnets and flannel bathrobes! What he hasn't counted on is a wife who either interrupts his newest Madison Avenue jape with, "You'll have to call the carpenters, honey, about that storm window," or greets its point with a chill stare.

Nor is he prepared at parties to have her snatch the same story away from him and finish it herself. Perhaps half the wife-murders in history would have gone uncommitted if the murderee had not, at some time during a convivial evening, stopped her husband dead in the middle of a story with an impatient, "Oh, Harry, you're getting it all wrong! The dog doesn't come in till later. You see there were these two sailors. . . ."

I happen to be married, myself, to a genuine wit; I *know* that his most off-hand dinner-table observation is far funnier than anything Abe Burrows ever said, and it makes for an agreeable life. But a good many husbands might be coruscating at dinner, too, if they were nicely applauded.

Let's see — that's three items on the list and it seems very skimpy advice for a woman to have accumulated after more than twenty years. My daughters would laugh at me, and quite rightly, if I handed them this trio of tenets. What about the hot meal at night and the good breakfast? What about being tactful to the president of his company? Is there to be no sound counsel on staying slimly seductive, on asking intelligent business questions, on Getting One's Way without a Fuss?

I'd have to admit I was a poor oracle. I've seen marriages fly apart at the seams and I've seen them firmly welded as a battleship, and there was never a rule of thumb to go by. Good housekeepers come to grief and bad ones prosper; but I have also seen Craig's wife enthroned like Hera in Mr. Craig's heart. I know happy women who understood more about business than their husbands and equally happy ones who thought a Dow-Jones average had something to do with golf. For my part, I think the more distance a wife puts between herself and the head of her husband's firm the better.

As for glamour, even that is moot. There's a friend of mine who, although she can scarcely make out the name on a restaurant marquee, leaves her glasses at home because her husband thinks they are unbecoming, and *she's* happy. I also know a witty woman novelist who buttons her sweaters unevenly and forgets her lipstick, and *her* husband hasn't spoken a cross word to her in years. There are executive-type women who do the driving in the family and who replace the fuses and beard the furnace in its den; and then there are the ones — like me — who go into trauma when faced with an automatic pencil sharpener. We all seem to fare about the same. And when it came to the final question, I'd have no answer at all. In a successful marriage, there is no such thing as one's way. There is only the path of both, only the bumpy, dusty, difficult, but always mutual path.

Pressed, I might add two trifles so old-fashioned as to seem fresh. I wish that every girl who marries might have a dot. Not a fortune — that might unbalance a relationship. But the woman with a little money of her own, a bit of change in her pocketbook which is not part of the domestic budget, is delightfully situated. It gives her confidence and kindness, like having naturally curly hair.

The other concerns the selection of a proper family tree. Nothing helps so much in getting along with a man as seeing to it that he stems from a long line of monogamous ancestors.

And there the list would have to end. Gratitude, an attentive ear, a sharing of faults; pocket money and a stout conviction that marriages were meant to last — those are the only recipes I have to offer. I hope no man sees the meagre roster, for it might seem to him condescending. And condescension is the poorest weapon in a woman's arsenal. But then, I and my kind do not own an arsenal, having no need of one. Who wants weapons when she has — and is aware that she has — all the luck?

CARY GRANT was born in England and started his career in America as a child acrobat on stilts with the Pender Troupe in the Folies Bergère, the first American cabaret. Since then, he has put sixty-four roles behind him and remains still devastating, witty, durable, and adored. His newest venture is *Operation Petticoat*.

Henry Clarke

WOLFE AND THE ANGEL

BY ALLENE TALMEY

KETTI FRINGS WITH ANTHONY PERKINS, JO VAN FLEET, AND HUGH GRIFFITH, THREE PRINCIPALS IN HER PLAY BASED ON WOLFE'S "LOOK HOMEWARD ANGEL"

Penn

Thomas Wolfe undoubtedly would have loved the play *Look Homeward, Angel*. It is impressive. It is enormously successful. It is big and it is about him. For Wolfe, six feet six, with a rapacious appetite for almost everything, was big and impressive and the centre of his writings. Whether he called the boy Eugene or George, the boy was always Tom, with "strange dark eyes . . . and a passionate and obscure hunger for voyages." When he described his mother's extraordinary memory in his first great novel, *Look Homeward, Angel*, he actually described his own. "Her memory moved over the ocean-bed of event like a great octopus, blindly but completely feeling its way into every seacave, rill and estuary, focussed on all she had done, felt and thought . . ."

At some time in his thirty-seven years of life, Wolfe wrote a small autobiographical note, really to himself. He promised, "Someday I shall write a book about a man who was too tall — who lived forever in a dimension that he did not fit and for whom the proportions of everything — chairs, beds, door, rooms, shoes, clothes, shirts, and socks, the berths of Pullman cars, and the bunks of transatlantic liners, together with the rations of food, drink, love and women which most men on this earth have found sufficient to their measure — were too small. . . . The

368 [1953 – 1963]

world that I have lived in is the world of six feet six, and that is the strangest and most lonely world there is." That long, cataloguing, lonely, rhythmic sentence is completely Wolfe.

It is part of the accumulated and vast paper residue of his life, some of it valuable, some of it debris, that lies among the papers, documents, notebooks and photographs in maroon cases at the Houghton Library at Harvard College in the depths of the William B. Wisdom collection of Wolfiana. In another maroon box, on one of his innumerable pieces of paper, Wolfe wrote this broken bit of autobiography: "Thomas Clayton Wolfe was born in Asheville, North Carolina, Oct. 3, 1900. He was the youngest of a family of eight children of whom seven were living at his birth . . . his mother, Julia Elizabeth Westall, a member of a family which had been among the first settlers in the Blue Ridge." On another scrap he wrote that he began to scribble at fourteen but never seriously until he was about twenty-six. He called *Look Homeward, Angel* a "huge leviathan," and he dreamed of finding a publisher and a public, but it was a "kind of intoxicating illusion which sustained me during the period of creation." Wolfe added that the first publisher who read it sent it back speedily, saying in effect, "it was too long, too autobiographical, too amateurish, and too like other books which he had published and lost money on." The second publisher took it and published it in October 1929, a few weeks after Wolfe's twenty-ninth birthday.

In that same autobiographical sketch, he added that he had to "struggle against indolence, against insatiable and constantly growing interest in life around me, my desire to get out and explore with an encyclopedic thoroughness, my desire to travel . . . my liking for companionship, food and drink and having a good time. I also have to struggle constantly against self-doubt. My knowledge of the craft and technique of my profession is still very imperfect. . . . I learn very slowly and at a cost of almost infinite error, waste and confusion. I do too much of everything. I write millions of words in the course of shaping out and defining a volume of a few hundred thousand." He added more about his torrential production. Then he wrote, "The core of an artist's life is in his work and the deepest knowledge, his greatest power, his profoundest social feelings come through the work as a great current of electricity pulses and surges through a dynamo. . . ."

The Houghton Library also owns the original manuscript of "L.H.A.," as Wolfe eventually and often referred to it. He wrote that long, difficult work in nineteen large and varied notebooks that look like ledgers. Some have marbleized covers, some are black, bound with maroon. One of them is bright royal blue, but most of them are the grey of dust under a bed. He wrote in pencil. His handwriting is sprawling, big, and usually legible with five words to a line, the "y's" full of curlicue, the "f's" straight. His cry to the world, his fury at life, his uncontrolled love of America, his massive fountain of loneliness was spelled carefully, the punctuation correct. He was sure of what he was writing — this withdrawn young man who seemed to hate his own gropings, who shrank sometimes from his own gusto. For four or five pages in a row he only crossed out such small words as *that* for *than;* or changed *make* to *put*.

On some richly beige-brown thin paper, like rather elegant wrapping paper, he explained to himself, "The book shall represent the emergence of an individual — not towards freedom — but rather towards creative [illegible] and an inner solitude of freedom from certain forces and of [illegible] towards others."

The physical labour of these notes and the nineteen ledgers is enormous. When he still called the novel *O Lost*, Madeleine Boyd, his literary agent, tried to sell four excerpts. On the typescript of the fourth excerpt, Wolfe wrote in handwriting, "The Death of Ben Gant — this is probably too long as it stands for a magazine but it might be shortened." *The Bookman*, it seems, had returned the four chapters on April 11, 1929, with a note informing him that the magazine was interested in his work and wanted to see anything he wrote in shorter form.

Perhaps the shortest of his writings were his revisions of the *Look Homeward, Angel* dedication. On the first of four revisions he wrote:

To
The Memory of his Brother
Benjamin Harrison Wolfe
(Oct 1893 — Oct 1918)
And to the proud and bitter
briefness of his days

In 1937 Wolfe's compulsion for lists had become fantastic. Among the Harvard papers are his rough estimates of his journeys from 1922 to 1937. He figured that he had travelled some 129,000 miles. The same year that he worked out the mileage of his life, he listed the people he would never have known if he had not lived in New York, England, France, and New England. When the General Alumni Association of the University of North Carolina sent him a questionnaire, he filled it out. To the question, "Are you married?" he answered. "Yes. I am wedded to my art." To the question, "Where was your wife educated?" he answered, "First at Athens, later at Rome, Elizabethan England, 17th cent. France, and more recently in Scandinavia, Germany, Russia, Austria, Italy, France, England, and at present in America."

That last answer has the long roll of rhetoric that sounds like Wolfe's descriptions of his father, whom he called in "L.H.A." Oliver Gant, and of whom he wrote, "Day after day he became maniacally drunk, until he fixed himself in a state of constant insanity." Earlier Wolfe wrote of Gant, "And he thought of how he had set out to get order and position for himself, and of the rioting confusion of his life." There are many similarities between old man Gant and thirty-five-year-old Tom Wolfe — the unbridled love of words, the drink, the stubbornness, the fury. But Thomas Wolfe did not end in a red waste of his youth.

[1953 – 1963] 369

THE ROYAL WEDDING

BY SARAH RUSSELL

"Dearly beloved, we are gathered here . . . to join together this man and this woman. . . ." For centuries these words have been spoken at weddings of commoners and of kings. Never before in Westminster Abbey have they been spoken at the marriage ceremony of a plain "Mr." with a Royal Princess. At the wedding of Her Royal Highness the Princess Margaret and Antony Armstrong-Jones in Westminster Abbey, the assemblage included queens and prime ministers, lords and ladies, and might well have been splendidly overwhelming. But this was Princess Margaret's own wedding: her friends were there *en masse*, gay, young, well-dressed, happy to see her happy, glad and proud to be there. Gold braid to be sure, ecclesiastical splendour, scarlet tunics, and a measure of pomp and circumstance, but through it all a sense of warmth and atmosphere of intimacy.

The beautiful Countess of Rosse, mother of the groom, attracted great attention. Opposite, seated each in his own choir stall, were the prime ministers of the Commonwealth of Nations: Mr. Macmillan and all the rest. The groom arrived looking pale. Obviously nervous as any other groom, he talked animatedly to his groomsman, Dr. Roger Gilliatt. The Royal Family began to enter the Abbey: the Duke and Duchess of Gloucester, the Duchess of Kent, Princess Alexandra, the young Duke of Kent, and Prince Charles. Then came the Queen Mother, in white and gold lamé and feathered hat; and the Queen, in turquoise, regal and calm.

Suddenly a loud trumpet fanfare; everyone rose and Princess Margaret swept into view on the arm of Prince Philip while the choir sang "Christ is made the sure foundation." As they came up the aisle, one realized that this was a new princess; her dress, unadorned, struck a clear true note. She tried unsuccessfully not to smile at her groom. Antony came forward; took her hand; the bride promised to love, honour, and obey, and, as she had requested, there was a reading of the Beatitudes by the Dean of Westminster, in place of a sermon. The choir sang the lovely Psalm "I will lift up mine eyes unto the hills." Then members of the Royal Family slipped into the Chapel of Edward the Confessor to sign the Register; the Queen returned to her gold-and-black throne chair and a moment later the bride reappeared, radiant and beaming, turned and dropped a curtsy to her sister, and moved down the Abbey on the arm of her Mr. Jones.

THE ROYAL PROCESSION AT THE GATES OF BUCKINGHAM PALACE. SKETCHED BY FELIKS TOPOLSKI

OPPOSITE: QUEEN ELIZABETH II, THE QUEEN MOTHER, AND OTHER MEMBERS OF THE ROYAL FAMILY THROWING ROSE PETALS, AS THE CAR WITH THE BRIDE AND GROOM LEAVES THE PALACE COURTYARD

Mirrorpic

MODERN ARCHITECTURE IN AMERICA

BY PETER BLAKE

Just as Paris, during the first three decades of the century, was the centre of modern art, so America is now the centre of modern architecture. All over the world, the names of great American architects — native as well as foreign-born — are known and their work admired. Much early modern architecture in Europe and elsewhere received its impetus from the work of the great Chicago architects of the late nineteenth and early twentieth centuries, from Louis Sullivan to Frank Lloyd Wright. Now architecture in Europe, Asia, and Africa is receiving *its* impetus from the work of living Americans. Impetus comes from Louis I. Kahn, perhaps the most creative United States architect since Wright. It comes as well from the work of Philip Johnson, Edward D. Stone, Paul Rudolph, Craig Ellwood, and Minoru Yamasaki — from the American buildings by such European-born American pioneers as Ludwig Mies van der Rohe, Walter Gropius, Marcel Breuer, Richard Neutra, and Eero Saarinen.

Laymen, of course, recognize the names of the great pioneers — may recognize the names of Saarinen and Johnson and one or two of their contemporaries. But many would be hard put to identify the work of these men, or to separate it from that of lesser architects. The ferment itself is practically unknown. To some laymen, modern architecture looks much the same: glass and metal "graph paper" draped over rectangles of steel and concrete, with little variation in detail, little allowance for "beauty." They are reconciled to this sameness because they have come to believe that modern architecture is cheap, and that the sameness is the reason it *is* cheap.

The facts, however, are rather different. Although it is certainly cheaper to build a modern building than it would be to build Chartres today, modern architecture is anything but cheap — nor does it all look the same. Indeed, it would be very difficult to find a contemporary art form in America, or anywhere else, in which there are so many vehemently opposed splinter groups at work. As a matter of fact, the great diversity in American architecture and the lack of consensus among its practitioners are among its diverting pleasures. While it is certainly true that glass-and-metal "graph paper" is one characteristic surface of modern buildings, glass and metal do not become architecture until employed by a glass-and-metal artist. The glass-and-metal Seagram Building in New York, designed primarily by Mies van der Rohe, is as different from the jerry-built glass-and-metal junk of much of Park Avenue as the poetry of T. S. Eliot is from his prose. (Furthermore, the Seagram may be one of the most expensive buildings, per square foot, put up by anyone since Angkor Wat.)

In short, it should be understood that (a) many modern buildings are not architecture; (b) modern architects may build with almost anything from prehistoric rock to irradiated plastics, and their forms and spaces may recall anything from the piazza at Vigevano to twenty-first-century science fiction; (c) modern architecture is not particularly cheap; and (d) modern architects do not think that ugliness is synonymous with goodness.

It is much harder to say what American architects do believe. One article of faith held by many of them is that the structural frame of a building is a kind of ethical basis for architecture. Because much of modern architecture began with *structures* rather than buildings — with bridges, dams, silos, railroad sheds, and airplane hangars, all shaped primarily by considerations of engineering — a good many architects now seem to have a fixation about "expressing structure."

372 [1953–1963]

FRANK LLOYD WRIGHT,
WHOSE LATEST GREAT ACHIEVEMENT IS THE
SPIRALLING GUGGENHEIM MUSEUM IN NEW YORK

William Short

This fixation has, on occasion, produced some very odd results. On the one hand — quite validly — a young virtuoso like Victor Lundy, in Florida, may engage in fabulous acrobatics with laminated wood arches; or another man of outstanding talent, like Ulrich Franzen, in New York, may become just as fascinated by hinged arches of steel. But on the other hand, a number of Lundy's and Franzen's contemporaries have begun to decorate their buildings with *symbols* that are meant to "express structure" but in truth have little, if anything, to do with the structure that actually holds up the roof. Philip Johnson's new Amon Carter Museum in Fort Worth, a lovely piece of outdoor decoration, has a great portico of sculptured arches that *look* like formed concrete, but are actually a Texas variation of travertine, carefully fitted around thin steel-pipe columns that are the *true* structural supports — but would look like toothpicks if left exposed to the eye.

Mies van der Rohe has been doing this kind of thing for some time. Although his tall glass towers are supported on fairly conventional steel columns and beams, encased in concrete to comply with the building codes, he has for years applied vertical steel rails to the exteriors of these towers to *symbolize* structure. Shaped like I-beams, these rails hold up nothing much except themselves, but look as if they had some connection with the actual structure.

This cult of "expressing structure" through applied pilasters and porticos is about to receive quite a workout at New York's Lincoln Center. There, almost every building will be faced with arched porticos that do nothing but "decorate a plaza," as the great German neo-classicist of the early nineteenth century, Karl Friedrich Schinkel, once put it. Philip Johnson had no qualms whatever about going back to Schinkel when he designed his Fort Worth museum; he takes an almost sadistic delight in parading his eclecticism before his more purist (and utterly infuriated) contemporaries.

Indeed, some of the early pioneers of the modern movement must be turning in their graves. The great Auguste Perret, who was Le Corbusier's teacher some fifty years ago, used to say that "decoration always hides an error in construction." And Perret's contemporary, the Viennese Adolf Loos, once wrote that decoration was "a crime"! It has taken only fifty years to render Perret and Loos obsolete: by a quick twist of semantics, "decoration" has become "symbolism," and what was once a "crime" has been legitimized.

By now, most of our "structural exhibitionists" have calmed down; they have learned to let the engineers tell them the rules of the shell-game and use the new forms with increasing discretion. Such architects as I. M. Pei, Gordon Bunshaft, John Johansen, and Victor Christ-Janer have demonstrated not only that shells, domes, arches, and so forth are fine in their places — but that their places are not everywhere.

Quite a few modern architects, on the other hand, do not really believe that "expressing structure" is all-important. Because most of the cost of a building goes into services (like heating, air conditioning, and plumbing), these men have begun to "express services" rather than structural forms. The outstanding exponent of this approach is Louis Kahn, the remarkable sixty-year-old Philadelphia architect whose new Richards Medical Research Building at the University of Pennsylvania is an astonishing complex of brick, concrete, and glass, dominated by a series of tall brick shafts that contain all the elaborate services required by research labs. These great shafts are as vigorous as the towers of San Gimignano (which Kahn admires greatly), and, while they contain the services which they are meant to symbolize, they also dramatize those services in a way that no cost accountant could possibly justify.

The Blue Cross Building in Boston, by Paul Rudolph, the head of Yale's School of Architecture, is another attempt to "express services": the air-conditioning ducts of this building have been applied to the facade (rather than concealed within), and these ducts rise to the full height of the structure looking, for all the world, like small concrete columns. Undoubtedly, there will be more buildings that "express services" rather than structure, for both Kahn and Rudolph influence their peers. Indeed, we may soon see buildings with mail chutes, telephone wires, pneumatic tubes, and soft-drink dispensers all applied to, or expressed on the outside. Or we may not; for there are many who agree with Mies van der Rohe, who said recently, "You can't make architecture out of pipes."

While no architect has ever been able to define beauty to anybody else's complete satisfaction, some modernists have tried very hard indeed. Edward D. Stone, whose screens of concrete grillwork are famous from New Delhi to his native Fayetteville, Arkansas, speaks quite lyrically in his charming, southern voice when describing his own romantic pavilions. Minoru Yamasaki, the Detroit architect, who talks about harmony and serenity, manages to achieve them in his delicate temples of precast concrete.

But there are some modernists who deride the beauty-seekers and say that their buildings are pretty rather than beautiful. One English critic, Dr. Reyner Banham, has called some of the beauty-seekers the "ballet school" of American architecture; and other critics are less polite, muttering darkly about "exterior decoration" and other offenses against purity. Louis Kahn (who is *very* polite) feels that it is more important for a building to have "character" than to have beauty — an argument brazenly stolen from the sisterhood of spinsters; Mies van der Rohe believes that if a building represents "truth" it will also be beautiful — *his* argument having been borrowed from the equally chaste beliefs of St. Augustine. Le Corbusier, since 1945, has been working exclusively in *béton brut*, and some of his many admirers have decided to call themselves the "New Brutalists," producing buildings deliberately violent in form and deliberately crude in surface and detail. To the "New Brutalists," as to Louis

LUDWIG MIES VAN DER ROHE AND PHILIP JOHNSON, DESIGNERS OF NEW YORK'S HANDSOME SEAGRAM BUILDING, ALL BRONZE AND GREY, SHOWN HERE IN A SMALL MODEL (KAHN AND JACOBS WERE THE ASSOCIATE ARCHITECTS)

Penn

Kahn, beauty is to be found in the virile ruthlessness of their buildings — or, to coin a phrase, "Beauty is ugliness." This, one feels, is the Marlon Brando school of modern architecture. (The "New Brutalists" in Japan have spoiled everybody's fun, because it is absolutely impossible for Japanese craftsmen to build *im*perfectly — hence, the "New Brutalist" architecture around Tokyo and Kyoto turns out to be rather pretty.)

The "New Brutalists" are, of course, a perfectly serious group: they bear some relation to the "Action Painters" of the New York School and to the "Angry Young Men" of the English stage. They believe that a building bearing the imperfect imprint of man's hand — rather than the impersonal imprint of a rolling mill — can speak more forcefully than a too polished building. Unhappily, however, some men's hands are clumsier than others. While a "Brutalist" building by Le Corbusier, Kahn, or the young Japanese genius, Kenzo Tange, may have the grandeur of an Easter Island head, a "Brutalist" building by a second-rater can look like the back of the A & P.

But the central problem of American architecture is no longer the individual building, but the entire city and its environs. Recently one American critic started to talk about "Chaoticism" as a movement in architecture in this country. "Chaoticism" is, of course, not a movement — it is a non-movement. It is the by-product of an apparent absence of civilization. Every new highway built across our land seems to be an invitation to string out more honkytonk developments. Too often, new space opened in the cities seems to invite further vulgarity.

More and more architects of the younger generation in this country are trying to do something to halt this blight, to create a civilized, even beautiful American townscape. The first step, to them, is simply to create a sense of order, without which neither civilization nor beauty seems attainable. These younger men have approached the problem in two ways: some consider every new building on

LOUIS I. KAHN, "PERHAPS THE MOST CREATIVE U. S. ARCHITECT SINCE WRIGHT," WITH A MODEL OF HIS RICHARDS MEDICAL RESEARCH BUILDING IN PHILADELPHIA.

their draughting boards an element within an architectural "continuity," and consider what each new building will do to existing structures and spaces nearby. Others have concentrated upon broader projects of city planning and urban renewal — projects that will take five or ten years to come to fruition.

A good example of "continuity" is Paul Rudolph's new Arts Center for Wellesley, which duplicates the scale of older campus buildings nearby, uses some of the same materials, and contains a number of details that *recall* those of the neo-Gothic campus without copying them. Another example is Saarinen's complex of dormitories at Yale, modern in fact but not in feeling, designed in a vaguely mediaeval pattern that recalls the ramparts of Harlech Castle — and some of the neo-Gothic romanticism of older buildings on the Yale campus. (The "ivy" on this Ivy League campus, provided by the Sardinian-born sculptor Tino Nivola, is something to see.) Among such younger New Orleans architects as Nathaniel Curtis and Arthur Davis, the buildings of the French Quarter and the Garden District have served as a powerful inspiration: colonnades, porticos, balconies, grilles of iron or tile reappear, admitting their debt to the past.

In short, wherever modern architects congregate, the talk is not about Perret, Loos, or the Bauhaus — but about Schinkel, San Gimignano, mediaevalism, pilasters, St. Augustine, decoration, and similar heresies. Only the jerry-builders in cities and suburbs still talk about functionalism.

Unlike these jerry-builders, whose deplorable mark is on every United States street, the younger idealists in urban renewal and city planning do not yet have much to show for their efforts. It takes a long time to raze and rebuild a sizable portion of an old, dilapidated city — it takes a long time, that is, if you care about what you are doing. Among those who care is Edmund Bacon, the effective head of the Philadelphia City Planning Commission, who was trained at the Cranbrook School in Michigan by Eero Saarinen's great father, Eliel. Bacon and his chief architect, Willo von Moltke, together with their assistants, have begun to change the face of Philadelphia dramatically over the past ten years — and the change will become more dramatic in the next ten. Harry Weese, the Chicago architect, who was trained by Finland's Alvar Aalto, is another dedicated renewer of cities (his plans include a part of Washington, D.C.); John Carl Warnecke, trained by Gropius at Harvard, is now busy trying to renew San Francisco and environs — the "environs," in this case, encompass areas of Honolulu; and New York's I. M. Pei works on urban renewal in almost every part of the country.

Unhappily, these excellent, idealistic architects and planners have made hardly a dent on the great face of the United States. The reason is simple enough: so long as unbridled speculation in land is perfectly legitimate, most of our building will be shaped not by considerations of aesthetics or urban design, but by considerations of tax accountancy and rapid return on investment. The basic decision that must be made by Americans is whether they want their land to be used for the making of money or for the making of a civilization. Perhaps the two objectives can be attained jointly.

To many an investment builder, good architects are anathema — and for perfectly valid reasons: such architects think, and thinking takes time. Hacks are safe, fast, cheap, and untroubled by ideas. Meanwhile, exhibitions of outstanding new American architecture are admired all over the world, and foreign magazines praise these new American architects in every issue. By comparison, the work of the hacks looks duller and sleazier every day. Unfortunately, it is also more numerous every day.

Still, the new American architects continue, with the zeal of missionaries. It has been said that it took this country close to two hundred years to create a workable political system, and that the next step is to create a civilization. These new architects have that sense of historic mission, and men with that sense are hard to stop.

EERO SAARINEN, BRILLIANT DESIGNER OF THE GENERAL MOTORS TECHNICAL CENTER IN DETROIT

GORDON BUNSHAFT, DESIGNER OF THE PARK AVENUE LANDMARK, LEVER HOUSE, GLIMPSED IN THE BACKGROUND

[1953 – 1963]

POPULARITY   BY SIR OSBERT SITWELL

It was in May 1923, when the *inquilini* were still many of them living in the Castle, that my father asked me to go for a walk with him in the Great Court. The summer heat, which in certain years begins in Tuscany as early as the second week in May, was not yet in full glow and the shafts of sunlight, instead of piercing like spears, lay light as feathers on the dark stone of the pavement, and even from this distance the bees could be heard swarming in the dark-leaved golden blossoms of the ivy which completely covered the stone mediaeval tower at the garden's end.

As we strode up and down, my father talked, I remember, of the translation of books, and remarked to me what a pity it was that if the English bishops of King James I's reign had felt obliged to translate a volume of some kind, they could not have found for their purpose a more interesting book than the Bible. I did not attempt to enter into argument with him as it did not seem that it would lead very far. Occasionally, as he talked, the shutter of an upper window would silently shift a little, and a face would be seen behind it glowering and glaring down at us.

My father seemed pleased, taking it to be a token of interest and popularity; indeed, he observed to me that it was nice to feel that you could always make yourself liked if you wanted. But facts have an awkward way of asserting themselves and when, shortly afterwards, an old woman was arrested by the police, she was found to be carrying on her a list of people whom she meant to kill when the Revolution came: my father's name was at the head of the list. Yet even if his assumption had been rather too sanguine, there were fragments of truth in it. He could make himself generally and lightly popular with great numbers but had no gift for intimacy.

In this respect I think the house-to-house canvassing that was formerly conducted in between general elections by the candidates of both parties must have been a great strain on him, for he had difficulty in remembering people (as I have written elsewhere, he could pass his own children in the street without recognizing them) and, if he remembered them, in associating them with their names. Thus, on one occasion he went into a small house under the Castle Hill at Scarborough and asked a woman who was ironing shirts to obtain for him her husband's vote. She looked at him and said, "But I am *Mrs. Jones*, Sir George." This information conveyed nothing to my father, who did not identify her as the wife of his personal servant who had been his scout at Christ Church and who had remained with him to serve him ever since.

A more obvious instance of the falsity of my father's happy conviction comes back to me when I think of my first visit to Chiswick House. It proved a memorable occasion and took place in the early twenties when the building was still in use as a private mental home. It was necessary beforehand to obtain permission to go over it from the Commissioners of Lunacy, who kindly granted my request. Accordingly, my brother Sacheverell and I went there about four o'clock one hot afternoon in July.

The house, built for the great patron Lord Burlington by Colin Campbell, then existed on a larger scale than it does today, when the two later eighteenth-century wings have been blown up or pulled down to show the purity of design of the original Palladian Villa. . . . We were to have tea with the resident doctor, but on arrival we were not certain by which of the doors to enter. However, we opened one of

AUDREY HEPBURN, whose immense enchanting eyes have the effect of making half the audience feel slightly in love and the other half feel a vague impulse to write out checks for war relief or the Fresh Air Fund, emerges improbably in the new movie *Breakfast at Tiffany's* as Truman Capote's Holly Golightly, a girl who calls El Morocco Elmer's, lives on other people's expense accounts, and thinks, like Becky Sharp, that she could be good if she had so much a year.

them and there, coming down the staircase, was a good-looking grey-haired man already wearing a dinner jacket — it seemed an odd hour to be clad in this manner. We inquired from him where the doctor lived and he replied by whistling, but — this was the most extraordinary part of it — the words were absolutely distinct, yet enunciated by — not through — the whistling. He was, in short, whistling and not speaking. It was obviously a natural and original gift, though he must have cultivated it, too, to the highest degree.

This virtuoso, then, informed us that we were on the right track. . . . When we reached the doctor upstairs, we found a most splendid and impressive tea ready for us, sandwiches very thinly cut and bearing flags on them, cut out of paper on which were written such descriptions as "Pâté de foie gras" and "Caviare." My brother commented on this smart labelling to our host, who asked, "Did you happen, when you came in, to notice the whistling man who was wearing a dinner jacket?"

We said: "Yes."

"Well," he explained, "he arranged the tea. He always does it for me. A most curious history. His father was one of the Marshals of France during the reign of Napoleon III and a great favourite at court. His son inherited a fine fortune, but dissipated it on prima donnas. I had known him for a long time, but some ten years ago we received a letter from him telling us that he felt he was going off his head, and asking whether we would take him in here to be under my care, in return for which he would act as a servant — but every now and then he asks permission to go out for the evening and the next day we read in the *Morning Post* that he was at some social gathering to which I should never be invited."

It was, as I was saying, a peculiarly sultry day, and after tea the doctor led us through the suites of rooms which, richly decorated, formed a strange setting for the wretched lunatics, all overexcited by the heat. Many of them shook as if with fever, and their faces were yellow from the glow of the gilding as much as from illness. You could hear cries and roars and screams on every side.

When we had completed our tour we went out onto the platform at the top of the staircase leading down to the garden. The vista was a perfect instance of the aesthetic beauties caused by neglect. It was not a flower garden, but a large pleasance, though owing to the skillful planning it looked immensely larger than it really was. An idyllic rusticity prevailed, aided by the greensward, stone vases, pools of bracken, and groves of old trees. We wandered about there for a while and talked. Then, as we turned to climb up to the portico, we saw approaching a tall, lank man with an air of some distinction, who carried over his shoulder a bag of golf clubs.

"Oh, I am so glad," the doctor remarked to me, "that this particular patient has come out. Don't feel the slightest alarm: he has never been violent and is a very charming person."

The doctor beckoned to him to join us and formally introduced him to me.

"This is Mr. Osbert Sitwell," the doctor announced.

"Are you Sir George's son?" the lunatic at once demanded.

I admitted it, and his demeanor changed. Rather hastily selecting a golf club, he shouted, "Then I should like to kill you."

By some means or other the doctor persuaded him to disarm and go away without any of us incurring injury. But it was a breath-taking moment. Having successfully spirited the patient away, the doctor hurried back to us, saying, "Oh, I am so sorry! What a dreadful thing to happen! He has never been known to behave like that before."

In the same instant I recalled my father striding along in the Great Court at Montegufoni, and the faces peering down at him, and I wondered by what precise act of his I had so nearly, if vicariously, shared his popularity. I never found out.

THE FAMOUS SITWELL TRIO — SACHEVERELL, EDITH, AND OSBERT — OUT FOR A STROLL IN 1927

QUEEN SIRIKIT OF THAILAND, ONE OF THE WORLD'S MOST SERENE BEAUTIES, STANDS HERE IN FRONT OF A JEWELLED TEMPLE IN THE ROYAL COMPOUND OF BANGKOK

Horst

ON STAGE 1958-1962

What is the magnet that fixes the public eye on a play, that stirs enough people to make the play a hit? That, any producer will tell you, is the catch. There is no specific formula, as witness these five dissimilar successes. *The Miracle Worker* succeeds because it is a magnified documentary of the struggle for speech, hearing, sight, by a brilliant mind encased in a small girl, Helen Keller. *A Man for All Seasons* is a philosophic piece of history that comes alive through the performance of Paul Scofield. *Camelot* is rescued by the engaging performances of Richard Burton, Julie Andrews, and (not photographed) Robert Goulet. *Sweet Bird of Youth* has the magic of pure theatricalism that holds the audience whether they want to be held or not. And *How to Succeed in Business without Really Trying* succeeds, quite probably, because the three male characters have been entrusted to three foolproof stage presences — Rudy Vallee, Charles Reilly, and (photographed here) Robert Morse.

OPPOSITE: ROBERT MORSE, YOUNGER THAN SPRINGTIME, IN "HOW TO SUCCEED IN BUSINESS WITHOUT REALLY TRYING"

ANNE BANCROFT AND PATTY DUKE IN "THE MIRACLE WORKER"

PAUL SCOFIELD AS SIR THOMAS MORE IN "A MAN FOR ALL SEASONS"

RICHARD BURTON AND JULIE ANDREWS IN "CAMELOT"

FAR LEFT: PAUL NEWMAN, WHO STARS OPPOSITE GERALDINE PAGE IN "SWEET BIRD OF YOUTH"

HOW TO FACE OUTER SPACE

BY ANTHONY WEST

The scene is the terrace in front of a pleasant small house in the country not far from New York. Mr. Blount and his friends Mr. and Mrs. Truscott are discovered, on a balmy autumn night filled with stars, looking attentively at the horizon. After a moment they all say, "There it is," together, and their heads turn slowly as they follow the course taken by Sputnik II as it flies across the sky.

MRS. TRUSCOTT: Poor little dog!

MR. TRUSCOTT: Oh, no! Darling, you just can't take that line.

MR. BLOUNT: I don't see why not. I feel rather that way myself. I don't really see the point of the dog myself.

MR. TRUSCOTT: Well, I guess Laika or Limonchik or whoever it is doesn't either — but then he or she is just a dog. We ought to realize that she's dying for a cause — to get necessary information so that we can send men up there with some idea of what they're going to be up against when they go.

MR. BLOUNT: Well, it's just that that makes me wonder what the point of sending the dog is.

MR. TRUSCOTT: Don't tell me that you're one of these blind men who can't see what a really important thing this breakthrough into outer space is?

MR. BLOUNT: It's a very great achievement from a technical point of view — yes. That it's a breakthrough — no. That it opens anything to men that wasn't open before — no it doesn't.

MR. TRUSCOTT: Don't say that you believe that people have been whizzing about outer space for years, only nobody has known about it except you and members of flying saucer clubs.

MR. BLOUNT: No and yes. I think people began to explore space just as soon as the men of the Renaissance caught onto the idea that the sun was one star among many, and that there might be millions of suns and earths.

MR. TRUSCOTT: So what? Now we have a hope of really going to some of them, and in a space ship that will reel off a hundred million miles an hour.

MRS. TRUSCOTT: Darling!

MR. TRUSCOTT: It seems fantastic — but it's possible. Some kind of electronic motor that would discharge a jet of ionized particles could do it. It's just a matter of working out the details, and then we're off to the stars!

MR. BLOUNT: A hundred million miles an hour — do you realize that's only a seventh of the speed of light?

MR. TRUSCOTT (laughs): Well, that's certainly too bad.

MR. BLOUNT: It is. The nearest star to the solar system is four light-years away.

MRS. TRUSCOTT: Mmmn?

MR. BLOUNT: Well, if you insist, a light-year is the distance light will travel, going at six hundred and sixty-nine million six hundred thousand miles an hour in a year of eight thousand seven hundred and sixty hours. Get it?

MRS. TRUSCOTT: No.

MR. BLOUNT: I'm never quite sure how much it means to me. What I hang onto is just this. Nothing travels faster than light and it looks as if nothing ever could. So when it's said that something is four light-years away, it means that there's just no way at all of getting there in less than four years. Do you see? But anyway, if this nearest star is four light-years away, it means that Bill's hundred-million-mile-an-hour space ship will take twenty-eight years to get there.

MR. TRUSCOTT: Well, that's possible.

MR. BLOUNT: Put a crew of twenty-year-olds aboard and you'll get them back as men of seventy-six.

MRS. TRUSCOTT: They'd run out of Kleenex.

MR. TRUSCOTT: For heaven's sake....

MR. BLOUNT: It's a point, though, isn't it? Imagine yourself at the age of twenty climbing into a tin can the size of a New York apartment, loaded up with all the food and drink you're going to need for a lifetime....

MR. TRUSCOTT: But what an adventure — it would be worth it. . . .

MRS. TRUSCOTT: Being shut up in a box with the same two or three people from the time you were twenty till the time you were seventy-six — and wearing one of those ghastly space suits too . . . do you call that an adventure?

MR. TRUSCOTT: Yes. I'd go through anything to find out if there were other creatures like men out there.

MRS. TRUSCOTT: Do you think there are people — things — we could get in touch with in space?

MR. BLOUNT: I'm almost sure of it. We know from our own experience that life is the sort of thing you'd find on a planet like ours, circling round our sort of sun. There are a million suns like it in our galaxy. Beyond our galaxy there are a hundred million others, and there are good grounds for thinking that every one of these galaxies has a million planetary systems like ours in it.

MR. TRUSCOTT: Well, there it is, the mission for our space ship. First we go round our galaxy trying to make contacts; and if we draw a blank there, why we go on to the next galaxy.

MR. BLOUNT: Our galaxy happens to be a hundred thousand light-years wide. We're about twenty thousand years in from the outer edge, and eighty thousand years away from the far side. The whole period of human history covers only about four thousand years — can you imagine the journey?

MRS. TRUSCOTT: Why, the crew would have to have babies and train them as their replacements.

ISAK DINESEN (BARONESS BLIXEN)
AT RUNGSTEDLUND,
PHOTOGRAPHED BY JOHN STEWART

[1953 – 1963]   385

MR. BLOUNT: For generations... at any given moment the space ship's crew would have to consist of the operating group, the breeders and baby minders, and the babies. Halfway across the galaxy there would be some kind of celebration as the thousandth generation of the crew took over the controls.

MRS. TRUSCOTT: It'll be *squalid* in that space ship.

MR. BLOUNT: They'll run into some interesting psychological and genetic problems aboard, that's for sure. The conditions should make the crew neurotic, and unless you're going to make very elaborate preparations for artificial insemination, they're going to get pretty inbred. Of course, if the ship is going to take an intergalactic trip, the problems are more complicated.

MR. TRUSCOTT: Just what do you mean?

MR. BLOUNT: M 31, the nearest galaxy — you can see it as a faint haze in the constellation Andromeda with your naked eye — is one million five hundred thousand light-years away. By the time the space ship gets there, its crew will be farther from us in time than Neanderthal man is. Before they leave they'll have to adopt a policy and decide whether they'll go with the evolutionary tide or put up a fight to stay like modern man. The select breeding group on board might breed true, but then they might start adapting to the artificial environment in the space ship. By the time they got to M 31, they might be something quite unique — space-ship man.

MR. TRUSCOTT: How silly can we get!

MR. BLOUNT: For a start, we can try talking about the physical conquest of space in rockets and things of that kind. But perhaps that isn't even silly, I'd rather call it simply childish.

MR. TRUSCOTT: What makes you so negative about this tremendous thing?

MR. BLOUNT: I don't think I am being negative. It's just that I think the human mind is a much superior vehicle for space travel to any material thing or mechanical device. The farthest galaxies that we can see are one thousand two hundred million light-years away. We can go there instantly in thought, but the idea of setting out on a physical journey over that vast gulf of space and time is grotesque. The estimated time of arrival would be never. One of the odder things about the universe is that it seems to be expanding. The farthest galaxies seem to be rushing away from us at such speeds as thirty-four thousand miles a second, and they are going faster all the time. If you set out for one of them in Bill's super space ship, travelling at a hundred million miles an hour, you would be dropping behind from the word go. The galaxy would be twelve million miles farther off than when you started at the end of the first hour, and the gap would widen every hour. There isn't any point in even thinking about such journeys, even if you could find a crew.

MRS. TRUSCOTT: Is there any point in even thinking about space? It doesn't seem quite real to me — it's all too big.

MR. BLOUNT: There's no trick to space — it's nothing special. You live in it. When you get a sunburn, you're having a space adventure, you're being browned by something ninety-three million miles away. Your favourite flower grows in space. The earth you live on is on a space journey, circling round the galaxy with its sun at a speed of two hundred miles per second. The trip round the galaxy is going to take two hundred million years, we're on our thirtieth trip round, so far as we know. It doesn't matter though, but you are travelling in space even when you're in your bath. You don't have any choice. You just *are* a space traveller whether you like it or not.

MRS. TRUSCOTT: You mean I don't have to worry about it?

MR. BLOUNT: You don't have to.

MRS. TRUSCOTT: You said that in an awfully odd way.

MR. BLOUNT: I've made enough priggish noises already to throw Bill into a fit of the sulks, I feel hesitant about going further. Suppose I just quote Thomas Wright. "By proper objects, attended with just reflections, we may raise our ideas almost to the pitch of the immortals; how far the human imagination may possibly go, or by how much minds like ours may be improved, is a question not easily determined...." He thought the stars were proper objects, "a subject worthy of our speculations." Not just the stars themselves but how they came to be there, and what they are. He was right. The secrets of the universe aren't locked up, they're all written across the sky waiting to be read. The greatest human adventure of all is to try to understand this material thing that has no beginning and no end, but which perpetually renews itself....

A silence falls. Mr. Blount, deep in an interplanetary reverie, wonders if one of the qualities of space is that it breeds hydrogen particles from nothing as Bondi, Gold, and Hoyle think. For aesthetic reasons he prefers this idea to any other, but for the life of him he can't figure out how something can come from nothing.

Beside him Bill Truscott is dreaming along his own lines. Square-jawed under a white space helmet, he is at the controls of a space rocket which is heading out of the solar system. The blast-off has gone well, and a minute after passing the moon, the big rocket is pushing on the speed of sound. Truscott leans forward towards the microphone of the ship's intercom. "Hold on men, we're going through the light barrier." He reaches for the controls of the Zeta wave accelerators. There is a moment of nausea, and then the needles on the ultra speed dials begin to flicker, five light-years an hour, ten, fifteen, twenty... man, those accelerators have really fixed that stick-in-the-mud Blount.

Both men suddenly return to the terrace at the speed, at least, of light. They have received an urgent recall signal. Mrs. Truscott's neat hand is over her mouth, silently she is suppressing a tiny yawn. When she sees that she has been spotted, her mind is jolted into action. She thinks of the little Russian dog hurtling along at seventeen thousand miles an hour on a journey it cannot possibly ever understand. For a moment she pities it, and then has her flash of insight. "Poor little dog," she says again, and then, "Poor us."

WILLIE MAYS, joy boy of the New York Giants, is the happy young outfielder whose genius lies in catching murderous fly balls high in the air against the bleacher walls, in hitting home runs when they count almost double for lifting the spirits of his team. A kind of physical intuition, backed by almost perfect reflexes, tells him where the ball is coming from; "Willie just goes on back and grabs it."

A LITTLE GAME BY LAWRENCE DURRELL

"The case of Wormwood," said Antrobus gravely, "is one which deserves thought."

He spoke in his usual portentous way, but I could see that he was genuinely troubled.

"It is worth reflecting on," he went on, "since it illustrates my contention that nobody really knows what anybody else is thinking. Wormwood was cultural attaché in Helsinki, and we were all terrified of him. He was a lean, leathery, saturnine sort of chap with a goatee and he'd written a couple of novels of an obscurity so overwhelming as to give us an awful inferiority complex in the Chancery. He never spoke. He carried this utter speechlessness to such lengths as to be almost beyond the bounds of decency. The whole Corps quailed before him. One slow stare through those pebble gig lamps of his was enough to quell even the vivid and charming Madame Abreyville, who was noted for her cleverness in bringing out the shy. She made the mistake of trying to bring Wormwood out. He stared at her hard. She was covered with confusion and trembled from head to foot. After this defeat, we all used to take cover when we saw him.

"One winter, just before he was posted to Prague, I ran into him at a party, and finding myself behind the piano with no hope of escape, cleared my throat (I had had three Martinis) and said with what I hoped was offensive jocularity, 'What does a novelist do at parties like these?'

"Wormwood stared at me for so long that I began to swallow my Adam's apple over and over again as I always do when I am out of countenance. I was just about to step out of the window into a flower bed and come round by the front door when he . . . actually spoke to me. 'Do you know what I am doing?' he said in a low tone full of malevolence.

"'No,' I said.

"'I am playing a little game in my mind,' he said, and his expression was one of utter, murderous grimness. 'I am imagining that I am in a sleigh with the whole Diplomatic Corps. We are rushing across the steppes, pursued by wolves. It is necessary, as they keep gaining on us, to throw a diplomat overboard from time to time in order to let the horses regain their advantage. Who would you throw first . . . then second . . . and then third . . .? Just look around you.'

"His tone was so alarming, so ferocious and peremptory, that I was startled; more to humour him than anything else, I said, 'Madame Ventura.' She was rather a heavily built morsel of ambassadress. He curled his lip. 'She's gone already,' he said in a low, hoarse tone, glowering. 'The whole Italian mission has gone — brats included.'

"I did not quite know what to say.

"'Er, how about our own Chancery?' I asked nervously.

"'Oh, they've gone long ago,' he said with slow contempt. 'They've been gobbled up — including you.' He gave a yellowish shelf of rat-like teeth a half-second of exposure, then sheathed them again in his beard. I was feeling dashed awkward now, and found myself fingering my nose.

"I was relieved when I heard he had been posted.

"Now, old boy, comes a series of strange events. The very next winter in Prague — that was the severe one of thirty-seven when the wolf packs came down to the suburbs — you may remember that two Chancery guards and a cipher clerk were eaten by wolves? They were, it seems, out riding in a sleigh with the First Secretary Cultural. When I saw the press reports, something seemed to ring in my brain. Some half-forgotten memory . . . It worried me until I looked up the Prague Mission. It was Wormwood. It gave me food for thought.

"But time passed, and for nearly ten years I heard no more of Wormwood. Then came that report of wolves eating the Italian Ambassador on the Trieste-Zagreb road in midwinter. You remember the case? The victim was in a car. I do not have to tell you who was driving. Wormwood.

"Then once again a long period of time passed without any news of him. But yesterday . . ." Antrobus' voice trembled at this point in the narrative and he drew heavily on his cigar.

"Yesterday, I had a long letter from Bunty Scott-Peverel, who is head of Chancery in Moscow. There is a passage in it which I will read to you.

"'We have just got a new Cultural Sec., rather an odd sort of fellow — a writer, I believe. Huge fronded beard, pebble specs, and glum as all highbrows are. He has taken a *dumka* about twenty miles outside Moscow where he intends to entertain in some style. Usually these hunting lodges are open only in the summer. But he intends to travel by droshky and is busy getting one built big enough, he says, to accommodate the whole Dip. Corps, which he will invite to a housewarming. It is rather an original idea, and we are all looking forward to it very much and waiting for this giant among droshkies to be finished.'

"You will understand," said Antrobus, "the thrill of horror with which I read this letter. I have written at length to Bunty, setting out my fears. I hope I shall be in time to avert what could easily become the first wholesale pogrom in the history of diplomacy. I hope he heeds my words. But I am worried, I confess. I scan the papers uneasily every morning. Is that the *Telegraph*, by any chance, protruding from the pocket of your mackintosh?"

OPPOSITE: ELIZABETH TAYLOR AS CLEOPATRA, PHOTOGRAPHED IN ROME BY BERT STERN
OVERLEAF: THE GLORY OF VENICE'S SAN MARCO, PHOTOGRAPHED BY ALEXANDER LIBERMAN

JOHN STEINBECK'S NOBEL PRIZE ACCEPTANCE SPEECH

DELIVERED IN 1962

I thank the Swedish Academy for finding my work worthy of this highest honour.

In my heart there may be doubt that I deserve the Nobel award over other men of letters whom I hold in respect and reverence — but there is no question of my pleasure and pride in having it for myself.

It is customary for the recipient of this award to offer scholarly or personal comment on the nature and the direction of literature. However, I think it would be well at this particular time to consider the high duties and the responsibilities of the makers of literature.

Such is the prestige of the Nobel award and of this place where I stand that I am impelled not to squeak like a grateful and apologetic mouse, but to roar like a lion out of pride in my profession and in the great and good men who have practised it through the ages.

Literature was not promulgated by a pale and emasculated critical priesthood singing their litanies in empty churches — nor is it a game for the cloistered elect, the tin-horn mendicants of low-calorie despair.

Literature is as old as speech. It grew out of human need for it, and it has not changed except to become more needed. The skalds, the bards, the writers are not separate and exclusive. From the beginning, their functions, their duties, their responsibilities have been decreed by our species.

Humanity has been passing through a grey and desolate time of confusion. My great predecessor, William Faulkner, speaking here, referred to it as a tragedy of universal physical fear, so long sustained that there were no longer problems of the spirit, so that only the human heart in conflict with itself seemed worth writing about. Faulkner, more than most men, was aware of human strength as well as of human weakness. He knew that the understanding and the resolution of fear are a large part of the writer's reason for being.

This is not new. The ancient commission of the writer has not changed. He is charged with exposing our many grievous faults and failures, with dredging up to the light our dark and dangerous dreams, for the purpose of improvement.

Furthermore, the writer is delegated to declare and to celebrate man's proven capacity for greatness of heart and spirit — for gallantry in defeat, for courage, compassion, and love. In the endless war against weakness and despair, these are the bright rally-flags of hope and of emulation. I hold that a writer who does not passionately believe in the perfectibility of man has no dedication nor any membership in literature.

The present universal fear has been the result of a forward surge in our knowledge and manipulation of certain dangerous factors in the physical world. It is true that other phases of understanding have not yet caught up with this great step, but there is no reason to presume that they cannot or will not draw abreast. Indeed, it is a part of the writer's responsibility to make sure that they do. With humanity's long, proud history of standing firm against natural enemies, sometimes in the face of almost certain defeat and extinction, we would be cowardly and stupid to leave the field on the eve of our greatest potential victory.

Understandably, I have been reading the life of Alfred Nobel; a solitary man, the books say, a thoughtful man. He perfected the release of explosive forces capable of creative good or of destructive evil, but lacking choice, ungoverned by either conscience or judgment.

Nobel saw some of the cruel and bloody misuses of his inventions. He may even have foreseen the end result of his probing — access to ultimate violence, to final destruction. Some say that he became cynical, but I do not believe this. I think he strove to invent a control — a safety valve. I think he found it finally only in the human mind and the human spirit.

To me, his thinking is clearly indicated in the categories of these awards. They are offered for increased and continuing knowledge of man and of his world — for *understanding* and *communication*, which are the functions of literature. And they are offered for demonstrations of the capacity for peace — the culmination of all the others.

Less than fifty years after his death, the door of nature was unlocked and we were offered the dreadful burden of choice. We have usurped many of the powers we once ascribed to God. Fearful and unprepared, we have assumed lordship over the life and death of the whole world, of all living things. The danger and the glory and the choice rest finally in man. The test of his perfectibility is at hand.

Having taken God-like power, we must seek in ourselves for the responsibility and the wisdom we once prayed some deity might have. Man himself has become our greatest hazard and our only hope. So that today, Saint John the Apostle may well be paraphrased: In the end is the *word*, and the word is *man*, and the word is *with* men.

CLAUDIA CARDINALE, the young Italian screen actress. Of seven films made last year in which the Cardinale grin will appear, two, *Rocco and His Brothers* and *Girl with a Suitcase*, have already shown why Miss Cardinale has soared into the same planetary system as Miss Bardot. Of CC, BB said, "She will succeed me."

MARILYN MONROE,
THE MAGNIFICENT BLONDE IMAGE
IN THE AMERICAN MEMORY-STREAM;
TRAGIC, BEAUTIFUL, UNREPEATABLE

Bert Stern

SPACE HEROES

In his silver space suit, the armour of the mid-twentieth century, Colonel Glenn, on February 20, 1962, hit that "keyhole in the sky," as he described it, thereby crossing the soundless barrier between the past and the future, the familiar and the uncharted. He returned in four hours and fifty-six minutes. Later on television he said, "I know I still get a real hard-to-define feeling when the flag goes by — and I know you all do, too."

In Colonel Glenn's mind, there circulate two companionable streams, that of the spirit and that of common sense. As he orbited the world, he needed both — one to help him get off the earth, the other to keep him off; one to cause him to remark early in orbit on how impressive the view was, and the other to enable him to control and guide the capsule's movements by hand, when the automatic control system failed — an unrehearsed feat of flexibility, concentration, and mental dexterity.

Although some thirty-five thousand technicians and scientists had worked to perfect the capsule, alone he took the risk, a small word for so enormous an achievement.

Glenn's single orbit showed the way for Cooper's twenty-two. On May 16-17, 1963, Major Gordon Cooper was absent from earth for thirty-four hours' travel in outer space, at 17,000 miles per hour, landing almost precisely when, and almost precisely where the incredibly exact calculations had scheduled him. At left, Major Cooper in his space suit, aboard the U.S.S. *Kearsarge*, after his capsule landed in the Pacific Ocean, 7:24 p.m., May 17, 1963. At right, Colonel Glenn drawn for *Vogue* by Feliks Topolski.

ROBERT FROST: BEST LOVED OF AMERICAN POETS

A distinguished professor of English literature at Queen Mary College, London University, writing for *Vogue* about Robert Frost in 1954, gave evidence of the admiration in which Frost, who died on January 29, 1963, is held in England. This was Mr. J. Isaacs, himself a writer and critic of modern poetry, Shakespeare expert, and book collector. Of Frost, Mr. Isaacs said, "His fame began in England, and had he stayed there, he might have become one of the glories of English literature rather than American." And in discussing Frost's methods of writing, Mr. Isaacs told us of Frost's own account of the writing of one of his best known, best loved poems, "Stopping by Woods on a Snowy Evening." Frost said that it was "written off in a flash." He had spent all night writing the long poem, "New Hampshire." But "next morning," said Frost, "I wrote this. I was so tired and intoxicated, I couldn't stop."

ROBERT FROST — R. Thorne McKenna

Whose woods these are I think I know.
His house is in the village though;
He will not see me stopping here
To watch his woods fill up with snow.

My little horse must think it queer
To stop without a farmhouse near
Between the woods and frozen lake
The darkest evening of the year.

He gives his harness bells a shake
To ask if there is some mistake.
The only other sound's the sweep
Of easy wind and downy flake.

The woods are lovely, dark and deep,
But I have promises to keep,
And miles to go before I sleep,
And miles to go before I sleep.

"That poem," he said, "contains all I ever knew."

Right: LEONTYNE PRICE, whose lyric voice swells like a spinnaker under full wind, has sung the star roles in *Aida, Madame Butterfly, Ernani, Don Giovanni, Tosca,* and other operas. (She once said that she prepared for *Tosca* by singing Bess in *Porgy and Bess,* for "both were strumpets, only Tosca dressed better.") A reasonably good actress as well as a great soprano, she knows the worth of economy of gesture and accurate spanning between her upper and lower registers. This Mississippi-born star, with shell-shaped eyes, brought to Salzburg audiences performances of undimmed magnificence when she sang Leonora in the Herbert Von Karajan production of *Il Trovatore*. With her world reputation, loved as much in Australia as in Austria, Miss Price has settled in comfortably at the Metropolitan Opera as America's new prima donna.

Penn

THERE IS SO ALAS ABOUT A PIGEON

BY PATRICIA COLLINGE

Dear Mr. Thurber:

Quite a little time ago, you wrote a piece called *There's an Owl in My Room*. Actually, it dealt more with pigeons, which was all right with me. When you said there was no alas about a pigeon I was right with you, agreeing with every word. In fact I cut the piece out of *The New Yorker* in which it appeared and kept it. My favourite bit was: "You could dress up a pigeon in a tiny suit of evening clothes and put a tiny silk hat on his head and a tiny gold-headed cane under his wing and send him walking into my room at night. It would make no impression on me. I would not shout 'Good god a'mighty, the birds are in charge!' But you could send an owl into my room, dressed only in the feathers it was born with, and no monkey business, and I would pull the covers over my head and scream."

I cherished that. I used to say it over to myself every time I passed a pigeon, and chuckle.

Well, I've stopped chuckling, Mr. Thurber, because I don't feel like that any more, and I'm sorry to have to tell you this, but you were wrong about pigeons. They *can* take charge, and, so far as I am concerned, they have, and they are led by a small one who is a bright reddish colour. I will refer to him, from now on, as Homer.

Homer is in charge. I'll modify that. He may not be in charge of the world, but he is definitely in charge of me, and yet, that may be the world, too, because one of the actors in *Look Homeward, Angel* points out that there is no world; that a person is the world, and if I'm a person, which up to now I have thought more or less probable, then I'm the world and if Homer is in charge of me, then — I'm terribly sorry, I'm upset, and that makes me sound confused. Well, if it comes to that, I *am* confused. All I know for certain right now is that my own world is chaos and all because of a small red pigeon who looks like James Cagney, and behaves like him, too. Not Mr. Cagney in private life, but Mr. Cagney in *Public Enemy No. 1*. Homer walks like James Cagney, squares off like James Cagney, and any day now he's going to fly in and push a grapefruit in my face.

Maybe I had better begin at the beginning. It might be easier for you, and I might be calmer that way.

The beginning was two years ago when I heard they were going to tear down the nice low brownstone houses

JAMES THURBER
Penn

next door to me and put up a very high apartment building. It was going to cut off a lot of light and sun and a pretty nice view from my bedroom window, but I resigned myself. It's a changing world, anyway, and liable to go up in flames at any moment, so the loss of a view seemed a small matter. The one thing that bothered me was that the new apartments would be so close that I would be practically sharing them with their tenants, including their radios, hi-fi's, and television programs; in other words, I thought it was going to be noisy, but my husband said in two years we would probably be dead, so not to worry about the noise *now* for pity's sake, so I didn't. I lived through the building and the tearing up of Beekman Place and the "Dig we must" signs that I was always walking into, and then last spring we went abroad, and when we came back the apartment house was up and my bedroom was dark and sunless as the grave, but, Mr. Thurber, it was also as quiet because the new building is air-conditioned and all the windows are shut tight, and never a sound comes from behind them. I can't tell you how happy and relieved I was. I sang and whistled and everybody said how well I was looking, and then Homer moved in.

Now, 30 Beekman Place, where we live, is not air-conditioned, but many of the tenants have installed the kind that comes in boxes, as I understand it. These boxes jut out from the window sills, but they don't fit close. They leave narrow spaces on each side that are sheltered and cosy, and that's where Homer hangs out. That is also where he hangs his etchings, because he does not occupy these havens alone. He has a wide circle of acquaintants, and an inexhaustible list of addresses, and he starts entertaining with the first streak of dawn. That is not what concerns me. Homer's amours are his own business if he would just shut up about them. But he coos, Mr. Thurber, and the new apartment building makes a sort of well, and the acoustics are magnificent. So every daybreak it begins. *Coo-oo-oo, coo-oo-oo*, with a rise in the second coo.

Sharp, insistent, repetitious, and unceasing. At first, I just got up and shut my window, but that was a mistake, because it caught Homer's attention and he moved up one floor nearer to me. The next morning I shut my window, and then opened it again quickly and leaned out and said, "Shoo." I said a little more than that, actually, but "Shoo" was the idea. Homer's companion fluttered away, all girlish confusion, but Homer stood his ground. He didn't exactly reach for his gun but he gave me a long, appraising look. "O.K., sister, if that's the way you want it, that's how it's going to be." That's what the look meant, Mr. Thurber, but I still thought pigeons were just pigeons and I'm afraid I laughed. Did you ever see anyone laugh at James Cagney? Did you ever see the look they got in return? The narrowed eyes, the tight smile? Well, then you know what I got. Homer gave it to me, took one slow insolent circle, and wheeled off into the dawn.

Next morning he was back with everything planned, everything right on the line. I changed my tactics. I got ready a glass of water, and at the first coo I let him have it. Sure enough, off he went, shaking his wings, making the getaway *fast*.

And that's that, I thought. But, Mr. Thurber, it was not. The next dawn Homer was back, and this time he waited till I threw the water, side stepped it as it came, winked at his companion, and as one bird they moved to the conditioner just above my window, and you can't throw water *up*, Mr. Thurber, I soon found *that* out. I tried throwing wads of wet newspaper, but all that got me was a complaint from a window cleaner who happened to be working outside an apartment just below.

So I decided to give Homer the silent treatment. What happened was that Homer got a stand-in. When Homer got tired the stand-in took over, and boy, was he hand-picked! Homer's note was bad enough, but at least it was firm. It had a certain timbre, a certain strength, but the stand-in, a disreputable piebald, had a coo that was low and depressed and whining. He sounded like a displaced mourning dove, and for all I know he may have been one. Homer had me hysterical, but the stand-in had me suicidal. And also helpless, Mr. Thurber. It wasn't like the old days when I had trouble with a chimpanzee. He lived in the apartment above me at 39 Fifth Avenue, and he used to go *whoop-whoop-whoop-whoopwhoopwhoop-whoooooop* on a rising note that had me rising with it. But I could have dealt with that, I could have had it moved out, or I could have moved out myself, because in those days there was always someplace to move *to*, but nowadays you're stuck. The chimpanzee trouble took care of itself anyway, because one day it just got quietly into a taxi with its owners, and they all went back to the jungle. But no one owns Homer, and there's no place for him to go back to, even if he wanted to go.

Right now, I'm pretty sure he just wants to stick around me, because he's taken me over, Mr. Thurber. He has sent out the word, and I'm surrounded. The gang is moving in. For the moment, they just coo and stay out of my reach, and laugh their heads off. But it's ominous, Mr. Thurber. They're taking it easy, but the day is coming when Homer is going to come in and lock the door and turn the radio up loud. I'm a marked woman, Mr. Thurber, and if Homer walked in right now in the feathers he was born in, I wouldn't just scream, I'd yell bloody murder. And that's why I'm writing you before it's too late. I have heard that the one thing that terrifies a pigeon is an owl. I have heard that an owl scares the living daylights out of a pigeon, and I cannot help feeling that if *anyone* can contact an owl, you can. So, please would you use your influence and have one come over and police my window? It's in the back, and it's the one without an air-conditioner.

Please help me, Mr. Thurber, because, while there may be no alas about a pigeon on a grassplot, on an air-conditioner he reeks of it.

Desperately,
Patricia Collinge

DR. CLAUDE E. SHANNON

Massachusetts Institute of Technology's eminent authority on the Information Theory looks forward to man and machine talking back and forth. For Doctor Shannon, why not? "Out of his research," wrote Dr. Frank Stanton, president of the Columbia Broadcasting System, "there grew what eventually became . . . the Mathematical Theory of Communications (or Information Theory) regarded by many scientists as the most important statement in physics since the Quantum Theory."

Henri Cartier-Bresson

VLADIMIR NABOKOV

A novelist who wheedles words into the brilliance of the butterflies he collects, a big man with a voice tuned for Chekhovian drama, a writer with a magician's trickeries, a humorist who plagues his books with puns, Vladimir Nabokov has written twenty-three books, the most discussed of which is *Lolita*. Thirteen of these creations he wrote in his native Russian; one of them, *The Gift*, published in 1963, but written in 1937, is about those who were, like Nabokov, expatriates in Berlin.

Horst Tappé

1958–1960s

WOMEN CHOOSE THEIR OWN FIGURES; WEAR OUTRAGEOUS HATS

PLUS CA CHANGE, PLUS C'EST LA MEME CHOSE
(SEE THE FASHIONS OF FIFTY YEARS AGO)

Cecil Beaton

MRS. ALFRED G. VANDERBILT
IN AN ALMOST HOUR-GLASS DRESS
DESIGNED BY MAINBOCHER

404   [1953 – 1963]

MRS. PATRICK GUINNESS
WEARS A CARDIN HAT

William Klein

LIFE MUST SURPASS ITSELF

BY RENE DUBOS

The human future is not what is inevitably bound to happen, a situation determined by antecedent events and by the blind operation of natural forces. What happens to man is conditioned largely by human imagination and human will.

As judged from history, the most common human desire has been to improve what already existed rather than to set on a new course. Often in the past this attitude has resulted in what Arnold Toynbee has called "arrested societies." The Polynesian Islanders and the Eskimos, for example, had arrived many centuries ago at a formula of existence admirably suited to their particular environment; their ancestral ways of life provided the kind of comfort and the satisfactions that come from carrying out the functions required for group survival. But "arrested societies" are rapidly disintegrating or at least are being profoundly transformed, as a result of the enormous increase in means of communication. They die or they must evolve when they come into contact with competitive cultures.

The predominant attitude in much of the Western World is to substitute for the desire to maintain the traditional state of affairs, the desire to plan the future so as to maintain the same kind of life, only with more of everything and with perfected mechanical operations.

The willingness to accept change as a matter of course became very early a trademark of life in the United States. The French sociologist Alexis de Tocqueville emphasized this as one of the typical American traits in his *Democracy in America*, published in 1839. He recognized that this attitude was the extension of a general faith in the endless perfectibility of man, which the Western world, and especially America, had adopted enthusiastically from the Enlightenment philosophers. With time, however, this concept has deteriorated, and refers now to mechanical convenience and to an increase in quantity of goods rather than to real qualitative changes.

To the extent that we want only more of what we already have, we are in the process of becoming a self-satisfied society without vital thoughts of renewal. But stability, comfort, and even high refinements are not enough to nourish human nature; the body survives but the spirit loses its vitality unless stimulated by new models created by imagination. Human life is not concerned only with perpetuating itself and satisfying itself. It must surpass itself; otherwise it merely awaits death.

Few of us are capable of devoting all our energies to causes that transcend our personal interests. But all of us can cultivate the awareness that we do not function as self-sufficient entities, that we are a part of a continuous creative effort which is making mankind. The least we can do is to leave for those who will follow us a world as good as that which we have inherited from the past. The ultimate symbol of irresponsibility and of decadence are the words attributed to Louis XV: "*Aprés moi, le déluge.*"

Among the obvious responsibilities to the future is the preservation of natural resources which have accumulated in the course of time. As an excuse for the thoughtless destruction of these, it is commonly said that the loss is of no consequence, because science will eventually provide new materials and new sources of power to take their place. In reality, it is unjustified to believe that the possibilities of technological development are unlimited. Modern technology is geared to abundant supplies of cheap raw materials, to natural available resources.

Furthermore, technology is based on theoretical scientific knowledge which we have inherited from the past. Theoretical science must be continually added to, for the sake both of understanding the universe and of continued technological growth. This sense of the continuity of knowledge is not new. It was expressed by Diderot in his Encyclopaedia. "The purpose of an Encyclopaedia," he wrote, "is to assemble the knowledge scattered over the surface of the Earth, and to transmit it to the men who come after us, in order that the labours of centuries past may not be in vain during the centuries to come; that our descendants, by becoming better instructed, may as a consequence be more virtuous and happier, and that we may not die without having deserved well of the human race."

In contrast to Diderot's words, it is rather distressing to note the present insistence that all learning be directed to immediate practical ends. It is true, of course, that our present prosperity results in large part from scientific research pointed to very practical questions. But the very processes of modern thinking, and the fundamental basis on which all modern science is erected, have their origin in the abstract speculations of Greek philosophers and in the theoretical studies of scientists of the past three centuries.

We are the beneficiaries of wisdom that our ancestors acquired through centuries of painful effort. Most of the splendours of our civilization are not of our own making; we enjoy a heritage rich in material goods, in experience, in knowledge. To the extent that we exploit this inherited intellectual wealth, without making the effort to accumulate theoretical knowledge, we act as selfish tenants who exhaust the land of their ancestors and prepare the intellectual dust bowls of the future.

RICHARD LIPPOLD, ONE OF THE PRIME FORCES IN SCULPTURE THAT IS PART OF THE ARCHITECTURAL DESIGN OF THE NEWEST BUILDINGS — THE SKY-REACHING BUILDINGS — THAT ARE THE LANDMARKS OF OUR ERA

Elliott Erwitt Magnum Photos

RADIO TELESCOPE, NEWEST PROBE INTO
SPACE BEYOND SPACE. THIS, THE WORLD'S LARGEST,
WAS COMPLETED IN 1962 BY THE NATIONAL RADIO
ASTRONOMY OBSERVATORY, GREEN BANK, WEST VIRGINIA.
THE PURPOSE: EXTRA-GALACTIC STUDY.
ONE HOPE: FUTURE CONTACT WITH INTELLIGENT
LIFE BEYOND OUR OWN SOLAR SYSTEM

All of us, for example, have derived pleasure and inspiration from the architectural monuments that have survived from the past. These monuments symbolize the fact that human existence transcends the life of each particular individual. How much the world would lose emotionally and aesthetically, if it were deprived of the venerable structures that men have left as witnesses of their passage — the Celtic dolmens and the Greek temples; the Tibetan monasteries and the Gothic cathedrals; the Roman aqueducts and the Renaissance palaces; the great public monuments and memorials to heroes. By the same token, should we not give thought to what our own civilization will leave for the generations to come? Where are the monuments of today that will still be standing two thousand years hence? Where are the gardens, parks, and avenues of trees made of lasting species, planted in a noble style, that could become increasingly poetic and majestic with added centuries?

To build nothing capable of surviving our times is a sign of irresponsibility, a refusal to continue the tradition which has carried mankind beyond its brutish origins. In contrast, to create for the future is not only a duty but a source of deep satisfaction that gives significance to the most trivial tasks.

Man differs from the rest of creation by the greater extent to which he exercises free will. It is the inescapable need to choose which gives its grandeur to the human condition, yet accounts for its tragic quality.

The spirit of human brotherhood, the urge to attempt the impossible for the sake of greatness without any hope of material reward, arise from expectations, from visions, from dreams. They are so real and powerful that they are the most effective forces in changing the face of the earth. Thus it is certain that man cannot be completely understood merely by considering him as a piece of machinery to be analyzed objectively by the methods of the exact sciences. To be understood man must be "known" in the Biblical sense; he must be encountered and experienced as a dreaming and throbbing creature.

National Radio Astronomy Observatory

NOTES AND ACKNOWLEDGMENTS

With the passage of time, and after two world wars, many of the original photographs, drawings, and plates used in *Vogue* were no longer available. But the editors felt that some of these pictures were too important to be omitted from the book; so reproductions of them (including some in color) were made directly from the pages of various issues of *Vogue*, with a consequent lack of sharpness in some instances. We regret these occasional imperfections, but we would have regretted still more the omission of these particular pictures. In a few (very few) cases new photographs, almost identical to those reproduced in *Vogue*, taken at the same time and in the same place, were substituted for missing original prints.

The material in the book has been arranged chronologically, as closely in order, year by year, as the arrangement of pictures and text would allow. Dates, by decades, are indicated next to the folio, and where especially important the exact year of publication in *Vogue* is also stated on the page.

Credits, where space has permitted, have been given next to the illustrations. In the "Seven Decades" feature, newly created for this book (pages 10 to 21), the publishers are indebted to the following sources for the small photographs: Acme Photos, Astor Release, A. T. and T., Bettmann Archive, Brown Brothers, Culver, I.N.P., The Museum of Modern Art, National Archive Record, National Foundation of Infantile Paralysis, Topical Press, Underwood and Underwood, U.P.A., U.P.I., United States Air Force, Vandamm, and Wide World; also to E. O. Hoppe, Max Haas, Hurrell, Charles R. Joy, Max Kleppein, Charles E. Kerlee, and Paul Thompson; the photographs by Elliot Erwitt, Henri Cartier-Bresson, and Edward Steichen are reduced from pages in *Vogue*.

For the print of Barney Oldfield (pages 30 and 31) the publishers are indebted to the Automotive History Collection of the Detroit Public Library. For the war photographs (pages 82 and 83) credit is due the American Press Association, Brown Brothers, Campbell, Harris and Ewing, Paul Thompson, Underwood and Underwood, Sarony, Western Newspaper Union, and White Studio. For "Family Portraits" (pages 84 and 85) acknowledgment is made to David and Sanford, Medem Photo Service, Rochlitz, and Walter Scott Shinn. For the photographs on pages 126 and 127, our thanks to Cameragrams, Cameranews, Hoyningen-Huene, I.N.P., Edwin Levick, Remie Lohse, Pacific and Atlantic Photos, Photoschall, Pictorial Press; the photograph of Katharine Hepburn is by Steichen. In "The Armory Show" article (pages 66 to 69) we are grateful to The Art Institute of Chicago; The Lamont Art Gallery of The Phillips Exeter Academy; The National Gallery, London; The Philadelphia Museum of Art; and Mrs. Amos Pinchot for permission to photograph paintings which were in their collections at the time of the Armory Show or which have been acquired by them since. On pages 382-383: Paul Scofield was photographed by Angus McBean; Paul Newman, Richard Burton, and Julie Andrews by Friedman-Abeles; Robert Morse by Bert Stern; and the scene from *The Miracle Worker* by A. Cantor.

Except as noted below, the copyright on the texts belongs to The Condé Nast Publications Inc. Acknowledgment is hereby made to:

George Allen & Unwin Ltd. for "My Grandmother and Mr. Gladstone" by Bertrand Russell

Curtis Brown Ltd. for "The Light in the Dark" by Elizabeth Bowen

Curtis Brown Ltd. for "The Revolution of the Women" by Joyce Cary

Curtis Brown Ltd. for "Just Idling Along" by Daphne du Maurier. Copyright 1946 by Daphne du Maurier

Curtis Brown Ltd. for "Meditation on Simplicity" by Rumer Godden

John Mason Brown for "Thanks to Casey Jones" by John Mason Brown. Copyright 1937 by John Mason Brown

Estate of Albert Camus for "The Crisis of Man" by Albert Camus. Copyright 1946 by the Estate of Albert Camus

Jacques Chambrun, Inc. for "The Man Who Planted Hope and Grew Happiness" ("The Man Who Planted Hope") by Jean Giono

Jacques Chambrun, Inc. for "The Vamp" ("The New Vamp") by Anita Loos

Jacques Chambrun, Inc. for "Fashion and the Fine Arts" by André Maurois

Mary Ellen Chase for "There Was No More Sea" by Mary Ellen Chase

Jean Cocteau for "The Best of Talk" by Jean Cocteau. Copyright 1949 by Jean Cocteau

Patricia Collinge for "There Is *So* Alas about a Pigeon" by Patricia Collinge

Pierre Daninos and Georges Borchardt for "What Is an Englishman?" by Pierre Daninos

Agnes de Mille for "The Art of Ballet" by Agnes de Mille, republished in *The Book of the Dance*

William Pène du Bois for "The Armory Show 1913: From One Extremist to the Other" by Guy Pène du Bois

René Dubos for "Life Must Surpass Itself" excerpted from "Mankind Does Become Better" by René Dubos, also published in *The Torch of Life*

E. P. Dutton & Co., Inc. and Faber and Faber Ltd. for "Cry Wolf" ("A Little Game") from *Esprit de Corps* by Lawrence Durrell. Copyright © 1957, 1958 by Lawrence Durrell

Farrar, Straus & Co., Inc. and Maurice Goudeket for "Mannequins" by Colette

Donald Gallup, David Higham Associates Ltd., and Alice B. Toklas for "Pierre Balmain, Remembered Before Darker Days" by Gertrude Stein

Paul Géraldy for "The Marrying Age" by Paul Géraldy

Harper & Row Publishers, Inc. for "Edna St. Vincent Millay" ("'Between the Birds and the Poets': A Millay Memoir") from the book *The Indigo Bunting* by Vincent Sheean. Copyright 1951 by Vincent Sheean, copyright 1951 by Norma Millay Ellis

Estate of Ernest Hemingway for "The Clark's Fork Valley, Wyoming" by Ernest Hemingway. Copyright 1939 by Ernest Hemingway

Holt, Rinehart and Winston, Inc. and Laurence Pollinger Ltd. for "Stopping by Woods on a Snowy Evening" from *Complete Poems of Robert Frost*. Copyright 1923 by Holt, Rinehart and Winston, Inc., copyright renewed 1951 by Robert Frost

President John F. Kennedy for "Brothers, I Presume?" by John F. Kennedy

Little, Brown and Co. – Atlantic Monthly Press and Hutchinson & Co. Ltd. for "Popularity" by Sir Osbert Sitwell from his book *Tales My Father Taught Me*. Copyright © 1961 by Sir Osbert Sitwell

Little, Brown & Co. – Atlantic Monthly Press and A. M. Heath & Company, Ltd. for "The Eye of a Soldier" by Geoffrey Household. Copyright © 1957 by Geoffrey Household

Harold Matson Company, Inc. for "The Old Home Town" by William Saroyan. Copyright © 1940 by William Saroyan

Elsa Maxwell for "What Makes or Breaks a Party?" by Elsa Maxwell

William Morris Agency, Inc. for "How to Face Outer Space" by Anthony West. Copyright © 1958 by Anthony West

Sir Harold Nicolson for "Are the English Hypocrites?" by Harold Nicolson

Harold Ober Associates, Inc. for "Modern Architecture in America" (part of a series of *Vogue* articles entitled "Are You Illiterate about Modern Architecture?") by Peter Blake

Harold Ober Associates, Inc. for "Don't Flatter Yourselves, Girls" by Paul Gallico

Pantheon Books, a division of Random House, Inc. for "Revisitation" from *Unicorn and Other Poems* by Anne Morrow Lindbergh. Copyright © 1956 by Anne Morrow Lindbergh

A. D. Peters for "Conversational Kleptomania" by G. B. Stern. Copyright © 1939 by G. B. Stern

Katherine Anne Porter for "The Charmed Life" by Katherine Anne Porter. Copyright © 1942 by Katherine Anne Porter

Emily Post Institute, Inc. for "Enter Gwendolyn!" by Emily Post

Random House, Inc. for "Call It New York" reprinted from *Local Color* by Truman Capote. Copyright 1948 by Truman Capote

Random House, Inc. for "Nobel Prize Acceptance Speech" by William Faulkner. Reprinted from *The Faulkner Reader*. Copyright 1954 by William Faulkner

Leah Salisbury, Inc. for "The Art of Laughter" by Christopher Fry. Copyright © 1950 by Christopher Fry

Harlow Shapley for "You and the Queen of Sheba" by Harlow Shapley

Mrs. Edward Speares for "Sophisticated Ladies Kiss Everybody" by Mary Borden. Copyright 1932 by Mary Borden Speares

Howard Taubman for "They Pack Them In" by Howard Taubman

The Viking Press, Inc. for "How to Get Along with a Man" from *The Province of the Heart* by Phyllis McGinley. Copyright © 1958 by Phyllis McGinley

The Viking Press, Inc. for "Nobel Prize Acceptance Speech, 1962" by John Steinbeck. All rights reserved

VOGUE 1893-1963

PUBLISHERS	Arthur Turnure	1893-1909
	Condé Nast	1909-1942
	Iva S. V.-Patcévitch	1942-
EDITORS, AMERICAN VOGUE	Josephine Redding	1893-1900
	Marie Harrison	1901-1914
	Edna Woolman Chase	1914-1945
	Jessica Daves	1946-1962
	Diana Vreeland	1963-
ART DIRECTORS, AMERICAN VOGUE	Harry McVickar	1893-1909
	Heyworth Campbell	1910-1927
	M. F. Agha	1928-1943
	Alexander Liberman	1943-
	Priscilla Peck, Art Editor	1954-
EDITORS, BRITISH VOGUE	Elspeth Champcommunal	1916-1922
	Dorothy Todd	1922-1926
	Alison Settle	1926-1934
	Elisabeth Penrose	1934-1940
	Audrey Withers	1940-1960
	Ailsa Garland	1961-
EDITORS, FRENCH VOGUE	Cosette Vogel	1922-1927
	Main Bocher	1927-1929
	Michel de Brunhoff	1929-1954
	Edmonde Charles-Roux	1954-

Of particular importance in the making of this book: H. W. Yoxall, Chairman, British Vogue; Allene Talmey, Feature Editor, American Vogue; Margaret Case, Personalities, American Vogue; Priscilla Peck, Art Editor, American Vogue.

INDEX

Aalto, Alvar, 377
Adams, Esther, 275
Adams, Franklin P., 269
Adams, Maude, 43, 44
Addams, Charles, 337
Agnelli, Signora Gianni, 342
Alajalov, Constantin, 154-55
Alcock, John, 13
Alexandra, Princess (England), 370
Alexandra, Queen (England), 46
Alexandre, Mr. and Mrs. J. Henry, 194-95
Alexis, Grand Duke of Russia, 13, 47
Alfonso, King, of Spain, 46, 53, 207
Alix, Empress, of Russia, 13, 47
Allais, Emile, 342
Allegret, Marc, 356
Allen, Fred, 303
Allison, William B. 325
Alonso, Alicia, 330
Altemus, Elizabeth, 126
Amato, Pasquale, 63
Ambler, Eric, 236
Ambrose, Marilyn, 254
Anastasia, Grand Duchess, of Russia, 13, 47
Anderson, Judith, 158
Anderson, Marian, 216
Anderson, Maxwell, 236
Andrews, Julie, 341, 382
Anglesey, Marquis and Marchioness of, 292
Anson, Hon. Alfred, 194-95
Appleton, Frank, 74

Arliss, George, 44, 110
Armstrong-Jones, Antony (Earl of Snowden), 371
Armstrong, Louis, 210
Arthur, Julia, 25
Astaire, Adele, 16, 116
Astaire, Fred, 116, 148, 207, 209
Astor, Ava Willing (Mrs. John Jacob IV), 43
Astor, Mrs. John Jacob (Caroline), 43, 44, 106
Astor, Michael, 293
Astor, Lady (Nancy Langhorne, wife of Waldorf Astor, second Viscount), 75, 312, 313
Astor, Stella, 293
Astor, Vincent, 72
Astor, Mrs. Vincent, 72, 167
Astor, Waldorf (second Viscount), 312
Astor, William, 75
Astor, Mrs. William, 44, 103, 105, 106
Attlee, Clement, 19
Auden, W. H., 237
Ayres, Agnes, 118

Bacon, Edmund, 377
Bacon, Mrs. Robert L., 194-95
Bagby, Albert Morris, 44
Bailey, Buster, 210
Bailey, Mildred, 210
Baker, Josephine, 15
Baker, Lee, 157

Bakst, Leon, 77, 140, 301
Balcom, Mrs. Ronald B., 213
Baldwin, Hon. and Mrs. Joseph Clark, 194
Ball, Lucille, 302
Balmain, Pierre, 228
Balzac, Honoré, 94, 140
Bancroft, Anne, 382
Banham, Dr. Reyner, 374
Bankhead, Tallulah, 204
Banting, Sir Frederick Grant, 13
Bara, Theda, 337
Bardot, Brigitte, 337, 355, 356, 357, 393
Barker, Margaret, 128
Barkley, Alben W., 288-89
Barrès, Maurice, 265
Barrie, J. M., 28
Barry, Philip, 144, 197
Barrymore, Ethel, 28, 86, 233
Barrymore, John, 111, 158
Barrymore, Lionel, 28
Barzun, Jacques, 246
Basie, Count, 210
Baudelaire, Charles, 264, 301
Beale, Mrs. Truxtun, 194-95
Beaton, Cecil, 162
Beck, James, 194-95
Bedaux, Charles, 162
Beiderbecke, Bix, 210, 211
Belasco, David, 62
Bell, Dr. and Mrs. Alexander Graham, 54
Bellew, Hon. Sir. George, C.V.O., 319

412

Belmont, Mrs. August, 82
Belmont, Oliver, 42
Belmont, Mrs. Oliver, 44
Benchley, Robert, 270
Ben-Gurion, David, 19
Bennett, Helen, 254
Bennett, Joan, 127
Bennett, Wilda, 208
Benny, Jack, 302
Benois, Alexandre, 236, 301
Bérard, Christian, 178, 179
Bergman, Ingrid, 232
Berigan, Bunny, 210
Berlin, Irving, 206-209
Berlin, Mrs. Irving (Ellin Mackay), 207
Berman, Eugene, 362-63
Bernhardt, Sarah, 26
Bernstein, Leonard, 344, 345
Berry, Chu, 210
Berwind, Mrs. E. J., 74
Berwind, Miss Julia A., 194-95
Bettoni, Count Alessandro, 126
Biddle, Mrs. Alexander, 194-95
Bishop, Mrs. Francis C., 194-95
Bjoerling, Jussi, 238
Blake, Peter, 372
Blanch, Lesley, 182
Blériot, Louis, 50, 54
Blondell, Joan, 150
Boissevain, Eugen, 275
Boldini, Giovanni, 10
Bolger, Ray, 204
Bolm, Adolf, 77
Bonnard, Pierre, 361, 362-63
Borden, Lizzie, 10
Borden, Mary, 143
Bori, Lucrezia, 189
Bose, Sterling, 210
Bouché, René, 313, 338, 339, 344, 345
Bouvier, Jacqueline Lee, see Kennedy, Mrs. John F.
Bowen, Elizabeth, 291
Bowes-Lyon, Lady Elizabeth, see Elizabeth, Queen Mother
Boyd, Madeleine, 369
Boyer, Charles, 147
Brady, Alice, 157
Brady, William A., 207
Brancusi, Constantin, 95
Brando, Marlon, 236, 376
Braque, Georges, 298-99, 362
Breese, Robert, 73
Breuer, Marcel, 372
Brown, Arthur W., 13
Brown, John Mason, 197
Brown, Reverend Doctor Wesley, 43
Brox Sisters, 208
Bruce, Virginia, 118
Bruguière, Louis, 194-95
Bryan, William Jennings, 15
Brynner, Yul, 284
Buchanan, Jack, 166
Bunshaft, Gordon, 374, 377
Burden, William, 194-95
Burke, Billie, 109
Burlington, Lord, 379
Burton, Richard, 382

Cabot, Bruce, 150
Caesar, Sid, 302
Cagney, James, 147, 401
Callas, Maria, 337, 352
Calvé, Emma, 10, 44
Camargo, Marie, 330
Campbell, Colin, 379
Campbell, Mrs. Patrick, 28
Camus, Albert, 226
Cannon, Harry, 38
Cantor, Eddie, 207, 302
Capone, Al, 286
Capote, Truman, 261, 379
Caracciolo, Donna Marella, 326
Caraman-Chimay, Princesse de, 265
Cardin, Pierre, 405
Cardinale, Claudia, 392
Carlson, Lily, 255
Carnegie, Andrew, 107

Carol, Prince, of Rumania, 47
Carpenter, John Alden, 207
Carpenter, Scott, 20
Carr, Elmendorf L., 194-95
Carrel, Alexis, 307
Carrington, Kay, 209
Carstairs, Mrs. Carroll, 126, 213
Carter, Benny, 210
Caruso, Enrico, 63, 187, 211
Cary, Joyce, 314
Casey, Mrs. A., 342
Cassatt, Mary, 67
Castle, Irene, 13, 207, 208
Castle, Vernon, 207, 208
Cather, Willa, 274
Cavalieri, Lina, 89
Cavanaugh, Inez, 210
Cavendish, Lady, see Astaire, Adele
Cazalet, Mr. and Mrs. Peter, 233
Cézanne, Paul, 67, 68, 69, 300
Chadbourne, William M., 194-95
Chaliapin, Feodor Ivanovitch, 189
Chamberlain, Neville, 182
Chambers, Hadden, 25
Chandler, Mrs. Otis, 342
Chandler, Robert L., 68, 69
Chanel, Gabrielle, 168, 171
Chaplin, Charlie, 15, 110
Charles, Prince, of Wales, 370
Charpentier, Gustave, 189
Chase, Mrs. Edna Woolman, 102
Chase, Ilka, 145, 204
Chase, Mary Ellen, 175
Chevalier, Maurice, 142
China, Dowager Empress of, 10
Chopin, Frédéric François, 207
Christ-Janer, Victor, 374
Churchill, Arabella, 319
Churchill, Lady, 319
Churchill, Sir Winston, 19, 223, 316, 320, 321
Claire, Ina, 213, 340
Clark, Bobby, 302
Claudel, Paul, 350
Clayton, Buck, 210
Clemenceau, Georges, 13
Cleveland, Mrs. Grover, 11, 104
Clinton, Larry, 211
Cobb, Lee J. 249
Coca, Imogene, 166
Cochran, Jacqueline, 181
Cocteau, Jean, 264
Cohan, George M., 13
Cole, Cozy, 210
Coleman, Bill, 210
Colette, 121, 350
Collinge, Patricia, 401
Colman, Ronald, 147
Coolidge, Calvin, 15
Cooper, Gary, 150, 232, 396
Cooper, Gordon, 20, 396
Cornell, Katharine, 14, 128, 236
Cortese, Valentina, 263
Cot, Pierre Auguste, 24
Courbet, Gustave, 67
Couturier, Père, 353
Covarrubias, Miguel, 286
Coward, Noel, 89, 130-31
Cowl, Jane, 109
Crane, Stephen, 10
Crawford, Joan, 118
Crawford, Kathryn, 118
Cromer, Harold, 204
Crosby, Bing, 209, 302
Crosby, Bob, 211
Crouse, Russel, 204
Crowninshield, Frank, 102, 193
Cruger, Mrs. Van Rensselaer, 38, 104
Cuevas, Marquis de, 326
Cugat, Xavier, 211
Curie, Mme. Marie, 10
Curie, Pierre, 10
Curtis, Charles, 286
Curtis, Nathaniel, 377
Curtiss, Glenn H., 54, 55
Cushing, Dr. Harvey, 300
Cutting, Brock, 38
Cutting, Fulton, 167

Daché, Lilly, 199
Dali, Salvador, 16, 170, 200
Danilova, Alexandra, 328
Daninos, Pierre, 346, 347
Darlington, Bishop, 107
Darrow, Clarence, 15
Daudet, Alphonse, 22
Daumier, Honoré, 67
Davidson, Duncan, 318
Davies, Arthur B., 67
Davis, Arthur, 377
Davis, Bette, 199
Davis, Mrs. Joseph E., 74
Day, Clarence, 204
Debussy, Claude, 10, 211
Degas, Edgar, 34, 67
De Gaulle, General Charles, 19, 224
De Kooning, Willem, 364
Delacroix, Ferdinand Victor Eugène, 67, 140
De Mille, Agnes, 329
Dempsey, Jack, 15
Denis, Maurice, 69
De Peyster family, 102
Derain, André, 92, 140
De Segurola, Andrés, 63
Deslys, Gaby, 207, 208
De Staël, Mme., 92
Destinn, Emmy, 63
De Wolfe, Elsie (Lady Mendl), 82, 106, 213
Diaghilev, Sergei Pavlovich, 76, 77, 301, 334
Diderot, Denis, 406
Didur, Adamo, 63
Dietrich, Marlene, 149, 296
Dillingham, Charles, 207
Dinesen, Isak (Baroness Blixen), 385
Dior, Christian, 19, 235
Disney, Walt, 16
Dooley, Mr. (Finley Peter Dunne), 270
Dorsey, Jimmy, 210, 211
Dorsey, Tommy, 210, 211
Dos Passos, John, 287
Dostoevsky, Feodor, 296
Doyle, Arthur Conan, 24
Dreyfus, Alfred, 10
Drummond, James, 318
Dubos, René, 406
Duchamp, Marcel, 66, 68
Dufy, Raoul, 362-63
Duke, Mrs. Angier Biddle, 84
Duke, Angier Biddle, Jr., 84
Duke, Doris, 127
Duke, Patty, 382
Du Maurier, Daphne, 244
Duncan, Isadora, 112, 334
Dunn, Josephine, 118
Dunnock, Mildred, 249
Durante, Jimmy, 204
Durrell, Lawrence, 388
Duse, Eleonora, 86, 113
Dyer, Brigadier-General, 83
Dyer, Elisha, 38, 105

Earhart, Amelia, 15
Eckstein, Gus, 233
Eden, Sir Anthony, 20
Edinburgh, Duke of, 316, 317, 370
Edward VII, King, of England, 10, 46, 53
Edward VIII, King, of England, see Windsor, Duke of
Eglevsky, André, 330
Einstein, Albert, 13, 216, 310, 311, 355
Eisenhower, Dwight D., 20, 288-89
Eisenhower, Mrs. Dwight D., 288-89
Eldridge, Roy, 210
Eliot, T. S., 246, 270, 340, 372
Elizabeth, Princess, of Rumania, 47
Elizabeth, Queen Mother, of England, 13, 16, 123, 161, 316, 370, 371
Elizabeth II, Queen, of England, 161, 316, 317, 371
Ellington, Duke, 210
Ellwood, Craig, 372
Epstein, Jacob, 233
Eric, see Erickson, Carl
Erickson, Carl, 219, 228, 229
Erickson, Lee, 219

413

Evans, Maurice, 158

Fairbanks, Douglas, 114, 149
Fargo, Clara, 73
Farman, Henry, 55
Farrar, Geraldine, 29, 44, 187
Farrell, James T., 287
Faulkner, William, 272, 273, 393
Fauré, Mme. Hubert, 326
Faye, Alice, 209
Fell, Mrs. John, 343
Ferdinand, Archduke, of Austria, 13
Fermi, Enrico, 16
Fish, Mrs. Stuyvesant, 37, 59, 106, 107
Fisher, Most Reverend and Right Honorable Dr. Geoffrey Francis (Archbishop of Canterbury), 319
Fiske, Minnie Maddern, 44
Fitzgerald, Ella, 210
Fitzgerald, F. Scott, 13, 275, 287, 314
Flagstad, Kirsten, 186, 187, 188, 238
Fleming, Sir Alexander, 15
Flynn, Errol, 147
Fokine, Michel, 301
Fonda, Henry, 147
Fonssagrives, Lisa, 254
Fontanne, Lynn, 207, 239
Fonteyn, Margot, 333
Ford, Henry, 116
Fosburgh, Mrs. James, 300
Foy, Mrs. Byron C., 213
Francis, Joseph, 54
Frank, Jean-Michel, 170
Franklin, Frederic, 329
Frazier, Brenda, 177
Frelinghuysen, Mr. and Mrs. Frederick, 194-195
Frick, Henry Clay, 72
Frings, Ketti, 368
Froeba, Frankie, 210
Frost, Robert, 270, 398
Fry, Christopher, 282
Fuller, Loie, 104

Gable, Clark, 149, 193, 256
Gagarin, Yuri, 20
Gallico, Paul, 149
Galli-Curci, Amelita, 13, 110
Galsworthy, John, 78, 165, 166, 324
Ganay, Count Charles de, 326
Gandhi, Mahatma, 19
Garbo, Greta, 17, 150, 261
Garden, Mary, 89
Gardner, Mrs. Jack, 74
Garner, John N., 286
Garson, Greer, 352
Gaston, Mrs. William, 126
Gates, Charles G., 54
Gates, Frederick T., 304, 305
Gauguin, Paul, 68, 173
Gaxton, William, 287
Gaynor, Janet, 15
George V, King, of England, 60, 61
George VI, King, of England, 13, 16, 164, 233, 316
George, Grace, 109
Géraldy, Paul, 115
Gerard, Hon. and Mrs. James W., 194-95
Gerry, Elbridge T., 39
Gerry, Mrs. Elbridge T., 39, 106
Gershwin, George, 117, 211, 214, 287
Gershwin, Ira, 287
Gibbons, Elizabeth, 255
Gibbons, Stella, 166
Gibson, Charles Dana, 75
Gibson, Mrs. Charles Dana, 75, 312
Gielgud, Sir John, 158
Gilbert, W. S., 207
Gilliatt, Dr. Roger, 370
Gilly, Dinh, 63
Giono, Jean, 308
Gish, Dorothy, 109
Gish, Lillian, 89, 108
Givenchy, 338, 339
Gladstone, William Ewart, 258
Glaenzer, Jules, 167
Glanville-Hicks, Peggy, 307

Glenn, Colonel John, 20, 396, 397
Gloucester, Duke and Duchess of, 370
Godden, Rumer, 247
Goodman, Benny, 210, 211
Gordon, Ruth, 233
Grahame, Kenneth, 166
Grant, Cary, 149, 367
Greenwood, Joan, 340
Gregory, Elizabeth H., 53
Griffith, Hugh, 368
Grissom, Virgil, 20
Grofé, Ferde, 211
Gropius, Walter, 372, 377
Grosvenor, Rose, 106
Grosvenor, Mrs. William, 106
Gude, Mrs. O. J., 127
Guest, Winston, 342
Guest, Mrs. Winston, 271
Guilbert, Yvette, 86
Guinness, Sir Alec, 358-59
Guinness, Mrs. Patrick, 405
Gunther, Mr. and Mrs. John, 353

Haggard, Mr. and Mrs. Godfrey, 194-95
Haines, Willie, 118
Hamilton, Clayton, 86
Hamilton, Duchess of, 61
Hammerstein, Oscar, 258, 284-85, 352
Hammond, Hon. and Mrs. Ogden H., 194-95
Hampton, Lionel, 210
Hand, Judge Learned, 352
Harding, Warren G., 13, 15
Harlow, Jean, 16
Harriman, Mrs. J. Borden, 82, 194-95
Harris, Sam, 207
Harrison, Rex, 341
Hart, Moss, 204, 207
Hartley, Marsden, 362-63
Haugwitz-Reventlow, Countess, see Hutton, Barbara
Havemeyer, Theodore Augustus, 103, 104
Hawkins, Coleman, 210
Hayes, Helen, 152
Haymes, Joe, 210
Hearst, Mrs. W. R., 167
Hebuterne, Jeanne, 92
Hellman, Lillian, 204
Hellström, Dr. Gustaf, 273
Hemingway, Ernest, 15, 140, 153, 233
Henderson, Fletcher, 210
Henri, Robert, 68
Henry, Prince, of Prussia, 44
Hepburn, Audrey, 379
Hepburn, Katharine, 127, 196
Herbert, Lord David, 218
Hernan, Kay, 255
Herrick, Mrs. Parmely W., 194-95
Hewitt, Peter Cooper, 54
Hillary, Sir Edmund, 20
Hiller, Wendy, 249
Hirschfeld, Albert, 288, 289
Hitchcock, Alfred, 352
Hitchcock, Helen, 72
Hitchcock, Thomas, Jr., 72
Hitchcock, Thomas, Sr., 74
Hitler, Adolf, 16, 286, 355
Holiday, Billie, 210
Hoover, Herbert C., 13, 16, 286
Hoover, Mrs. Herbert C., 286
Hope, Bob, 19, 302
Hopper, Edna Wallace, 28
Household, Geoffrey, 359
Howard, Leslie, 145, 146, 158
Hughes, Charles Evans, 286
Hutton, Barbara, 127, 213
Hutton, Ina Ray, 210
Huxley, Aldous, 246, 257, 314, 315

Ingres, Jean Auguste Dominique, 67, 69
Iselin, Mrs. Arthur, 85
Iselin, Edith Hope, 126

Jaipur, Maharaja of, 260
James, Harry, 210, 249, 287
James, Henry, 78
Jay, William, 84
Jeanmaire, Renée, 327

Jenney, Dana, 254
John, Augustus, 67, 69, 233
John XXIII, Pope, 20
Johnson, Andrea, 255
Johnson, Jimmy, 210
Johnson, Philip, 372, 374, 375
Jolson, Al, 15, 208
Jones, Bobby, 120
Jones, Jesse, 83
Jones, Joe, 210
Jones, Jonah, 210
Joyce, James, 13, 140, 246
Junyer, Sebastia, 190

Kahn, Louis I., 372, 374, 376
Kahn, Maude, 82
Karsavina, Tamara, 77
Kaufman, Beatrice, 233
Kaye, Danny, 204, 205, 353
Kaye, Nora, 330
Kazan, Elia, 249
Keats, John, 140, 276
Keith-Johnston, Colin, 129
Kelly, Grace, 290
Kennedy, Arthur, 249
Kennedy, Edward, 182, 184
Kennedy, Eunice, 183
Kennedy, John F., 20, 183, 322
Kennedy, Mrs. John F. (Jacqueline Lee Bouvier), 20-21, 301, 322
Kennedy, Joseph, 182, 184
Kennedy, Mrs. Joseph, 182, 184
Kennedy, Kathleen, 184
Kennedy, Patricia, 183, 322
Kennedy, Robert, 182, 184
Kennedy, Rosemary, 184
Kent, Duke of, 370
Kent, Marina, Duchess of, 18, 370
Kern, Jerome, 206
Khrushchev, Nikita, 20
King, Charlie, 118
Kipling, Rudyard, 10, 140
Kirk, Andy, 210
Kissel, Mrs. W. Thorn, 194-95
Kokoschka, Oskar, 362-63
Korda, Alexander, 136
Krupa, Gene, 210
Kubitschek, Juscelino, 20

Lahr, Bert, 303
Lanchester, Elsa, 136
Landi, Elissa, 129
Langley, Prof. S. P., 53
Langtry, Lily, 144
Lanvin, Madame, 96-97, 171
Lardner, Ring, 270
La Rocca, Nick, 210
Latham, H., 55
Lattuada, Alberto, 263
Laughton, Charles, 137
Lawford, Peter, 322
Lawrence, D. H., 314, 315
Lawrence, Gertrude, 130-31, 167, 204, 205, 285
Le Corbusier, 374, 376
Lee, Gypsy Rose, 209
Lehmann, Lotte, 188, 189, 238
Lehmbruck, Wilhelm, 362-63
Lehr, Harry, 107
Leigh, Dorian, 255
Leigh, Vivien, 16, 174
Lejeune, Baron Hubert, 194-95
Lelong, Lucien, 170, 171
Lenglen, Suzanne, 120
Leonard, Mr. and Mrs. Edgar, 194-95
Leontovich, Eugenie, 129
Lerner, Alan Jay, 340
Lewis, Jerry, 302, 303
Lewis, Sinclair, 15, 166
Liberman, Alexander, 278, 390-91
Lillie, Beatrice (Lady Peel), 134, 166, 233
Lindbergh, Anne Morrow, 281
Lindbergh, Charles A., 15
Lindsay, Howard, 204, 205
Lipchitz, Jacques, 362-63
Lippmann, Walter, 198, 324, 352
Lippold, Richard, 407
Lloyd, Harold, 15

414

Lloyd George, David, 13
Lodge, Senator Henry Cabot, 74
Loew, William Goadby, 194-95
Loewe, Frederick, 340
Loftus, Cissie, 44
Lombard, Carole, 118
Lonsdale, Frederick, 167
Loos, Anita, 337
Lord, Pauline, 147
Loren, Sophia, 354-55
Losch, Tilly, 123
Lowndes, Marie Belloc, 294
Loy, Myrna, 199
Luce, Henry R., 312
Luce, Mrs. Henry R. (Clare Boothe Luce), 312
Ludington, Wright Saltus, 362
Luks, George, 68
Lunceford, Jimmy, 210
Lunt, Alfred, 239
Lvnd, Sylvia, 165
Lynes, Russell, 286

MacArthur, General Douglas, 19
MacDonald, Ramsey, 15
Macgowan, Kenneth, 113
MacIver, Loren, 259
Mackay, Clarence, 207
Mackay, Mrs. Clarence, 44
Macmillan, Harold, 20, 370
Magnani, Anna, 262
Mailer, Norman, 19
Maillol, Aristide, 362-363
Mainbocher, 170, 171, 404
Manet, Édouard, 67
Manners, Lady Diana, 12
Manuel, King, of Portugal, 207
Mao Tse-tung, 20
March, Fredric, 147, 149
Marconi, Guglielmo, 10
Margaret Rose, Princess, of England, 161, 316, 370, 371
Marie, Grand Duchess, of Russia, 13, 47
Marié, Peter, 37
Marie, Princess, of Rumania, 47
Markova, Alicia, 331
Marlborough, Ninth Duke of, 42, 43
Marquand, John P., 246
Martial et Armand, 96-97
Martin, Mrs. Bradley, 43
Martin, Dean, 302, 303
Martin, Mary, 259
Marx, Groucho, 353
Mary, Queen, of England, 60, 61, 82
Mather, Victor C., 74
Mathews, Dorothy, 128
Matisse, Henri, 69, 140, 151, 252, 300
Matthews, Jessie, 166
Mature, Victor, 204, 205
Maude, General Sir Frederick Stanley, 84
Maugham, Somerset, 78, 199, 240
Maurois, André, 140
Maxwell, Elsa, 132, 133, 166, 167
Maxwell, Muriel, 255
Mays, Willie, 386
McAdoo, Mrs. Francis, 138
McAdoo, Mrs. Robert, 126
McAllister, Ward, 37, 102, 103, 106, 107
McCormack, John, 208
McCullers, Carson, 352
McGinley, Phyllis, 365
McGregor, Kenneth, 343
McKenzie, Red, 210
McKeever, Marianne, 82
McKinley, William, 10
McLauchlen, Betty, 254
McVickar, Harry, 37, 104
Melba, Nellie, 110, 238
Melbourne, Lord, 325
Melchior, Lauritz, 187, 188
Méliès, Mme., 10
Mencken, H. L., 353
Mendl, Lady (Elsie De Wolfe), 82, 106, 213
Meneghini, Giovanni Battista, 352
Menotti, Gian-Carlo, 344
Menuhin, Yehudi, 217
Merman, Ethel, 166, 167, 204, 205

Meux, Lady, 10
Michener, James A., 258
Mielziner, Jo, 249
Mies van der Rohe, Ludwig, 372, 374, 375
Milanov, Zinka, 238
Milburn, Mrs. Devereux, 74
Millay, Edna St. Vincent, 15, 274, 275
Miller, Arthur, 249
Miller, Gilbert, 233
Miller, Mrs. Gilbert, 167, 213
Miller, Marilyn, 98, 207, 209
Mills Brothers, 210
Mills, Mrs. Ogden, 37, 44, 106
Miró, Joan, 241, 362-63
Modigliani, Amedeo, 92, 93, 363
Molyneux, 171
Mondello, Toots, 210
Monet, Claude, 67
Monnet, Jean, 20
Monroe, Marilyn, 394-95
Moore, Mr. and Mrs. Clement C., 38
Moore, Fanny, 126
Moore, Grace (Mrs. Valentin Parera), 167, 189, 207, 208
Moore, Marianne, 321
Moore, Valerie, 194-95
Moore, Victor, 287
Moran, Lois, 287
Morehouse, Marian, 122
Morgan, Anne, 43, 53, 82
Morgan, J. P., Jr., 107
Morgan, J. P., Sr., 106, 107, 184
Morgan, Mrs. Pierpont, 37
Morisot, Berthe, 67
Morris, William, 267
Morse, Robert, 382-83
Mozart, Wolfgang Amadeus, 189, 237
Mundy, Meg, 254
Munroe, Lieut. John G., 194-95
Murray, Huntly, 79
Musso, Vido, 210
Mussolini, Benito, 13, 16, 287
Myers, Carmel, 118

Nabokov, Vladimir, 402, 403
Nasser, Gamal Abdel, 20
Nast, Condé, 167
Nathan, George Jean, 157, 353
Nazimova, Alla, 157
Nehru, Jawaharlal, 20
Neutra, Richard, 372
Newman, Paul, 382
Newton, Frankie, 210
Nicholas II, Czar, of Russia, 13, 47
Nichols, Red, 210
Nicolas, Prince, of Rumania, 47
Nicolson, Harold, 135
Nijinsky, Vaslav, 76, 77, 301
Nixon, Richard, 20, 288-89
Noailles, Comtesse Anna de, 264, 265
Nobel, Alfred, 393
Norfolk, Duke of, 319
Norvo, Red, 210
Novarro, Ramon, 118

Oberon, Merle, 136
Obolensky, Prince Serge, 167
O'Brien, Floyd, 210
Oelrichs, Mrs. Hermann, 57
O'Hara, John, 323
Oldfield, Barney, 30-31
Olga, Grand Duchess, of Russia, 13, 47
Oliver, King, 211
Olivier, Sir Laurence, 174
O'Neill, Eugene, 156, 157, 207
Orlando, Vittorio Emanuele, 13
Ormandy, Eugene, 216
Owens, Jesse, 16

Page, Anita, 118
Page, Geraldine, 382
Paget, Lady Henriette, 292
Paige, Lips, 210
Paley, Mrs. William, 300
Palmer, Mrs. Potter, 10
Pankhurst, Mrs. Emmeline, 10
Paquin, 96, 170

Parker, Dorothy, 99
Parker, James, 37, 39
Pasternak, Boris, 20
Pastor, Tony, 210
Patou, 15, 170
Paulhan, Louis, 54
Pavlova, Anna, 10, 101
Peabody, Helen, 83
Peary, Commander Robert Edwin, 10
Peel, Lady Robert, see Lillie, Beatrice
Pei, I. M., 374, 377
Pell, Mrs. George, 57
Pembroke, Countess of, 218
Pendar, Kenneth W., 194-95
Pène du Bois, Guy, 66
Perkins, Anthony, 368
Perret, Auguste, 374, 377
Perugia, 171
Picabia, Francis, 68
Picasso, Pablo, 92, 190, 191, 230-31, 252, 363
Pickford, Mary, 13, 114
Pignatelli, Princess, 342
Pinero, Sir Arthur, 28
Pinza, Ezio, 188, 189
Pissarro, Camille, 67, 69
Plank, George, 90
Polignac, Princesse de, 265
Polk, Mr. and Mrs. Frank Lyon, 194-95
Pons, Lily, 189
Porter, Cole, 166, 167
Porter, Katherine Anne, 201
Post, Emily, 70, 71
Powell, William, 147, 199
Power, Tyrone, 147
Prévert, Jacques, 263
Price, Leontyne, 399
Price, Vincent, 152
Proust, Marcel, 13, 140, 149, 264, 265
Puccini, Giacomo, 62, 237, 344
Puvis de Chavannes, Pierre, 67
Pyne, Mrs. Grafton H., 194-95

Quartermaine, Leon, 129

Rachmaninoff, Sergei, 214
Radziwill, Princess, 343
Rains, Claude, 340
Ramsay, Sir William, 356
Rathbone, Basil, 249
Rawlings, Marjorie Kinnan, 172
Raye, Martha, 302
Rayleigh, Lord, 356
Reboux, 125, 132
Redfern, 10
Redman, Don, 210
Redon, Odilon, 67, 68, 362-63
Reid, Whitelaw, 107
Reid, Mrs. Whitelaw, 105, 107
Reilly, Charles, 382
Renoir, Jean, 263
Renoir, Pierre Auguste, 67
Revalles, Flore, 77
Reynolds, Marjorie, 209
Rice, Dr. Hamilton, 194-95
Richier, Ligier, 362-63
Richman, Harry, 207, 208
Rickover, Hyman, G., 20
Rimsky-Korsakov, Nikolai Andreevich, 77, 301
Robbins, Jerome, 332
Robinson, Edward Arlington, 270
Roche, Ensign Francis Burke, 83
Roche, Captain Maurice Burke, 83
Rockefeller, David, 185
Rockefeller, John, 185
Rockefeller, John D., Jr., 185, 305
Rockefeller, Mrs. John D., Jr., 305-307
Rockefeller, John D., Sr., 304, 305
Rockefeller, Laurance, 185
Rockefeller, Nelson, 185
Rockefeller, Winthrop, 185
Rodgers, Richard, 258, 284-85, 352
Rodin, François Auguste René, 94
Rogers, Buddy, 118
Rogers, Ginger, 207, 209
Rogers, Will, 13, 16
Rohde, Eleanour Sinclair, 321
Roosevelt, Alice, 42, 44

415

Roosevelt, Archibald, 74
Roosevelt, Cornelius, 85
Roosevelt, Franklin D., 16, 19, 74, 222, 223, 286, 288
Roosevelt, Mrs. Franklin D., 203, 233, 286
Roosevelt, Grace, 85
Roosevelt, Mr. and Mrs. James A., 74
Roosevelt, Mrs. Kermit, 84, 85
Roosevelt, Kermit, Jr., 85
Roosevelt, Colonel Theodore, 10, 84
Roosevelt, Lt. Colonel Theodore, 84, 85
Roosevelt, Theodore, III, 85
Roosevelt, Mrs. Theodore, 84, 85
Rose, Dr. Wickliffe, 305
Rosenstein, Nettie, 199
Rossellini, Roberto, 263
Rossetti, Christina, 323
Rouff, Maggy, 170, 171, 178
Rousseau, Henri, 33
Roxburghe, Duchess of, 61
Rudolph, Paul, 372, 374, 377
Rushing, James, 210
Russell, Bertrand, 257, 349
Russell, Mrs. Henry Potter, 82
Russell, Lady, 257, 258
Russell, Lillian, 45
Russell, Pee Wee, 210
Russell, Lady Sarah, 370
Ruth, Babe, 15
Rutland, Eighth Duke of, 13

Saarinen, Eero, 372, 377
Saarinen, Eliel, 377
Saki (H. H. Munro), 165
Salk, Dr. Jonas, 20, 337
Salm-Hoogstraeten, Countess Ludwig, 126
Sandburg, Carl, 270, 353
Sanger, Margaret, 365
Sard, Mrs. Russell Ellis, 75
Sargent, John Singer, 10
Saroyan, William, 159
Sartre, Jean-Paul, 246
Satterlee, Mrs. Herbert, 107
Savonarola, Girolamo, 314
Sayao, Bidú, 238
Schiaparelli, Elsa, 170, 171, 179
Schinkel, Karl Friedrich, 374, 377
Schirra, Walter, 20
Schwartz, A. Charles, 194-95
Schweitzer, Albert, 19
Scofield, Paul, 382
Searle, Ronald, 347
Sears, Eleonora, 74
Sedgman, Frank, 343
Selfridge, Lieutenant, 52
Selznick, David Oliver, 193
Serrell, Mrs. Howard, 343
Serret, Pierre-César, 67
Seurat, Georges, 32
Shannon, Dr. Claude E., 402
Shapley, Harlow, 355
Shaw, Artie, 210, 211
Shaw, George Bernard, 13, 238, 266, 267, 325, 340
Shearer, Norma, 149, 158
Sheean, Vincent, 274
Shepard, Alan B., Jr., 20
Sherwood, Robert, 352
Shevlin, Mrs. Thomas H., 213
Shutt, Arthur, 210
Signac, Paul, 67
Sillman, June, 166
Silvers, Phil, 302
Simone, Madame (Pauline Benda), 264
Simpson, Mrs. Wallis Warfield, see Windsor, Duchess of
Sinatra, Frank, 19
Sirikit, Queen, of Thailand, 380-81
Sisley, Alfred, 67
Sitwell, Edith, 141, 380
Sitwell, Osbert, 379, 380
Sitwell, Sacheverell, 380
Skelton, Red, 303
Slayton, Donald, 20
Sloane, Mrs. William D., 106
Smith, Kate, 209
Smith, Stuff, 210

Snead, Sam, 342
Spencer, Lorillard, 74
Spiess, Jan, 211
Spock, Dr. Benjamin, 19
Stalin, Joseph, 15, 19
Stanley, Lady, of Alderley, 257
Stanton, Dr. Frank, 402
Steele, John, 207
Stein, Gertrude, 16, 211, 228, 229, 252, 253
Steinbeck, John, 287, 393
Steinberg, Saul 250-51
Stern, G. B., 165
Stevens, Mrs. Paran, 38
Stewart, James, 147, 291
Stickney, Dorothy, 204, 205
Stieglitz, Alfred, 23
Stone, Edward D., 372, 374
Strange, Michael, 85
Strauss, Richard, 188, 237
Stuyvesant family, 102
Sullavan, Margaret, 243
Sullivan, Louis, 372
Sullivan, Maxine, 166, 210
Sullivan, Captain R. O. D., 181
Swanson, Gloria, 88

Taft, Robert H., 352
Taft, William Howard, 10, 54
Taglioni, Maria, 330, 333
Talbert, Mr. and Mrs. William, 343
Talmey, Allene, 206, 368
Tange, Kenzo, 376
Tatiana, Grand Duchess, of Russia, 13, 47
Taubman, Howard, 187
Taylor, Elizabeth, 389
Taylor, Laurette, 248
Taylor, Mary, 127, 138
Taylor, Robert, 147, 149
Teagarden, Charles, 210
Teagarden, Cub, 210
Teagarden, Jack, 210
Tearle, Conway, 86
Tempest, Marie, 38, 104
Tetrazzini, Luisa, 238
Thomas, John Charles, 189
Thomas, Mrs. Leonard M. (Michael Strange) with Leonard Jr. and Robin, 85
Thurber, James, 400-401
Tibbett, Lawrence, 189
Tocqueville, Alexis de, 406
Todd, Miss E. L., 53
Toklas, Alice B., 228, 252
Topolski, Feliks, 223, 349, 370, 397
Toscanini, Arturo, 182, 189, 215, 216
Tough, Dave, 210
Toulouse-Lautrec, Henri Marie Raymond de, 67, 300
Toynbee, Arnold, 406
Tracy, Spencer 353
Traina-Norell, 339
Truman, Harry S., 19, 288-89
Truman, Mrs. Harry S., 288-89
Trumbauer, Frankie, 210
Tucker, Sophie, 208
Tuckerman, Bayard, 74
Tweed, Harrison, 74

Ustinov, Peter, 236
Uxbridge, Earl of, 292

Vadim, Roger, 356
Valentino, Rudolph, 118, 119
Vallee, Rudy, 209, 382
Van Alen, James, 39
Van Alen, Mrs. James, 342
Van Cortlandt family, 102
Vanderbilt, Alfred G., 40-41
Vanderbilt, Mrs. Alfred G., 404
Vanderbilt, Brigadier General Cornelius, 193
Vanderbilt, Mrs. Cornelius, Jr., 192, 194-95
Vanderbilt, Mrs. Cornelius, II, 42, 106
Vanderbilt, Consuelo, 36, 42
Vanderbilt, Gladys, 42
Vanderbilt, Harold, 74
Vanderbilt, Mrs. Murray, 343
Vanderbilt, William H., 193
Vanderbilt, William K., 103, 104

Vanderbilt, Mrs. W. K. (Alva Vanderbilt), 39, 72, 82
Van Fleet, Jo, 368
Van Gogh, Vincent, 68
Van Rensselaer family, 102
Venuti, Joe, 210
Verdura, Duc di, 200
Victor Emanuel III, King, of Italy, 10, 53
Victoria, Queen, of England, 10, 337
Vinson, Frederick M., 288-89
Vionnet, 171
Vitale, Joe, 261
Volk, Vic, 210
Von Bernstorff, Count, 107
Von Karajan, Herbert, 398
Von Moltke, Willo, 377

Waldron, Charles, 128
Wales, Prince of, see Windsor, Duke of
Waller, Fats, 210
Walsh, Mary Jane, 166
Ward, Mr. and Mrs. Newell, 343
Warnecke, John Carl, 377
Warner, Sylvia Townsend, 165
Waters, Ethel, 207, 209
Waugh, Evelyn, 314
Webb, Chick, 210
Webb, Clifton, 209
Webster, Ben, 210
Weese, Harry, 377
Welles, Orson, 242, 287
Wells, H. G., 78, 166
Wenman, Henry, 129
West, Anthony, 385
West, Mae, 15
West, Rebecca, 166, 294
Wharton, Mrs. Edward (Edith), 43, 44, 104
Whistler, James Abbott McNeill, 10
White, T. H., 166
Whitehouse, Mr. and Mrs. J. Norman de R. 194-95
Whitehouse, Worthington, 105
Whiteman, Paul, 210, 211
Whitney, Mr. and Mrs. Cornelius Vanderbilt, 181
Whitney, Flora, 74
Whitney, Mrs. Harry Payne, 74, 75
Whitney, Joan (Mrs. Charles S. Payson), 185
Whitney, John Hay, 185
Whitney, Mrs. John Hay, 300
Whitney, William C., 103, 104
Whitney, Mrs. W. C., 104
Wiborg, Mary Hoyt, 83
Wilde, Oscar, 25, 67, 301
Wilder, Thornton, 233, 353
Wilhelm II, Kaiser, 46
Williams, Charles, 283
Williams, Mrs. Harrison, 139, 213
Williams, Hope, 129
Williams, Mary Lou, 210
Williams, Midge, 210
Williams, Tennessee, 249
Wills, Helen, 120
Wilson, Bettina, 169
Wilson, Teddy, 210
Wilson, Woodrow, 13, 83, 131, 324
Windsor, Duchess of (Mrs. Wallis Warfield Simpson), 16, 162, 163, 212, 287
Windsor, Duke of, 16, 61, 162, 163, 287
Winmill, Mrs. Robert, 343
Winnington, Richard, 262
Wisdom, William B., 369
Wolfe, Thomas, 368, 369
Woollcott, Alexander, 207
Worth, 10
Wray, Fay, 150
Wright, Frank Lloyd, 372, 373, 376
Wright, Orville, 10, 52, 53, 54
Wright, Wilbur, 10, 53, 54
Wylie, Philip, 352
Wynn, Ed, 302

Yamasaki, Minoru, 372, 374
Young, Loretta, 199

Ziegfeld, Florenz, 208
Zola, Émile, 10